DOMINIC GOWER

The Kingdom of God

JOHN BRIGHT

THE
KINGDOM
OF
GOD

The Biblical Concept and Its Meaning
for the Church

ABINGDON PRESS
Nashville

THE KINGDOM OF GOD

ISBN 0-687-20908-0

Library of Congress Catalog Card Number: 53-8131

MANUFACTURED IN THE UNITED STATES OF AMERICA

97 98 99 00 01 02 03— 40 39 38 37 36 35 34 33

To my teacher

William Foxwell Albright
as a token of gratitude and high esteem

Preface

THIS BOOK, AS ITS TITLE INDICATES, IS CONCERNED WITH AN IDEA OF CEN-
TRAL IMPORTANCE IN THE THEOLOGY OF THE BIBLE. IT SEEKS TO TRACE
for the benefit of the general Bible reader the history of that idea and
to suggest its contemporary relevance. By this means, it is hoped, a contribution may be made to the understanding of the Scriptures. For the
concept of the Kingdom of God involves, in a real sense, the total
message of the Bible. Not only does it loom large in the teachings of
Jesus; it is to be found, in one form or another, through the length
and breadth of the Bible—at least if we may view it through the eyes
of the New Testament faith—from Abraham, who set out to seek "the
city . . . whose builder and maker is God" (Heb. 11:10; cf. Gen. 12:1 ff.),
until the New Testament closes with "the holy city, new Jerusalem, coming down out of heaven from God" (Rev. 21:2). To grasp what is meant
by the Kingdom of God is to come very close to the heart of the Bible's
gospel of salvation.

But the book has a broader aim: to come to grips, if possible, with
one of the fundamental reasons for the current neglect of the Bible. It
is unnecessary to furnish proof that there exists even among Christians
a widespread biblical illiteracy, and gratuitous to deplore that fact as
disastrous. Indeed, one might go so far as to say that Protestantism will
not forever survive if steps cannot be taken to remedy it. We may not
forget that the Protestant churches all began in a very biblical protest,
have always claimed the Bible as the final source of authority, and have
never allowed that any hierarchy may stand between the believer and
that Bible to bar his way to it or to mediate its interpretation. Uprooted
from the Bible we have no proper place to stand; we cannot, in fact, be

7

Protestant. It is therefore no light thing that the Bible should have become so strange a book to the average churchgoer and (tell it not in Gath!) to many a minister as well.

Now the reasons for this are no doubt manifold, and we cannot pause here to analyze them. But surely many a reader will complain that the Bible is a most confusing book of very unequal interest, so varied in content that he is unable to follow a line through it. Much of it is scarcely comprehensible, much is perplexing, and much plainly dull. (How many a person has set out manfully to read it through only to come a cropper somewhere in the middle of Leviticus!) Even its thrillingly told narrative has a most ancient flavor. The reader feels that much of it says nothing to him, and he is tempted to skip. In the end, if he persists in reading his Bible at all, he confines himself to favorite snippets here and there.

In any case there has grown up in the Church, alongside a total neglect of the Bible, a dangerous partial use of it. As a Church we declare that the Bible is the Word of God, and we draw no distinctions between its parts. But in practice we confine our use almost entirely to selected sections—the Gospels and the Psalms, portions of Paul and the prophets —and ignore the rest as completely as if it had never been written. The result is that we not only neglect much that is valuable but, what is worse, miss the deepest meaning of the very parts we use because we lift them from their larger context.

This is nowhere more acutely evident than where the relationship of Old Testament to New is concerned. The two testaments are sharply separated both in our printed Bibles and in the minds of most readers. And, because the New Testament has Christ, it is quite natural and right that the Christian should turn first and most frequently to it, and should find there the ultimate source of his faith. But that raises a question: In what sense does the Old Testament have authority over the Christian at all? Its ceremonial law has been set aside in Christ and is no longer binding. Its prophetic hope, it is affirmed, was fulfilled in him. Has not the Old Testament, then, in some way been superseded? In what relationship does it stand to the New in the canon of Holy Scripture? If that is a question which puzzles the layman, he may comfort himself that it has exercised scholars no less. At present it appears that the Church is not sure of her answer. We continue to affirm that the scriptures of the Old and New Testaments are the Word of God, and vaguely we believe this to be so; but it is to be feared that we have no clear idea of what we mean by the statement. In practice we tend to relegate the Old Testament to a position of little importance and to regard it, one might say, as scripture of the second rank. An ambiguous and unofficial sort of neo-Marcionism has arisen.

The question of the unity of Scripture must be taken seriously if the Bible is to be saved from disuse and misuse. But it is not a question that can be brushed aside with an easy answer. In one sense the Bible exhibits more diversity than unity. It is a very variegated book; rather, it is not a book at all, but a whole literature. It was written over a period of well above a thousand years by men of the most diverse character and circumstance; its parts are addressed to all sorts of situations; it contains every conceivable type of literature. To level the Bible off, as it were, and to impose upon it an artificial unity, or equality of value, which ignores this amazing diversity would be to manufacture a strait jacket. It would also be to leave unanswered the question, In what sense is Christ the crown and norm of revelation?

But is there in the Bible some unifying theme which might serve to draw its diverse parts together into a complete whole? Is there, amid its admitted discontinuity, any essential continuity?

There are those who would find little. One thinks of those scholars, fewer today than formerly, who would trace through the Bible the course of man's development in the realm of religion (or, theistically conceived, the progress of divine revelation), which began with the tribal god and primitive faith of early Israel, moved upward through the prophets into ethical monotheism, and finally reached its culmination in the teachings of Jesus.[1] That such an approach had an atomizing effect on the Bible cannot be doubted. To be sure, a certain continuity was observed, but it lay in the evolutionary pattern itself, not the Bible. The biblical religion was set apart into its various stages of development, the later of which had little or nothing in common with the earlier. It was impossible even to speak of a biblical theology. Now it would be dishonest to sneer at this critical scholarship, for it produced much for which we must be grateful. In particular it reminded us that revelation is not a picture

[1] So most critical scholars of the past generation. An excellent example of this approach in popular language is Harry Emerson Fosdick, A Guide to Understanding the Bible, the Development of Ideas Within the Old and New Testaments (New York: Harper & Bros., 1938).

gallery but a process in history. Of course there was progress! But the scheme of straight-line evolution was a framework imposed on the Bible from without, and it has proved far too rigid to accommodate the data. It can bring no solution to the problem of Scripture.

But one nurtured in the mainstream of Reformation theology may find the answer very simple: the unity of Scripture is in Christ. That this is in a real sense true I trust will be made clear as we proceed. To the mind of the New Testament faith not only all Scripture, but all history, centers in Christ. Yet this fact, true as it is, must be asserted with considerable care lest, in our zeal to make Christ all in all, we be guilty of imposing him arbitrarily on the Old Testament. It was once quite customary to do this, and there are those today who, it is to be feared, go too far in this direction.[2] If this is done consistently, the Old Testament becomes simply a Christian book, and biblical theology assumes a static quality which violates its very nature. In careless hands Old Testament studies tend to degenerate into a game of which the object is to find types of Christ and the prefigurement of Christian truth in unlikely places. This is, of course, to discard sound exegetical method. As Christians we read our Old Testament in the light of Christ, and from it we preach Christ. But we are not permitted to attribute to the Bible writers ideas which they did not have in mind, only to discover as best we can what they actually intended to say. To save the Old Testament by reading into it ideas which are not there is to save it at too high a price.

This book arises out of a concern for the problems just raised. It is submitted in the belief that while the complexity of the Bible is by no means to be minimized, there nevertheless runs through it a unifying theme which is not artificially imposed. It is a theme of redemption, of salvation; and it is caught up particularly in those concepts which revolve about the idea of a people of God, called to live under his rule, and the concomitant hope of the coming Kingdom of God.[3] This is a

[2] Wilhelm Vischer is perhaps an example: cf. *Das Christuszeugnis des Alten Testaments* (7th ed., Vol. I; 2nd ed., Vol II; Zürich: Evangelische Verlag, 1946); Eng. trans. Vol. I, from 3rd Ger. ed., A. B. Crabtree, *The Witness of the Old Testament to Christ* (London: Lutterworth Press, 1949).

[3] This insight is of course not original. I must acknowledge indebtedness to W. Eichrodt, whose *Theologie des Alten Testaments* (1st ed., Vol. I, Leipzig: J. C. Hinrichs, 1933; 3rd ed., Vol. I, Berlin: Evangelische Verlagsanstalt, 1948; cf. p. 1) first brought the importance of it home to me.

note which is present in Israel's faith from earliest times onward, and which is to be found, in one way or another, in virtually every part of the Old Testament. It also unbreakably links Old Testament to New. For both have to do with the Kingdom of God, and the same God speaks in both.

It is, of course, impossible to subsume all that the Bible has to say under a single catchword, and no attempt to do so has been made here. The title does not imply that the New Testament concept of the Kingdom of God may be imposed on the Old, nor does it seek to disguise the fact that the idea of the rule of God underwent considerable development within the Old Testament itself. But ideas are ever larger than the words that carry them. The roots of this idea lie in the very earliest period of Israel's history. Development is undeniable, but it must be viewed less as an evolution upward from lower forms to higher, than as a development outward from a concept which was normative in Israel's faith from the beginning onward. It was a concept which by its very nature pointed beyond itself and demanded its fulfillment.

As was said in the beginning, this book is addressed primarily to the general reader of the Bible. For this reason, although it is hoped that no indefensible position has been taken, every effort has been made to keep the text of the book free of technical discussion lest the reader, called upon to follow the thread of the argument through piles of scholarly baggage, should lose it altogether. The aim throughout has been clarity. It has not, of course, been possible to avoid footnotes. The reader who does not wish to go into them may well pass them by. It is because of the hope that the book may also be of use to teachers and more advanced students, and because candor demands that indebtedness be acknowledged and important areas of disagreement be indicated, that they have been included. Wherever it has been possible to do so, the effort has been made to refer to such works as may be expected to assist the student in further reading. Because of the limitations of space no attempt has been made to give full bibliography.

The historical approach has been chosen because, in the last analysis, biblical theology can be treated in no other way. Abstract it, discuss it as a system of ideas divorced from history, and it is no longer biblical theology. It is hoped, however, that the historical approach, far from dismaying the reader, will assist him to fit the various parts of the Bible—

particularly the Old Testament prophets—into their proper historical perspective.

If this book should make the Bible in any way clearer, or should stimulate in any the desire to study it, I shall be deeply gratified. But if it should be the means of causing some to hear again from the Bible page the summons to citizenship in the Kingdom of God, it will have more than succeeded.

JOHN BRIGHT

Acknowledgments

THE PREPARATION OF A BOOK IS AN ARDUOUS TASK, AND IT IS PROBABLE
THAT FEW HAVE EVER CARRIED IT THROUGH TO COMPLETION WITHOUT
the assistance and encouragement of others. This book has been no exception. I must, therefore, express my thanks to those friends who have
helped me along the way. I am grateful, first of all, to the Rev. Dr.
Barclay Walthall and the Rev. Dr. Holmes Rolston, both of the Board
of Christian Education of the Presbyterian Church, U.S., Richmond,
Va. It was the invitation of the former to deliver a series of Bible lectures
at a leadership conference for laymen at Montreat, N. C., in the summer
of 1950 that first gave occasion for thinking through the subject matter
of this book and presenting it orally; and but for the friendly interest
and insistence of the latter the labor of writing might never have been
undertaken at all. I must also thank Dr. Henry M. Brimm, librarian,
Union Theological Seminary, Richmond, Va., who called the Abingdon-
Cokesbury Award Contest to my attention and whose encouragement
it was that emboldened me to enter it. Especial thanks are due to Professor G. Ernest Wright of McCormick Theological Seminary, Chicago,
Ill., who read the completed manuscript and made numerous suggestions for its improvement. The present book is far the better for his
help, as well as for that of Professor W. F. Albright of Johns Hopkins
University, who made yet further suggestions; but it must be emphasized
that the shortcomings which remain are entirely my own. Not least, I
owe thanks to my wife—without whose assistance in the typing and
correcting, the manuscript would never have been ready in time.

Quotations from Scripture, except where otherwise indicated or where
I have ventured my own translation of the original, follow the R.S.V.

13

Contents

I. The People of God and the Kingdom of Israel 17

II. A Kingdom Under Judgment 45

III. A Remnant Shall Repent 71

IV. The Broken Covenant and the New Covenant 98

V. Captivity and New Exodus 127

VI. Holy Commonwealth and Apocalyptic Kingdom . . . 156

VII. The Kingdom at Hand: Jesus the Messiah 187

VIII. Between Two Worlds: The Kingdom and the Church . 215

IX. Even to the End of the Age 244

Index of References 275

Index of Subjects 283

CHAPTER ONE

The People of God and the Kingdom of Israel

THE GOSPEL ACCORDING TO MARK BEGINS THE STORY OF JESUS' MINISTRY WITH THESE SIGNIFICANT WORDS: "JESUS CAME INTO GALILEE, PREACHING the gospel of God, and saying, 'The time is fulfilled, and the kingdom of God is at hand; repent, and believe in the gospel'" (1:14-15). Mark thus makes it plain that the burden of Jesus' preaching was to announce the Kingdom of God; that was the central thing with which he was concerned. A reading of the teachings of Jesus as they are found in the Gospels only serves to bear this statement out. Everywhere the Kingdom of God is on his lips, and it is always a matter of desperate importance. What is it like? It is like a sower who goes forth to sow; it is like a costly pearl; it is like a mustard seed. How does one enter? One sells all that he has and gives to the poor; one becomes as a little child. Is it a matter of importance? Indeed it is! It would be better to mutilate yourself and enter maimed than not to get in at all. So paramount, in fact, was the notion of the Kingdom of God in the mind of Jesus that one can scarcely grasp his meaning at all without some understanding of it.

But for all his repeated mention of the Kingdom of God, Jesus never once paused to define it. Nor did any hearer ever interrupt him to ask, "Master, what do these words 'Kingdom of God,' which you use so often, mean?" On the contrary, Jesus used the term as if assured it would be understood, and indeed it was. The Kingdom of God lay within the

17

vocabulary of every Jew. It was something they understood and longed for desperately. To us, on the contrary, it is a strange term, and it is necessary that we give it content if we are to comprehend it. We must ask where that notion came from and what it meant to Jesus and those to whom he spoke.

It is at once apparent that the idea is broader than the term, and we must look for the idea where the term is not present. Indeed, it may come as a surprise to learn that outside of the Gospels the expression "Kingdom of God" is not very common in the New Testament, while in the Old Testament it does not occur at all. But the concept is by no means confined to the New Testament. While it underwent, as we shall see, a radical mutation on the lips of Jesus, it had a long history and is, in one form or another, ubiquitous in both Old Testament and New. It involves the whole notion of the rule of God over his people, and particularly the vindication of that rule and people in glory at the end of history. That was the Kingdom which the Jews awaited.

Now the Jews looked in particular for a Redeemer, or Messiah, who should establish the Kingdom of God victoriously. And since the New Testament declared that Jesus was that Messiah who had come to set up his Kingdom, we are at once driven back into the Old Testament to consider the messianic hope of Israel. We think particularly of Isaiah, who gave the hope of the coming Prince of the line of David its classic form. There leap to mind the words so often read as the Christmas lesson: "For to us a child is born, to us a son is given; . . . and his name will be called 'Wonderful Counselor, Mighty God, Everlasting Father, Prince of Peace' " (Isa. 9:6). But since the expectation of the coming redemption is expressed repeatedly in the Old Testament in passages which make no explicit mention of the Messiah,[1] it is clear that we have to do with a subject as wide as the entire eschatological hope of Israel. For the hope of Israel was the hope of the coming Kingdom of God.

But we cannot consider that hope in a vacuum, as it were, by an analysis of the various passages that express it. That hope had its roots in Israel's faith and in Israel's history, and we must attempt to trace

---

[1] Properly speaking, the messianic hope is the hope of the coming Prince (Anointed One) of the line of David, as in the passage just quoted. A messianic passage, then, is one that specifically mentions the Messiah. In a loose and popular sense, however, "messianic" has come to be a designation for all passages which speak of the future hope of Israel, whether the Messiah is mentioned or not.

18

them. This is not idle antiquarian curiosity, as a moment's reflection would show. Isaiah, for example, although he gave the hope of the Messiah Prince its definitive formulation, and although we may declare that he was surely inspired of God to do so, clearly did not shape his idea out of the blue. Revelation, here as always, was organic to the life of the people, and its shape was hammered out of tragic experience. Before there could have been the hope for a Prince of David's line, there had to be—David. Before the hope of a messianic Kingdom there had to be —the Kingdom of Israel. In short, before Israel's hope of the Kingdom of God could assume such a form, she had first to build a kingdom on this earth. We shall therefore have to go back and consider the rise of the Davidic state and those ideas which it released into the Hebrew soul.

The Davidic state would, however, be a very poor place to begin, for it created neither Israel's faith nor the notion of the Kingdom of God. True it powerfully shaped and colored both for all time to come, but Israel's faith had already assumed its normative form long before David was born. The idea of the rule of God over his people was already there. Indeed, the Davidic state was itself no little limited by that idea, and there were some, as we shall see, who even felt that it was in fundamental contradiction to it. So we are driven back into that earliest and formative period of Israel's history in which both people and religion took shape. There, in the heritage of Moses himself, we shall find the beginnings of her hope of the Kingdom of God. For this was no idea picked up along the way by cultural borrowing, nor was it the creation of the monarchy and its institutions, nor yet the outgrowth of the frustration of national ambition, however much all these factors may have colored it. On the contrary, it is linked with Israel's whole notion of herself as the chosen people of God, and this in turn was woven into the texture of her faith from the beginning. Only so can its tenacity and its tremendous creative power, both in Old Testament and New, be explained.

We have opened a subject as wide as the Old Testament faith itself, and one to which we shall find it difficult to do justice in so brief a compass. But we have no course but to essay it. There is no other way.

I

We must, then, begin our story in the latter half of the thirteenth century B.C., for it was then that Israel began her life as a people in the Promised Land.

19

Let us look briefly at the world of the day. The long reign of Ramesses II (1301-1234) [2] was moving toward its end, and Egypt's great period of empire had not long to go. Egypt was now an ancient country with well-nigh two thousand years of recorded history behind her. Some three hundred years before, under the dynamic pharaohs of the XVIII Dynasty, she had entered her period of greatest military glory, at the height of which she ruled an empire which stretched from the fourth cataract of the Nile to the great bend of the Euphrates. The instruments of power were in her hands, and she knew how to use them. Her army, based on the horse-drawn chariot and the composite bow, possessed a mobility and a fire power few could withstand. Her navy ruled the seas. And in spite of temporary weakness in the early fourteenth century, as the XVIII Dynasty gave way to the XIX, and in spite of Hittite pressure in the north, the empire had been maintained fundamentally intact. Ramesses II was able to fight the Hittites to a bloody stalemate in Syria and to end his days in peace and glory—and considerable vainglory.

But the great Ramesses died, and under his successors the glory of Egypt slipped away. His son Marniptah came to the throne, already an old man, and in his short reign (1234-1225) had to fight twice for Egypt's life. Hordes of strange peoples, whom the Egyptians called the "Peoples of the Sea," were pressing upon the land down the invasion route from Libya, that route most recently traversed by Rommel's famed *Afrika Korps*. Only by the most strenuous effort was the pharaoh able to repel them. Then Marniptah died, and there ensued twenty years of weakness and anarchy followed by a dynastic change. Although the XX Dynasty took over and restored order, troubles were by no means at an end. Ramesses III (1195-1164), who might be called the last of Egypt's great pharaohs, had need of all his strength in order to deal with yet further invasions of the "Peoples of the Sea" from Libya, from the direction of Palestine, and by sea.

The "Peoples of the Sea" are an intriguing subject into which we can-

[2] For the sake of consistency the dates given for this period of Egypt's history will follow those in W. F. Albright, *From the Stone Age to Christianity* (Baltimore: Johns Hopkins Press, 1940), which are those of L. Borchardt. If the chronology of M. B. Rowton (*Journal of Egyptian Archaeology*, 34 [1948], 57-74) be correct—and Albright himself is inclined to accept it (*American Journal of Archaeology*, LIV-3 [1950], 164, 170)—the date for Ramesses II must be lowered to 1290-1224, that for Ramesses III to ca. 1180-1150, and others correspondingly.

not go.[3] Their names: Ruka, Tursha, Aqiwasha, Shardina, Perasata, etc., show them to be Aegean peoples in a great race migration. They interest us chiefly because in the Perasata (Pelasata, biblical Peleshet) we recognize the Philistines—of whom more later. Although Egypt was able to save herself, she was internally sick. Bled white by incessant war, her army depending ever more largely on mercenaries, the drive which had sustained her for so many centuries had nearly played itself out. Apparently the will to empire had been lost. At any rate, under the successors of Ramesses III, the futile Ramessides (IV-XII), all traces of the empire vanished, never to be recovered again. By the latter part of the twelfth century Egypt was but a memory in Asia—albeit a potent one, as later history illustrates.

On the northeastern frontier of Egypt lies Palestine, the stage of the drama with which we are concerned. For centuries Palestine had been an Egyptian province. She had developed no political unity; Egypt had allowed none.[4] Her population, predominantly Canaanite, was organized into a patchwork of petty city states, each with its king, subject to the pharaoh. In addition Egyptian governors, with their garrisons and tax-gatherers, were spotted through the land in a sort of dual control. Since the Egyptian bureaucracy was notoriously corrupt and rapacious, the land went from bad to worse. And when at last the power of the pharaoh slipped away, there remained a political vacuum. Left without a master were the Canaanite kinglets, each behind the ramparts of his pitiful walled town. Virtually every man's hand was against his neighbor in a sordid tale of rivalries too petty for history to notice. No unity existed, and Canaan was incapable of creating any.

Now Palestine is geographically defenseless, as all who have seen it on the map know.[5] Not only is it sandwiched between the great powers of the Nile and the Euphrates and condemned by its position and small size to be a helpless pawn between them; it is also wide open to the desert on the east. Its entire history has been a tale of intermittent infiltration from that quarter. Beginning at least in the fourteenth cen-

[3] For the latest discussion see the article of Albright mentioned above: "Some Oriental Glosses on the Homeric Problem," *American Journal of Archaeology*, LIV-3 (1950), 162-76.

[4] What little had once existed had apparently been broken up some centuries previously by the Hyksos invaders; cf. A. Alt, *Die Landnahme der Israeliten in Palästina* (Leipzig: Druckerei der Werkgemeinschaft, 1925).

[5] For all matters of biblical geography the reader is urged to consult G. E. Wright and F. V. Filson, *The Westminster Historical Atlas to the Bible* (Philadelphia: The Westminster Press, 1945).

tury, if not as early as the sixteenth, and continuing progressively in the thirteenth, just such a process had been going on. Palestine and the surrounding lands were in course of receiving a new population. The Amarna Letters of the fourteenth century, where some of the invaders are called Ḥabiru,[6] are a witness to this process, while by the thirteenth century Edomites, Moabites, and Ammonites had established themselves in their lands east of the Jordan. The Egyptians apparently could not stop these incursions, or did not care to.

In the decades after 1250 B.C., however, utter catastrophe struck Palestine. The Canaanite population sustained one of a series of blows that was ultimately to cost them nine tenths of their land holdings in Palestine and Syria. This is the story that we may see through the eyes of the book of Joshua. It is a story of bloody war; the smoke of burning towns and the stench of rotting flesh hang over its pages. It begins as the Israelite tribesmen, who have already run wild through the Amorite kingdoms of eastern Palestine, are poised on the bank of Jordan in sight of the Promised Land. Suddenly they are across the river dry-shod, the walls of Jericho fall flat at the sound of the trumpet, and Canaanite hearts melt with terror. Then follow in rapid succession three lightning thrusts—through the center of the land (chs. 7–9), into the south country (ch. 10), and into the far north (ch. 11)—and the whole mountain spine of Palestine is theirs. Were it not for the iron chariots (Judg. 1:19) which no foot soldier could face, they would have had the coast plain as well. Having occupied the land, they divide it among their tribes. It is a land made desert: the inhabitants have uniformly been butchered, the cities put to the torch.

Did the Canaanites know who these people were? Probably they thought them Ḥabiru (Hebrews) like others who had preceded them. Perhaps they knew, though, that they called themselves the Benê Yisrā' ēl, the children of Israel. Perhaps they learned, too—first with amusement, then with horror—that these desert men were possessed of

---

[6] The Amarna Letters were written by vassal kings of Palestine and Syria to the court of Amenophis IV (1377-1360) at Tell el-Amarna, where they were found. The name Ḥabiru (in other texts ʿApiru or Khapiru) seems to be etymologically the equivalent of Hebrew, although there is much debate on this point. But the presence of the name over a span of centuries in places as far removed as Nuzi in Mesopotamia, Boghaz-Köi in Asia Minor, Ras Shamra in northern Syria, as well as in Egypt, forbids us simply to identify the two. Ḥabiru seems to have been a class, not a racial, designation. While the Hebrews of the Bible were no doubt Ḥabiru, the latter term included far more than the biblical Hebrews.

the fantastic notion that their God had promised them this land, and they were there to take it!

It is not to be imagined, of course, that the Israelite conquest of Palestine was either as simple, as sudden, or as complete as a casual reading of Joshua might lead one to suppose. On the contrary, that book gives but a partial and schematized account of an incredibly complex process. New blood had, as we have seen, been in process of infiltrating Palestine for centuries. Many of these peoples, no doubt of kindred (Ḥabiru) stock to the people of the conquest, came to terms with the latter and were incorporated into their tribal structure.[7] Nor are we to suppose that when the conquest was over, the land was cleared of its original inhabitants and entirely occupied by Israel. A careful reading of the records will show that Canaanites continued to hold the plain, and even enclaves in the mountains, such as Jerusalem (cf. Judg. 1). Side by side with these people the Israelites had to live. The occupation of Palestine was thus partly a process of absorption which went on at least until David consolidated the entire land. It is clear from this that the nation Israel, which came to be, was not by any means composed exclusively of the descendants of those who had come from Egypt, a fact which partly explains her vulnerability to pagan notions. Still, for all these qualifications, the historicity of a concerted onslaught in the thirteenth century can no longer be questioned in view of overwhelming archaeological evidence.[8] It was then that Palestine became the home of Israel.

[7] Josh. 24 seems clearly to reflect the integration of new blood into the Israelite tribal league. It will be noted that some of the participants, unlike the Israelites of the Exodus, were still pagans (vss. 14 ff.). That Canaanites were also gradually absorbed is witnessed by a variety of evidence: e.g., Canaanite cities such as Shechem (Gen. 34), Hepher, and Tirzah (Josh. 12:17, 24) appear also as subclans of Manasseh (Josh. 17:2-3).

[8] Towns such as Bethel, Lachish, Eglon, and Debir (all mentioned in Josh. 10 or Judg. 1) are known to have been put to the torch and reoccupied at this time. Jericho and Ai (Josh. 6–8) raise particular problems but cannot be used to impeach the essential historicity of the Joshua narrative. For a statement of the evidence see W. F. Albright, "The Israelite Conquest of Canaan in the Light of Archaeology," *Bulletin of the American Schools of Oriental Research*, 74 (1939), 11-23; cf. idem, *The Archaeology of Palestine* (Harmondsworth: Pelican Books, 1949), pp. 108-9. For an excellent popular summary cf. G. E. Wright, "Epic of Conquest," *The Biblical Archaeologist*, III-3 (1940), 25-40; cf. idem, "The Literary and Historical Problem of Josh. 10 and Judges 1," *Journal of Near Eastern Studies*, V-2 (1946), 105-14. The latest and most complete discussion of the whole problem of Exodus and conquest is H. H. Rowley, *From Joseph to Joshua* (London: Oxford University Press, 1950). My views are expressed at greater length in the Introduction and Exegesis of Joshua in *The Interpreter's Bible*, Vol. II (New York and Nashville: Abingdon-Cokesbury Press, 1953).

Of this climactic phase of the conquest the book of Joshua tells, in its own way, the story.

II

So Israel began her history as a people in the Promised Land. That was in itself an event of no great importance, and history would scarcely have remembered it at all had it not been for the fact that these tribesmen brought with them a religion the like of which had never been seen on earth before. Israel's faith was a drastic and, one might say, a rationally inexplicable break with ancient paganism.[9] The father of that faith was Moses. The exact nature of the Mosaic religion is, of course, a vexed question, and we cannot launch into a lengthy discussion of it here. Yet it is important that we pause to point out its salient features.

1. The faith of Israel was unique in many respects. First of all, it was a monotheism.[10] There is but one God, and the command, "You shall have no other gods before [i.e., beside] me," sternly forbade the Israelite to worship any other.[11] Whether the Israelite at this period actually denied that other gods existed is a point that has occasioned much debate. Certainly monotheism was not so early a logically formulated doctrine, and, equally certain, the full implications of monotheistic belief were centuries in being drawn. Further, it is to be admitted that Israelite practice, especially as Israel came into contact with the older

[9] For an excellent introduction to the mind of ancient paganism, pointing up its radical difference from that of Israel, cf. H. Frankfort, ed., *The Intellectual Adventure of Ancient Man* (Chicago: University of Chicago Press, 1946). A splendid statement of the peculiar nature of Israel's faith is G. E. Wright, *The Old Testament Against Its Environment* (Chicago: Henry Regnery Co., 1950).

[10] It is no longer possible to view early Israel's faith as a tribal religion which gradually evolved into monotheism, as was the fashion in the Wellhausen school; recently I. G. Matthews, *The Religious Pilgrimage of Israel* (New York: Harper & Bros., 1947). The authoritative statement of the evidence for Mosaic monotheism is W. F. Albright, *From the Stone Age to Christianity*, ch. iv. Unwilling to define Mosaic religion as more than an incipient monotheism, but strongly asserting the unity of Israel's faith, are, e.g.: W. Eichrodt, *Theologie des Alten Testaments* (3rd ed.; Berlin: Evangelische Verlagsanstalt, 1948), I, 1-6, 104 ff., *et passim*; in popular language H. H. Rowley, *The Rediscovery of the Old Testament* (Philadelphia: The Westminster Press, 1946), ch. v.

[11] The Decalogue, in a form underlying the parallel versions in Exod. 20 and Deut. 5, must, in the writer's opinion, be regarded as the very charter of Mosaism. Cf. P. Volz, *Mose und Sein Werk* (Tübingen: J. C. B. Mohr, 1932), pp. 20 ff., for a strong defense; in English, H. H. Rowley, "Moses and the Decalogue" (*Bulletin of the John Rylands Library*, 34 [Sept., 1951]) with full bibliography.

24

population of Canaan, was frequently anything but monotheistic. Yet in that Israel's faith not only commanded the exclusion of other gods from Israel, but also deprived them of all function and power in the universe and rendered them nonentities, it certainly deserves to be called a monotheism. And all this the Mosaic faith did. Its God stands quite alone. It is he who, even in the old creation story (Gen. 2:4 ff.), created all things without assistance or intermediary; his very name Yahweh claims for him this function.[12] No pantheon surrounds him. He has no consort (the Hebrew does not even have a word for "goddess") and no progeny. Consequently the Hebrews, in sharpest contrast to their neighbors, developed no mythology. No doubt their zeal for this newly found faith does much to explain their almost fanatical fury in the days of the conquest.

Furthermore, Israel's faith was aniconic: its God could not be depicted or imaged in any form. The words of the Second Commandment, "You shall not make yourself a graven image," make this clear. No ancient paganism could have said such a thing. Yet it is consistent with the whole witness of the Old Testament which, however much it says about the worship of false gods, affords no clear reference to any attempt to make an image of Yahweh. That a strong feeling against doing such a thing existed in Israel at all periods of her history is clearly illustrated by the fact that archaeology has not yet found a single male image in any ancient Israelite town so far excavated. It is only in the light of such an aniconic, monotheistic tradition, centuries old, that it is possible to understand the fierce prophet hatred of all pagan gods and idols.

But there is another point, in many ways the most striking of all: Israel believed that her God both could and did control the events of history, that in them he might reveal his righteous judgment and saving power. Here is the sharpest break with paganism imaginable. The ancient paganisms were all polytheistic, with dozens of gods arranged in complex pantheons. These gods were for the most part personifications of the forces of nature or other cosmic functions; they were in and of nature and, like nature, without any particular moral character. Their will could be manipulated in the ritual (which re-enacted the myth) so that they would bestow on the worshiper the desired tangible benefits. In

---

[12] *Jehovah* (Heb. *Yahweh*) seems to be part of a formula (cf. Exod. 3:14) meaning, "He who causes to be what comes into existence." Cf. W. F. Albright, *From the Stone Age to Christianity*, pp. 197-98.

such religions no moral interpretation of events, nor indeed any consistent interpretation, was possible, for no one god ruled history. The God of Israel is of a totally different sort. He controls sun, moon, and stars; works now in the fire, now in the storm—but he is identified with none of these. He has no fixed place of abode in heaven or on earth, but comes to the aid of his people and exhibits his power where he will, be it in Egypt, at Sinai, or in Canaan. He is no personification of natural force to be appeased by ritual (in Israel's faith nature is "de-mythologized"); he is a moral Being who controls nature and history, and in them reveals his righteous will and summons men to obey it.

This notion of God is no late development in Israel, but is very ancient. As far back as the biblical records go, we see the God who is powerful over nature and history.[13] It is he who, having created all things, disposes of the destinies of all the families of men and calls Abraham to serve his purpose. It is he who humbles the pride of pharaoh to the dust and engulfs his army in the sea. He delivers his people from all their foes, provides sustenance for them in the wilderness, dries up the flood of Jordan, brings Jericho's walls tumbling to the ground, and paralyzes the Canaanites with terror. The dark powers of the plagues do his bidding, as do the sea waters and the wind (Exod. 15:1-17), the sun and the moon and the stars (Josh. 10:12-13; Judg. 5:20), and the rain (Judg. 5:4, 21). It is he, too, who when his people have sinned, turns the battle against them and delivers them to their foes (Josh. 7; I Sam. 4).

2. The God of Israel stands before us as one God—invisible, Creator of all things, Ruler of nature and history—absolutely unique in the ancient world. But that is not all. Israel did not believe merely that such a God existed; she was convinced that this God had, in a historical

---

[13] A much larger body of literature goes back to the earliest period (tenth century and before) than was formerly thought. This includes poems—e.g., the Song of Deborah (Judg. 5); Josh. 10:12-13; the Blessing of Jacob (Gen. 49); the Blessing of Moses (Deut. 33; cf. Cross and Freedman, *Journal of Biblical Literature*, LXVII [1948], 191-210); the Balaam poems (Num. 23–24; cf. Albright, *idem*, LXIII [1944], 207-33); the Song of Moses (Exod. 15; cf. Albright, *Studies in Old Testament Prophecy*, H. H. Rowley, ed. [Edinburgh: T. & T. Clark, 1950], pp. 5-6); numerous psalms (e.g., 29, 67, 68). Besides these are the David biography (II Sam. 9–20; I Kings 1–2) and no doubt others of the Samuel-Saul-David cycles. Further, even if we were to grant that the stories of the Patriarchs, Exodus, and conquest (in their oldest recension commonly called J) received final form only in the ninth century (the writer prefers an earlier date), they must be assumed to contain material and to rest on a chain of tradition centuries older.

act, chosen her, entered into covenant with her, and made her his people.[14]

We can find no period in her history when Israel did not believe that she was the chosen people of Yahweh. And this choosing had taken place in history. The Bible story traces this history of election back to Abraham, but it was in the Exodus events that Israel saw her real beginnings as a people.[15] The memory of the Exodus towered over the national consciousness for all time to come. The prophets harked back to it repeatedly. Here is the unforgettable example of the power and grace of God (Amos 2:9-11; Mic. 6:2-5; Ezek. 20:5-7), here he carried infant Israel as a little child (Hos. 11:1), here he married her in the covenant ceremony and claimed her loyalty forevermore (Hos. 2; Jer. 2:2-3). But this was no esoteric notion advanced by the spiritual leaders; the people were saturated with it. Indeed, so confident were they that they were God's chosen and favored people, that the prophet preaching of doom could only seem to them the most utter nonsense. It was a conceit that the prophets, from Amos to Jeremiah, found it impossible to penetrate.

A confidence so powerfully entrenched can have had its origin only in the memory of the Exodus events themselves. The hypercritical attitude toward the Exodus narrative, formerly so popular, can no longer be maintained.[16] There can be no doubt that a band of Hebrews were slaves in Egypt; that Moses, under the impetus of a tremendous religious experience, led them thence to the accompaniment of happenings so stupendous that they were never forgotten; and that they then came to the mountain in the wilderness where there took place those events which made them a people and gave them that distinctive religion which would mold the whole course of their history. Israel's origins are thus linked to historical events as surely as are those of Christianity.

[14] The covenant idea is so important that W. Eichrodt, op. cit., has reconstructed the entire Old Testament theology around it. The writer is in fundamental agreement. It is true that the word "covenant" is rarely used in the earliest sources, but the idea is larger than the word. It is linked with Israel's whole notion of election and with the very structure of the tribal league. Cf. Wright, op. cit., pp. 54-68.

[15] On the Old Testament idea of election cf. H. H. Rowley, The Biblical Doctrine of Election (London: Lutterworth Press, 1950); also Wright, op. cit., ch. ii. The patriarchal narratives are not to be viewed with the once-fashionable hypercriticism: cf. Albright, From the Stone Age to Christianity, pp. 179-89; Rowley, "Recent Discovery and the Patriarchal Age" (Bulletin of the John Rylands Library, 32 [Sept., 1949]) with full bibliography.

[16] Cf. Albright, From Stone Age to Christianity, pp. 189-96, for the evidence.

As Israel absorbed new blood into her tribal structure, the Exodus tradition extended itself and became normative for all, even for those whose ancestors had not participated in the Exodus.[17]

Since this is so, far more important than the actual events is the interpretation Israel laid upon them in the light of her faith. The Exodus was viewed as a sheer act of God's grace. The signs and wonders in Egypt, the wind that drove the sea waters back, the deliverance from pharaoh's army—all are illustrations of that grace (hesed). It was grace because it was absolutely unmerited. The Old Testament never suggests that Israel was chosen for any merit that was in her; on the contrary, the Exodus narratives are at pains to depict a people who are cowardly, ungrateful, and utterly unworthy. The Exodus was the act of a God who chose for himself a people that they might choose him. The covenant concluded at Sinai could, then, be understood in Hebrew theology only as a response to grace: man's hesed for God's hesed.[18] The Old Testament covenant was thus always properly viewed, like the New, as a covenant of grace. This ought to be kept in mind. The strictures of Paul and others (e.g., Gal. 4:24-25; Heb. 8) against a covenant of works, however justified they may have been, were far more apropos to the Judaism of their own day than to the Old Testament faith. For Israel had begun its history as a nation summoned by God's grace to be his people, to serve him alone and to obey his covenant law. *The notion of a people of God, called to live under the rule of God, begins just here, and with it the notion of the Kingdom of God.*[19]

3. These ideas were tremendously dynamic and creative. On the one hand, a deeply moral note was injected into Israel's notion of her place as a chosen people which she was never allowed to forget, however much

---

[17] Perhaps somewhat as the traditions of early America have become normative for all Americans, even those but recently arrived. Thus the child of immigrant parents may speak—and with justice—of our Pilgrim Fathers.

[18] The word hesed cannot be exactly translated. The usual rendition in the English Bible ("lovingkindness," "mercy," etc.) is most inadequate. The word is intimately related to the idea of the covenant. When it is used of God, it is very nearly the equivalent of "grace." It refers to the favor of God which summoned Israel into covenant and the steadfast love which he shows them even in spite of unworthiness. When used of man, the word denotes that proper response to grace which is utter loyalty to the covenant God and obedience to his will. Cf. N. H. Snaith, *Distinctive Ideas of the Old Testament* (Philadelphia: The Westminster Press, 1946), ch. v; and, more briefly, idem, in A *Theological Word Book of the Bible*, A. Richardson, ed. (New York: The Macmillan Co., 1951), pp. 136-37.

[19] Cf. Eichrodt, op. cit., I, 8, et passim. This does not mean that we may read either the New Testament doctrine or later Old Testament concepts of the kingship of Yahweh back into this primitive theocracy.

she might try. On the other hand, there was kindled a lively hope which nothing could erase. This note is sounded in the oldest Exodus narrative, and it is not too much to say that the entire prophet preaching is based upon it: "Now therefore, if you will obey my voice and keep my covenant, you shall be my own possession among all peoples" (Exod. 19:5). In this sentence, and in the faith that produced it, there lie the germs both of the prophet preaching of doom and of their eschatological hope.

Conditioned by this faith Israel could never properly take her status as a chosen people for granted; it was morally conditioned. She was no superior race, favored because she deserved it. Her God was not a sort of national genius, blood kin to her, whose worship and favor were posited in the scheme of things. Hers was a cosmic God who in a historical act had chosen her, and whom she in a free, moral act had chosen. The covenant bond between them was thus neither mechanical nor eternal. While it could not be called a bargain—it was not between equals—it nevertheless partook of the nature of a bargain in that it was a bilateral compact. God would give Israel a destiny as his people, would defend and establish her, but only so long as she obeyed him. The covenant laid heavy demands on Israel. Specifically it demanded *hesed*, a grateful and complete loyalty to the God of the covenant to the exclusion of all other gods. Equally, it demanded strict obedience to the laws of the covenant in all human relationships within the covenant brotherhood. Before these demands Israel had to live continually in judgment. That judgment the prophets pronounced, and it is in the light of this theology that we must understand their verdict upon the nation.

But at the same time this covenant-people idea imparted to Israel a tremendous sense of destiny and a confidence that would not down. Every reader knows that the Old Testament faith housed a glorious hope which no tragedy, however total, could defeat. The careful reader knows, too, of a fatuous popular optimism which had no business to exist, but which the fist of the prophet word was powerless to demolish. Israel's faith was strongly eschatological in orientation, because history itself was to the Hebrew mind eschatologically orientated: it was guided to a destination by God. And this gave to the Israelite a robust confidence in the future.

This, too, is no late development. To be sure, a definite notion of

29

"the last things" emerged only in a later period, and it may be misleading to use the word "eschatology" in connection with the faith of early Israel. But the germs of it are there. In the earliest literature that we have (see note 13 above), we may observe the confidence that events are moving toward a destination, an effective terminus beyond which one need not look. We see it in the ancient epic of the Patriarchs, told for centuries about nomad campfire and at pilgrim shrine: there is a good land "flowing with milk and honey" which our God has promised us (Exod. 3:8, 17); there is a mighty nation which we shall one day be (Gen. 12:2). God will defend us from all our foes (Num. 23:21-24; 24:8-9) and will make us great (Num. 23:9-10; 24:5-7). He will make us to live in unimagined peace and plenty (Gen. 49:25-26; Deut. 33:13-17), until the divinely sent leader appears whom all the nations will serve (Gen. 49:10; Num.24:17-19). He has called us to a destiny, to serve his purpose in the world (Gen. 12:3; 18:18; 22:18). Such a faith, we may believe, filled the future with light and carried Israel over insurmountable obstacles into the Promised Land.

Thus to expect great things of the future, it must be emphasized, lay in the very nature of Israel's faith from the beginning. If God be the Lord of history who works his will in history, and if he has chosen Israel to serve his purpose, then surely he will bring that purpose to its conclusion. And if he has, in the covenant bond, demanded of Israel full obedience, he has also promised that if they obeyed, he would defend them and establish them in the Promised Land. And he is powerful to do so, and his word is faithful. What outcome, then, could history have but the fulfillment of promise, the establishment of God's chosen people under his rule in peace? The future leads on to the victory of God's purpose. The seeds of that tenacious confidence in the coming Kingdom of God thus lie here in the faith that made Israel a people.[20]

[20] In fairness to the reader it must be said that there is the widest divergence of opinion regarding the origins of Israelite eschatology. W. Eichrodt (op. cit., I, 240-57) has splendidly expressed what is essentially my own position, which has been briefly stated in an article, "Faith and Destiny" (Interpretation, V-1 [1951], 9-11). The effort of Gunkel, Gressmann, Breasted, and others (see references in above article) to explain Old Testament eschatology as a borrowing from Egypt or Babylon seems to me unsuccessful—so also that of Mowinckel and others to find its origin in an annual Enthronement Festival supposed to have taken place during the monarchy. Although Hebrew eschatology is superficially paralleled in pagan texts, and although a royal ideology and the frustration of national political hopes no doubt stimulated it and gave it shape, its origin must be sought in the very nature of Israel's faith itself.

III

But let us return to Israel as she first emerges into history in the Promised Land in the thirteenth century B.C.

1. It must be understood that the Israel of the early days in Palestine was not at all a nation as we would understand the term. On the contrary, she was a tribal league, a loose confederation of clans united one to another about the worship of the common God.[21] There was no statehood or central government of any sort. The clans were independent units unto themselves. Within the clans there was recognition of the moral authority of the sheikhs, or elders, but organized authority was lacking. Furthermore, society exhibited no class distinctions, no wide rift between rich and poor, ruler and subject, but that rather complete democracy characteristic of nomad life. The focal point of the clans was the shrine of the Ark, which moved from place to place and finally came to rest in Shiloh (I Sam. 1–4). Here the tribesmen gathered on feast days to seek the presence of their God and to renew their allegiance to him. This tribal structure corresponds perfectly to the covenant-people idea and may be assumed to be an outworking of it. The covenant league was a brotherhood; it was ruled only by the law of the covenant God.

One may best see how the primitive order in Israel operated from a reading of the book of Judges. Here we see the clans maintaining a precarious existence, surrounded by foes but without government, central authority, or state organization of any sort. In times of danger there would arise a hero, one upon whom the spirit of Yahweh rushed (Judg. 3:10; 14:6), called a judge (shôphēt). He would rally the surrounding clans and deal with the foe. While his victories no doubt gained him prestige, he was in no sense a king. His authority was neither absolute over all Israel nor permanent; in no case was it hereditary. The battle strength of the judge was the voluntary levy of the clans; he had no standing army, no court, no administrative machinery whatever. His authority rested solely in those dynamic qualities which made

---

[21] She was very like a Grecian amphictyony, such as the Delphic league, numerous examples of which are known, many of them with twelve members. The basic discussion is M. Noth, *Das System der zwölf Stämme Israels* (Stuttgart: W. Kohlhammer, 1930); in English, W. F. Albright, *Archaeology and the Religion of Israel* (Baltimore: Johns Hopkins Press, 1942), pp. 95-110.

him the man of the hour. This type of authority has aptly been called charisma.[22] And charisma well represented the primitive theocracy of Israel: it was the direct rule of God over his people through his designated representative.

2. Now this tribal theocracy was an incredibly stubborn and tenacious pattern. It did not give way quickly. The conquest, it is true, led Israel into an entirely new situation. It represented a shift from the nomad to the agrarian life. And while the shift was not at all uniform (on the desert fringe it was never completed), Israel speedily became a nation of small farmers. This meant some economic betterment, as archaeology abundantly shows. Indeed that is why the nomad covets the soil. It also meant the beginning of that long adjustment to the superior material culture—and the religion—of the Canaanites which was to be so portentous for Israel.

But Israel did not at once surrender the old order. On the contrary, for some two hundred years after the conquest (through the period of the judges) the old order persisted. Israel remained a tribal league, a racial (if such a hodgepodge as early Israel could be called a race) and religious unit, not a geographical or political one. The principle of leadership remained the charisma. She did not organize a state or make any move to do so. Specifically, she did not imitate the city-state pattern of Canaan.

Nor was this an accident. On the contrary, the idea of monarchy was consciously rejected. This is illustrated in the words with which stout Gideon spurned a crown: "I will not rule over you, and my son will not rule over you; the Lord will rule over you" (Judg. 8:23).[23] It echoes in the fable told by Jotham (Judg. 9:7-21), which makes it plain that only a worthless bramble of a man, who had no useful employment, would aspire to be a king. In both the spirit of old Israel, of the tribal league, speaks. Only in the light of such an ingrained feeling can one understand the conduct of Samuel, himself the father of the monarchy, when the people demanded a king. We hear the old prophet castigate

[22] See especially A. Alt, *Die Staatenbildung der Israeliten in Palästina* (Leipzig: A. Edelmann, 1930). The term is originally Max Weber's.

[23] I find it impossible to agree with those commentators (e.g., G. F. Moore, *Judges* [International Critical Commentary; New York: Chas. Scribner's Sons, 1895, 1923], p. 230) who regard the verse as the reflection of late, antimonarchical sentiment. It is part of an unimpeachably old narrative.

the notion of monarchy as a craven imitation of pagan ways and a flagrant rejection of Yahweh (I Sam. 8).[24]

3. So might matters have remained indefinitely had not a new menace appeared: the Philistines. Of Aegean origin (cf. Amos 9:7) they were one of the "Peoples of the Sea" who had battered at Egypt's door during the reigns of Marniptah and Ramesses III. They were a part of a great racial migration (not unconnected with the story of the Iliad) which had overrun all the Hittite Empire and the Syrian coast. Presumably they settled on the coastland of Palestine after their defeat by Ramesses III in 1188 B.C.[25] Thus their arrival fell approximately within the half century after that of the Israelites.

The Philistines put charisma to a new and severer test. The Israelite conquest had been possible, humanly speaking, because the Canaanite petty states could offer no unified resistance. And the tribal league had been able to survive in Palestine because its foes—petty kinglets or Bedouin raiders—were such that the informal rally of the clans could deal with them. In short, charisma had survived because Israel had never been called upon to meet a well-organized military state. But the Philistines were just that. They were a tightly-knit, well-armed, disciplined military people. They gradually began to dominate Palestine. It was their aim to inherit the hegemony over the land which had but recently slipped from the hand of the pharaohs.

It was an emergency which threatened Israel with permanent slavery. The decisive blow, of which we read in I Sam. 4, came about 1050 B.C., although border fighting such as that reflected in the Samson stories had been going on for years. It was utter defeat. Israel was cut to pieces; the Ark—the holy object of the covenant league—captured; Hophni and Phinehas, priests of the Ark, killed; and Shiloh with its shrine razed to the ground (as archaeology tells us). It was the deepest military and spiritual humiliation. Thereafter we see Philistine garrisons in the heart of Israel (I Sam. 13:4), and Israel itself disarmed and its war potential

---

[24] In I Sam. 8–13 the historian has woven together two parallel stories of the rise of Saul (see the commentaries), one of them tacitly favorable to the monarchy, the other bitterly hostile. Ch. 8 belongs to the latter. But it is not on that account to be regarded as a late, even exilic production (so, e.g., H. P. Smith, *Samuel* [International Critical Commentary; New York: Chas. Scribner's Sons, 1899, 1909], p. 55) reflecting disillusionment with the state. On the contrary, the two stories accurately reflect the tension which was there from the beginning.

[25] Cf. note 2 above. Perhaps a date some fifteen years later would be more correct.

destroyed (I Sam. 13:19-23). Charisma had failed; the people of Yahweh were crushed.

4. In the face of this emergency the first step toward statehood was made. It was made with reluctance, and it ended in failure. Now we are neither surprised that it was made nor that this was done reluctantly. It was done, as has been said, out of sheer necessity. The ill-trained, unorganized clan militia could not face the Philistine army. It was a case of do it or be enslaved, and for a freeborn Israelite the choice was clear. Yet this was a hard choice, for it represented a step toward an authority totally foreign to Israel's tradition. In the light of this tension we may understand the enigmatic figure of Samuel, who appears now as Saul's patron (I Sam. 9), now as bitterly reluctant (I Sam. 8), and who, when Saul got out of hand, deserts him and breaks him (I Sam. 13:8-15; 15).

Saul is a fascinating figure. Of giant size and fine looks (I Sam. 9:2; 10:23), fiercely courageous (11:1-11), modest (9:21), of magnanimous spirit (11:12-13), there was nevertheless in him the taint of a mental and emotional instability which was his undoing. We cannot here trace his story. The reader will find it in I Sam. 9–31. There he will read of the initial victories (13–14) which broke the Philistine hold on central Palestine; of the break with Samuel, who never did really approve; of that jealousy of David which drove the king to madness and suicide.

Now Saul, although king, was as little a change from the old order as possible. He rose in the old-fashioned way, as a charismatic man upon whom the spirit of Yahweh rushed (I Sam. 11:6-7). Indeed he scarcely differed from the judges at all except that he was acclaimed king [26] "for the duration" (11:15), and the "duration" outlasted the life of Saul (14:52). Nor did Saul alter the internal structure of Israel. While he no doubt made some effort to weld Israel together more tightly,[27] in no sense did he create a state. He had no administrative machinery, levied no taxes, and his court was so modest it hardly deserves the name (I Sam. 22:6). It is true that he began to gather about him a bodyguard

---

[26] It is interesting that the old narrative of I Sam. 9 refrains from using the word "king" (melek), preferring instead the word "leader" (nāgîd). Cf. Eichrodt, Israel in der Weissagung des Alten Testaments (Zürich: Gotthelf-Verlag, 1951), p. 22; cf. also II Sam. 5:2.

[27] His service to the people of Jabesh-gilead won their undying devotion (cf. I Sam. 11; 31:11-13). Perhaps the campaign against Amalek (I Sam. 15) was designed partly to woo Judah. At any rate, there were those in the south who preferred Saul to their own David (I Sam. 23:19-23; 26:1-2).

of tough soldiers (14:52), but, although this was an innovation that had in it the seeds of a standing army, it could hardly be regarded as more than plain military necessity. And when Saul died a suicide on the field of Gilboa (I Sam.31), all that he had worked for was lost. His army was dispersed, his three sons were slain and their bodies, together with his own, shamefully exposed, while the one surviving son—Ish-baal (Ish-bosheth)—fled as a refugee east of the Jordan (II Sam. 2:8-10). The Philistines regained control, and their garrisons were once more to be seen in the land (II Sam. 23:14). Night had returned to Israel.

IV

David was the one who saved his people, dramatically reversed their fortune, and brought them to undreamed of heights of glory. The familiar story of his career cannot be traced here. The fair-haired darling of Saul's court, military hero and giant killer, his exploits aroused popular adulation and provoked Saul's jealousy until he had to flee, first to the wilds of Judah and then into the arms of the Philistines. When Saul was dead, David became king over Judah in Hebron with Philistine consent (II Sam. 2:4).[28] When Ish-baal was subsequently removed, he became king over all Israel (II Sam. 5:1-5). It is with David that a new and different Israel emerges.

1. Now David, too, was in the old tradition: he was a man of charisma. His brilliant exploits were evidence to all Israel that the spirit of Yahweh was with him. Indeed the people began to say in effect that he, not Saul, was the true charismatic:

> Saul has slain his thousands,
> And David his ten thousands.
> (I Sam. 18:7)

Saul realized perfectly that this was tantamount to saying that David ought to be the leader, for he said: "What more can he have but the kingdom?" No doubt this feeling that the "spirit" was slipping away from him served to accelerate his disintegration, while that very dis-

---

[28] David had been a Philistine vassal (I Sam. 27), and he could hardly have taken such a step without at least their tacit approval. No doubt the Philistines wished to keep Israel divided between David and the house of Saul. A unified Israel was the last thing they wanted (II Sam. 5:17).

integration, plus David's continued success, but served to convince the people that the "spirit" had indeed passed to David.

It must be emphasized that early Israel recognized and followed only the charisma. The very language in which the people acclaim David king illustrates this (II Sam. 5:1-2). David could never have become king had he not been regarded as the man of charisma. Heredity counted for nothing, as the sad fate of Ish-baal (II Sam. 2–4) shows. Although Saul's son, and although acclaimed king by his uncle Abner, Ish-baal was apparently a weakling. The people never followed him, king's son or not, and when Abner quarreled with him and left him, nothing remained for the futile puppet but assassination.

Yet at the same time David was a long step from the older order. If he could not have arisen without the charismatic qualities, he did not owe his rise to these alone. For one thing, he had a rugged private army, and their victories contributed to his prestige. First an outlaw band of four hundred (I Sam. 22:2), it later grew to six hundred (I Sam. 27:2), and subsequently was to grow into a considerable foreign legion (II Sam. 8:18; 15:18).[29] He thus created a standing army responsible only to himself. Nor must we discount the sagacity with which David consciously set out to inherit the claims of Saul. He had long tried to win the affections of Judah (e.g., I Sam. 30:26-31). He had married Saul's daughter, and when he became king in Hebron, he demanded her return (II Sam. 3:12-15), although it is apparent that they did not greatly care for each other (II Sam. 6:20-23). And although he scrupulously refused to harm Saul (I Sam. 24:6; 26:10-11) and publicly honored his memory (II Sam. 21:12-14), he nevertheless ordered the execution of Saul's surviving male issue (II Sam. 21:1-10) save for Jonathan's son, the lame Mephibosheth, whom he made a pensioner of his court (II Sam. 9). Whatever David's motives actually were, the house of Saul could only regard this as ruthless political cynicism (II Sam. 16:5-8). Suffice it to say David represented a shift from the old order. He was a charismatic who, aided by his personal soldiery and his political acumen, was acclaimed king in a considered election (II Sam. 5:1-5).

[29] Cherethites and Pelethites are mentioned on several occasions (II Sam. 8:18; 20:23; 15:18). These were, as the names indicate, contingents recruited from the Aegean peoples of the coastal plain. With them on one occasion (II Sam. 15:18) are mentioned six hundred Gittites (men of Gath, a Philistine city).

2. No sooner was David king than he embarked upon that course of action that was utterly to transform Israel. The steps by which he welded the Israelite people into a united nation we can do no more than sketch. First, of course, the Philistine menace had to be dealt with, and David dealt with it for good. The Philistines could not tolerate a united Israel. Indeed their policy had been to play David off against the house of Saul under the principle "divide and rule." So when, with the death of Ish-baal, David was acclaimed king over all Israel, it was their signal to strike (II Sam. 5:17). But the victory was David's. With two crushing blows, both delivered near Jerusalem (II Sam. 5:17-25), he sent them reeling headlong from the Judean mountains. How David followed up his victory we do not know, but in the end the Philistines are subdued and tributary to Israel (II Sam. 8:1). Never again would they be a serious menace.

David went on from victory to victory. Seeing the need of unifying the country, he seized for himself a new capital—Jerusalem (II Sam. 5:6-10), a city hitherto non-Israelite—centrally located between north and south and the property of no one of the tribes (a step to be compared with that of our founding fathers who selected the site of Washington, D.C.). We should note that he took it with his private army (5:6). It was his personal property, and he called it "the city of David" (5:9). Subsequently he reduced one by one, as archaeology proves, the other Canaanite towns that had so far withstood Israel, and incorporated them into his state. The climax of his military glory came when in a series of incredibly brilliant campaigns (II Sam. 8; 10–12) he conquered the Moabite, Ammonite, and Edomite kingdoms of Transjordan and made them tributary, and then went on to extend his victories over the Aramean states of Syria. When the wars were over, David ruled an empire which stretched from the Gulf of Aqabah in the south to central Syria in the far north. Kings still farther to the north hastened to make peace with him (II Sam. 8:9-10).

A more dramatic reversal of fortune could hardly be imagined. In a few short years Israel had been changed from a disorganized league of tribesmen struggling for existence into the ranking nation of Palestine and Syria.

3. David's conquests had laid the basis for an unexampled economic prosperity, and Solomon had the genius to take advantage of it. Israel now controlled the trade routes from Egypt to the north, from the

37

Phoenician littoral to the hinterland, and from Damascus down through Transjordan to the Hedjaz. Solomon enlarged the state no further, but he was able, in spite of disturbances in Edom and Aram (I Kings 11:9-25), to hold the structure together. This he did by fortifying key defense points (I Kings 9:15, 17-19), by developing a formidable chariot arm (I Kings 4:26; 10:26)[30]—a thing never before done in Israel (cf. II Sam. 8:4)—and by a program of judicious alliances. These last, usually sealed by a marriage of convenience, serve to explain the astounding number of wives Solomon is said to have had (I Kings 11:1-3). Foremost among these was none other than the daughter of the pharaoh (I Kings 3:1), who brought with her as a dowry the Canaanite city of Gezer (I Kings 9:16),[31] which pharaoh's army took and handed over to Solomon.

Of all his alliances none was more profitable than that with Hiram, king of Tyre, an alliance already sealed by David (II Sam. 5:11). The Canaanites (whom the Greeks knew as the Phoenicians) were at this period entering the heyday of the overseas commercial expansion which was to make them the great trading people of the ancient world. Solomon linked hands with this expansion. Phoenician materials and Phoenician architects served his building projects (I Kings 5:1-12, 18); Phoenician sailors furnished the "know-how" in the new trading venture out of Ezion-geber down the Red Sea which brought back to the royal court the exotic products of the south (I Kings 9:26-28; 10:11-12, 22). Perhaps stimulated by this activity, the Queen of Sheba came from Arabia to visit Solomon (I Kings 10:1-13), no doubt in the interest of the overland camel caravan trade then newly developing.

Israel was filled with wealth as never before or since. A flourishing trade in horses and chariots between Egypt and Cilicia (I Kings 10:28-29)[32] fed the royal coffers. Vast copper smelteries, the largest known in

[30] One of Solomon's chariot cities, Megiddo (I Kings 9:15), has been excavated by archaeologists of the Oriental Institute. Large stables for horses were found. For a popular discussion cf. Robert M. Engberg, "Megiddo—Guardian of the Carmel Pass," Part II, *The Biblical Archaeologist*, IV-1 (1941), 11-16; cf. G. E. Wright, "The Discoveries at Megiddo, 1935-39," *ibid.*, XIII-2 (1950), 28-46.

[31] W. F. Albright has suggested that "Gezer" is a corruption of "Gerar" (in the Hebrew very similar in appearance), a town near the Egyptian frontier of Palestine (Gen. 26:1); Albright, *Archaeology and the Religion of Israel*, p. 214, and references there.

[32] Reading the Hebrew of I Kings 10:28, "And the source of the horses which Solomon had was . . . from Que [Cilicia]; the king's merchant's got them from Que at a [set] price." Cf. most recently W. F. Albright, *Journal of Biblical Literature*, LXXI (1952), 249.

the ancient world, belched their smoke to the skies at Ezion-geber.[33] Ambitious public works gave employment to thousands. Aside from the temple and the military installations mentioned above, there was a palace for the king—which took longer to build than the temple (cf. I Kings 6:37-38; 7:1)—an armory (7:2), the royal court (7:7), a palace for pharaoh's daughter (7:8), and many other things. The Bible does not tire of telling of the wealth and splendor of the court of Solomon (I Kings 10:11-29).

V

That all this represented a fundamental change is obvious, and it is important that we evaluate it.[34] It was a change which affected the whole structure of Israelite society. The people of Yahweh had become the Kingdom of Israel, the citizens of the Davidic state.

1. Little was left of the old order. The tribal league had given way to the state centered in the king. Such a development was inevitable as David conquered the Canaanite cities of the land and incorporated their population into Israel's structure, and then went on to subdue a polyglot empire. There was need for a standing army, administrative and judicial machinery, the levying of taxes, if such a state was to be governed. But the tribal league had no such machinery. In fact David, not the tribal league, had created the structure. It centered in David, and it was up to him to hold it together. Even the capital city, Jerusalem, was his personal holding. The state had to be organized under the crown. No doubt David's census (II Sam. 24) was a step, and a bitterly resented one, toward measures for conscription and the raising of taxes—both anathema to Israel. The process reached its climax when Solomon virtually abolished the tribal league and substituted for it twelve administrative districts subject to the crown (I Kings 4:7-19). Two of the district governors were the king's own sons-in-law (4:11, 15). The people of Yahweh's covenant had become the people of Solomon's state.

In the process charisma gave way to the dynasty. This, too, was a gradual and inevitable change. Saul had been a charismatic hero ac-

---

[33] These are known from the excavations of Nelson Glueck. Surprisingly the Bible does not mention them. Cf. N. Glueck, *The Other Side of the Jordan* (New Haven: American Schools of Oriental Research, 1940), pp. 89-113.

[34] The work of A. Alt, *Die Staatenbildung der Israeliten in Palästina*, is basic. For a brief discussion of the Davidic state in English see my article, "The Age of King David," *Union Seminary Review*, LIII-2 (1942), 87-109.

claimed king. David, too, was a charismatic; but a private army and considerable political skill had furthered his rise, until he was formally elected king. But the state which David built was so personally his own that it needed an heir of David to hold it together. By the time David grew old, the question was not *if* his son would succeed him, but only *which* son would do so—and the reader of the court history of David (II Sam. 9–20; I Kings 1–2) knows what a rivalry that was. When Solomon came to the throne (I Kings 1), it was by palace plot, without reference to charismatic qualities or popular will at all. Charisma would never again select a leader in Jerusalem. The leader designated by Yahweh's spirit had given way to the anointed son of the anointed king.

Nor was there much left of the ancient tribal simplicity. Israel, which had passed from the nomad to the agrarian life with the conquest, was now by way of becoming a commercial society with a considerable industrial superstructure. There was wealth; and some grew rich, while others, especially by contrast, grew poorer. There was the makings of a proletariat. There were princes, and there were also slaves. And above it all was the resplendent court of Solomon with its standing army, its functionaries and flunkies, its harem, and its princelings to the manner born. The nomad ideal persisted, and was to persist, but it was less and less of a reality. Such a state could never exist without tension, a tension which more than once flared into open rebellion. The feeling grew in the hearts of many: "We have no portion in David" (II Sam. 20:1).

2. Yet the state produced Israel's Golden Age. Never again would she see the like. In one brief generation she had been transformed from a loose, disjointed tribal league, fighting for its life, into a united, self-conscious nation of some importance in the world. Most of the land thought of as "promised" was now, for the first and last time, in Israelite hands—a fact she never forgot. Literature and culture flourished as never before, and there was unexampled material prosperity. It was a proud thing to be an Israelite in the tenth century B.C.

So the Davidic state made an unforgettable impression. It must have seemed to many that Israel's destiny had been realized in it beyond fondest dreams: that the promise to Abraham—"I will make of you a great nation" (Gen. 12:2)—had been amply fulfilled, and God had indeed established his Kingdom under his anointed in peace. In any case, we shall have to reckon from now on with the "David idea." In the hard times which the future was to bring there grew a nostalgic yearning for "the good old days" of David. David himself suffered a transformation; the evil that he did forgotten, he was remembered as the man after God's own heart whose house was to rule forever (II Sam. 7:16; 23:5). The age of David became no less than the lost Age of Gold. It would be impossible for a man of Judah to think of the coming Messiah save as a David redivivus, a new David.

This could only have been intensified as David and Solomon centered the national religious feelings upon Mount Zion. Now the religion of old Israel had never been tightly centralized. The worshiper might without sense of sin offer his sacrifices, as Samuel did, at any one of dozens of shrines. Yet the heart of the tribal league had always been the Ark shrine, which had last stood at Shiloh (I Sam. 1–4). But this had long lain in ruins, and the Ark had languished in neglect at Kiriath-jearim (I Sam. 7:1-2). David was the one who at length brought the Ark to Jerusalem (II Sam. 6) and set it up in a tent shrine there with Zadok and Abiathar (the latter of the house of Eli) as priests (II Sam. 20:25). It was a step of consummate acumen. For David thus linked his state to the Ark, to Shiloh and the tribal league, to the Mosaic heritage, and made claim to be the patron and protector of that heritage. The magnificent temple which Solomon built could only have served to enhance the prestige of Jerusalem as the rallying place of the national faith, the very dwelling place of Yahweh's presence on earth.[35] Other shrines were not, of course, ruled out, but they were overshadowed. The process which was to weld all the hope of Israel to Jersualem the holy city had begun.

3. But it must be said that this brought in a mortal danger. An official, state-supported religion had been created, and where such exists, the danger is immense that it will place itself wholly at the service of the state and will begin to hallow the state in the name of its God. To be sure, there were factors that prevented Israel from deifying the state to the extent that this was done elsewhere in the ancient Orient. The king was not a god, as he was in Egypt. Nor could he properly be regarded as a divinely ordained mediator of the national "salvation," a sort of "liv-

---

[35] For further reading on the architecture and symbolism of the temple the following may be suggested: W. F. Albright, *Archaeology and the Religion of Israel*, pp. 142-55; G. E. Wright, "Solomon's Temple Resurrected," *The Biblical Archaeologist*, IV-2 (1941), 17-31; *idem*, "The Significance of the Temple in the Ancient Near East," Part III, *ibid.*, VII-4 (1944), 65-77; P. L. Garber, "Reconstructing Solomon's Temple," *ibid.*, XIV-1 (1951), 2-24; also F. M. Cross, "The Tabernacle," *ibid.*, X-3 (1947), 45-68.

ing Messiah," as he was in Babylon.[36] The Israelite state was too near its beginnings for this. It had not existed, as it were, from all eternity. There still lived men who could remember that the state had been founded by the action of their own fathers, and that it had replaced the older order of the covenant league. To many of them the old order seemed both preferable and normative, the new a dangerous innovation. Israel could never with good conscience hallow the state as a divine institution.

Yet inevitably state and cult were integrated with each other. We must not forget that the shrine on Mount Zion was a royal installation; David had founded it, and Solomon had lavished all the wealth and prestige of the state upon it. David's own sons were ordained as priests there (II Sam. 8:18 [Heb.]). Although the details are not clear to us, it is likely that the king himself played a central role in the cult (e.g., II Sam. 6; I Kings 8). The king in turn was hailed in the ritual as the (adopted) son whom God would surely defend from his foes (Pss. 2:7; 89:27; II Sam. 7:14). How much of a pagan royal ideology Israel absorbed, and how rapidly, cannot be said with assurance. But as the monarchy absorbed foreigners and came into contact with foreign nations, it must have assimilated foreign ideas as well.[37] We may believe that not a few in Israel became accustomed to view the state in a wholly pagan light.

In any case the temptation was insidiously present to place religion at the service of the state. That the king had power over the clergy is illustrated by the fact that when the veteran priest Abiathar was so ill-advised as to hew to the wrong political line (I Kings 1:7, 25), he was summarily dismissed by Solomon (I Kings 2:26-27), past faithful serv-

[36] Strong arguments have been made, especially by certain Scandinavian scholars, for the existence of the notion of the divine king in Israel, and of an annual Enthronement Festival patterned upon the Babylonian New Year. Discussion of this complex issue is forbidden, but the evidence for these things seems to me tenuous in the extreme. See the judicious remarks of G. E. Wright, The Old Testament Against Its Environment, pp. 62-68. Cf. also H. Frankfort, Kingship and the Gods (Chicago: University of Chicago Press, 1948), pp. 337-44; A. Alt, "Das Königtum in den Reichen Israel und Juda," Vetus Testamentum, I-1 (1951), 19-22; M. Noth, "Gott, König, Volk im Alten Testament," Zeitschrift für Theologie und Kirche, 47-2 (1950), 157-91.

[37] Egypt as well as Canaan would be a likely source of such ideas (cf. Alt, ibid.). Solomon was a son-in-law of the pharaoh, and at least some of the organization of the court at Jerusalem was patterned on Egyptian models. See the writer's article mentioned in note 34 (pp. 93, 98) and references there, especially K. Elliger, "Die dreissig Helden Davids," Palästinajahrbuch, 31 (1935), 29-75; R. de Vaux, "Titres et fonctionnaires égyptiens à la cour de David et de Salomon," Revue Biblique, XLVIII (1939), 394-405.

ice to the contrary notwithstanding. It was inevitable that as the years passed, the aims of the state and the aims of religion should tend ever more closely to coincide: the state supports the cult, and the cult in turn exists for the state. It is the business of the cult to intercede with the Deity on behalf of the state, with the aid of its ritual to maintain that harmonious balance which would protect the state from ill fortune within and without. If this be done, the state need have no fear; for it is God's "kingdom," composed of God's chosen people, and ruled by his anointed "son," the king: God will eternally defend the state. Thus are all the purposes of God in history equated with the existing order and made realizable in terms of it.

Such was the temptation. Would Israel succumb to it wholly? Would her sense of destiny as the people of God be transferred lock, stock, and barrel to the state? Would that cohesive sense of peoplehood that was hers be satisfied by the privilege of citizenship in the Kingdom of Israel? Would that robust confidence in the future which had activated her and driven her on toward a Promised Land, and written in her spirit— though she may not have known it—the vision of a city not made with hands, be satisfied with the city of Jerusalem and the material plenty which Solomon could provide? In other words, would Israel mistake the Davidic state for God's, and imagine that in it God *had* established his Kingdom?

That was Israel's question. It is a question which is neither ancient nor irrelevant, but is asked of us today. We are, it is true, in no external particular to be compared with the people Israel. But we, like them, are a people not very far from our origins, from the patterns of the past and the great faith of the past—yet very far indeed. Like Israel we were lured on by a vision and a promise: a land of plenty, of freedom and human dignity. And we pressed toward that goal as if to that Promised Land "flowing with milk and honey." We have created a nation greater than David's, prosperity such as Solomon never dreamed of, and with it a complete metamorphosis of the national character. A few years have brought many changes.

So it is that the question before us is not unlike that which the monarchy posed for Israel. Perhaps, so far, it is only a question. But it is a question which cannot be evaded, and it matters greatly how we answer it. Will our destiny as a nation which calls itself Christian be satisfied in terms of the economic prosperity and the national might which we have created? Will we seek no higher salvation than the present order can provide in terms of increased income, automobiles, and television sets? What is worse, will we, because we have churches and because our political forms are hospitable to their growth, assume that the present order is the God-ordained order which God—if he be just—may be called upon to defend always? The people that answers the question so, will see it as the sole function of religion to support and to hallow in the name of God its own material best interests. But it will never begin to understand the meaning of the Kingdom of God.

It is therefore of interest to see how that question was answered in Israel. And to that we must now turn.

CHAPTER TWO

A Kingdom Under Judgment

WE HAVE SEEN HOW THE VERY NATURE OF HER COVENANT FAITH HAD GIVEN ISRAEL A DEEP SENSE OF DESTINY AS THE PEOPLE OF GOD AND, WITH IT, THE hope and the confidence that God would bless her and establish his rule over her in the Promised Land. We have also seen how the rise of the Davidic monarchy, although it drastically altered the tribal structure of Israel and made changes which effected every aspect of her society—changes bitterly resented by some—nevertheless made much of that hope a reality. God had indeed established his people and made them great. This left us with the question: Would all the hope of Israel, and all her sense of destiny, be transferred bodily to the Davidic state and find its fulfillment in terms of it? In short, would the Kingdom of God be made equal to the Kingdom of Israel?

I

The danger was very real, but it was not to be. Israel's heritage was such that she could never rest content with such an identification. On the contrary there were many in Israel who found Solomon's state an intolerable institution: not only was it not a kingdom established by God; it was not even compatible with the Israelite ideal.

1. There was a grave sickness in the state; the schism of society had begun, and there was severe social tension. As was previously mentioned, the simple democracy of the tribal order had increasing difficulty in maintaining itself amid the changes which the monarchy brought. An

ever wider rift between those that had and those that had not was inevitable. The royal court had by this time nurtured a whole generation born to the aristocracy; as Solomon consolidated power under the crown, there are hints of that nepotism and favoritism which one would expect.[1] There grew up a privilege, insulated from popular feeling and imbued with the notion that the people were subjects to be possessed body and soul, of which Prince Rehoboam and his cronies (I Kings 12:1-15) are sufficient illustration. There also grew in many an Israelite heart the feeling: "What portion have we in David?" (I Kings 12:16.)

This tension was only accentuated by a fiscal crisis which developed. It was probably as simple as only arithmetic can be: Solomon's court, his harem, his building projects, and his army had to be paid for. David seems to have supported the state by the plunder and the tribute which he was able to exact from conquered peoples (II Sam. 8:2-12; 12:30-31). So far as we know, he levied no systematic taxes from his own people, although his census (II Sam. 24) was no doubt a prelude to such, as well as to military conscription. But with Solomon the state ceased to grow; there were no new lands to loot, and there was no doubt—even in those days—a limit to the plunder which could be taken from already subject peoples. Meanwhile, we may imagine, expenses mounted far above income.

At any rate Solomon laid a heavy hand on his people. His reorganization of the land (I Kings 4:7-19), no doubt based on David's census, was certainly for the purposes of taxation and probably of conscription— things hitherto unknown in Israel. What was worse, in order to recruit the labor force needed for his building projects he introduced the hated corvée. While this was at first laid on non-Israelites (I Kings 9:20-22),[2] it was subsequently extended to Israelites as well (I Kings 5:13-14; 11:28; 12:18) and was a heavy drain upon manpower.[3] No dose more bitter for

---

[1] This can be suspected rather than proved. A court and harem such as Solomon had inevitably breeds favoritism. Certainly Solomon did not stint his household any luxury. Favored wives, such as pharaoh's daughter, naturally received preferred treatment (I Kings 7:8-12). While we know nothing of the merits of the two sons-in-law who were made district governors (I Kings 4:11, 15), their presence certainly indicates a desire to consolidate power in the family.

[2] David had also subjected conquered peoples to forced labor (II Sam. 12:31).

[3] I Kings 5:13 speaks of a levy of thirty thousand Israelites. It has been estimated that this would be comparable to five million Americans today. Cf. W. F. Albright, "The Biblical Period," The Jews: Their History, Culture and Religion, L. Finkelstein, ed. (New York: Harper & Bros., 1949), p. 28. This article, incidentally, is highly recommended as an accurate thumbnail sketch of Israel's history.

a freeborn Israelite could be imagined. As if this were not enough, Solomon ceded certain towns in Galilee to Hiram, king of Tyre, in order to raise much-needed cash (I Kings 9:10-14).[4] A part of the Promised Land traded to a Canaanite! It is unthinkable that this could have been a popular transaction.

Nor could Solomon's state have been the Israelite ideal religiously. For in spite of its lavish patronage of the national religion, it made many adjustments to the pagan world and was tolerant of it. True, it was remembered by posterity for the temple it built in Jerusalem to Yahweh, God of Israel. But at the same time, in pursuit of its commercial policy, it turned outward into the wide world and concluded treaties and alliances with many foreign peoples. Far the most profitable of these, of course, was that with Tyre, trade emporium of the world and center of Canaanite culture. Now religious isolationism can hardly go hand in hand with internationalism in trade and politics. Nor did it in Israel. Solomon's alliances were mostly sealed by judicious marriages, and Solomon did not compel his highborn foreign wives to discontinue their native religions upon coming to Jerusalem. That would have been poor politics indeed! On the contrary, he saw to it that the state fostered these religions (I Kings 11:4-8)—much, we may imagine, to the disgust of the purists. And were there even some who had their misgivings about that magnificent temple on Mount Zion? After all, it was built on a Canaanite pattern by Canaanite architects on an erstwhile Canaanite high place.[5] Almost certainly there were men to be found in Israel who thought it a gaudy, parvenu structure: Yahweh the God of the tent-dwelling ancestors has no need for fine churches of cedar and stone (II Sam. 7:5-7).

2. In any case we are not surprised that there was a violent reaction against Solomon's state. The monarchy had never escaped tension. The old antimonarchic feeling of Gideon, Jotham, and Samuel never died out. The feeling persisted in many circles that the new order was a departure from, or at best a compromise with, Israel's proper destiny. This feeling, nurtured by popular grievances, had fed the rebellions of Absalom and of

---

[4] The background of the transaction is not clear. A casual reading would leave the impression that the cities were ceded to Hiram in payment for materials received (vs. 11), but vs. 14 (Hiram pays Solomon!) shows that the real purpose was to raise cash. Cf. most recently J. A. Montgomery, *The Books of Kings* (*International Critical Commentary* [New York: Chas. Scribner's Sons, 1951]), p. 204; he believes that the towns were pawned against a cash loan.

[5] Concerning the temple cf. Chap. I, note 35.

Sheba even in the lifetime of David (II Sam. 15–20). Prophets, them-selves on good terms with the state, were alive to these dangerous trends and attempted to act as a brake upon them. Gad the seer pronounced the judgment of God upon David for taking the census (II Sam. 24:11-13); and Nathan the prophet, when David had done his faithful retainer —Uriah the Hittite—to death in order to have his wife, called David a murderer to his face (II Sam. 12:1-15)· and reminded him that not even the king might flout the law of the covenant God with impunity. To these men there was an older and higher order than the state, God's order, to which the state must simply be made to conform.

But the tension continued, and Solomon's oppressive policy brought matters to a head. This tension was particularly severe among the north-ern tribes. How far Solomon's favoritism to his own household, to Jeru-salem, and to Judah, may have carried him is not clear,[6] but a feeling of profound alienation from the house of David was abroad in the north.

The corvée was the nub of their quarrel, as subsequent events were to show (I Kings 12:4, 18). The leader of the unrest was one Jeroboam, who was himself the labor gang boss for the tribes of Ephraim and Manasseh (I Kings 11:28), and who had no doubt been thoroughly sickened by his job. And although Solomon's police got wind of the plot, so that Jeroboam had to flee to Egypt (I Kings 11:40), all the makings of an explosion were present. Solomon's death touched it off. The northern tribesmen, with Jeroboam at their head, presented their petition to Rehoboam (I Kings 12:1-4) for an amelioration of their burdens; and when this was insolently refused (vss. 6-15), they forthwith seceded from the state. The royal taskmaster, Adoram, was lynched on the spot (vs. 18).

Now we must understand that this was not merely a social revolution, although economic grievances set it off. It had strong prophet backing. One remembers that a prophet, Ahijah of Shiloh (I Kings 11:26-39), was the one who in the name of God put Jeroboam up to the whole thing in the first place. And when Rehoboam mustered his forces to quash the

---

[6] A. Alt ("Israels Gaue unter Salomo," *Alttestamentliche Studien für Rudolf Kittel; Beiträge zur Wissenschaft des alten Testaments,* 13 [1913], 1-19) has argued that Solomon exempted his own tribe, Judah, from his district organization. W. F. Albright ("The Ad-ministrative Divisions of Israel and Judah," *Journal of the Palestine Oriental Society,* V-1 [1925], 17-54) has disagreed. The debate hinges about the very ambiguous verse, I Kings 4:19. Regardless of the correct reading of the verse in question, one may doubt if Solomon could have afforded to favor his own tribe to such an extent.

uprising, another prophet—Shemaiah (I Kings 12:21-24)—commanded him to desist, declaring that the rebellion was God's will. We may easily guess what these prophets hoped to gain. They certainly stood opposed to the excesses of the new order and hoped for an abatement of them; they probably favored a return to the charismatic principle as against the dynasty of David; it is probable, too, that they disliked the toleration of the state toward foreign cults and desired that these be removed.[7] It should be noted that in all this there was no rejection of the institution of monarchy as such. The north itself set up a monarchy. But the feeling was deep-seated in northern circles, a feeling reflected in the law of Deuteronomy (17:14-17), that a king ought to be as little like Solomon as possible.

In short, the majority of Israelites could not view the Solomonic state as the fulfillment of Israel's destiny. On the contrary, it was felt that Israel could find her destiny only by correction in the light of a more ancient pattern. And the feeling existed that this could be brought about by *political action*.

3. But we do not need to be told that mere revolution could not realize Israel's destiny as the people of God. The price of that revolution was total political disaster from which Israel never recovered. The schism was followed by some fifty years of intermittent sectional warfare, fought to no conclusion. In the course of it the land was dealt a devastating blow by Egypt, whose pharaoh was now Shishak—Libyan noble and founder of the XXII Dynasty. Apparently hoping to recoup Egyptian power in Asia, and possibly in response to a plea from Jeroboam—who had once found asylum at his court (I Kings 11:40)—for aid against Rehoboam, Shishak invaded Palestine. His armies ranged far and wide, ravaging Judah and its dependencies and looting Jerusalem (I Kings 14:25-28). If Jeroboam was indeed implicated, he had cause to rue his action: for the Egyptians then proceeded to lay waste the northern state as well.[8] Suicidal madness reached its climax a generation later when Asa of Judah

---

[7] Cf. J. Morgenstern, *Amos Studies I* (Cincinnati: Hebrew Union College Press, 1941), pp. 202-5.

[8] The extent of Shishak's depredations is known from his own inscription, found at Karnak, which lists over 150 places—many of them in northern Israel and Edom as well as in Judah. Cf. Albright, "The Biblical Period," p. 30. The reader will find excerpts from Shishak's list conveniently in G. A. Barton, *Archaeology and the Bible* (7th ed.; Philadelphia: American Sunday School Union, 1937), pp. 456-57.

(913-873),[9] hard pressed by Baasha (900-877), bought in the aid of Ben-hadad—king of the Aramean state of Damascus. The latter cheerfully ravaged much of northern Galilee (I Kings 15:16-22). In the course of this fraternal throat-cutting the empire which David had built collapsed like a house of cards. Damascus succeeded to the dominant position which Israel had held. Two centuries later Isaiah could still remember the schism as the worst disaster that had ever befallen his people (Isa. 7:17).

In such a situation Jeroboam could not, even had he wished, deliver what his prophet backers expected. An amelioration of taxes and conscription in the midst of war could hardly have been hoped for. On the contrary, expenses must have mounted. And to return to the loose charismatic leadership would have been to compound disaster. To bring stability to his state Jeroboam sought to found a dynasty. But the north apparently did not want a dynasty. No sooner did Nadab the son of Jeroboam take the throne (901-900) than he was murdered by Baasha. And when Baasha's son, Elah (877-876), attempted to succeed his father, he in turn was murdered by a cavalry officer, Zimri.[10] And both plots were prophet inspired (I Kings 14:6-16; 15:25-29; 16:1-12).

What was worse, Jeroboam was obliged to set up his own state cult to rival Jerusalem. It is clear (I Kings 12:26-29) that Jeroboam realized the enormous prestige of Solomon's temple—housing as it did the sacred Ark of the tribal league—and knew that if he could not wean his people from it, he would lose them. So he set up a rival shrine in Bethel. Now this shrine was a temple of Yahweh, God of Israel (in spite of the language of vs. 28), and the golden bulls which adorned it were not idols but—like the cherubim in the Jerusalem temple—pedestals for the throne of the invisible Yahweh.[11] But the bull motif was apparently too closely

[9] Dates given for the kings of the Divided Monarchy are those of W. F. Albright and will be found in table form on the back cover of the reprinted article mentioned in note 3 above. Cf. idem, "The Chronology of the Divided Monarchy of Israel," *Bulletin of the American Schools of Oriental Research*, 100 (1945), 16-22.

[10] A. Alt ("Das Königtum in den Reichen Israel und Juda," *Vetus Testamentum*, I-1 [1951], 2-22) has recently related the inability of the northern state to achieve a stable dynasty to the lively charismatic tradition that existed there. It seems to me that Alt is correct. But the dynastic stability of Judah cannot be explained by the supposition that such a tradition was largely lacking in the southern state. The strong prestige of the Davidic house, and the growing influence of the "David idea" must be taken into account.

[11] On the function of the cherubim and the winged bulls cf. Graham and May, *Culture and Conscience* (Chicago: University of Chicago Press, 1936), pp. 248-60; W. F. Albright, "What Were the Cherubim?" *The Biblical Archaeologist*, I-1 (1938), 1-3.

associated with the symbolism of the Baal cult for the taste of purists. No doubt ignorant people did come to worship them. Jeroboam was to live in the hearts of posterity as the man who "made Israel to sin" (I Kings 15:34). His cult was probably the entering wedge for all sorts of paganism. In any case pagan practices did enter (as the reader of Hosea well knows). What was worse, Yahweh—God of Israel—became, in the minds of many, all too very much like Baal.

So the northern state did not succeed at all in breaking with the new order. It broke from the Davidic dynasty—and never ceased to try to found a dynasty. It rebelled from the tax policy of Solomon—and itself followed exactly the same administrative pattern, as the ostraca of Samaria show.[12] It parted company with Solomon's state cult—and got Jeroboam's. One day prophets would be silenced in the name of that cult (Amos 7:10-13). And the schism of society went on unchecked. By the time of Amos we see a society torn asunder.

II

1. In the northern state, therefore, to the end of its existence, there was tension between the old order and the new. The gravest crisis came in the middle of the ninth century B.C. The able Omri (876-869) had seized the throne (I Kings 16:15-28), to be succeeded by his notorious son, Ahab (869-850). These kings sought to recapture a measure of the prosperity of Solomon, and to do that they had to recreate his policy. This called for internal unity, a strong hand in Transjordan—particularly against Damascus—and, above all, a close liaison with Phoenicia. Omri and Ahab achieved their goal by a series of steps which we cannot here trace. Suffice it to say that in a succession of victories the Arameans (Syrians) were repressed, while alliance with Phoenicia was sealed by the marriage of Ahab to Jezebel, the daughter of Ittobaal, king of Tyre (I Kings 16:31).[13] Meanwhile the fratricidal quarrel with the southern

[12] The Samaria ostraca are a group of inscribed potsherds which list quantities of oil and wine received as revenue at the court. They date from the reign of Jeroboam II (contemporary of Amos), but the administrative system which they represent may be assumed to be much older. Cf. W. F. Albright, *Archaeology and the Religion of Israel* (Baltimore: Johns Hopkins Press, 1942), pp. 141-42. For a translation of some of them with bibliography cf. *Ancient Near Eastern Texts Relating to the Old Testament*, J. B. Pritchard, ed. (Princeton, N. J.: Princeton University Press, 1950), p. 321.

[13] The Bible speaks of Jezebel's father as "king of the Sidonians." The power of the Sidonian Phoenicians (Canaanites) was now at its height. Tyre was the chief city. Cf. Albright, "The Biblical Period," p. 33. For an excellent, brief discussion of Phoenician civilization, idem, "The Role of the Canaanites in the History of Civilization," *Studies in the History of Culture* (Menasha, Wis.: Banta Pub. Co., 1942), pp. 11-50.

state was patched up by the wedding of Athaliah, daughter of Ahab and Jezebel, to Jehoram, son of Jehoshaphat—king of Judah (II Kings 8:18, 26). That the purpose of this alliance was partly commercial is shown by the abortive attempt to recreate the Red Sea trade out of Ezion-geber (I Kings 22:48).[14]

This might have been all to the good had it not been for Jezebel. Born and raised a worshiper of the Tyrian Baal, she was allowed by Ahab—it being the custom, and he not being narrow-minded—to continue her native religion in Samaria, and a temple of Baal was built for her there (I Kings 16:32). But it did not stop at that. Jezebel was a strong-minded woman who appears to have been no less than a missionary for her god. Infuriated by those that opposed her (notably Elijah), she turned all the repressive measures at her command against them, even the threat of death (I Kings 18–19). It was a question who should be the God of Israel: Yahweh or Baal Melqart (18:20-24).

The danger to Israel was immense. The more we know of Canaanite paganism the clearer this becomes.[15] Here was a paganism of the most degrading sort. Its gods and goddesses—Baal, Astarte, Asherah, Anat, and the rest—represented for the most part those forces and functions of nature which have to do with fertility. Its myth was closely linked with the death and rebirth of nature. Its cult was concerned to control by means of its ritual the forces of nature, and thus to produce the desired fertility in soil, in beast, and in man. As in all such religions sacred prostitution of both sexes and other orgiastic and ecstatic practices of the most disgusting sort were involved.

Clearly the question, Yahweh or Baal? was not a trivial one. We moderns tend to view it as a sort of denominational quarrel, and to find the prophet hostility to Baal rather fanatical and narrow. But we are wrong. For these were not two rival religions, one of which was somewhat superior to the other; they were religions of wholly different sorts; they could have nothing to do with each other. It must be understood

[14] Cf. Chap. I, p. 38.

[15] Far our richest source of knowledge are the texts discovered at Ras Shamra on the Syrian coast in the decade prior to World War II. For a useful introduction cf. C. F. A. Schaeffer, *The Cuneiform Texts of Ras Shamra-Ugarit* (London: Oxford University Press, 1939). For a complete translation of the texts cf. C. H. Gordon, *Ugaritic Literature* (Rome: Pontifical Biblical Institute, 1949); cf. idem, *The Loves and Wars of Baal and Anat* (Princeton, N. J.: Princeton University Press, 1943) for a popular treatment. For an excellent and brief discussion of Canaanite religion cf. Albright, *Archaeology and the Religion of Israel*, ch. III.

that Israel's very being as a people rested in her confidence that Yahweh had called her, entered into covenant with her, summoned her to live in obedience to his righteous law, and given her a sense of destiny as his people. Baal, on the contrary, would have been destructive of the very faith that made Israel what she was. Here was a religion which summoned men not at all beyond their animal nature, and even fostered that animal nature; which posed no moral demands, but provided men with an external ritual designed to appease the deity and to manipulate the divine powers for their own material ends; which was incapable of creating community but rather, by pandering to the selfish desires of the worshiper, was destructive of real community. Paganism was, then as now, no trivial thing. As long as men take on the character of the gods they serve, so long does it greatly matter who those gods may be. Had Israel embraced Baal it would have been the end of her; she would no longer have lived as the peculiar people of God. Not one scrap of her heritage would have survived.

Of course the menace of Baal was not new with Jezebel. It had been there since the conquest, when Israel first confronted the superior material culture of Canaan and, in taking over her land, took over her agrarian way of life, her cities, and her shrines. The temptation was always present to imagine that the worship of the gods of fertility was a necessary part of the agrarian life. Many were quick to apostatize to Baal or to address Yahweh as if he were Baal. The incorporation of new blood into Israel,[16] no doubt much faster than it could be assimilated, and the tolerant attitude of Solomon and others in such matters, could only have facilitated the process. Baal was no stranger to Israel.

Yet we must not allow this to obscure the magnitude of the threat which Jezebel posed. Here for the first time was an overt attempt on the part of the state to impose a foreign paganism by force. Jezebel, as we said, resorted to persecution, and this persecution had far-reaching effects. It fell with especial force on the prophets of Yahweh (I Kings 18:4; 19:14). For the first time in Israel the prophet was faced with reprisals for speaking the Word of Yahweh. In the face of pressure some of them gave way and surrendered to the state. We see thereafter groups of prophets, in the pay of the court or the shrine, clustering about the king to lick the royal hand and to say—unanimously—what the royal ear wished to hear (I Kings 22). But we see also a succession of lone in-

[16] Cf. Chap. I, pp. 23, 37.

53

dividuals who like Micaiah, because they refused to compromise their
prophet Word, were ever more completely alienated not only from the
state but from their fellow prophets as well. To these prophets *Yahweh
was against the state.*

2. That the policy of Jezebel should produce violent reaction was
inevitable. For not only was it intolerable to conservative Israelites, but
the feeling still persisted that the state could be purged, brought back
to its destiny by political action. The fact that the reaction bided its
time until both Ahab and Elijah had passed from the scene diminished
none of its violence. The reader will find the story in II Kings 9–10. It
is the tale of a blood purge with few parallels for brutality in history.
Jehu, a general who wanted to be king, carried it out. It did not end until
King Jehoram had been killed with an arrow, Jezebel thrown from a
window, and the entire house of Ahab exterminated to the smallest
child. It struck down Ahaziah—King of Judah—who was visiting his
cousin Jehoram at the time, as well as others of his family. The purge
reached its gory climax when Jehu summoned the worshipers of Baal
into their temple in Samaria, then turned his soldiers loose on them and
butchered them to the last man.

This is an ugly tale indeed. But although it furthered the political
ambitions of Jehu and other opportunists, it was by no means primarily
a political or social upheaval. It was an upsurge of conservative Israel
against the corrosion of the national spirit which Ahab's policy entailed.
The exponents of the blood purge were men of the ancient ways. Its
father was Elijah himself (I Kings 19:15-18), although he now was no
more. Elijah was a Gileadite (I Kings 17:1), a man of the desert fringe
where the old order still lived. His appearance (II Kings 1:8) recalls the
Baptist (Matt. 3:4) with the Nazirite costume of hair mantle and
leather girdle. In the name of the God of Israel he declared holy war on
Ahab and his pagan state, his pagan queen and her pagan god. When
Jezebel sought his life, he fled away to Horeb, the mount of Israel's
covenant origins (I Kings 19): a flight to the desert and the past, there
to encounter the God of the ancient ways. And at last we see him cross-
ing the Jordan and going east into the desert (II Kings 2), to be seen
nevermore by mortal eyes. Elijah was the very embodiment of the ancient
order and all that it stood for. He and the prophets he gathered about
him could never rest while Jezebel sat on the throne.

These prophet orders, "the sons of the prophets," are a further illustration of the fact that the purge of Jehu fed on a deep-seated feeling for the ancient ways. Both Elijah and Elisha had consorted with them, as had Samuel long ago. They were the ones who bore the brunt of Jezebel's wrath. And while some of them gave in, it was one of their number (II Kings 9:1-10) who anointed Jehu and set him to his bloody task. They present an intriguing picture.[17] Prophesying in groups, often to the accompaniment of music (I Sam. 10:5-13; II Kings 3:15), often in the wildest frenzy (I Sam. 19:18-24), they represent an ecstatic, "pentecostal" substratum in Israel's faith psychologically akin to similar manifestations in other religions (cf. Acts 2:1-13; I Cor. 14:1-33). Endowed with the divine fury they inspired men to fight the holy wars of Yahweh against his foes. First appearing in the Philistine crisis in the days of Saul, the height of their later activity coincided with the Aramean wars of Ahab. They accompanied the army in the field (II Kings 3:10-19; II Chr. 20:14-18); for the enemies of Yahweh they had scant pity (I Kings 20:31-43).[18] So stout a prop was Elisha to Israelite morale that he was called "the chariots of Israel and its horsemen!" (II Kings 13:14)— the man was worth divisions! A tradition so sturdily nationalistic could have had no willing truck with foreign ways.

Then there was Jonadab ben Rechab. It was he who (II Kings 10:15-17) personally endorsed and physically abetted Jehu in the butchery of the Baal worshipers at Samaria. No clearer illustration of the intensely conservative nature of the reaction against Ahab's house could be wanted. That both Jonadab and his entire clan were Nazirites we know from Jer. 35. They had pledged themselves (vss. 6-7) never to drink wine nor cultivate vineyards nor build houses nor till the soil, but always to dwell in tents as their ancestors had done. This is not to be taken as a temperance lesson. It was rather a symbolic renunciation of the agrarian life and all that it entailed. It moved from the feeling that God was to be found in the ancient, pure ways of the desert, and that Israel had departed from her destiny the moment she came in contact

[17] For a thorough discussion of the prophet orders cf. A. R. Johnson, *The Cultic Prophet in Ancient Israel* (Cardiff: University of Wales Press Board, 1944).

[18] That one of them should curse Ahab for sparing the life of Ben-hadad is to be explained only in the light of the strongly nationalistic and isolationist bias of the early prophets. Ahab's clemency would ordinarily seem not only humanitarian but politically wise in view of the impending Assyrian menace. Cf. note 21 below.

with the contaminating culture of Canaan.[19] To such as these Jezebel was the ultimate anathema.

The purge, then, was no mere political turnover; it was an effort to correct Israel in the light of an ancient standard. There was a keen feeling that Ahab's policy had perverted Israel's destiny and that God was therefore against the state. Yet at the same time the rejection of the state was not total, for it was believed that the state could be, and was to be, purged by revolution.

3. But did that purge, shall we say, make Israel God's Kingdom, restore her to her destiny as the people of God? Well, no! It would seem that no political action, however total, can do such a thing.

Indeed if we were to call the purge a crime and a blunder, we should have no less a prophet than Hosea to agree with us (Hos. 1:4). Certainly enough hatred must have been aroused by it to rend Israel apart for generations to come. The cream of the national leadership had been killed off, for almost everybody of importance in Israel had been tainted with Jezebel's ways. Further, the alliances with Phoenicia on the one hand and Judah on the other, which had been the bases of prosperity, collapsed at once. How could they help doing so? After all Jezebel was of the ruling house of Tyre, and her daughter, Athaliah— whose son, Ahaziah, had also been swept away in the blood bath—was queen mother in Jerusalem. Political alliances do not survive such doings.

In any case the Arameans once again seized the opportunity to humble Israel to the dust. During Jehu's reign (842-815) Hazael, the new king of Damascus, stripped Israel of all her holdings east of the Jordan (II Kings 10:32-33) and even stormed down the coastal plain as far south as the Philistine cities (II Kings 12:17). In the next generation conditions became worse. The Arameans had Jehu's son, Jehoahaz (815-801), so at their mercy that they permitted him only a police-force army (II Kings 13:7) of fifty horsemen, ten chariots, and ten thousand infantry (Ahab had fielded two thousand chariots against the Assyrian in 853).

What was worse, the purge did not really purge. True, Israel had been saved from overt conversion to Baal, and that was no trivial thing.

[19] Although the prophets did not themselves go so far, some of them—especially Hosea and Jeremiah—to an extent sympathized with their feelings. After all, Jeremiah highly commended their loyalty to their principles; cf. Jer. 35; 2:1-2; Hos. 9:10 ff.; 11:1-7. Cf. W. F. Albright, "Primitivism in Western Asia," in A Documentary History of Primitivism, Vol. I (A. O. Lovejoy and G. Boas, Primitivism and Related Ideas in Antiquity [Baltimore: Johns Hopkins Press, 1935]), pp. 421-32.

But it is clear that Jehu was an opportunist who had no real zeal for a purified Israel. The Asherah, symbol of the high goddess of the Baal cult, remained in Samaria (II Kings 13:6). A foreign paganism had been drowned in blood that the native variety might flourish unhindered.[20] That it is possible to crush an overt paganism physically only to surrender to a subtler form of it in the spirit is tragically true. This Israel did. The feeling that the state had cleansed itself led many prophets who had not previously done so to make peace with it. Their patriotic fervor was placed at the service of the state, for the state was now God's state.

III

The latter half of the ninth century B.C. brought dark days to Israel. The Aramean state of Damascus was at the height of its power, and Israel could not cope with it. But the eighth century produced a great shift of fortune. A providential combination of circumstances gave Israel another chance.

1. A new and terrible world power had stepped upon the scene: Assyria. Assyria was an ancient nation. A state of importance as far back as the time of Abraham and before, she had held the balance of power in western Asia approximately as the Israelites were entering Palestine. But for centuries, beset by Aramean pressure from the desert and by internal weakness, she had been of no great importance. Now, however, she had once more begun to entertain ambitions of empire. As early as 870 B.C. Asshur-naṣir-pal II had overrun all upper Mesopotamia and burst across the Euphrates with insensate cruelty. His successor, Shalmaneser III (858-824), followed in his footsteps. In the year 853 the latter was met at Qarqar on the Orontes by a coalition of Syrian and Palestinian kings, including Ben-hadad of Damascus and Ahab of Israel, who had for the moment laid aside their quarrel in the face of danger.[21] The Assyrian boasted of a great victory, as was his wont, but it is plain that he was thoroughly checkmated. Whereupon Aram and

[20] Albright, "The Biblical Period," p. 38, points out that proper names compounded with Baal are quite frequent in the Samaria ostraca of the next century. In any case a reading of Hosea alone is enough to show that Baal worship was far from uprooted.

[21] The Bible does not mention this battle at all, but we know of it from Shalmaneser's own inscriptions. Awareness of the danger which the Assyrian posed for them both is the best explanation for Ahab's desire to make peace with Ben-hadad (I Kings 20:31-34). For translation of relevant portions of the cuneiform texts, cf. Pritchard, op. cit., pp. 278-79.

Israel took up their senseless little war again, and three years later (850) Ahab met his death (I Kings 22).

The next fifty years brought triumph to Aram, humiliation to Israel. The energetic Hazael, who had usurped the throne in Damascus (II Kings 8:7-15), had to endure at least two further invasions of Shalmaneser, but he never capitulated. The last of these came in 837, after which Assyria was for a generation plagued with internal disorders and did not march west of the Euphrates. This gave Hazael the respite he needed, and he used it, as we have seen, to humble Israel abjectly. But the shadow of Assyria still lay over the west. By 805 she was back, this time under Adad-nirari III, and in a few years Aram was broken and under heavy tribute to the conqueror.

Israel, on the other hand, escaped the blow. True, Jehu had once paid tribute to the Assyrian,[22] but it was nominal and did not represent permanent subjugation. Nor did Adad-nirari's armies, which subsequently ravaged Damascus, invade Israel. What is more, the successes of Adad-nirari were not followed up. After his campaigns, and for a full fifty years thereafter, Assyria entered a further period of weakness during which she was scarcely able to maintain a foothold west of the Euphrates. It must have seemed to many an Israelite that Providence had intervened: that Assyria could only be God's tool used to save Israel and punish her foes, for Israel was God's "kingdom."

2. In any case this was the signal for the resurgence of Israel. Jehoash (801-786) began it. He leaped upon faltering Aram and in three victories recovered all the land his father, Jehoahaz, had lost (II Kings 13:25). At the same time when Amaziah—king of Judah (800-783)—showed a disposition to renew the chronic quarrel between the two states, he first tried to dissuade him and then, when Amaziah would not listen, thoroughly trounced him (II Kings 14:8-14). But it was Jeroboam II whose long reign (786-746) brought Israel to the height of her glory. By aggressive action he extended Israel's frontiers farther to the north than they had been since Solomon sat on the throne (II Kings 14:25). Meanwhile the equally long-lived and able Uzziah of Judah (783-742), who had succeeded to the throne in Jerusalem upon the assassination of his father, Amaziah (II Kings 14:19), was won as a full partner in this aggressive program. Uzziah's conquests matched those of Jeroboam in the

[22] In 841 B.C. This too is known from Shalmaneser's inscriptions; cf. Pritchard, *op. cit.*, p. 280.

north and extended from the Philistine plain in the west to Ammon and the northern Hedjaz in the south and east (II Chr. 26:6-8). Except that it was a double state, it was very nearly the size of Solomon's.

And prosperity unmatched since Solomon ensued. The trade routes which Solomon had controlled were again in Israelite hands. The Red Sea port of Elath (Ezion-geber?) was restored (II Kings 14:22), and presumably the overseas trade to the south again flourished. This probably means that the Phoenicians, still at the height of their prosperity, were again brought into the program. The economic resources of the country were developed (II Chr. 26:10).[23] Israel could remember few periods to compare with the mid–eighth century B.C. The fact that it was the glory of the nation's sunset did not diminish its splendor. The fine ivories and great palaces which archaeologists have found in Samaria are proof that Amos did not exaggerate the wealth which the land enjoyed.

3. But, again as in Solomon's day, society is sick. Only now the sickness is unto death. The reader of Amos sees the schism of society on every line. There is wealth unheard of, which knows every luxury that money can buy, and there is bitter and hopeless poverty. There are greed and venality which have no conscience, but place property above men and above God. And religion is equally sick. The shrines are busy and rich and thronged with worshipers (Amos 4:4-5; 5:21-23). But religion is a mechanical quid pro quo, a nauseous attempt to purchase material favors of God with material gifts. It tolerates the grossest immorality (Amos 2:6-8; Hos. 4:4-14); it utters no rebuke—provided only that one support his church! It is totally at the service of the state, and will countenance no criticism of it (Amos 7:10-13).

This is clearly the mortal sickness of a nation. Yet in spite of it there flourished a complacent confidence in the future which is past believing. No doubt this sprang in good part from the pride of a victorious nation in its own strength (Amos 6:13)[24] and from the favor-

[23] This has been partially illustrated by archaeology; cf. Albright, "The Biblical Period," pp. 39-40.

[24] Most commentators see in the cryptic words of Amos 6:13, "thing of nought" (Heb. lō' dābār) and "horns" (Heb. qarnayim), the names of two places known from other references in the Bible to have existed in north-central Transjordan. The verse would then read, "You that rejoice over Lodebar, that say, 'Is it not by our might that we have seized Qarnaim for ourselves?'" Presumably allusions to victories of Jehoash or Jeroboam over the Arameans are intended.

able political situation beyond which shortsighted men could not see. But it must also be understood as a disease of theology. Israel's faith had always taught her to expect great things of the future. History, it was believed, moved onward to the victory of God's purpose, the establishment of his rule over his people in glory. There would come that eschatological day of triumph, the Day of Yahweh, when the victorious Kingdom of God would become reality. Nor did Israel doubt that she *was* the people of God, the kingdom chosen by him and defended by him. So she faced the future with confidence and even dared to yearn for that Day of Yahweh (Amos 5:18), for it would be the day of her triumph too.[25]

IV

To this prosperity and this sickness Amos spoke. The first of that succession of prophets whose utterances are preserved for us in the Bible, he is clearly something new in Israel. Yet he is equally clearly the voice of the ancient ways. Of his life we know almost nothing. A herdsman from the fringe of the Judean wilderness (1:1),[26] he had occasion to travel into the northern kingdom. He did not at all like what he saw there, and at the great shrine of Bethel he gave vent to himself. No priest or professional prophet (7:14),[27] his only authentication was the Word of Yahweh which had come to him and demanded to be spoken (3:8; 7:15). He was thus a man of the charisma like the judges of old. Only charisma now no longer summoned to leadership in the state, but to the severest criticism of it.

1. The message of Amos seems to the reader rather plain and altogether thrilling. It is the classic ethical protest. It is classic because every

[25] I am in agreement with those who regard the popular notion of the Day of Yahweh as eschatological, i.e., the time when Yahweh would break into history to judge his foes and establish his rule. See my article "Faith and Destiny," *Interpretation* V-1 (1951), 9 ff.

[26] His home was Tekoa (1:1), a site which still wears its ancient name (*Khirbet Taqû'*), a few miles southeast of Bethlehem overlooking the steep pitch down to the Dead Sea.

[27] It is difficult to agree with those—recently A. Haldar, *Associations of Cult Prophets Among the Ancient Semites* (Uppsala: Almqvist & Wiksells, 1945), p. 112; Miloš Bič, "Der Prophet Amos—Ein Haepatoskopos," *Vetus Testamentum*, I–4 (1951), 292-96—who maintain that the words (1:1; 7:14) *nôqēd* and *bôqēr* ("herdsman") denote a cultic functionary. Even granting that the words may on occasion have had a cultic significance, this is no proof that they must always do so. The fact that the early prophets were closely linked to the cult must not be driven to such extremes. The sense of Amos 7:14 is that Amos was *not* a professional religionist at the time of his call; cf. H. H. Rowley, "Was Amos a Nabi?" *Festschrift Otto Eissfeldt*, J. Fück, ed. (Halle: Max Niemeyer, 1947), pp. 191-97.

prophet after Amos was to take it up; it is classic because it was never said better—it could not be said better. With savage anger Amos lashes at those who have placed gain above rectitude:

> Ah, these that turn justice to poison,
> thrust righteousness down to the ground
>
> . . . .
>
> They do hate him who rebukes crookedness in the court,[28]
> abhor him who speaks with integrity!
> Wherefore, because you trample on the weak
> take from him "presents" of grain,
> Houses of hewn stone you have built,
> but you'll not get to live in them;
> Delightful vineyards you have planted,
> but you'll never drink their wine.
> For I know that many are your crimes
> and countless your sins,
> Who harass honest men, take bribes,
> and push aside the needy in the court.
> (5:7, 10-12; cf. 2:6-16; 8:4-10)

But Amos knew that society's sin is far more than overt crookedness and greed. It is also a luxury-loving ease that places its comfort above human beings and is unconcerned about the deep schism in the social order. How the prophet scores the gentle ladies of the kingdom, calling them fat "Bashan cows" of Samaria (4:1)! How he excoriates a pampered society amusing itself before the Deluge!

> Ah these careless ones in Zion,
> complacent ones in Samaria's mount,
> Elite of the very top nation,
> to whom the house of Israel must resort,
>
> . . . .
>
> Who put far off the evil day,
> and make unjust assizes present fact,[29]
> Who lounge on ivory divans,
> are sprawled upon their couches,

[28] Literally, "that reproves in the gate." The city gate, as we know from numerous references in the Old Testament, was where the elders sat to administer justice. It thus corresponds to the court, as we would understand it.

[29] Literally, "and bring near the seat (sitting) of violence." Reference seems to be to courts where violence, instead of justice, is dispensed. But the sense is uncertain; see the commentaries.

61

> And eat choice lambs from the flock,
>   together with stall-fattened calves;
> Who improvise to the sound of the harp,
>   just like David, they compose all sorts of songs,[30]
> Who drink wine by the bowl,
>   and anoint themselves with the finest of oils;
> But over the rupture of Joseph they are not sick!
>
>   (6:1, 3-6)

Nor can a society so broken possibly heal itself by much religion. The busy religion of a people that has flouted all righteousness will avail nothing with God; nay more, it is a positive offense to him. Never has it been put better than Amos put it!

> I do hate, I do despise your pilgrim feasts,
>   take no pleasure in your high holy days,
> Though you offer to me (your) burnt offerings
>   and your meal offerings, I won't accept them;
> And to the peace offerings of your fat animals I'll pay no attention.
> Take away from me the noise of your songs;
>   to the melody of your harps I'm not listening.
> But let justice roll down like waters,
>   and righteousness as an ever-flowing stream.
>
>   (5:21-24)

Thus it was at a time when society desperately needed criticism, yet when established religion could not deliver that criticism, nor even criticize itself, that the protest had to come from outside the organized church. And that, plainly, was a horrible state of affairs.

The intent of Amos' message, then, is plain—as plain as a blow in the face. Nor is there need to argue that it is a relevant message in all ages; it is desperately relevant. It tells us what we need to hear: that a society that cares more for gain than for honor, for its living standard than for God, is sick to the death; that a church which has no rebuke for society, which demands lavish support before righteous behavior, is no true church but a sham of a church. Amos tells us that no amount

---

[30] The Hebrew, which the English follows, reads, "like David they devise for themselves instruments of music." To many commentators this seems unlikely because: (a) while David was famed as a composer of songs, we do not hear that he invented musical instruments; and (b) the context speaks of banquets with music, which is a place where ditties might be improvised but scarcely the place to devise novel musical instruments. The proposed emendation, following Nowack, etc., changes but one Hebrew letter. It is, however, a conjecture.

of religious activity and loyalty to church can make a man's conduct in business and society of no concern to God, nor can a correct creed play substitute for plain obedience to the divine Will in all aspects of life. He tells us that a church which makes a dichotomy between faith and ethics, to the point of making small insistence upon the latter, is under the judgment of God along with the society of which it has become a part.

2. Relevant indeed! But one might well ask what this has got to do with the hope of the Kingdom of God? Amos' message is one of almost unrelieved doom. True, he called for repentance (5:4, 14-15), and to the repentant he held out hope. But it is plain that he did not expect repentance: the doom is both sure and soon. Israel is a tottering, jerry-built wall out of line with the plumb line of God (7:7-9)—tear it down! Israel will be left "the crumbs of a lion's meal" [31]—two legs and a piece of an ear (3:12). So real was the coming ruin to Amos that he set up a wailing over the doomed nation as if for the dead:

> She has fallen, never again to rise,
>   has virgin Israel;
> Hurled headlong upon her land,
>   there is none to pick her up.
>   (5:2)

One might well ask what such black doom has to do with our topic.

But we shall badly mistake Amos and the other eighth century men if we do not understand their preaching as a powerful reactivation of the covenant faith. It is rooted and grounded in that sense of the intimate relationship between God and people which was the heart of all Israelite believing. It addresses the people as nothing other than the people of Yahweh, the subjects of his rule and partners of his covenant, and reminds them what that relationship means.

Now it is not to be supposed that Israel really needed to be reminded of her election. On the contrary, it was a fixed idea with her; she believed it all too well. Her whole tradition asserted with unanimous voice that God had chosen her out of all the families of the nations to be his people, and she cherished that belief with all her heart. Yahweh was her God, and she his people; Yahweh had therefore blessed her and

---

[31] The expression is George Adam Smith's in *The Book of the Twelve Prophets* (rev. ed.; New York: Harper & Bros., 1928), I, 148.

would continue to do so. As Yahweh's own people she might face the future without fear and even look forward with confidence to the Day of Yahweh (5:18), when he would intervene in history to judge his foes and establish his rule upon earth. Why should Israel not be confident? Is not the establishment of God's rule the establishment of his people? And the Israelite state *is* the people of God.

In short, the whole notion of covenant and election had been made a mechanical thing, the deeply moral note inherent in it blurred and obscured. It had been forgotten that the covenant was a bilateral obligation, requiring of its people the worship of Yahweh alone and the strictest obedience to his righteous law in all human relationships. Or if the obligation was remembered at all, it was imagined that lavish sacrifice and loyal support of the shrines discharged it. The bond between God and people was thus made into a static, pagan thing based on blood and cult—a total perversion of the covenant idea. And religion was accorded an altogether pagan function: to coerce the favor of God by the sedulous manipulation of the ritual so that protection and material benefit might be secured for individual and nation.

Amos totally rejected this mechanized notion of the covenant. But this did not involve either Amos or any of the other prophets in a rejection of the belief that Israel was a chosen people. On the contrary, they affirmed it again and again. Indeed it seemed to Amos that the whole national past had been no less than a history of God's grace— a grace repaid by the grossest ingratitude (2:9-12). But to be chosen, said Amos, is not to be pampered; it is to shoulder double responsibility. To sin against the light of grace is felony compounded, nay capital crime. All nations, Israel included, stand equally before the bar of God's justice (chs. 1–2). There are no pet nations, elite races: "Are you not just like Ethiopia's sons to me, sons of Israel? . . . Did I not bring Israel up from the land of Egypt—and the Philistines from Caphtor, and the Arameans from Kir?" (9:7.) Election is for responsibility. With what logic, and yet a logic so hard for favored people to grasp, Amos reasons (3:2)! He moves from plain premise to unheard-of conclusion. This is the premise: "Only you have I known (i.e., chosen) of all the families of the earth." And this is the inexorable conclusions: "Wherefore I will visit upon you all your iniquities"!

But in saying this Amos is only harking back from a perverted notion of the covenant to the true one. The people of God is a community knit to one another by its bond with the covenant God. It is a brotherhood, for within it all human relationships are regulated by the righteous law of that God; and all stand equally under that law. The covenant is not mechanical and in the nature of things; it is a bilateral, moral agreement and can be voided. Mistreatment of the brother voids it, for he who crowds his brother spits on the law of God and, in that fact, does not keep covenant with him. In short, Israel is the people of God, but only as she keeps his law and exhibits his righteousness. Because Israel has not done so, but has egregiously violated the covenant brotherhood, *Israel is no true people of God!*

It is in the light of this theology that we must understand Amos' ethical preaching. It is important that we note this, for it is too often missed. We take the ethical attack without the idea pattern upon which it was marshaled, and that attack becomes a noisy, angry thing—and Amos something he was not at all. He was no revolutionary summoning the downtrodden masses to the barricades. He was no humanitarian, moved by the plight of the poor, who advanced a program of social reform designed to cure the national malady. He was—let us not mistake it— no teacher of a new ethic which would ultimately, so the handbooks used to tell us, tame the rough-and-ready morality of the people and lift them to the heights of ethical monotheism. Amos was no innovator, but a man of the ancient ways. His ethical protest was drawn from a well five hundred years deep. His were the ethics of the Decalogue; of Nathan, who called David a murderer to his face (II Sam. 12:1-15); of rugged Elijah coming down to Jezreel to meet his enemy Ahab and curse him for his crime against Naboth (I Kings 21). Yet for all his roots in the past, Amos was no Nazirite, no Rechabite, who thought to cure the ills of society by a flight to a past that never was. Amos was plainly and simply a man of the covenant who denounced all greed, immorality, and social iniquity as a sin against the covenant God. He advanced no cure for the schism of society save a restoration of the covenant brotherhood which had created Israelite society in the first place:

> Seek good and not evil, that you may live;
> And so Yahweh God of Hosts may be with you, as you say he is.
> (5:14)

3. Just here is the tremendous contribution of Amos to the notion of the Kingdom of God apparent. With Amos the rejection of that

blasphemous identification of the people and the Kingdom of God with the Israelite state had become *total*. Resistance to that identification, as has been said, was not new. It went back to the ancient feeling that the monarchy was not God's order and, even if looked upon as a tolerable and necessary order, was to be brought into line with God's order. It was this feeling that was behind purge after purge, revolution and attempted revolution, which had torn the body politic of Israel for generations. But heretofore the hope had persisted that the state could be made God's order, or at least driven into some conformity with it, by political action. Amos quite gave up any hope of this. Indeed, after Jehu's horror any sensible man might. It is true that Amos was taken for a revolutionary, another *nābî'* plotter preaching sedition against the state (7:10-13), but his indignant denial (7:14-15) is borne out by the facts. Here is a new thing: *never again*, so far as we know, did a prophet seek to reform the state by direct political action.

But we certainly cannot see in this any lessening of tension with the state, but rather a heightening of it. There is no attempt to purge the state, because the state is beyond external correction. It is under the judgment of God. The bond between Israel and God has been broken; idolatry, gross immorality, and unbrotherly greed on a nationwide scale have broken it. "Call his name Lo-ammi, for you are not my people and I will not be your God," said Hosea (1:9). And since Israel has parted company with God, is truly no longer his people, all her exuberant confidence in the future is a false confidence. She has no future but utter and inescapable ruin. Thus it was that Amos leaped upon the popular desire for the Day of Yahweh, the day when Yahweh would intervene in history to establish his rule and to judge his foes. Israel has nothing to hope for from that day—for Israel is herself among Yahweh's foes:

> Ah you that eagerly desire the Day of Yahweh,
> What do you want with the Day of Yahweh?
>   it is darkness, not light;
> As if a man were fleeing from a lion,
>   and a bear attacks him;
> Or were to come home and lean his hand on the wall,
>   and a snake bites him.
> Is not the Day of Yahweh darkness and not light,
>   even black darkness with not a ray of light in it?
>   (5:18-20)

Here is the most shockingly novel note in all eighth-century prophecy: that God can and will cast off his people. This note runs through Amos' preaching and rises to a thundering crescendo: "Behold, the eyes of Lord Yahweh are on the sinful kingdom, and I will destroy it from off the face of the earth" (9:8a). God has rejected the Israelite state, and has rejected it totally.

This meant that the hope of the establishment of the Kingdom of God—the hope embodied in the dream of the Day of Yahweh—began to be divorced from the Israelite state and driven beyond it. The northern kingdom is under sentence of death; Israel's hopes can never be fulfilled in terms of that kingdom. If we had to put Amos' message in a word, might we not paraphrase it thus? *The Kingdom of Israel is not the Kingdom of God!* It can neither be that Kingdom nor inherit it. It cannot be the Kingdom of God, because it has flouted the laws of God and violated the covenant brotherhood. The Kingdom of Israel is under the judgment of God—*and the judgment is history!*

4. Let us not suppose that the words of Amos are ancient words. They are very modern. They are spoken to us and clamor for our attention. We dare not refuse to listen, for it is very late. We are, to be sure, in all externals as little like ancient Israel as possible. Yet in us there is written her hope, and also her delusion and her failure.

We, too, have longed and do long for the Kingdom of God, and dark days heighten the longing. Of course, tongue-tied as we are in the language of faith, we would never put it that way. We would speak of an end to war and fear, a community of nations, the triumph of justice and brotherhood, a moral world order. But there is small difference, in the stuff of it, between what we long for and the hope of ancient Israel that God's people would one day be established under his rule to live out its days in peace and plenty. We earnestly desire the Kingdom of God, although we do not know by what name to call it. With but a recollection of a parent's recollection of a grandparent's faith in that Kingdom, we desire it because we cannot help doing so.

But we might ask to what extent Amos' indictment of society is applicable to us today. In one sense the answer is obvious: it is fully applicable. It takes no skill, nor even a very sharp conscience, to point out that our society, like that of ancient Israel, is shot through with the crimes which Amos denounced: injustice and greed, immorality, pleasure-loving ease, and venality. Nor does one have to be a Cassandra to understand that these things are society's sickness, for which a doctor's bill will surely have to be paid. The indictment of Amos is an indictment of all societies, including our own.

But are we then to apply directly to our society the thundering negation which Amos gave to the hope of the Israelite kingdom? Have we nothing to look forward to but an impending and well-deserved doom? There is a sense in which to say so would not seem fair. To admit that we are guilty before the indictment of Amos is to say but half the truth. For, if compared with other societies that have existed and do exist, ours is not a bad society at all but a very good one. We are a nation founded on Christian principles; our political institutions and our national dogma of the rights and the dignity of man have grown out of these principles. We have so many churches, and these have so many active members, that we can claim to be a Christian nation. What is more, the shadow of the Church and her teachings falls across the nation and the national character more powerfully than most of us realize. The indictment of Amos, and of the other prophets and of Christ, has been, in a measure, taken seriously: stupendous efforts have been made to better the lot of mankind; injustices have been corrected and will continue to be corrected. Ours is a society as good to live in as any that has ever been. We ought to give thanks for it. For all its obvious faults it is worth defending; if we do not defend it, we are forty times purblind. Surely we may pray for God's guidance as we do so!

But will we then commit the fatal error? Will we, like Israel, imagine that our destiny under God and God's purposes in history are to be realized in terms of the society we have built? The temptation to do so is subtle. After all, we may claim a Christian heritage from which human liberties have flowed; we have churches and support them lavishly; but Communism, for example, is totally godless and so destructive of all that is noble in man that scarcely one redeeming thing can be said of it. Between the two there is simply no comparison. Surely God, if he be just, will further our efforts and will defend us from his foe and ours—for we are his good Christian people! As for ourselves, we will labor and pray for the winning of the world to Christ and the victory of his Kingdom—for it is either that sort of world or a chaos in which nothing which we value would be safe. And if the victory of Christ—which we tend to equate with our own best interests—seems remote, we will turn to yet busier activity, for that is all we know how to do. Surely if we thus energetically serve him, God will protect us and give us the victory!

To this hope Amos speaks a resounding *No!* Let us understand his words clearly: God does not in that sense have favored people. No earthly state is established of God, guaranteed of God, and identified with his purposes. Nor has any earthly order, however good, the means of setting up God's order in terms of its own ends. On the contrary, all societies are under the judgment of God's order, and those that have been favored with the light doubly so! Indeed, before we can have any hope of a righteous order established by God, we must, like Israel, learn that our order is not God's but must conform to it or perish. Wherever, says Amos, the schism of society is set forward, there is society perishing. Wherever men who have known of righteousness can speak only of their right to crowd for what they can get; wherever men who have known of Christian brotherhood behave as if they believed in favored races; wherever men who have heard a higher calling grow soft in the enjoyment of the ease that money can buy—there is society under judgment. And the judgment is history. Nor will it greatly matter to those who have to face it whether the barbaric tool of that judgment is Assyria or Russia.

Does Amos then leave society no hope? For sinful society, as sinful society, none! Man's disorder cannot inherit the Kingdom of God but must, on the contrary, live ever in history's judgment. The very hope of peace must remain for it a Utopian dream, which it pursues as a will-o'-the-wisp. Nor are there any external means by which an unrighteous society may avert the judgment that awaits it. Certainly the busy activity of its religion, and the formal correctness of its worship, is of no avail. It is true—although Amos does not mention it—that a nation may, by wise statecraft and sufficient strength, manage to postpone the judgment and survive through centuries of time. Because this is so, it is not irrelevant what policies a nation pursues; and we ought to pray that our nation may choose its course wisely. Amos, however, is not concerned with political realities, but with moral ones. And his verdict stands: a society which flouts the righteous laws of God is none of his and cannot forever endure. No comfort there, to be sure, but the alternative mankind must face. And if that alternative seems to brush aside the political realities which conditioned Israel's survival, and which govern ours, it may nonetheless be accorded a deeper relevance. For the choice before man remains this: to enter anew into covenant with God to live as his people under his rule—or the judgment of history without end.

So Israel yearned for the Day of Yahweh, the day of the victory of God's Kingdom. And week by week our prayer goes up: "Thy kingdom come." It is well that we so pray; it is our proper prayer. But how is it that we dare to pray it except as his obedient children? If we are to pray, "Thy kingdom come," we must also learn to pray, and to mean it quite seriously, "Thy will be done, on earth as it is in heaven."

CHAPTER THREE

A Remnant Shall Repent

THE ISRAELITE STATE, THOUGH PRIDING ITSELF THAT IT WAS THE CHOSEN PEOPLE OF GOD, SHOWED ITSELF BY ITS CONDUCT TO BE ANYTHING BUT that. We saw how, after repeated efforts to purge that state by direct political action had failed, Amos gave it up for lost and pronounced doom upon it: the Israelite state is not the Kingdom of God, and God will not defend it as if it were. The hope of Israel began thus to be broken irrevocably from the nation, and to be made something not realizable in terms of it. This was, however, not a thing to be accomplished quickly, but by a long process. We must now consider it further.

I

The doom pronounced by Amos came with incredible speed. Total disaster fell upon Israel in the latter half of the eighth century B.C., destroying the north entirely and leaving the south in shreds. Yet, paradoxically it might seem, it was precisely through the prophets of this period—particularly Isaiah—that the hope of the Kingdom of God was transfigured and given definitive form.

1. Israel's debacle is a sorry story, but a short one. The great Jeroboam II died in 746, and in twenty-five years the northern state had been wiped from the map. The picture which II Kings 15–17 paints is one of almost total anarchy. King follows futile king, six of them in that quarter century, usually by plot and assassination. There is no semblance

71

of stability. Zechariah, the son of Jeroboam, took his father's throne only to be murdered within six months by one Shallum ben Jabesh (15:8-10). Shallum, for his part, lasted but one month before he was in turn knifed by Menahem ben Gadi (15:13-14). This last took place to the accompaniment of civil war remembered for its unspeakable atrocities (15:16).

Of Menahem the Bible tells us little, and that not to his credit (15:17-22). Virtually all that we know of him is that he succeeded in keeping his seat on the throne for a somewhat longer period than his predecessors (745-738), and that he gave tribute to Pul, king of Assyria. This tribute he raised by means of a head tax levied on every landholder in the country. From the language of vs. 19 the significance of this act of Menahem is all too clear: he had bought Assyrian help to prop him on his shaky throne, and had sold his country into political servitude as the price of it.

This Pul, we know, was none other than the great Assyrian conqueror, Tiglath-pileser III (746-727). His own records tell us that he took tribute from Menahem of Samaria[1] and that, having conquered Babylonia, he reigned there under the throne name of Pulu. It was he who, coming to the throne in the year of Jeroboam's death, snatched Assyria from that lethargy which had permitted the world a half century of peace and set it upon the path of empire in earnest. He also, it would seem, instituted a policy of ominous portent which would be aped by all his successors: to deport and resettle conquered populations and to incorporate their lands as Assyrian provinces. Apparently it was hoped that this ruthless method would serve to eradicate all traces of national sentiment capable of nurturing resistance. Israel would, in its turn, learn what this policy meant. For the next century the name of "the King of Kings, the Great King, King of the land of Asshur" would be hated and feared throughout western Asia.

That Menahem could not have resisted such a colossus as Assyria is obvious. Yet his policy of appeasement was scarcely one that could have gone down well with patriotic Israelites, but must, on the contrary, have been resented bitterly. In any event when Menahem shortly died and was succeeded by his son, Pekahiah, the latter was murdered without much delay by Pekah ben Remaliah, a general of the army (15:23-25). It is possible that a sectional grievance played a part in this coup, for Pekah was assisted in his bloody deed by a gang of Gileadites (vs. 25);

---

[1] A translation of the inscription of Tiglath-pileser mentioning Menahem will be found conveniently in Pritchard, *op. cit.*, p. 283.

but it went far deeper than that. This was a blow for a change of policy; and when Pekah took the throne, he soon began whipping up an anti-Assyrian bloc to strike for independence. And this unleashed a chain reaction of disaster.

2. No less menacing than the international situation was the internal decay of Israel. The book of Hosea is the best possible commentary upon it, and it deserves a whole chapter. For Hosea lived through the collapse, and it tore at his heart.[2] He pictures graphically the political vacuum, the mad plotting for power, the collapse of law and order, civil anarchy in which life is no longer safe (e.g., 4:1-2; 7:1-7; 8:4; 10:3). Even worse, the heart has gone clean out of religious faith, and there is complete moral decay. The priests are timeservers who utter no moral rebuke but who are, through the practices they countenance and abet, themselves the corrupters of religion (4:8-9; 5:1; 6:9-10). Instruction in the true religion has lapsed, and with it all knowledge of the God of Israel; the land is permeated with the poison of paganism. Parents set for their children examples of immorality which the children only outstrip (4:6, 11-14). No more revolting or truer picture than this could be drawn of what the breakdown of religion really means. Nor did this sick nation know any way to cure itself save by political maneuvering (5:13). Yet even here was its bankruptcy evident. They trimmed their foreign policy to every political wind that blew, and they were always wrong—because they were morally wrong. Israel is a half-baked cake (7:8); "a silly dove without any sense" (7:11), fluttering and cooing this way and that in a panic; a worn-out roué who will not wake up to the fact that he is growing old (7:9). Israel is done for!

Clearly there could be no peace between Hosea and such a nation as that! But Hosea's attack differed somewhat from that of Amos. Although it moved from the same theology, it was delivered at a different point. Hosea has less to say of idle luxury and unethical behavior—although he is well enough aware of these things. After all, he spoke not to national prosperity but to national collapse, and his message was shaped by his own peculiar temperament. The target of his attack was idolatry, Baal wor-

---

[2] That Hosea began his ministry before the death of Jeroboam in 746 is evident from 1:4, which pronounces doom upon Jehu's dynasty. But the whole tenor of his prophecies (especially from ch. 4 onward) reflects the chaos which subsequently prevailed. On the other hand, there is little convincing evidence that Hosea lived to see the fall of the northern state. He was active, then, just before 746 and in the fifteen or twenty years thereafter.

ship, apostasy. This is the seat of the disease, the sin in which all sin consists, the poison in the body politic. It is this that has separated Israel from her God, and is the cause of all her calamity. An apostate nation cannot be the people of God.

Most interesting of all is the formulation Hosea gave to the covenant bond which bound Israel to her God. It is a formulation which became classic, and which was taken up by many a subsequent prophet—particularly Jeremiah and Ezekiel. The covenant is a wedlock; in it God "married" Israel and made her his "wife." To worship other gods as Israel has done is plain "adultery," and, if no sincere reconciliation is effected, the end of it will be "divorce"—national ruin. God demands of his people *hesed*,[3] that utter loyalty which is the only proper response to God's *hesed*, his covenant favor. No amount of protestations of loyalty through the external forms of religion can play substitute for it:

> For it is *hesed* that pleases me, and not sacrifice;
> And the knowledge of God rather than burnt offerings.
>   (6:6)

Now it is plain from chs. 1–3 that this formulation of the matter was shaped by Hosea's own tragic experience. He had married a weak creature who in spite of his love for her, turned out to be no better than a prostitute.[4] It would seem that she bore him nameless children.[5] Pleading with her did no good, and finally there was nothing left but divorce. But then, in agony of spirit, it became clear to Hosea that God had told him to marry this woman (1:2) in order that through his suffering he might learn what he had to say: for Israel was just like Gomer, an adulteress (2:2-13). Her very repentance was the facile wheedling of Gomer, her

---

[3] Cf. Chap. I, note 18.

[4] The precise relationship of Hosea and Gomer, and Gomer's actual character, have been much discussed. The reader should consult the various commentaries for the details. It has been suggested that the whole experience was an allegory or vision, but the plain language is against this. It has been argued that Gomer was a common whore, a sacred prostitute, or not a woman of reprehensible character at all. The last seems to me again contrary to the plain sense of ch. 1, while the word used to describe Gomer ('ēshet zenûnîm, 1:2) is neither that commonly used for a streetwalker (zônāh) nor for a sacred harlot (qedēshāh). But while I am inclined to believe that she was merely a wife who, like Israel, drifted into a life of immorality, it is impossible to be certain.

[5] Cf. the language of 1:6, 8 (and also of 2:4) with 1:3. In 1:3 the first child is said to be Hosea's, but such a statement seems pointedly to be omitted in the case of the other two.

hesed was "like a morning cloud, like the dew that goes early away" (6:4). It wasn't in her to go straight (5:4).

Hosea, therefore, rejected the Israelite nation as resoundingly as did Amos. Where a people worships false gods, attributes its material prosperity to false gods (2:8, 12), takes on the morals of false gods (4:11-14), and then tries to save its hide without reference to God (5:13)— *there is neither the people of God nor the Kingdom of God.* "Call his name Lo-ammi; for you are not my people and I will not be your God" (1:9). For all his loving nature Hosea turned upon his people with a ferocity that beggars description (cf. 9:11-17):

> Woe to them, for they have wandered from me;
> destruction to them, for they have rebelled against me!
> And I, I would have redeemed them;
> but they, they spoke lies against me!
>
> (7:13)

The state was doomed. Although Hosea was not sure which nation would be the agent of that doom (cf. 8:13; 11:5; 9:3), the fact of it was a moral certainty.

The hope of the fruition of God's Kingdom is thus completely divorced from the Israelite state.[6] But it is not thereby dissipated. On the contrary, it begins to take new form. God, who must "divorce" and destroy his people, nevertheless has a future for them. Partly, it would seem, this confidence issued from Hosea's own great heart. For his love for Gomer reached out beyond sin and tragedy to woo her and to restore her (ch. 3).[7] Would God, then, be less merciful than Hosea? Would he not restore his erring people? Hosea's faith in God would

---

[6] It would seem from the language of 13:9-11 that Hosea even went so far as to denounce the monarchy as such as a sinful institution. If he did so, he was in line with an ancient sentiment; but other prophets, notably Isaiah, did not go so far: cf. below pp. 85-86.

[7] Ch. 3 tells how Hosea once more purchased a woman of loose character and put her on probation, as it were, in his house. This is usually taken as the sequel of chs. 1–2: Hosea, having divorced Gomer because of her conduct, at the command of God buys her back. But the relationship of ch. 3 to chs. 1–2 is much debated. Ch. 3 not only does not mention Gomer by name, it is couched in the first person; whereas ch. 1 is in the third. It has therefore been suggested that ch. 3 is not the sequel, but a parallel, to ch. 1. On the other hand, the word "again" in 3:1 indicates (however interpreted) that ch. 3 reaches back to something that has gone before. In any case, it is plain, if only from the language of 2:14-23, that a restoration of Gomer-Israel is contemplated. The suggestion that the woman of ch. 3 is another woman than Gomer does not commend itself. It is against the whole drive of the book. God does not divorce one people and take back another.

75

not allow him to believe otherwise. Man's *hesed* may fail, but God's— never! It is precisely because he is God, not man, that he will not make a total end of Israel (11:8-9). The doom, to be sure, remains inescapable. Israel will be stripped of all that she has (2:3, 9, 12-13), ejected from the land, sent back literally to her desert days when she had nothing. But there she will learn again of her ancient purity and loyalty (2:14-15), now so long forgotten (9:10; 11:1-4; 13:4-6). From there she will have a new start, a new betrothal to her God.

> And I will betroth you to me forever;
>   yes, betroth you to me in righteousness and justice,
>   in *hesed*, and in tender compassion;
> Yes, betroth you to me in faithfulness;
>   and you shall know Yahweh.
>   (2:19-20; Heb. vss. 21-22)

Here indeed is Israel the true bride of God! Here lie the seeds of things of which we shall hear much more: the hope beyond tragedy of a new Exodus, a new beginning, a New Covenant.

3. But let us return to our story. Pekah (737-732),[8] seizing power by the assassination of Menahem's son, was the one who set in motion the march of disaster. He had come to the throne on a wave of anti-Assyrian feeling, and his policy precipitated war with Judah. A coalition was whipped together, no doubt with Egyptian prompting, the leaders of which were Israel and the Aramean state of Damascus, whose king was now one Rezin. In such a business, of course, unanimity is essential, and the reluctant must be bludgeoned into line. Because Judah—now ruled by Jotham, son of Uzziah (ca. 742-735) [9]—wanted no part of it, the confederates exerted pressure to bring her to terms (II Kings 15:37). Matters went badly for Judah. When Ahaz (735-715) came to the throne, the situation had become serious. Aramean troops had stripped Judah of all her holdings east of the Jordan, south to the Gulf of Aqabah (II Kings 16:6), and the allies were closing in on Jerusalem

---

[8] II Kings 15:27 gives Pekah twenty years, but this is impossible and some error must be assumed. Samaria fell in 721, less than twenty years after Pekah began to reign, and the total years between the death of Jeroboam (746) and the fall of the northern state is only twenty-five. Cf. W. F. Albright, *Bulletin of the American Schools of Oriental Research*, 100 (1945), 22, note 26.

[9] The sixteen years given Jotham (II Kings 15:33) must be understood to include the years when he acted as regent for his ailing father (vs. 5); cf. *ibid.*, p. 21, note 23.

itself (16:5). It was their intention to depose Ahaz and put an Aramean, one ben Tabeel (Isa. 7:6), in his place as king.

Ahaz was at his wit's end and did not know what to do. "His heart trembled, and the heart of his people, as the trees of the forest tremble before the wind." (Isa. 7:2.) It seemed to him that nothing was left but to appeal to Assyria for help. One day, as the king was inspecting his water supply in preparation for the worst (Isa. 7:3), there came to him a young prophet named Isaiah,[10] who urgently appealed to him to take no such step. Let the king only have faith! Rezin and Pekah are two burnt-out faggots (Isa. 7:4), little nobodies; Assyria will soon attend to them anyway (Isa. 7:7-9; 8:4). As for Assyria if Ahaz tries to shave with this "hired razor," God will shave him, and thoroughly, with the same razor (Isa. 7:20). To court Assyria will be the sure path to slavery. But Ahaz would not listen; the narrow walk of faith was not for him. His mind was made up, and he wanted no Word of God (Isa. 7:10-12). And so he took the fatal step, sending Tiglath-pileser large tribute and imploring his aid (II Kings 16:7-8).

This was no doubt the excuse Tiglath-pileser had been waiting for. In 733 B.C. his armies jumped off and, bypassing Aram, stripped Israel of all Galilee and Transjordan (II Kings 15:29) as well as the coastal plain. These territories were then annexed into the Assyrian Empire. The following year Damascus was taken (II Kings 16:9) and its land, in turn, incorporated as Assyrian provinces. Israel was left but a fragment of herself, with holdings confined to the central mountain range from the Plain of Esdraelon south to the frontier of Judah. We may be sure that Tiglath-pileser would have returned to destroy her entirely had it not been for the timely murder of Pekah by one Hoshea ben Elah (II Kings 15:30), who straightway submitted to the Assyrian and gave tribute.

But Israel's mad progress to ruin was not halted. Hoshea (732-724) had not brought his country into the Assyrian bloc through any love for the Great King, but only because there seemed to be no other course. His was a loyalty, therefore, that was not likely to last any longer than constrained by force. As a matter of fact it did last until Tiglath-pileser died (727) and was succeeded by Shalmaneser V (727-722). Shalmaneser

[10] Presumably Isaiah was yet young. He was called to his ministry in the year of Uzziah's death (742) some eight years previously. But since he continued active until late in Hezekiah's reign (d. 687), he must have been quite a young man at the time of his call. His prophecies are found in chs. 1–39 of the book that bears his name. On chs. 40–66, cf. Chap. V.

must have seemed to Hoshea an easier mark than his predecessor, for after a few years, with Egyptian encouragement (II Kings 17:4), he withheld tribute.

This was a step of utter folly, and it was fatal. Egypt, which was in process of building up a deserved reputation for being a "broken reed" (Isa. 36:6), was at this time even less in a position to give help than usual.[11] Shalmaneser, on the contrary, immediately invaded the rebellious state. Hoshea, whether by surrender or capture, was taken prisoner (II Kings 17:4). And although the capital city of Samaria held out against the might of Assyria for more than two years, with what must have been a heroic stubbornness with few parallels in history, it was no use. It is true that Shalmaneser died before the job was done, but his successor, Sargon II, finished it. In 721 B.C. Samaria fell, and the northern state came to an end. The cream of the population—27,290 in number[12]—was deported to Upper Mesopotamia (II Kings 17:6), there ultimately to lose its identity, while deportees from Babylon and elsewhere (17:24) were brought in to mingle with the surviving population. There was thus left of Israel only an Assyrian province with a bastard population (one day to be the Samaritans) and the hope, poignantly expressed by Hosea and taken up movingly by Jeremiah (31:1-6, 15-22), that God in his mercy would somehow, sometime, beyond tragedy give Ephraim a second chance.

II

1. All the hope of the people of God now rested with Judah. But although Judah had escaped physical catastrophe, she was in a pitiful state. Ahaz had signed away his liberty. The price that Assyria charged for saving him from the coalition was no less than that, as the language of II Kings 16:7-8 makes clear. Ahaz was a puppet. What was worse, this had involved, as a matter of diplomatic courtesy, numerous concessions to the overlord's religion. Assyrian innovations were introduced into the temple at Jerusalem (II Kings 16:10-18). Nor was that all. Paganism breeds paganism, and Ahaz' policy, as might be expected, led to a general

---

[11] The King So of II Kings 17:4 appears in Assyrian inscriptions as Sib'e, but is otherwise virtually unknown. Apparently Egypt at this period had disintegrated into a number of petty states. In any case Sargon utterly routed Sib'e when the latter tried to make good his promise of aid. Cf. Sargon's inscription, J. B. Pritchard, op. cit., pp. 284-85.

[12] The figure is taken from Sargon's inscription. See the references in note 11.

aping of foreign fashions and cults by the people of Yahweh (II Kings 16:3-4; Isa. 2:6-8).

Nor was Judah free of the moral rot which had destroyed Israel. Although it is unlikely that social deterioration had gone as far there as it had in the northern state, there was much that needed reform. A reading of the little book of Micah at least makes it plain that there were those who thought so. Who Micah was, we do not know, except that he seems to have been a villager from southwestern Judah (1:1);[13] but he lashed at social unrighteousness with all the fury of an Amos. It seemed to him that the blow that had slain Israel must surely strike Judah down as well (1:5, 9)—and does she not deserve it! Unbrotherly greed dispossesses the poor (2:1-2, 9); the judges are venal and have made their courts instruments of injustice (3:1-3). The prophets are shams who counterfeit the divine Word and trim their oracles to the size of the fee (3:5); and the priests are no better (3:11). Yet these people sit in the midst of the wreckage they are making of their little world with the smuggest complacency: for they are Yahweh's people, and Yahweh is their God, and the temple—Yahweh's earthly habitation—is in their midst on Zion (3:11). Micah can have no word for this but an unqualified No! This is not the people of Yahweh nor the kingdom he is bound to protect. On the contrary, because of their doings Jerusalem with its temple will become a ruin heap in the forest (3:12). Again the rejection of the state is uncompromising.

2. But Ahaz died, to be succeeded by his son, Hezekiah (715-687)— a man of totally different stamp. Where Ahaz had chosen the path of submission to Assyria, Hezekiah favored a policy of independence and nationalism. In this he was probably in line with the sentiments of the majority of his patriotic subjects, who must have hated their shameful position. And the time might have seemed ripe. In the earlier years of his reign Sargon was far too busy elsewhere to pay much attention to Palestine and Syria. Numerous campaigns into the northern mountains, especially against the kingdom of Urartu,[14] were necessary to consolidate Assyrian power in that quarter. Meanwhile Babylon, under

[13] Micah (1:1; cf. Jer. 26:18) is called "the Morashtite." His home, therefore, was probably Moresheth-gath (mentioned in 1:14), although the nearby Mareshah (mentioned in 1:15) is a possibility. Cf. Wright and Filson, op. cit., p. 110 and Pl. IX.

[14] This land, the name of which is the equivalent of the biblical Ararat (Gen. 8:4; Jer. 51:27), was located in the mountains of Armenia in what is now partly Turkey, partly Russia, and partly Iran. Cf. ibid., Pl. XI.

the patriot Marduk-apal-iddina (the Merodach-baladan of the Bible: II Kings 20:12; Isa. 39:1), had driven the Assyrian from its borders and made itself independent. Not for a dozen years was Sargon able to re-establish control. At the same time, we may imagine, Egypt continued to sing her Lorelei song, encouraging the Palestinian states to resistance with promises of aid which never materialized in effective proportions.

This independence movement had, as we might expect, its religious aspects. As with Ahaz political submission had meant religious syncretism, so with Hezekiah nationalism led to reform: let Judah be Judah religiously also. While it is impossible to say exactly when Hezekiah took the various steps recorded of him, it is clear that he made a thoroughgoing effort to purge out all pagan cult objects and practices, and even to an extent to centralize worship in Jerusalem (II Kings 18:1-5). According to II Chr. 30:1-12 an invitation was even sent out into the erstwhile northern state, now divided into Assyrian provinces, to share in the program.[15] Although the effort was only partially successful,[16] it would seem that the dream of a reconstituted Israel under the throne of David in Jerusalem had not been given up. Yet while the reform undoubtedly fed on nationalistic sentiment, and no doubt popular revulsion at the excesses of Ahaz as well, it must not be overlooked that it had strong prophet prompting, notably in the preaching of Micah (cf. Mic. 3:12; Jer. 26:16-19) and no doubt of Isaiah also. In any case Hezekiah was a sincere Yahwist, the sort of man with whom an Isaiah could speak.

The decision, however, was postponed as long as Sargon lived. We will not here trace the history of the revolts, attempted revolts, and abortive revolts that shook the west of the empire at this period. While Judah was in it hand and glove, she was apparently not so deeply committed that she could not draw out and escape Assyria's wrath. If this

[15] No reason exists to mistrust the account of this reform, particularly as recorded by the Chronicler, as many commentators do: e.g. W. A. L. Elmslie, *The Books of Chronicles*, (The Cambridge Bible [2nd ed.; New York: Cambridge University Press, 1916]), p. 308; E. L. Curtis, *The Books of Chronicles* (International Critical Commentary [New York: Chas. Scribner's Sons, 1910]), pp. 470-71. In its main features Hezekiah's reform followed the same pattern as that of Josiah a century later (II Kings 22–23) and had, we may be sure, a similar objective. Assyria was having difficulty in holding the Israelite population of Samaria in line at this period, and Hezekiah was apparently playing upon this unrest. Cf. W. F. Albright, "The Biblical Period," p. 42.

[16] II Chr. 30:10 asserts as much. Albright links this with the reorganization of the shrine at Bethel by the Assyrians (II Kings 17:27-28). Destruction of ancient shrines would inevitably cause resentment, as the similar measures of Josiah were to do (II Kings 23:8-9). The Assyrians sought to play on this resentment (II Kings 18:22).

was so, it was partly at least because of Isaiah's uncompromising opposition to the whole thing. The prophet who had opposed submission to the Assyrians now opposed rebellion against them! When rebellion broke out in Ashdod (711 B.C.), and an effort was made to entice Judah to join in,[17] Isaiah walked about Jerusalem "naked and barefoot" (Isa. 20:2) as a symbol of the disaster such a course promised. Here, as previously (Isa. 7:3-9) and subsequently (28:14-22; 30:1-5), his burden was not merely that Egyptian help was a great delusion, but that the only path for Judah to walk was the narrow path of faith: "In withdrawal and rest will you be saved; in quiet and in trust is your strength" (Isa. 30:15).

3. But when Sargon died (705) and his son, Sennacherib, came to the throne, the fierce patriotism of the people could no longer be held in check. Again the time seemed ripe. In Babylonia Marduk-apal-iddina, whom Sargon had finally succeeded in crushing, again struck a blow for freedom and, although it failed, it gave Sennacherib no little trouble. Meanwhile a coalition was being formed in the west backed by Shabako, pharaoh of the newly arisen XXV (Ethiopian) Dynasty. A number of Syrian and Palestinian states were drawn into it, and a deputation from Marduk-apal-iddina himself waited on Hezekiah (Isa. 39:1-8=II Kings 20:12-19).[18] Casting Isaiah's earnest warning to the winds, Judah joins in. The reluctant are whipped into line, and this time Judah wields the bludgeon.[19] At the same time Hezekiah dug in for the inevitable blow, seeing to his water supply[20] and his fortifications (II Kings 20:20; II Chr. 32:3-5, 30; Isa. 22:9-11).

Of course, it was not to be expected that the Assyrian would overlook this, nor did he. On the contrary, in 701 B.C. his armies "came down like the wolf on the fold" to wreak bitter vengeance. The story of Sennacherib's invasion, as we know it both from the Bible and his own

[17] This we know from Sargon's inscription (Pritchard, op. cit., p. 287), as well as from Isa. 20.

[18] This is the most logical date for the overtures of Marduk-apal-iddina to Hezekiah, but a date early in Hezekiah's reign is not excluded.

[19] Sennacherib tells us in his inscription how Hezekiah held Padi, king of Ekron, prisoner because of his refusal to co-operate; cf. Pritchard, op. cit., p. 287. Perhaps the Bible reference to Hezekiah's campaigns in Philistia (II Kings 18:8) refers to the same events.

[20] It is probable that II Kings 20:20 and II Chr. 32:30 refer to the digging of the Siloam Tunnel under the hill of Jerusalem. The tunnel was dug from both ends; and at the point where the two crews met, an inscription was cut in the rock. A translation of the inscription, discovered in 1880, will be found in Pritchard, op. cit., p. 321.

inscriptions, raises many problems which would be out of place in this discussion. It is a moot question whether the story of II Kings 18–19 (= Isa. 36–37) covers one campaign or two.[21] Suffice it to say that the revolt was utterly crushed. The Assyrian juggernaut burst into the land with terrific force; nothing could halt it (cf. Isa. 10:28-32). All the fortified cities of Judah, forty-six in number,[22] were reduced and razed to the ground. An Egyptian army hastening to Hezekiah's aid was swept aside like the straw it was. Hezekiah, shut up in Jerusalem "like a bird in a cage," [23] had no course but to give in and pay the heavy tax which Sennacherib laid upon him (II Kings 18:14-16).[24] But, subsequently, unconditional surrender was demanded (II Kings 18:17–19:19), and that was too much; Hezekiah resolved to die fighting. Jerusalem was in desperate straits.

Isaiah's attitude in the course of all this is truly remarkable. In view of his previous attitude we might expect an "I told you so" coupled with advice to give in. But instead he emerges as a tower of courage to king and people. Have faith, he says, do not fear! The Assyrian has blasphemed God in his pride and will surely be cut down to size. He will not take the city, but will be sent limping home with his tail between his legs (II Kings 19:6-7, 20-34=Isa. 37:6-7, 21-35). God will by all means defend Zion! The enemy "shall not come into this city nor shoot an arrow there. . . . For I will defend this city to save it, for my own sake and for my servant David's sake" (Isa. 37:33, 35=II Kings 19:32,

---

[21] The Assyrian texts (cf. Pritchard, op. cit., pp. 287-88) give us a story in all essentials parallel to the account in II Kings 18–19 except that, as one would expect, there is no mention of a miraculous intervention which saved Jerusalem. Most scholars hold that there was but one campaign of Sennacherib (in 701). Others, recently W. F. Albright ("The Biblical Period," p. 43; cf. note 102 for bibliography), believe that II Kings 18–19 combines the accounts of two campaigns. The first of these took place in 701 and ended with Hezekiah's surrender and payment of tribute, mentioned in II Kings 18:14-16 and, in greater detail, by Sennacherib. Then at a later date, after Tirhakah (II Kings 19:9) had come to the throne of Egypt (and he did so only in 689), Hezekiah again rebelled. In this campaign there took place the siege and deliverance mentioned in the Bible. It must be admitted that the transition between II Kings 18:16 and 18:17 is very sharp. Hezekiah has paid the tribute demanded and then, at once, the city is under siege. Either Sennacherib raised his demands beyond reason or reference is to another occasion. The mention of Tirhakah necessitates a later date, unless Tirhakah is identified as king—although at the time of the events described in II Kings 19, he had not yet ascended the throne.

[22] II Kings 18:13. The exact number is from Sennacherib's inscription.

[23] The expression is Sennacherib's.

[24] Sennacherib adds that Hezekiah was forced to cede certain border cities to the Philistines.

34). And in fact, so we read, deliverance came in the nick of time. The plague struck; "the angel of Yahweh went forth" in the Assyrian camp (Isa. 37:36; II Kings 19:35) and inflicted heavy casualties. Tidings of trouble, too, came from home (Isa. 37:7=II Kings 19:7). The Assyrian army retired. Yahweh had indeed saved his people!

So Judah escaped with her life—but no more! Jerusalem had been spared, but the rest of the land had been utterly ravaged. Hezekiah's bold bid for freedom had brought his people unspeakable suffering. And although in 681 B.C. Sennacherib was assassinated (Isa. 37:38=II Kings 19:37), his successors, Esarhaddon and Asshurbanapal, enlarged Assyrian power to yet more fearsome dimensions. Hezekiah and his son Manasseh after him remained vassals of the Great King. Judah was not free.

III

Surprising as the fact may seem, it was in this time of high courage and brute agony—when any hope at all might seem to be a luxury beyond affording—that the Old Testament hope of the messianic Kingdom was given both its most eloquent expression and its definitive form. This we may see particularly in the book of Isaiah, but also in that of Micah.[25]

1. The reader of Isaiah senses at once that denunciation and doom are balanced there by a glorious hope, and that far more strikingly so than in Amos or even in Hosea. This is, of course, not at all that Isaiah was either blind to the sins of his people or willing to overlook them. On the contrary, he assailed them with a fury and a lofty ethical sense which made him every inch an eighth-century prophet. He could abide no more than Amos that greed for gain which places property above men and above God:

> Ah these that join house to house,
> lay field to field,
> till there is no room.
>
> (5:8)

[25] Especially in question here are such passages as Isa. 2:2-4=Mic. 4:1-4; Isa. 9:1-6; 11:1-9; Mic. 5:2-4. There was once quite a strong tendency to regard these and similar passages as later—even exilic and postexilic—additions to their respective books, but recent opinion has been much less decided in this direction. For full discussion the reader must refer to the various commentaries. While, of course, the genuineness of such passages cannot be proved mathematically, the arguments for relegating them to a later era are more than dubious. They may safely be regarded as expressions of the prophetic mind of the late eighth and early seventh centuries and may, therefore, be used as evidence here. They fit perfectly into the theology of Isaiah. Of course the fact that Isa. 2:2-4 is repeated almost exactly in Micah, makes it a special problem; but the very fact that it is found among the oracles of two eighth-century prophets may be regarded as an accurate index of its date.

> Ah these that enact hurtful enactments,
>   and, busily writing, do write hardship,
> To push aside the weak from judgment
>   to snatch away the right of the poor of my people,
> That widows may become their prey,
>   and that they may plunder orphans.
>
>   (10:1-2)

Equally did he loathe an effete society, concerned for its living standard above all things (3:16–4:1; 32:9-14) and all too often besotted with debauchery (5:11-12, 22; 28:1-8). And worst of all he hated that pride, complacent in its power, which seeks to dispose of life itself without reference to God. That pride is the very essence of sin (2:9-22)! This people must learn that God does not tolerate such behavior; and if they will not hear the lesson spelled out in plain Hebrew, then God will be forced to teach it to them in Assyrian (28:9-13)!

Isaiah's attack on the sins of society was uncompromising. And it proceeded from precisely the same feeling for the covenant relationship between Israel and God which had moved in Amos and Hosea. God has indeed called Israel to be his people. But the bond between them is not mechanical, existing because Israel is Israel, but reciprocal: it demands obedience. The people are God's vineyard (5:1-7), upon which he has lavished the very best of care, and from which he expects the very best fruit of justice and rectitude. And he will simply turn a vineyard which does not produce such fruit over to the thorns and briers. If just conduct is not given, nothing that is given is acceptable. Without it all the sacrifices and sacred observances on Mount Zion are so much pious mummery and positively an offense to God:

> What is the multitude of your sacrifices to me? saith Yahweh.
> I am fed up with burnt offerings of rams and the fat of fat animals,
> And in the blood of bullocks and of lambs and of he-goats I take no pleasure.
> .   .   .   .
> Your new moons and your set feasts my very being hates,
> They have become a burden to me that I am tired of carrying.
> And when you spread forth your hands, I will hide my eyes from you;
> Yes, when you make many prayers, I am not listening.
> Your hands are full of blood!
> Wash yourselves; cleanse yourselves!
> Put away the evil of your doings from before my eyes!
> Cease to do evil! Learn to do good!

Seek justice! Restrain the oppressor!
Do justice to the orphan! Espouse the cause of the widow!
(1:11, 14-17)

Now it is clear from this that Isaiah could not make peace with the state and hallow it as the kingdom of God's people any more than Amos had done. Certainly he could never do so with Ahaz' state. Nor could he have agreed that even the reformed state of Hezekiah satisfied Israel's destiny as the people of God. On the contrary, even that state—though repeatedly summoned to the walk of faith—had rebelled against its divine Father and sought help elsewhere. In fact it did not display the sense of a stupid ox or a jackass, for even these know who feeds them (1:2-4).[26]

For such a state there can only be a judgment. And the judgment comes in history. The day of Yahweh's anger on proud men is near (2:12); the hand of his anger is stretched out (9:12, 17, 21; 10:4); in it is his chastening rod—Assyria (10:5-6)! Nor let this state which has refused divine aid and counsel think to save itself with Egyptian help (31:1-3). "The Egyptians are men, and not God"; the outstretched hand of God's anger will strike down both those that seek help and those that give it. There will come a day when the very pillars of society will crumble (3:1-8). So great will be the chaos that they will be glad to lay hold on anyone who has so much as a coat to his back (vs. 6) and make him ruler, so that someone may take responsibility for the utter mess they have created. "Jerusalem has stumbled; Judah has fallen"! (3:8.)

Yet in spite of this Isaiah did not pronounce a doom of total proportions. He did not believe—quite contrary to Amos' verdict on the northern state (9:8a)—that his nation would be utterly destroyed. He believed that the line of David would continue, and he could look forward to a coming Prince who should establish the rule of that line forever (Isa. 9:6-7). So it was that where Amos (Amos 5:18-20) had described the Day of Yahweh's judgment as "thick darkness with not a ray of light in it" for Israel, Isaiah could see "a great light" bursting upon the "land

[26] I am in agreement with those commentators who place ch. 1 (especially vss. 2-9) in the setting of Sennacherib's invasion: e.g. B. Duhm, *Das Buch Jesaja* (Hand-kommentar zum Alten Testament [4th ed.; Göttingen: Vandenhoeck and Rupprecht, 1922]), p. 24; G. A. Smith, *The Book of Isaiah* (*The Expositor's Bible* [New York: A. C. Armstrong & Son, n.d.]), I, 3; J. A. Bewer, *The Book of Isaiah* (New York: Harper & Bros., 1950), I, 15. Other commentators, it must be admitted, prefer other dates.

of deep darkness" (9:2). And where Amos had totally rejected the cult of Bethel (Amos 9:1), and where Micah had in turn rejected that of Jerusalem (Mic. 3:12), Isaiah could regard Mount Zion as the very throne room of Yahweh's Kingdom, founded by him and defended by him (6:1-5; 14:32; 28:16; 31:4-9).

Isaiah gave dramatic illustration of this confidence when he was shut up in Jerusalem's siege. We do not forget that he had urged Ahaz not to sell out to Assyria in the first place. And when this had nevertheless been done and rebellion was planned, he stoutly opposed it. He, too, had announced the Assyrian as the rod of God's avenging wrath (10:5-6). And yet when the Assyrian tide lapped at the very walls of Jerusalem, he almost alone had the incredible optimism to declare that the Assyrian would never take the city: God would defend the city for his own sake and for David's sake (37:33-35). That, indeed, calls for explanation. It sounds very like a lapse into the popular theology. It sounds, one might say, too confident—as if in the crisis Isaiah proved to be more of a patriot than a prophet. He might well have been understood to say just what the people wanted most to hear: God will save Zion no matter what—for here are God's people, God's anointed king, and God's Kingdom. It must be said that in later generations Isaiah's words were exactly so understood, as Jeremiah knew to his sorrow (Jer. 7; 26). Although we may not doubt that this would have caused Isaiah to turn in his grave had he known it, it nevertheless had strong support from his words.

2. But we would be quite wrong if we were to regard this tenacious confidence of Isaiah's merely as an expression of patriotic sentiment, or his messianic hope as the projection into better days to come of frustrated national longing. To be sure, the importance of these factors—and of many others—for the intensifying and shaping of Israel's national hope ought not for a moment to be discounted. And Isaiah was a patriot. After all, he was a citizen of Jerusalem and apparently of good family. He had easy access to the king, if he was not actually a member of the court. And about Jerusalem and that court clustered, as nowhere else, all the memories of David. Here the confidence was cherished of the eternity of David's line (cf. II Sam. 7:13-16; 23:5); here the ruling king (even if he were an Ahaz!) was a Davidide, and thus a representative of something greater than himself. In the coronation ritual each king was hailed as the adopted "son" of Yahweh (e.g., Ps. 2:7) and, in what cultic ceremonies we do not know, the promises made to David were kept alive in popular

imagination.[27] In this seedbed of faith messianic expectations were nurtured. Nor ought we to forget that it was in the temple—which housed the sacred Ark, holiest symbol of Israel's heritage—that Isaiah himself had had that vision of God which made him a prophet (ch. 6). It would have been strange indeed if Isaiah's message had not been colored by these things, and stranger if he had cast them all off without pity.

But important as these factors were, we cannot explain the prophetic hope merely in terms of them. We must remember that the hope entertained by the prophets rooted, no less than did their condemnation of national sin, in the very nature of the God in whom they believed and in their feeling for the covenant relation which bound Israel and God together.[28] Israel's God is the Lord of history. Creator of all things, all things are in his hands; in the events of history he works his purpose. And the issues of history are his also; history moves toward his victory, the triumphant establishment of his rule over his people. True, he called Israel to be the people of his rule, and Israel had egregiously failed and fallen under condemnation. But that fact could not in prophet theology cancel out the victory of God, for that would be to allow that the failure of man is also the failure of God. And no prophet would have dreamed of saying such a thing.

Least of all Isaiah! His was the God of Israel, and no one ever painted that God with bolder strokes. Here is the thrice-holy God of the inaugural vision (ch. 6) whose glory filled the temple, burst out of the temple, shook the temple, clearly could not be contained in any temple made with hands. Before him the pride of men is nothing (2:11-22); mortal eyes may not behold him and live (6:5). The powers of this earth, even great Assyria, are but the merest utensils in his hands; he whistles for them to come (7:18-19); he uses them and casts them off (10:5-19). Clearly they would have no power at all except it were given them of God! True, Israel is judged by that holy God and cannot escape punishment; but God has a purpose in history, and he does not abdicate it—not even to Assyria. God will work his purpose in history, and he will work it with stubborn Israel: *he will save some for his purpose!* And now that the northern state is gone, with whom could this be done but with

[27] One thinks especially of such Psalms as 2; 45; 72; 89:3-4, 19-37; 110; and 132. We cannot debate the moot question of the place of the king in Israelite theology and cult, but the evidence for a belief in the eternity of the royal line is unmistakable.

[28] Cf. Chap. I, pp. 28-30.

Judah and Jerusalem? The future is with God: though all else be uncertain, that much is unshakably certain!

Coupled with this, too, was Isaiah's feeling that, in spite of her shortcomings Judah was not wholly irredeemable. In point of fact there is evidence that the southern state never actually sank to such depths of apostasy and social deterioration as did her northern sister.[29] There was never a time when there were not good men, even kings, in Judah who were amenable to the prophet preaching and willing to reform. Hezekiah, though he might be called politically unwise, was by any standard a brave and good man who certainly did not deserve utter condemnation. Isaiah never lost the confidence that there was a "holy seed" (6:13) [30] in the country, a good element over which God could rule if only it could be separated out. Dire calamity might leave the house of David like a cut-down tree; but there is sap in the stump, and it will put forth "a shoot" which will one day again become a fruitful tree (11:1).

Thus it was that Isaiah could never speak of the judgment on the state as total destruction. It is to be seen as a discipline, a purge out of which will come the pure Remnant of God's people. The nation goes down into the fiery furnace, but pure metal will come out—a clean people:

> What a harlot she has become,
>   the (once) faithful city!
> (Once) she was full of justice;
>   righteousness abode in her,
>   but now murderers!
> Your silver has become dross,
>   your wine cut with water;
> Your rulers are unruly,
>   confederates of thieves!
> Every one of them loves a bribe
>   and runs after graft!
> To the orphan they don't do justice,
>   and the case of the widow never comes before them.

[29] For example, proper names compounded with Baal seem to have been much rarer in the south than in the north—a fact which indicates a stronger resistance to pagan tendencies. There is evidence, too, that there wealth was not so concentrated in the hands of a few. Cf. Albright, "The Biblical Period," pp. 38, 41.

[30] The text of Isa. 6:13 is exceedingly obscure, but the evidence is against the omission of the words in question. So recently, I. Engnell, *The Call of Isaiah* (*Uppsala Universitets Arsskrift* 1949:4 [Uppsala: Lundequistka Bokhandeln, 1949]), pp. 14-15. For further bibliography H. H. Rowley, *The Biblical Doctrine of Election* (London; Lutterworth Press, 1950), p. 73, notes 4 and 5.

Wherefore saith the Lord, Yahweh of Hosts, the Champion of
Israel:
"Ah, I will have satisfaction from my adversaries,
will take vengeance on my foes.
And I will turn my hand against you
and purge out your dross in the furnace[31]
and remove all your alloy.
And I will restore your judges as at the first,
your counsellors as at the beginning.
After that you shall be called
City of Righteousness, Faithful Town."
(1:21-26)

The notion of a pure Remnant of God's people, cleansed in fiery trial
and made amenable to God's purpose, is one of the most characteristic
of all the ideas of Isaiah (4:2-4; 10:20-22; 37:30-32), and one that was to
exert a profound influence on his people for centuries to come. In fact
so basic was it to Isaiah's thinking, that he even named his two sons
(7:3; 8:1) Maher-shalal-hash-baz ("The Booty Hurries; the Plunder
Comes Quickly") and Shear-jashub ("A Remnant Shall Return"; i.e.,
"Repent").[32]

3. There will always be a Remnant! This does not mean, it must be
repeated, that Isaiah was able to identify the existing state or any group
in it with the true people of God over whom God would establish his
rule. On the contrary, the hope of the Kingdom of God is sharply divorced from the existing state. It is not realizable in terms of it as it
presently is: that Isaiah would have said, and did say, as strongly as did
his predecessors. But hope could neither be given up nor exist vaguely
and without form. It was, therefore, pushed into the future and projected
upon the ideal state of the Messiah, the Israel of the Remnant. In the
process the messianic hope of Israel was given its classic expression.

To be sure, the imagery of the Remnant and the purge were drawn
from the bitter present. After all, compared with the glories of David

---

[31] This emendation is acceptable with many commentators. The change involves only
the transposition of two Hebrew consonants (*bkr* for *kbr*). The present text: "I will purge
away thy dross as (with) lye" is rather clumsy.

[32] Some take the name as a threat: *"Only a remnant will return."* So, for example,
Sheldon H. Blank (*Journal of Biblical Literature*, LXVII [1948], 211-15). But in
either case the idea of a surviving few is present. To deny Isaiah the notion of a purged
Remnant, as Blank does, involves an unwarranted ruling out of the evidence.

and Solomon—especially as longing memory had idealized them—Hezekiah's state was a remnant, and a pitiful one at that. Isaiah, in fact, looked upon the schism of the state at the death of Solomon as the worst calamity of the past (7:17), for then the brave structure which David had built was destroyed. And we must remember that in 733 Tiglath-pileser had reduced the northern state to a shadow of itself, and in 721 Sargon had destroyed it utterly. At the same time the southern state had saved its skin only at the price of shameful servitude and, when it had tried to get free, had been butchered by Sennacherib. The body politic had been left a mass of festering wounds and, but for the mercy of God who left a tiny remnant, would have joined Sodom and Gomorrah in total oblivion (1:5-9).

Judah was the remnant. And yet, as we have said, Isaiah was not able simply to identify the hoped-for Remnant with his decimated nation. There is reason to believe, indeed, that he would have liked to do so. He had hoped, it would seem, that each succeeding blow would prove to be the discipline needed to purify his people and drive them back to God. It is interesting, at least, that the great proclamation of the Messiah Prince of 9:1-7 is addressed precisely (vs. 1; Heb. 8:23) to those areas ravaged by Tiglath-pileser (II Kings 15:29).[33] Certainly the language of 37:30-32 indicates that the prophet expected that those who escaped Sennacherib's siege would turn out to be the Remnant which God would bless. But if he had such hopes—hopes that the present crisis would purify the nation—they were bitterly disappointed. When he observed the behavior of his people on the glad day when the Assyrian army lifted the siege (22:1-14) [34]—up on the rooftops wild with joy, banqueting, carousing, celebrating, but with never a thought for the God who had saved them or for the repentance to which he had been trying to drive

[33] So with many commentators. A recent and able defense of this date, and of the genuineness of the passage, is that of A. Alt, "Jesaja 8:23–9:6, Befreiungsnacht und Krönungstag" (*Festschrift für Alfred Bertholet* [Tübingen: J. C. B. Mohr, 1950], pp. 29-49). Alt even sees in the passage a rejection of the ruling Davidide, Ahaz. The recent effort of H. L. Ginsberg ("Judah and the Transjordan States from 734 to 582 B.C.E." *Alex Marx Jubilee Volume*, S. Lieberman, ed. [New York: Jewish Theological Seminary, 1950], pp. 347-68) to relate Isa. 9:1-6 to the reign of Josiah (pp. 357 ff.) does not carry conviction.

[34] While most commentators assign 22:1-14 to the period of Sennacherib's invasion, the exact circumstances are much debated. I have agreed with those who see here the rejoicing over deliverance: e.g., J. Skinner, *Isaiah* (*The Cambridge Bible* [New York: Cambridge University Press, 1925]), I, 175; G. B. Gray, *Isaiah* (*International Critical Commentary* [Edinburgh: T. & T. Clark, 1912]), p. 364.

them—the old prophet could no longer contain himself. This is no clean Remnant! The purge has not purged! In the bitterest words we have from his lips, he cries out (22:14): "Surely this iniquity will not be forgiven you till you die"! The Remnant hope, then, could have nothing to do with the actual nation, but must await its fruition in the ideal state which God should produce in the future.

The hope of Israel is thus driven ahead beyond the existing nation. But with this forward look there is coupled a nostalgic gaze into the lost past. Over this Remnant, that shall one day be, there shall rule the Messiah Prince of the line of David. Now men have always turned with homesick longing from the agony of the present to the "good old days" of the heart's imagination. Many in Israel had of course idealized the desert days of Israel's beginnings, and this had always created a tension with the present. But Isaiah is of Jerusalem, and Jerusalem is the City of David where the "David idea" lived with tenacious power. The age of David was Israel's Golden Age. How better, then, could the bliss of the future be described than as the reign of a transfigured David? Isaiah's hope of the coming Kingdom of God is not to be explained, as we have said, merely as a child of the "David idea"; it springs, rather, from the mainstream of Israel's theology. But it is not at all strange that Isaiah should have used the ideology of royal David to express it. There will come a new David, a David redivivus; he will rule over a new and a redeemed Israel (9:1-7; 11:1-5; cf. Mic. 5:2-4).

> For a child is born to us;
> a son is given to us.
> And the dominion is upon his shoulder,
> and his name is called:
> "Wonderful Counsellor, Mighty God,
> Father forever, Prince of Peace."
> Great[35] is the dominion
> and of peace no end,
> On the throne of David,
> and over his kingdom,
> To establish it and to support it
> in justice and in righteousness,

[35] So with many commentators. The first two consonants of the first word (lmrbh) seem to be a dittography of the last two of the last word of the preceding verse (note the m is written as a final letter should be). The verse then begins, "Great is . . ." (rabbāh).

> Henceforth and forevermore.
> The zeal of Yahweh of Hosts will do this.
> (9:6-7; Heb. vss. 5-6)

Yet it is plain that this is something which lies far beyond the presently existing state, however much Isaiah may have hoped of that state. It is the Kingdom of God toward which all history moves.[36] There justice shall reign (11:3-5); there peace will be unbroken (Isa. 2:2-4=Mic. 4:1-3). There Israel shall find at last her destiny to be a blessing to the entire world (Isa. 2:3=Mic. 4:2; cf. Gen. 12:3). God is the real ruler of that Kingdom. The Prince of David's line is imbued with God's spirit, and by that spirit he rules; he is God's own charismatic (11:2). He stands before us as no fierce warrior, but as a little child (9:6) established in his rule by God's power (9:7). He reigns over a people transformed through their obedience to the divine Will. It is God's Kingdom and it will endure forever (9:7).

And, then, with a change of imagery that Kingdom is described not as a transfigured age of David, but as a recovery of the lost bliss of Eden. An Edenlike peace reigns in all the earth (11:6-9): peace among men, peace in nature, peace with God. The balance in creation, upset so long ago by sin, is now restored—for God's law is supreme. If the prophet had said that there will be a new Eden, a new Adam, it would hardly be surprising.[37] He did not, of course, but the idea is there. Keep it in mind! We shall in due time hear of a new Adam in whom all are made alive (I Cor. 15:22, 45-49).

4. The influence which these majestic concepts exerted is simply

---

[36] The concept of the Messiah cannot be denied eschatological quality. Perhaps it may not satisfy the definition of eschatology in later Jewish and Christian theology (end of the aeon, end of the world), but the rule of Yahweh over his people which it depicts nevertheless represented to prophet and people the *effective* goal of history. Nothing was thought of as lying beyond it. The fact that the language may have been drawn from cultic sources, and the fact that Israelites may have hoped that each succeeding Davidide would prove to be the Messiah, does not alter the case.

[37] I regard 11:6-9 as an integral part of the prophecy. Some have argued (e.g., A. Bentzen, *Messias-Moses redivivus-Menschensohn* [Zürich: Zwingli Verlag, 1948], pp. 37-42, etc.) that the concept of the Messiah is closely related to that of the Urmensch (the Primitive Man). Were this so, the hope of the Messiah's coming would inevitably suggest the return of Edenlike peace, and the presence of such a picture in a messianic passage would be very natural. While I am not convinced that there was any conscious connection in the prophet's mind between Messiah and Primitive Man, the language used may have had a prehistory. Israel's faith had a way of borrowing the language of myth and giving it an entirely new meaning.

beyond measure. The messianic hope of Israel was thus tied firmly to the line of David, to Jerusalem and the temple, and given a form which it would never lose. A mighty faith was therewith created which nothing could shatter. Indeed, the darker the days, the brighter its flame. For Messiah does not come to a proud nation glorying in its strength, but to a beaten nation, a cut-down stump of a nation, a nation tried in the furnace of affliction. No humiliation could be so abject, no torment so brutally severe, but that faith might whisper: Who knows but that this suffering is the purge that is even now producing the pure Remnant; who knows but that tomorrow Messiah, the Prince of David's line, may come?

That this was not all gain needs no saying. It meant that as long as the state lasted, each king, in the popular mind, was a potential Messiah—and how unfitted even the best of them were for that distinction! It helped to father the national delusion that, though Judah might be decimated, Jerusalem and the Davidic state could never be destroyed—a delusion that was to break the heart of Jeremiah. It meant that messianic expectations would attach themselves pathologically to a hundred pretenders, from Zerubbabel to Bar-Kokhba. It meant that when he who was the fulfillment of that longing should appear, men would demand of him things which were not in his nature to deliver: "Lord, will you at this time restore the kingdom to Israel?" (Acts 1:6.) Yet for all that, this concept was to provide faith with a rallying place secure even beyond exile, humiliation, and frustration of hope. No calamity could eradicate it—for the Kingdom of the Messiah comes precisely beyond calamity to a poor Remnant.

Into the Hebrew soul were released powerful ideas, which would in time bear fruit. Isaiah speaks here, it is true, of no suffering Messiah, but of a ruling king. Yet it is an unusual figure of a king: of humble and unlikely origins (Mic. 5:2), a sprout from the stump of a once-mighty tree (Isa. 11:1), whose power is not of the sword but over the spirits of men. And his Kingdom is one entered by the humiliated—that small Remnant who in suffering and tragedy have been purged of their sinful ways, who in that suffering have learned obedience to the will of God. Here lie mighty things, albeit in germ.[38] We shall hear more of another figure, disfigured yet in his disfigurement kingly, who was "a root out

[38] Cf. especially the excellent lecture of W. Eichrodt, *Israel in der Weissagung des Alten Testaments* (Zürich: Gotthelf-Verlag, 1951), pp. 35-37.

of dry ground" (Isa. 53:2); of a king, a lowly king, who comes "riding on an ass" (Zech. 9:9). We shall hear of One, every inch a King, who summoned the poor in spirit to his Kingdom (Matt. 5:3): clearly a Kingdom to which "not many . . . wise . . . , not many . . . powerful, not many . . . of noble birth" are called (I Cor. 1:26).

A further point, however, is perhaps even more important: in the Isaianic doctrine of the Remnant the hope of the Kingdom of God begins to shift markedly from the nation Israel to a "church" within the nation. It is not, of course, to be imagined that Isaiah was the first to be aware of a distinction between the faithful few and the sinful majority.[39] Yet heretofore we have dealt with Israel as a nation. Israel is the covenant people of God, the chosen people of his election, the heirs of his promises. We have seen how easily this idea could be prostituted until, in popular imagination, the people of God became identified with the Israelite state, and the victory of God's purpose with the glorification of that state. We have also seen that the prophets were obliged to reject that identification completely. Yet not completely, for they could never agree that Israel's failure involved the failure of God. In the notion of the Remnant, however, a distinction begins to be drawn between physical Israel and the true Israel, the actual Israel and the ideal Israel. The notion begins to take root in Hebrew theology that actual Israel will not inherit the Kingdom of God—that vision will ever be beyond her. Yet, along with this, there remains the confidence that one day there will emerge a true Israel, disciplined to obedience to God's will, fit to be the instrument of his purpose. It is an Israel, not of birth, but of individual choice for the calling of God. Over this true Israel, and over it alone, will God rule—for these are the people of his Kingdom.

This notion of a new and spiritual Israel, first foreshadowed in Isaiah's doctrine of the Remnant, did not yield its full meaning all at once; but it was to be taken up in many varying forms by the prophets that came after Isaiah. For they all understood that a new Israel "according to the spirit," and not the nation Israel, would be heir of the promise of the Kingdom. In all of them the notion of the Remnant appears, even where the term is not used. It is precisely as this new Israel, as we shall see later, that the New Testament church understood itself.

[39] Cf. especially Elijah and the remnant of seven thousand who had not bowed the knee to Baal (I Kings 19:18). On the Remnant cf. H. H. Rowley, op. cit., pp. 69 ff.

IV

But what has Isaiah to say to us who are the people of that Church and who proudly claim to be the heirs of that very promise? Much more than we can even suggest here. To be sure we no longer look forward to the coming of the Messiah King. As Christians we must affirm that that hope has been amply fulfilled in One born of the house and lineage of David and hailed in derision as "King of the Jews!" But the prophet vision of the Kingdom of God is before us yet. The Bible language is antique language, and we would never put it so, but when we read of swords beaten into ploughshares and of war forever ended, of the eternal reign of justice and peace (Isa. 2:2-4; 9:6-7; 11:1-9), we recognize our deepest longing. We may be so very modern that we have heard neither of Isaiah nor of the Kingdom of God, but we can no more escape that longing than we can escape ourselves. A world of peace, a moral world order, we desperately desire. We try to produce it in a thousand mutually canceling ways; for we know that if we do not achieve it, or at least some semblance of it, we shall perish.

Isaiah tells us things we need to know, but have forgotten. A moral world order is inconceivable and impossible save in submission to the righteous rule of God. The time shall indeed come—so faith makes affirmation—when "they shall not hurt nor destroy in all my holy mountain"; but it will come only when "the earth shall be full of the knowledge of the Lord as the waters cover the sea" (Isa. 11:9). The peace of man *is* the Kingdom of God, and he has no other peace. That being so, we will neither produce that rule of peace nor enter it as we are. The state cannot achieve it by its policies—though what those policies are is by no means irrelevant. Civilization will not ascend to it on an incline of washing machines and new automobiles. Organized religion cannot by its busiest programs open the doors to it, nor hallow society so that it may enter. We have no external program that can lead us to this idyllic peace. It is given ultimately only to a world which submits itself to the rule of the divine King in deed and in truth: there are no short cuts. Our programs, wise and good as they may be, are but temporary stopgaps. At best they may produce an approximation of that peace, at worst a travesty of it. We shall have peace only when men surrender their tools, their minds, and their wills to the Kingdom of God: "Thy will, not mine, be done."

That becomes to us a summons to read the lessons of history aright. History is a judgment upon sin. If the prophet so declared, it would not today take any great faith to agree with him. At least it certainly seems that the incurable sickness of the world is due, more than to any economic cause, to the total and corporate failure of man in the realm of righteousness. He has known no moral law, or knowing one, has not obeyed it. And for that he is being severely punished. But history is also a warning and a discipline. That men will heed this warning is perhaps too much to expect. But the warning is uttered each day with unmistakable clarity: that our best is not good enough; that we must find some higher righteousness, some higher citizenship, or perish. History is each day showing us the bankruptcy of all earthly states that we may be driven to seek redemption in some higher quarter. Without using the word, history is pointing us to the Kingdom of God and telling us that it is more than high time.

But may we not also be led to reflect that times that seem evil to us may serve a better purpose than times that are good? This may seem a strange thing to say, but there is much truth in it. The good times that we desire are times of freedom from disturbing bother—in which a man can read his paper without worrying, can get on with his business, can have gas for his car and the pleasures and luxuries which we all enjoy. Those, we would say, are good times. But perhaps from the divine point of view they are not. For the purpose of God for us is not the comfort of our bodies or the preservation of our interests, but the discipline of our spirits that we may become truly his people. Who shall say what times serve that end best? Let it be understood that there is nothing of the Pollyanna, no careless belittling of the tragedy of our times, in that statement. No one who has seen even a little of that tragedy can indulge in cheap moralizing about the virtues of suffering. Yet, let it never be forgotten, it is precisely in suffering that the people of God are selected; in suffering are they *known*. The tragedy of the times, therefore, becomes to us a personal summons to decide for the calling of God and, in tragedy, to serve him. We will have no patience with false cheerfulness. But we will learn the meaning of that hymn based on Isaiah's words:

> When through fiery trials thy pathway shall lie,
> My grace, all-sufficient, shall be thy supply,

The flame shall not hurt thee; I only design
Thy dross to consume, and thy gold to refine.

Let Isaiah, then, speak to our faith. As Isaiah cast longing eyes upon the Golden Age of David, and then spoke of the transfigured David that was to come, so we will look back to a Prince of David's line who needs no idealizing; then ahead with Isaiah, the New Testament church, and all Christendom, to Christ regnant and triumphant at the issue of history. And though we may not see how that Kingdom could come soon, or prove that it will come at all, we will face the dark future with faith and pray for its coming. And we will take courage. As civilization and material property, nations and churches, are tossed into the caldron of history and seemingly destroyed, we will reflect upon Isaiah's words: there is always a Remnant, a people of God, a true church. And with these God works his will. To them he says, "Fear not, little flock, for it is your father's good pleasure to give you the kingdom" (Luke 12:32). Indeed these have, by his grace, already received it and entered it, here and now.

The Broken Covenant and the New Covenant

THE LATTER PART OF THE EIGHTH CENTURY B.C. BROUGHT DESTRUCTION
TO THE NORTHERN STATE, FOLLOWED, AS THE EIGHTH CENTURY GAVE WAY
to the seventh, by the near annihilation of Judah at the hands of
Sennacherib. Yet we saw how the same years brought, on the lips
of the prophets who functioned then, a quickened hope that there
would emerge from the discipline of catastrophe a righteous Remnant
whom God might bless. Coupled with this we observed a heightened
longing for the coming of the Messiah Prince of the line of David
who should establish his just and peaceful rule over the people of
God's Kingdom, which should endure forevermore. The hope of the
Kingdom of God, progressively divorced from the actually existing
state, was thus projected upon the ideal state of the Messiah. It is to that
future state, and to it alone, that all the felicity of the Kingdom is to be
given.

We must now leap forward—all too quickly—another century, to the
days of the final collapse of Judah and the fall of Jerusalem. On our way
we shall encounter other prophets,[1] among whom one—for violence of

---

[1] Zephaniah, Nahum, Habakkuk, and especially Ezekiel, all fall in this period. Zephaniah
(cf. 1:1) flourished in the reign of Josiah and was thus a contemporary of the young
Jeremiah. Nahum prophesied just prior to the fall of Nineveh in 612. Habakkuk seems to
have been active in the reign of Jehoiakim (609-598), just as the Chaldean menace began

passion and tenderness of feeling, for agony of spirit and plain raw moral courage—stands out as a man of mark: the prophet Jeremiah. For many reasons, but especially for his comprehension of the inner and spiritual nature of man's relation to God, he has few peers in the history of religion.

I

1. Judah was tributary to Assyria and remained so for a hundred years. Ahaz, you will recall, first put her in that position. Menaced in the early years of his reign (735-715) by the anti-Assyrian confederacy headed by the kings of Damascus and of Israel, he had implored the aid of Tiglath-pileser and had surrendered his liberty as the price of it. And although Hezekiah struck a brave blow for freedom and Judah was providentially spared total destruction, she by no means gained independence. Hezekiah ended his life an Assyrian vassal, and his son—Manasseh (687-642)—continued all his long life in the same position.[2]

Indeed it could scarcely have been otherwise. Never did the petty states of western Asia have slimmer hope of gaining independence from the Assyrian master. Assyria was at this time reaching the very zenith of her power. Sennacherib was assassinated in 681, but he was succeeded by his son, Esarhaddon (681-669), who was in turn succeeded by his son, Asshurbanapal (669-ca. 630).[3] During the reigns of the latter two the Assyrian Empire reached greater dimensions than those of any power previously known on earth. Victory attended Assyrian arms everywhere. Babylonia, where perennial revolt had plagued both Sargon and Sennacherib, had momentarily been pacified. By 670 the Assyrian army had

---

to make itself felt (cf. 1:6); while Ezekiel (according to 1:2) began his ministry in the fifth year of Jehoiachin's captivity (593) and continued active until well after the final deportation of 587 (e.g. 40:1). While most of these datings have been questioned, I am strongly inclined, for reasons that cannot here be discussed, to accept them. Joel has also been placed in this period (A. S. Kapelrud, *Joel Studies, Uppsala Universitets Arsskrift 1948:4* [Uppsala: Lundequistska Bokhandeln, 1948], pp. 191-92), but most scholars locate this book well after the Exile.

[2] II Chr. 33:11 seems to hint of a rebellion on the part of Manasseh of which Kings says nothing. It may have been that the rebellion of Shamash-shum-ukin against Asshur-banapal (652-648) had tempted Manasseh to a similar step (Albright, "The Biblical Period," p. 44; R. Kittel, *Geschichte des Volkes Israel* [7th ed.; Stuttgart: W. Kohlhammer, 1925], II, 399). Ezra 4:2, 10 speaks of a further resettlement of population in Samaria by Esarhaddon and Asshurbanapal (Osnappar). Perhaps unrest in Palestine was at the bottom of it. In any case Manasseh's rebellion, if such it was, was not successful.

[3] The date of Asshurbanapal's death is uncertain. Dates as high as 633 and as low as 626 are given. Cf. Albright "The Biblical Period," p. 44 and note 104.

embarked upon a venture, often dreamed of no doubt but never before attempted: the invasion of Egypt. Before its might Egypt could not stand, and, although Esarhaddon died before victory was complete, within a few years Asshurbanapal had marched far south into upper Egypt. In 663 Thebes was taken and destroyed (cf. Nah. 3:8). Now Egypt had been the only nation in the west capable of maintaining any semblance of a balance of power against Assyria. Her fall meant not only that this balance was destroyed, but that the one nation capable of underwriting revolt in Palestine was gone. It was, for a brief time, one world—an Assyrian world. To rebel would have been futile and suicidal.

Under Manasseh, Assyrian underling that he was, Judah sank to unparalleled depths of apostasy. This is no mere coincidence. In good part it was sheer political necessity, for in the ancient world political subservience always entailed at least nominal acknowledgment of the overlord's gods. It is, therefore, with no surprise that we read that under Manasseh, as previously under Ahaz, Assyrian deities began to be worshiped in Jerusalem (II Kings 21:3b-5). Divination and magic, too (vs. 6), were fashionable, for these practices were then popular among the Assyrians as at no other time, and were even fostered by the royal court itself. Nor was this all. Laxity inevitably leads to laxity, and along with foreign paganism the native variety, severely repressed by Hezekiah, began again to flourish. (vss. 3a, 7). Altars were erected to the heavenly bodies in the temple itself (vs. 5),[4] as were the sacred objects of the fertility cult. Sacred prostitutes began to ply their loathesome trade there (cf. II Kings 23:7). Even the barbarous rite of ordeal by fire, if not actual human sacrifice, was practiced (II Kings 21:6a), as it had been in the days of Ahaz (II Kings 16:3).[5] The historian who gave us the books of Kings rates Manasseh as the very worst ruler ever to sit on the throne in Jerusalem (II Kings 21:9, 11), and declares that his sin was such that it could never be forgiven, but was alone enough to explain the national ruin (II Kings 21:11-15; 24:3-4; cf. Jer. 15:4).[6]

[4] It appears that in this period sun, moon, and stars were widely regarded as members of the heavenly assembly, and were accorded worship—a thing intolerable to purists (cf. Jer. 19:13). Cf. G. E. Wright, The Old Testament Against Its Environment (Chicago: Henry Regnery Co., 1950), pp. 30-41, for an excellent discussion of the point.

[5] The exact meaning of "pass through the fire" is uncertain. Perhaps it was some sort of ordeal to appease the deity, but Jer. 7:31 seems to speak of actual human sacrifice (cf. II Kings 17:31).

[6] II Chr. 33:12-17 tells of a repentance of which Kings says nothing (cf. also the apocryphal Prayer of Manasseh). It is of course possible that such a person as Manasseh

2. But the Assyrian Empire, for all its appearance of might, was not in a healthy condition. It was a jerry-built structure at best, held together by sheer force. Even in Asshurbanapal's lifetime, if not before, a clever observer might easily have detected the cracks which were beginning to appear. The strain of repeated campaigns necessary to keep subject peoples in line, scarcely one of whom had anything but hate for Assyria, must certainly have made itself felt. There were internal tensions, too, one of which flared into disastrous civil war. Shamash-shum-ukin, a brother of Asshurbanapal who was serving as Assyrian ruler in Babylon, revolted. The rebellion was beaten down, to be sure, and Shamash-shum-ukin chose the path of suicide. But the struggle was a bloody one lasting four years (652-648), and it shook the empire to its foundations. Meanwhile Egypt—now under the energetic Psammetichus I (663-609), first pharaoh of the XXVI Dynasty—had taken advantage of the confusion to make herself free once more. Assyria seems to have been powerless to prevent it. Besides all these dangers, just as in the last days of Rome, new semibarbarian peoples such as the Scythians and the Cimmerians, who had made their appearance during the preceding century, had become a real threat to the northern frontiers of the empire. The Assyrians sensed the danger and, again as the Romans were later to do, tried to use one barbarian people as a buffer against others and thus to channel the stream of race migration off to one side. But a sensitive observer might well have wondered what would happen if the dike were ever to break.

After the death of Asshurbanapal (ca. 630) the overstrained empire could postpone the inevitable no longer. With incredible speed the whole gargantuan structure fell to pieces and vanished from the face of the earth. We shall not dwell on the details of the story, which was in any case a very short one. Asshurbanapal was followed in succession by two of his sons, neither of whom proved equal to the emergency. Perhaps no one could have been; for Assyria was at last at bay, beset by powerful foes without and weariness within. Chief among these foes were the Medes, now masters of a considerable domain in the western Iranian highlands, and the Babylonians, at last free of the hated master under

---

might, had he been sufficiently frightened, or had the political situation seemed favorable, have repented more or less superficially. But it is quite certain that whatever repenting Manasseh did was not permanent; the abuses for which he was responsible continued until Josiah removed them (II Kings 23).

the patriot Nabopolassar (625-605). Between them they mounted a two-pronged attack upon the Assyrian homeland.

At this point there took place an astounding *volte-face*. Egypt—for centuries the archfoe of Assyria, and but recently invaded and occupied by her—is found fighting on the Assyrian side! Apparently Pharaoh Psammetichus sensed that the very civilization of which he, too, was a part was in peril, and he preferred that a weakened Assyria be kept in existence as a buffer against more dangerous forces beyond. Too, as the price of his aid, he hoped to secure a free hand in Egypt's historic sphere of influence—Palestine and Syria. But Egyptian aid, as Egyptian aid seemed fated to do, came too little and too late. In spite of initial successes it was soon plain that Assyria's time was up. In 614 the ancient capital of Asshur went down before the Medes, and in 612 Medes and Babylonians launched the final assault on Nineveh itself. The city fell; Sin-shar-ishkun, Asshurbanapal's son, died a suicide in the flames; and a shout of joy went up from the little people of the earth that great Nineveh, that "bloody city" (Nah. 3:1), that "well-favored whore" (Nah. 3:4), was fallen. No one at all was sorry (Nah. 3:7, 19).

True, Assyria did not die easily; having lived by the sword, she chose to die by the sword. Prince Asshur-uballit, with the remnant of the Assyrian army, resisting stubbornly, fell back on Harran; and then, driven from there but still fighting, back across the Euphrates into the arms of the Egyptians. But it was no use: Assyria was finished.

This is of interest to us, because it meant that by default, as it were, Judah was free. For within a few years after Asshurbanapal's death Assyria quite lost effective control of the western part of her empire, while it was to be some years before Egypt would be able to step in and claim the pieces. There was, meanwhile, on the throne of Judah a young lad named Josiah. Grandson of apostate Manasseh, he had come to the throne ca. 640 as an eight-year-old boy upon the assassination of his father, Amon (II Kings 21:19–22:1).[7] By the time he came of age the Assyrian hold upon his land was rapidly fading away, and by the eighteenth year of his reign the country was, to all intents and purposes, independent. In that year (621, cf. II Kings 22:3) there was launched Judah's greatest reform.

---

[7] The details need not concern us. Apparently Amon had continued the policy of his father, Manasseh (vss. 20-21), and his assassination reflected a growing discontent with it. Yet the fact that the assassins were at once punished (vs. 24) may indicate that many felt a change of policy to be unwise at that time.

II

The reform of King Josiah was an event of epoch-making importance in the life of Israel, yet its true significance is too often missed by the Bible reader.

1. The story of the reform is to be found in II Kings 22–23, and it is clear from ch. 23 what it set out to do. It was a thoroughgoing purge of all kinds of paganism. Specifically mentioned are foreign cults newly imported by Manasseh, including that in the valley of Hinnom where barbarous rites were practiced (vss. 10-12); the various native pagan cults, many of which were of very long standing (vss. 4, 6, 13-14), together with their sacred objects; the personnel of these loathesome rites, particularly the eunuch priests (vs. 5) [8] and sacred prostitutes of both sexes (vs. 7). But far more drastic than this, we read (vss. 8-9) that Josiah, as Hezekiah had essayed to do before him, abolished even the shrines of Yahweh—God of Israel—in the outlying towns and sought to centralize all worship in Jerusalem.[9]

As we learn from ch. 22, the reform was given direction by a law book which was found in the temple (vs. 8) in the course of repairs there. Brought to the attention of Josiah (vss. 10-13), it awakened in the godly young king the profoundest consternation. It seemed to him that if this were really the law of God, then God help the country; for it had been flagrantly disregarded. Assured that it was in fact such (vss. 14-20), the king summoned all the people to the temple (23:1-3), read the law to them, and engaged in solemn covenant with them before God to implement its demands with appropriate action. From that the reform took shape.

Now it has long been generally agreed that this law book was some form of the code of Deuteronomy.[10] Deuteronomy is a reform law. In-

---

[8] The word kemārîm, translated in the English Bible "idolatrous priests," really means "eunuchs"; cf. W. F. Albright, *From the Stone Age to Christianity* (Baltimore: Johns Hopkins Press, 1940), p. 178.

[9] That the priests of II Kings 23:8-9 were priests of Yahweh is evident from the fact that they were invited to Jerusalem. Had they been functionaries of pagan cults, they would have been executed. The passage is to be compared with the law of Deut. 18:6-8. Vs. 9 makes it clear that the measure met resistance—as one would expect.

[10] Deuteronomy was connected with Josiah's reform by several of the church fathers (e.g., Jerome), and this has become increasingly the accepted view since W. M. L. deWette developed it 150 years ago. For a recent discussion of the question with bibliography, cf. H. H. Rowley, "The Prophet Jeremiah and the Book of Deuteronomy," *Studies in Old Testament Prophecy*, H. H. Rowley, ed. (Edinburgh: T. & T. Clark, 1950), pp. 157-74.

deed, it might well be called a reform edition of the ancient *Lex Mosaica.* Regardless of when it was given its definitive form, its laws reach back to very ancient origins (probably by way of northern Israel) and reflect thoroughly the spirit of the Mosaic heritage. In any event the action taken by Josiah corresponds well to the Deuteronomic demands. With unparalleled vehemence Deuteronomy commands the destruction of all foreign cults (e.g., Deut. 12:1-3) and makes idolatry a capital crime (ch. 13). Alone of all the Pentateuch law codes, it explicitly forbids the worship of Yahweh at various places and directs that sacrifice be offered only at the one place which Yahweh chooses (12:13-14; 16:5-6). Furthermore, it declares over and over again with ringing eloquence that the very national existence depends upon the loyalty with which the people serve the covenant God and obey his will (6:1-15; 8:11-20; 11:26-28; 28; 30:15-20).

But a mere law book never made a reform—any more than the presence of a dust-covered Bible in the family parlor can of itself create character. In fact, be it noted, the reform was already under way when the law book was found.[11] The motivation for it was already present in the hearts of the people. The reform was, in part, a facet of high hopes born of independence and resurgent nationalism. There had undoubtedly been a popular revulsion at the excesses of Manasseh; there was a desire to put away all recollections of foreign rule, religious as well as political. The oscillation of apostasy and reform is no accident. As Ahaz the vassal had been an apostate, as Hezekiah the rebel had been a reformer, and as Manasseh the vassal had been again an apostate, it is no coincidence that Josiah, king of free Judah, should tread the path of reform. But Josiah's ambitions went beyond mere independence. Just north of Jerusalem lay the territory of the old northern state, for a century an Assyrian province but now, to all intents and purposes, a political vacuum. That Josiah extended his reform into the north, destroying the cult installations there —particularly the shrine of Bethel (II Kings 23:15-20)—can mean but one thing: he had *de facto* annexed the territory of Samaria.[12] This was

---

[11] Josiah had given orders (II Kings 22:3-8) that the temple be repaired, and it was only while this was being done that the book was found. But the repairing of the temple was itself the beginning of a reform effort.

[12] II Chr. 34:6 has Josiah extend the reform into Galilee (i.e., the Assyrian province of Megiddo) as well. This is not incredible, if Hezekiah's similar effort (cf. Chap. III, p. 80) be recalled. The royal house had since then kept in close touch with Galilee. The mothers of both Amon (II Kings 21:19) and Jehoiakim (II Kings 23:36) were of Galilean origin; cf. Albright, "The Biblical Period," p. 45.

a day of high hope and great promise: perhaps the David ideal could be realized again, a free Israel once more united under David's throne, the "fallen hut of David" (Amos 9:11) patched and restored!

But it went far deeper than that. In spite of the hopes which the situation engendered, this was a time when facile optimism was impossible. With Assyria's collapse the very foundations of ancient civilization were cracking, and who knew what the future would bring? All over the ancient world we may detect a nostalgic longing for the more secure days of the past, in Judah no less than elsewhere.[13] The book of Deuteronomy is shot through with such a longing. It not only tells the glories of the Mosaic heritage, but insistently asserts that the very hope of national survival lies in laying hold of that heritage in letter and in spirit. In this the theology of Deuteronomy but coincides with the mainstream of prophet preaching for centuries past, reinforced now no doubt by the voices of Zephaniah and the young Jeremiah. And Isaiah had been right: there was a right-thinking minority, a "holy seed," in the nation who took the prophet preaching seriously, who saw that all this paganism scarcely left Israel the people of Yahweh, but rather ripe for judgment. There were many, no doubt, who reasoned that perhaps God had destroyed the Assyrian colossus and allowed this moment of freedom that there might be one last chance to repent (cf. Zeph. 3:6-7a; 2:1-3). If Israel is to find her destiny as the people of God, nay, if she is to survive, she must put away foreign gods and serve Yahweh alone. If Israel is to be the people of God—she must reform!

2. It is in this context that we meet Jeremiah for the first time. Of Jeremiah's early life we know little or nothing. Born of a priestly family in Anathoth, a village about three miles north of Jerusalem,[14] he was probably a lad scarcely of age when his country's independence became a reality. At least when he felt the call to be a prophet, about the year 626 (Jer. 1:2), he protested that he was too young (1:6). Early in life he seems to have been haunted by that premonition of doom which was later to become well-nigh his entire burden (cf. 1:11-16). His earliest

---

[13] For evidence cf. Albright, *From the Stone Age to Christianity*, pp. 241 ff.

[14] The priests in Anathoth possibly claimed descent from Abiathar, whom Solomon banished thither (I Kings 2:26-27) for his complicity in Adonijah's attempted *coup d'état*. This, if correct, would mean that Jeremiah traced his ancestry to the house of Eli (cf. I Kings 2:27; I Sam. 22:20; 14:3), the ancient custodians of the Ark at Shiloh.

preaching shows him deeply shocked at the paganism of the land.[15] The entire national history, it seemed to him, had been a history of ingratitude (2:4-8). Israel has run after false gods with the unrestrained passion of an animal (2:23-25); her sin is a stain that will not wash (2:22); it has perverted the national character into a foreign thing (2:21). Never in the world has there been such apostasy! Even the heathen do not desert their gods, although these are, in fact, no gods at all (2:10-11). But Israel has! She has abandoned the "fountain of living waters" (2:13) for the stale cisterns of idolatry—and leaky cisterns at that! In the spirit and language of Hosea, Jeremiah declares that the nation is a "harlot" who has betrayed her divine husband and faces "divorce" (3:1-5; cf. vss. 6-10).[16] Yet, as was the case with Hosea, angry denunciation is coupled with a moving and impassioned plea for repentance (3:12-13, 21-22). Only by sincere repentance will Israel be spared; only so will she find again her historic destiny as the elect people of God (4:1-2; cf. Gen. 12:3; 18:18).[17]

Jeremiah's precise attitude toward the great reform, which took place some five years after he began his ministry, must remain a mystery. The records are quite ambiguous on the point and there is a total lack of agreement among scholars. We do not know if he concerned himself actively with regard to it or not. But it is hardly conceivable that he would not have approved heartily of the effort to abolish the paganism against which he had so uncompromisingly thundered. In any case his admiration for Josiah, whom he regarded as well-nigh the ideal king (22:15-16), was unbounded—which it would not have been had he disapproved of the major action of that king's reign. It even appears that as Josiah carried forward his political program in the north (II Kings

---

[15] Although chs. 2–3 contain material from the period after the death of Josiah and the Egyptian victory of 609, such as 2:14-17 (cf. vs. 16), 29-37 (cf. vs. 36), the vast majority of commentators find in the poetry of these chapters a sample of Jeremiah's preaching before the reform.

[16] The English translates 3:1, 4 badly. Neither is a plea to return, but both are indignant denunciations. Vs. 1 should be read with A.S.V. margin. Vs. 4 begins, "Have you not just now [i.e., even under the circumstances of your faithless behavior] called to me"; that is, Israel, though faithless to God, continues to address him as Father and to count on his forgiveness (vs. 5).

[17] Jer. 4:1-2 should be read approximately with A.S.V. margin. The wording of vs. 2b is a little surprising (we should expect "in me" or "in thee" in place of "in him"), and this has led some (e.g., A. S. Peake, Jeremiah [The New-Century Bible (Edinburgh: T. C. & E. C. Jack, 1910)], I, 116) to surmise a direct quotation of Gen. 18:18. While this cannot be proved, it is likely that a reference to the promise to Abraham is intended.

23:15-20), there was awakened in Jeremiah's breast the lively hope that Ephraim would soon return to the fold (3:12-14; 31:2-6, 15-22) and, like Judah, worship God on Mount Zion (31:6)—an attitude which betrays at least a measure of sympathy with the king's policy.[18] And in later years the men of the reform and their sons were the ones who stood by Jeremiah and saved his life (26:24; 36:12, 19, 25; cf. II Kings 22:12).[19]

But whatever Jeremiah may have thought of the reform in the first place, he was not long in seeing how shallow a thing it was.[20] It had produced only a great cloud of incense smoke and great throngs of worshipers in the temple, but no real return to the ancient paths (6:16-21). So men have always reformed: cutting out the grosser immoralities and participating more actively in the work of the church! The social sins which are society's sickness continue (5:23-29), and the clergy have come to terms with them to everyone's satisfaction (5:30-31). Real repentance there is not. On the contrary, the people are continuing on the path to ruin like a horse charging madly into battle (8:4-6). For all their pride in the possession of the law (8:8) they have not the sense of wild creatures, who at least instinctively obey the laws that govern their existence (8:7). Yet over it all is heard the voice of the clergy blandly announcing that peace with God has now been gained (6:13-14=8:10-11)—and this is an unmitigated lie!

In short, Jeremiah saw that it would take more than Josiah's reform to make Judah the people of God. How strange their delusion, yet how familiar! We yearn for a Christian society and know no way to gain it

---

[18] These passages are to be placed in Jeremiah's earliest period with the vast majority of commentators, against G. A. Smith (*Jeremiah* [4th ed.; New York: Harper & Bros., 1929], pp. 297-303) and J. Skinner (*Prophecy and Religion* [Cambridge: The University Press, 1922], pp. 299-305), who place 31:2-6, 15-22 in 587.

[19] It is frequently asserted (e.g., in great detail by A. F. Puukko, "Jeremias Stellung zum Deuteronomium," *Alttestamentliche Studien für Rudolf Kittel: Beiträge zur Wissenschaft des alten und neuen Testaments*, 13 [1913], 126-53) that the similarity of names in II Kings 22 and Jer. 26; 36 is coincidence. The coincidence is, however, too remarkable to be explained as such.

[20] Most treatments of Jeremiah, because no oracle of his can be surely dated in the latter part of the reign of Josiah, posit a long silence on his part from the reform (621) until the death of Josiah (609) or shortly before. I find such a thing incredible. Detailed argument is impossible here but, although it must be admitted that few of Jeremiah's oracles can be dated with certainty, I believe that many of them fit best precisely between 621 and 609. It would not take a Jeremiah many months to see the superficiality of the reform (cf. A. C. Welch, *Jeremiah: His Time and His Work* [London: Oxford University Press, 1928], pp. 76-96; W. A. L. Elmslie, *How Came Our Faith?* [New York: Charles Scribner's Sons, 1949], p. 316).

save by organizing meetings, financing programs, enacting laws, and pad-locking the more nauseous resorts of ill fame. And Israel yearned for covenant peace with God—and padlocked the false shrines and became very busy at the temple. We shall not decry reform measures any more than did Jeremiah. Indeed continuous reform measures are called for. But Jeremiah tells us that if we have no more than reform measures, we are chopping Hydra's heads, lopping at the leaves and branches of mortal frailty and touching the trunk of it not at all. Jeremiah told his people that the covenant bond is simply not to be restored externally. He wheeled upon their busy observance of the cultic law (7:21-23) and appealed from the external of the law to the heart of it. Said he: God does not care how fussily you regulate public worship. Offer your sacri-fices this way or that—it's all one to God! For the heart of God's demand is not busy religion, but obedience. Only an obedient people can remain in covenant with God; only over an obedient people will he rule. As for this people, it must repent from the heart (4:14); it must circumcise itself anew into the covenant relationship from the heart—or face the fire:

> For thus saith Yahweh to the men of Judah and to Jerusalem:
> "Break up for yourselves fallow ground,
>   and do not sow among thorns.
> Circumcise yourselves to Yahweh,
>   and remove the foreskins of your hearts,
>   O men of Judah and citizens of Jerusalem;
> Lest my wrath go forth like fire,
>   and burn so that none can quench it,
>   because of the evil of your doings."
>   (4:3-4; cf. Deut. 10:16)

The people of God are a people of clean heart. Paul (Rom. 2:25-29) is one day to declare that it is precisely this spiritual circumsion that marks the member of the true Israel.

III

1. Whatever misgivings Jeremiah may have had concerning the reform during the lifetime of good King Josiah, the latter's death saw his worst fears realized. Josiah's death was tragic and must have come as a terrific shock. Josiah, as we have said, had desired once more to unite all Israel under the scepter of David. Assyria could, of course, no longer prevent

it. But Egypt—under Psammetichus I and his son, Necho (609-594)—had conflicting ambitions. It was the dream of these pharaohs to recreate the ancient empire which Egypt had held in Palestine and Syria in the heyday of the XVIII Dynasty, nearly a millennium before; and it was as an aspect of this policy that they rushed to the aid of tottering Assyria. Josiah, we may well imagine, had no intention of exchanging an Assyrian master for an Egyptian one. In 609 B.C., when Necho marched northward to assist the Assyrian in a last futile attempt to retake Harran from the Babylonians, Josiah tried to intercept him at the pass of Megiddo. And in the attempt he met his death (II Kings 23:28-30).[21]

This was the end of Judean independence, and it had lasted scarcely fifteen years. The son of Josiah, Jehoahaz, was hastily made king, only to be deposed by the pharaoh and led away to exile in Egypt. Pharaoh then put Jehoahaz' brother, Jehoiakim, on the throne as king and laid the land under heavy tribute (II Kings 23:31-35). Judah was now a dependency of Egypt.

What made matters worse was the character of Jehoiakim. The people apparently did not want him, as is evidenced by the fact that on the death of Josiah, they passed him up for Jehoahaz—although the latter was the younger (cf. II Kings 23:31, 36). All that we know of Jehoiakim indexes a frivolous character, unfit to rule. What sort of man he was is clearly indicated by one of his earliest royal acts. With the land under heavy tax to Egypt and with the political situation explosive to the highest degree, we find him—having decided that his father's palace was not good enough for him—wasting his funds building a new and finer one, and using forced labor to do it (Jer. 22:13-14). This of course brought from Jeremiah his scathing best. "Does that make you a king," he demands (22:15a), "because you fuss about with cedarwood?" Then after advising this spoiled young man to consider his own father if he would like to know what really makes a man a king (vss. 15b-16), he sums the matter up by declaring that Jehoiakim will one day be buried with all the honor of a dead donkey—hauled out and dumped on the garbage heap with no one in the least sorry to see him go (vss. 18-19). Clearly Jeremiah and Jehoiakim were not going to get along!

[21] Vs. 29 says that Necho was going up "against" Assyria. But the evidence is incontrovertible that Egypt fought for, not against, Assyria. The preposition ‘al (translated "against") must be rendered "to," as it is a few words subsequently: "to (‘al) the river Euphrates."

Under Jehoiakim (609-598) the last vestiges of the reform collapsed. The fact that the king was spiritually shallow and without deep conviction undoubtedly had something to do with it. But deeper than this, we may imagine, was a widespread popular feeling that the blessings promised by Deuteronomy to a repentant people had not been forthcoming. The law demanded reform as the price of putting off the doom; reform was made, but calamity came anyhow! The reform, in short, collapsed because it did not seem to have paid off; and what paganized people, ancient or modern, cares to stick with a religion that does not pay off in tangible terms? In any case the pagan cults came back in force (e.g., Jer. 7:16-18; cf. Ezek. 8). Yet paradoxically (yet it is no paradox, for we, too, know how to behave as thorough pagans, and yet pride ourselves in being a Christian nation—because, forsooth, we have churches) the reform persisted in a way that it should not have: in the form of a blind confidence of rightness with God (Jer. 2:35). We have God's temple (7:4) and God's law (8:8); we are the holy people of God, and God will allow no evil to come near us—so the paid prophets assured them repeatedly (5:12; 6:14; 8:11; 14:13). Nothing that Jeremiah could say could crack this suicidal conceit. It persisted to the bitter end.

2. It is plain that there could be no peace between Jeremiah and Jehoiakim. Jeremiah broke completely with the corrupt nation and pronounced doom upon it. The state, in allowing the reform to be canceled, has broken covenant with God and lost all claim to his mercy. This slipping back into pagan laxity is no less than a conspiracy against the divine King (11:9-11), and it is in the light of it that the shameful subjugation to Egypt is to be explained: if "the sons of Memphis and Tahpanhes have cracked your skull," you did it to yourself by forsaking Yahweh (2:15-17).[22] But it is fatuous to settle down under the relatively easy yoke of Egypt and to imagine that trouble has been bought off so cheaply (2:36-37). A far worse foe is coming, the awful foe from the north—the Babylonian (e.g., 5:14-17; 4:5-9; 6:22-26).[23] He will de-

[22] Cf. note 15 above.

[23] From the language of 5:14-17 it is clear that such a people as the Babylonians are in mind. It used to be assumed that the background of these poems (mostly in chs. 4–6) was an invasion of Scythians which was supposed to have taken place ca. 625. Later the foe was reinterpreted as the Babylonians. This idea, popularized by B. Duhm (*Das Buch Jeremia*, Kurzer Hand-Commentar zum Alten Testament [Tübingen: J. C. B. Mohr, 1901]), was taken up by most commentators. But evidence for such an invasion is almost

stroy without pity, and it will be the finish of you. This will be a theological crisis, too, for you will learn that there is no peace between you and the God you have refused to obey (4:8-10).

But is not this nation the people of God, and is not his temple—his earthly habitation—in its midst? Is there not safety in that fact? An unqualified No! That religion is no bulwark! Trust in the mere presence of the temple is a great lie (7:4). That temple is not so large a structure that it can hide from the eyes of God the corrupt, the unbrotherly, the unrepentant behavior of the people who worship there (7:8-10). God is not so blinded by incense smoke that he cannot see (7:11). And if you do not believe that God can destroy the houses where men sing his praises, then go back to that other temple which once stood in Shiloh—the shrine of the old tribal league—and see what happened to it. God can, in the judgment of history, destroy even churches (7:12-15; 26:6)! That, of course, was a great blasphemy; and no sooner had Jeremiah said it, than a mob, incited by the outraged clergy, rushed upon him to lynch him (26:8).[24] Had not certain of the nobles (26:16-19)—notably Ahikam ben Shaphan, one of the men of Josiah's reform (vs. 24; cf. II Kings 22:12)—been possessed of the old-fashioned notion that a prophet might not be killed for speaking the Word of God, this would have been the end of Jeremiah.

Thereafter Jeremiah's life became a history of persecution. The details of the plots against him cannot be traced, but they were many (e.g., 18:18-20; 20:10). Jeers and ostracism were his lot (20:7; 15:10, 15-18). On one occasion, we do not know when, his fellow townsmen laid plans to kill him (11:18-23),[25] covering up their cowardly designs with words of friendship (12:6). Jeremiah declares that he felt (11:19) "like a tame lamb led to the slaughter." On another occasion, having smashed

---

nil, and since the strong criticism of F. Wilke, "Das Scythenproblem im Jeremiabuch" (Alttestamentliche Studien für Rudolf Kittel; Beiträge zur Wissenschaft des Alten und Neuen Testaments, 13 [1913], 222-54), the idea has somewhat lost favor. But although the northern foe is Babylon, we must not forget that a premonition of evil from the north may have been with Jeremiah for years before the Babylonian menace appeared.

[24] That 7:2-15 refers to the same occasion as ch. 26 is the opinion of all scholars, with a few exceptions (e.g., Smith, op. cit., p. 147). Its date, therefore (26:1), is 609 B.C. The substance of the two speeches is certainly the same, although the Biographer (ch. 26) has given us an abridged form of it.

[25] If Jeremiah was indeed an active proponent of the reform, hatred on the part of the people of Anathoth—whose local shrine would have been put out of business—would be understandable (e.g., Peake, op. cit., I, 182). But the uncertainty is too great to warrant assurance.

a clay pot (19:1-2, 10-13) and having declared that just so would Jerusalem be broken beyond repair, he was seized by a temple officer and
clapped into the stocks overnight (19:14–20:6). It is possible that for
some time he was forbidden to enter the temple at all (36:5).

3. Jehoiakim came to the throne in 609 and for four years remained
an Egyptian vassal. After 605 events ran rapidly downhill. That year
saw a dramatic upset of the world balance of power. Pharaoh Necho had
hoped to re-create Egypt's ancient empire and had, as Assyria lost control,
occupied Palestine and Syria up to the great bend of the Euphrates.
For a few years he was able to hold his gains. But in 605 Prince Nebuchadnezzar—son of the Babylonian ruler, Nabopolassar—leaped on the Egyptian army at Carchemish on the Euphrates and administered it a defeat
from which there was no recovering.[26] And although Nebuchadnezzar
was unable to follow up his advantage immediately, owing to the death
of his father which took place just at that time and necessitated his return
to Babylon, the way was open, and nothing was there to stop him. We
may well imagine that consternation reigned throughout Palestine and
Syria: when would Nebuchadnezzar advance; which side should they
take? Jehoiakim, an Egyptian vassal, was faced with a desperate choice.

In that year Jeremiah made a last effort to warn his king (ch. 36).
Forbidden to enter the temple (vs. 5), he dictated his message to his
friend Baruch, the scribe, and sent the latter to read it publicly (vs. 6).
This Baruch did. The nobles of the king's cabinet heard of it (vs. 12)
and, summoning Baruch, asked that it be read again (vss. 14-15). So
impressed were they that they felt it their duty to call it to the attention
of the king (vss. 16, 20). The king demanded to hear it (vs. 21), but
not that he might give heed to it! As each three or four columns were
read (vs. 23), he snatched the scroll from the hands of the reader, hacked
off with a penknife the portion he had just heard, and threw it into the
fire—and so on till all of it was consumed.[27] Thus did a very little
man show contempt of things far bigger than he. Had not Baruch and

[26] A. Dupont-Sommer (*Semitica*, I [1948], 57 ff.) holds that Necho was crushed
in 609. I follow the usual dating; cf. W. F. Albright, "The Seal of Eliakim and the Latest
preëxilic History of Judah" (*Journal of Biblical Literature*, LI [1932], 77-106).

[27] K.J.V. and A.S.V. do not bring out the meaning of vs. 23. One gets the impression that
the king listened only to three or four columns, and then in a burst of anger seized the
scroll, cut it up, and burned it. The Hebrew places his conduct in an even worse light:
"And it was, as Yehudi would read three or four columns, he (i.e., the king) would cut
it with the penknife and toss it on the fire." The king did not act in a fit of temper, but
with studied impudence.

Jeremiah hidden as the nobles had urged them to do (vss. 19, 26), it would have meant the lives of both of them.

With that Jeremiah quite gave the state up for lost. He ceased to ask for repentance or to expect any. The state has shown itself to be beyond prayer (15:1; 7:16; 11:14; 14:11)—though we may assume from the very repetition of the injunction no longer to pray that Jeremiah never ceased to do so. The destruction of the state is sure; it will be eradicated —and that *without remnant* (8:13). Looking into the future Jeremiah could see only ruin of atomic proportions, as if creation had been canceled and primeval chaos reigned again:

> I saw the earth, and behold, primeval chaos;
>   the heavens, and their light was gone.
> I saw the mountains, and lo, they were trembling,
>   and all the hills shook to and fro.
> I looked, and behold, there was no man,
>   and all the birds of the heavens had fled.
> I looked, and behold, the tilled land was desert,
>   and all its cities lay in ruins
>   before Yahweh, before the heat of his anger.
>   (4:23-26)

The ruin did indeed come soon, but it was not at once as total as Jeremiah had expected. By 603/602 B.C., the Babylonians had returned and rolled the last vestiges of Egyptian power out of Asia. Jehoiakim had the good sense to submit and transfer his allegiance to Nebuchadnezzar. But good sense was not with Jehoiakim an enduring quality, and three years later he rebelled (II Kings 24:1). Nebuchadnezzar promptly sent contingents from neighboring vassal states (vs. 2) to harry the land until the Babylonian army could arrive. When the latter got there, Jerusalem was promptly put under siege. Egyptian aid, as usual, did not materialize, and soon the city was in desperate straits. At that point, however, Jehoiakim conveniently died (vs. 6). Perhaps he was assassinated (cf. Jer. 22:18-19; 36:30). His eighteen-year-old son, Jehoiachin, took the throne only to surrender (II Kings 24:8-17). Whereupon Nebuchadnezzar deported him to Babylon together with the royal family, the officers of the court, and the cream of the population. He then set up the boy's uncle—Jehoiakim's brother, Zedekiah—to rule over the remnant as a Babylonian puppet. Judah had yet eleven years to live.

113

4. It was this Zedekiah (598-587) who presided over the end. One would think that chauvinistic patriotism would have learned its lesson, but it had learned nothing. As early as four years later a plot at rebellion was already being hatched.[28] Emissaries of the vassal kings of Edom, Moab, Ammon, Tyre, and Sidon (27:3) gathered in Jerusalem to formulate plans. Probably there was also the promise, or the hope, of Egyptian backing. But there was more. Optimistic prophets had whipped up a popular frenzy by declaring (28:2-4) that God had already broken the yoke of Babylon and would bring captive King Jehoiachin and all the people who had been deported, together with the sacred vessels of the temple, back to Jerusalem—and that *within two years!* There can hardly be any explanation for such folly except that these people were possessed of the fantastic notion that the purge predicted by Isaiah had already come to pass, and that they who were left were the pure Remnant over whom God would shortly set up his Kingdom (cf. Ezek. 11:14; 33: 24 ff.)!

To Jeremiah, as to Ezekiel, this was the most utter nonsense. Jeremiah himself entertained the hope that one day there would be a Remnant over which the Messiah King would rule (23:5-6). But this king, who should be called "Yahweh is our righteousness" has nothing to do with this Zedekiah who so unworthily wears that name.[29] As for Zedekiah and his crew, they are so many bad figs too rotten to eat (ch. 24); they are not God's people, and the Kingdom of God will not be established over them. The calamity of 598 has purged nothing (6:27-30), and it is useless to go on refining such base metal. And so Jeremiah appeared before the conspirators (27:2-11) wearing an ox yoke on his neck, and told them to submit to the yoke of Nebuchadnezzar— for it is God's judgment upon a sinful people and to rebel against it is to rebel against God. At the same time (29:1-14) he wrote a letter to

[28] The date in 27:1 is an obvious scribal error (cf. A.S.V. margin). The events of ch. 27 are of the same date as those of ch. 28 (cf. 28:1; 27:2; 28:10), i.e., the fourth year of Zedekiah. Probably 27:1 mistakenly copied 26:1, where its date is correct. The Greek lacks the verse altogether.

[29] There is apparently a pun in 23:5-6 on the name of Zedekiah. The name of the ideal king is "Yahweh is our righteousness" (*Yahweh ṣidqēnû*), which is essentially the same as that of Zedekiah (*ṣidqîyahu*, "Yahweh is my righteousness"). The genuineness of the passage has been widely impugned, but see the able defense of it in Peake, *op. cit.*, I, 260; also W. Rudolph, *Jeremia* (Handbuch zum Alten Testament [Tübingen: J. C. B. Mohr, 1947]), pp. 125 ff. I am in agreement with Peake, against Rudolf, that the king in question is the Messiah.

the captives in Babylon telling them to disregard the lying prophets that sought to inflame them with talk of immediate release, and to settle down for a long stay.

Whether because of Jeremiah's words or because of the cold logic of power politics which Zedekiah's nobles would be more likely to understand, the revolt of 594 fell through, and Zedekiah made his peace with Nebuchadnezzar (29:3; 51:59). But in a few years revolt flared again. Psammetichus II (594-588) and his son Hophra (588-569), never left off the attempt to whip up an anti-Babylonian coalition in Palestine. By 589 Zedekiah, who seems to have known better but who was not man enough to stand up to his nobles (cf. 38:5), was prodded into joining. The Babylonians reacted swiftly, probably by the summer of the same year. By January of 588 (52:4) Jerusalem was blockaded and the outlying strong points reduced until only Lachish and Azekah held out (34:7-8).[30] Zedekiah implored Egyptian aid,[31] which was sent in the summer of 588 (37:5) and forced the Babylonians to lift the siege. But Egyptian aid was of the usual quality and was speedily routed. Whereupon the siege was resumed. Although the city held out well-nigh another year, till the summer of 587 (52:5-6), its fate was sealed. When Nebuchadnezzar's siege engines breached the walls, Zedekiah fled, only to be overhauled, thrown into chains, blinded, and led captive. The destruction of the city and temple, and a further deportation of the population, ensued.

Through it all Jeremiah unwaveringly predicted the worst. He promised Zedekiah, who to the end hoped that God would intervene as in the days of good King Hezekiah (21:2), that there would be no miracles. On the contrary (21:3-7), God was actively fighting for the Chaldeans. When the siege was lifted by the Egyptian advance (37:5-10) and hopes soared, he promised not only that the enemy would return but that if the Chaldean army consisted only of wounded men, even these casualties would rise up and take the city. He even (and this was too much) advised the people to desert (21:8-10), and not a few took his advice (38:19; 39:9). For this he was put into a dungeon (ch. 38) and left to

[30] That Lachish and Azekah were the last two strongholds to go is dramatically illustrated by the Lachish Ostraca (cf. IV:10), a group of letters written on bits of pottery and, for the most part, dispatched from a military outpost to the garrison commander in Lachish, where they were found. They date from the last year before the fall of Jerusalem.

[31] Lachish Letter III:14-16 tells of a deputation sent to Egypt in that year.

die, and die he would have had it not been for the courageous action of a Negro slave, one Ebed-melech. He was released from jail only by the fall of the city.

We must leave the story here. Suffice it to say that Nebuchadnezzar installed one Gedaliah, a Judean noble (40:5), as governor over the ruined land. Jeremiah, offered by the conquerors the choice of staying behind or going to Babylon, elected to stay (40:4-6). Scarcely three months later, however, certain hotheads assassinated Gedaliah as a collaborator (ch. 41). Although the group about Gedaliah had not been implicated, they feared Babylonian reprisals and saw nothing but to flee to Egypt (chs. 42–43). Jeremiah, loudly protesting, was dragged along with them; and in Egypt he died.

IV

But, one might say, has not all this led us rather far from the subject? We were speaking of the hope of the Kingdom of God, and it would seem that this dourest of all doom criers could certainly have contributed nothing to it. But he did! Indeed, few men have ever contributed more. Posterity has remembered Jeremiah as "the weeping prophet," but if such he was, his tears were a catharsis of spirit. Perhaps such a man, who had gone clean down to the end of hope, who had lost confidence in all that men trust in, was needed to see clearly the enduring structure of God.

1. Jeremiah's message is, of course, a total rejection of the state as the vehicle of the Kingdom of God beyond which nothing could be more total. This does not mean that he was a revolutionary who called for the destruction of the state and the monarchy as a sinful institution. On the contrary—and this is true of all the prophets—Jeremiah never attacked existing institutions as such or advocated their replacement by other institutions. He assumed the monarchy as a matter of course. His God neither hallowed nor condemned forms of government. Indeed it seemed to him that the monarchy had a destiny under God (21:11–22:5) to secure on earth an approximation of God's order, and if it could do this, its existence was justified. And in Josiah he saw a king who was as pleasing in God's eyes as a man could be (22:15b-16).

But the state he knew, that of Jehoiakim and Zedekiah, was a godless state. With the injustice and the idolatry which it tolerated or fostered, it was anything but the kingdom of God's people. God was not going

116

to defend such a kingdom. It had turned on God like a wild beast (12:7-8); God must therefore hate what he had dearly loved and give it over into the hands of its enemies. Whatever covenant had existed between God and that state is broken, finished. Jeremiah's younger contemporary, Ezekiel, had exactly the same conviction. In one of those bizarre visions to which this strange prophet was subjected (Ezek. 10-11), it seemed to him that he saw the very Glory of Yahweh—conceived in Hebrew theology as enthroned in the awful darkness of the Holy of Holies and symbolizing the living Presence of Yahweh among his people —come out of the temple, hover over it, and then depart. Yahweh is no longer with this people and this city!

Nor was Jeremiah's gloom mitigated, as Isaiah's had been, by the confidence that there was a "holy seed" in the nation which the present tragedy would purify. To be sure, as we have seen before (23:5-6) and as we shall see again, Jeremiah powerfully played on the Remnant theme. For all his gloom he never gave up hope of a glorious future for the true people of God. But as he looked at the current scene he could not lay his hands on a single group and say: Here is the clean Remnant! No group would escape the destruction. For Jehoiakim and his toadies Jeremiah had naught but the bitterest scorn; Zedekiah and his nobles were rotten figs (ch. 24), fit for nothing at all. And although he felt that the true future of the nation lay with those deported in 598 with the boy king, Jehoiachin (24; 29:10-14), that is a long way off and involves a total change of heart. As for the people he knew, they were in his opinion without a redeeming feature. Like Diogenes with his lantern (5:1-9) he searched the streets of Jerusalem for an honest man, and vowed that he could not find a single one. No use to hope that a pure metal can be refined out of such low-grade ore, nay, such slag, as this (6:27-30)! They are rotten to the heart and cannot repent:

> Can the Ethiopian change his skin
> or the leopard his spots?
> Then you too may find it possible to do good
> who are accustomed to do evil.
>
> (13:23)

It was this total pessimism regarding the moral character of the nation that drove him to virtual treason against it. Certainly he sounded like a traitor (21:8-10). So his fellow citizens understood him (37:13-14;

117

38:2-4); so the Babylonians, who thought he was on their side, understood him (39:11-12); and so, it must be admitted, would we. But Jeremiah was neither a coward nor a pacifist nor a one-man Babylonian fifth column. He was a man who had confronted the awful realization that God and the plain moral right of the matter were no longer on the side of his country. He was, in this respect, somewhat in the position of an anti-Nazi German or an anti-Communist Russian, who dearly loving his country as he may, nevertheless feels obliged to break with it. The leaders of his country will no doubt brand him a traitor, but perhaps he may be accorded a higher sort of patriotism. Jeremiah could only see the Babylonian as the tool of God's punishment on a sinful state. The state must submit to that judgment, for to rebel is to rebel against God and to court certain destruction (27:5-11). God has parted company with the Kingdom of Judah and wars against that kingdom.

2. To take this course cost Jeremiah a terrific struggle, as his "confessions" tell us. The temptation to digress is irresistible, for these little glimpses which Jeremiah gives us into his inmost soul are priceless. Here we see a soul at war with itself and with God; so much so that Jeremiah did not hesitate to hurl at his God the bluntest accusations of unfairness. It is quite clear that denouncing his people gave him not the least pleasure. He reminded God that he had never wanted the job of prophet anyhow (17:15-16). He longed to run out on it (9:2); he declared that he would prefer a lodging in the meanest desert hovel to life among a people such as this. The butt of jeers, he lashed out at God in well-nigh blasphemous language, charging that God had "seduced" him (20:7), and he had let himself be taken in; he had struggled against his destiny, but God had simply overpowered him. Was that not a great victory for so mighty a God! Again, ostracized and lonely, he felt like a man suffering from an incurable wound (15:17-18); and when he turned to his God for strength, he found that very God whom he had once called "the fountain of living waters" (2:13) no better than a dry wadi. His spiritual resources were at an end. Yet he could not quit, try as he might; the compulsion of the divine Word was upon him:

> And if I say, "I will not mention him,
>   nor speak any more in his name,"
> Then there is in my heart as it were a burning fire
>   shut up in my bones;

And I wear myself out trying to hold it in,
　　but I can't!

(20:9)

The human spirit is not made to endure such tension. The end of it is despair—despair unparalleled, despair which outruns all words and yet for which Jeremiah found words surpassingly moving. They are words that might almost have been written to accompany some *symphonie pathétique* in which it seems to the hearer that the music rushes downward to embrace death. Jeremiah did not want to live:

> Cursed be the day on which I was born,
> The day on which my mother bore me,
> 　　let it not be blessed!
> Cursed be the man who brought good news to my father, saying,
> 　　"A son, a boy, is born to you!"
> 　　making him thus to rejoice.
> Let that man be like the cities
> 　　which Yahweh overthrew without pity!
> Let him hear an outcry in the morning
> 　　and the battle shout at noonday,
> Because he did not kill me in the womb;
> 　　that my mother might have been my grave,
> 　　　　and her womb ever pregnant (with me)!
> Why did I come forth from the womb
> 　　to see trouble and grief,
> 　　　　that my days might be ended in shame?

(20:14-18)

One might be tempted to say: Here is a great coward, a soul that has completely lost faith in God. Not so fast! Let us remember that we would not even have known of it if Jeremiah had not confided in us. Had we but the words he uttered in public, and the record of his deeds, we would never have guessed that such a struggle took place. It is safe to say that few of his foes did; there was nothing in his actions to betray it. Within there was a boiling tempest; but without there was an impregnable "wall of bronze" (1:18; 15:20). Within was all manner of fear and despair; without was a man who, so far as we know, never gave back so much as an inch! Here, indeed, we learn what faith really is: not that smug faith which is untroubled by questions because it has never asked any; but that true faith which has asked all the questions and received very few answers, yet has heard the command, Gird up your

119

loins! Do your duty! Remember your calling! Cast yourself forward upon God!

In this connection, it would seem, Jeremiah refutes the popular, modern notion that the end of religion is an integrated personality, freed of its fears, its doubts, and its frustrations. Certainly Jeremiah was no integrated personality. It is doubtful if to the end of his tor-tured existence he ever knew the meaning of the word "peace." We have no evidence that his internal struggle was ever ended, although the passing years no doubt brought an increasing acceptance of destiny. Jeremiah, if his "confessions" are any index, needed a course in pastoral psychiatry in the very worst way. No cheap slurs upon the function of faith in creating mental and spiritual health, or upon the necessary techniques to achieve this end, are, of course, intended. Yet the feeling cannot be escaped that if Jeremiah had been integrated, it would have been at the cost of ceasing to be Jeremiah! A man at peace simply could not be a Jeremiah. Spiritual health is good; mental assurance is good. But the summons of faith is neither to an integrated personality nor to the laying by of all questions, but to the *dedication* of personality— with all its fears and questions—to its duty and destiny under God.

Jeremiah emerged from this unending Gethsemane of the spirit a strangely Christlike figure. Not that we may make Jeremiah into a Christian saint! He did not suffer with meekness but with angry indig-nation, and in his anger he knew how to curse his enemies. As one reads 18:18-23, for example, he realizes that Jeremiah has spoken of his tor-mentors, as clearly as could be said, a parody of the words of Calvary: "Father, forgive them *not*, for they know very well what they are doing!" That is not at all Christlike, but all too like you and me.[32] Yet for all his outbursts of very human passion, and for all his bitter com-plaint against God and destiny, here was one who endured brutal suffer-ing for the sake of the Kingdom of God; who made himself obedient unto death; who, when his spirit flinched and he fain would have turned tail and fled, nevertheless found it within him to say, "Not my will, but thine, be done" (Luke 22:42), and so to take up his cross. Here was, more, a good man who suffered because of a sinful people and,

---

[32] So much so that some scholars, for purely sentimental reasons, refuse to believe Jeremiah could have said such a thing (e.g., Peake, op. cit., I, 234; Duhm, op. cit., pp. 158-59). But see the remarks of Smith (op. cit., pp. 329 ff.) and of Rudolph (op. cit., p. 107) on the point. We cannot remake Jeremiah according to our ideals of piety.

in his suffering, conferred on all posterity an inestimable benefit. And here was one who found precisely his deepest suffering in his compassion for those whose sins he must denounce:

> Grief has come upon me,
> my heart is sick! [33]

> There! Hark, the cry of the daughter of my people
> far and wide through the land,[34]

> "Is Yahweh not in Zion?
> or is her King not in her?"
> .   .   .   .
> "The harvest is past, the summer is ended,
> and we have not been saved!"
> For the mortal hurt of the daughter of my people I am hurt,
> I mourn, dismay has seized me.

> Is there no balm in Gilead?
> or is there no physician there?
> Why, then, has there not come
> the healing[35] of the daughter of my people?

> Oh that my head were waters,
> and my eyes a fountain of tears,
> That I might weep day and night
> over the slain of the daughter of my people!
>
> (8:18–9:1 [8:18-23, Heb.])

Such compassion is only to be compared with that of Another who cried that he would gladly have taken sinful Jerusalem under his wing as a hen might her chicks (Matt. 23:37)—but in vain!

3. Now these factors in Jeremiah's character and message are precisely those that contributed powerfully to the survival of Israel's faith.

---

[33] The English translation of vs. 18 is a guess. The first word in the Hebrew is untranslatable as it stands. Probably (cf. Rudolph, op. cit., p. 54) it should be transferred to the end of the preceding verse. With slight emendation that verse would then end, ". . . and they shall bite you so that there is no healing." Vs. 18 then begins: " 'ălay (= 'ālāh) yāgôn 'ălay"—"sorrow has come upon me."

[34] The English translates mē'ereṣ marhaqqîm "from a land far off," but vs. 20 indicates that the final blow has not yet fallen and deliverance is still hoped for. For the reading "far and wide through the land" (literally, "from a land of distances") cf. Isa. 33:17; see also the lexicons and commentaries.

[35] "Healing" is literally the "new skin" that grows over a wound.

Perhaps, therefore, we shall find our little digression into Jeremiah's inmost soul to be no digression at all.

That he and Ezekiel should have so totally rejected the state helped men to see that God's purposes could go on without it. This was a powerful cushion against the shock. Suppose the only voices of religion in that hour had been those of professional prophet promising speedy deliverance and of priest proclaiming the inviolability of Zion! It might have been something like total disillusionment. *That* religion went down with the state in smoke and ashes in the calamity of 587. Had all that Israel's faith had to give been fair promises, the fall of state and temple might well have been the defeat of God and the victory of paganism. Many were tempted so to see it, as we shall see.

But here were the best voices of that faith announcing the tragedy as the judgment of God, the instrument of his moral purpose. It was God who struck the blow; God was, is, and always will be in control of history. In the mouths of Jeremiah and Ezekiel Israel's faith proved itself great enough to survive even the most total catastrophe. And, let us not dare to forget it, the religion that cannot encompass all of history's tragedy in its framework, that cannot go down to the very depths of the hell of tragedy, but must leave it as a sort of a great, whining question mark—that religion can speak to tragedy not one single syllable of a word. It cannot face tragedy, and, because it cannot, it cannot face history nor survive in it. That Israel's faith could survive at all, that Israel could live to hope in anything at all, was in good part due to prophets who so ruthlessly demolished all false hope. The Kingdom which God will establish is not equal to the Kingdom of Judah and its temple. By the same token the destruction of that state and temple is not the defeat of God.

Further, in loneliness of spirit, Jeremiah laid great stress on the inner and individual character of religion. Now it certainly ought not to be said, as the handbooks too often do, that either Jeremiah or Ezekiel was the father of individualism in the Old Testament faith. It is true that the Hebrew had always had a strong sense of the corporate nature of society (and there is a truth in that which we do ill to belittle or forget), and it is also true that the prophets had hurled their challenge at the nation and addressed it as a whole in the light of its position as the covenant people. But the nation was composed of individual men, and there was never a time when the Old Testament mind was not aware of that fact. The "you shall" of the Decalogue is addressed to the indi-

122

vidual will. The whole ethical attack of the prophets moved from the plight of individual men to an assault on the conscience of those individuals who oppressed them.

Yet this ought not to blind us to the fact that few ever laid more weight on the inner and personal nature of a man's relation to his God than did Jeremiah. The external circumstances perhaps help to explain this. As the state crumbled about his ears, as the state religion became an abhorrent thing in which he could have no part, it was inevitable that a man such as Jeremiah must meet his God in the privacy of his inmost soul, or meet him not at all. To no one was religion ever a more intensely intimate matter than to Jeremiah. No prophet laid greater stress on the inward nature of repentance, the change of heart, than did he. His preaching was not merely an attack on the state, it was a call to individual men to decide for the Kingdom of God against the Kingdom of Jehoiakim. And his own life was an illustration of the immense cost of that decision. It may be added that Ezekiel in his own way followed the same path (e.g., ch. 18).

But this cleared the way for the possibility that faith, divorced from state and state cult, might live on in the hearts of individual men. The notion of the people of God shifts in Jeremiah entirely away from the Israelite state. And although the faith that a godly Remnant would one day emerge is retained, there could be no hope, such as Isaiah appears to have had, that a purified nucleus in the nation would somehow escape the catastrophe and continue to exist. For the catastrophe was total, and none escaped it. The notion of the elect people thus becomes far more individualized a matter than it had ever been before. Individual men of the humiliated residue of the nation who at all costs hear the Word of God and obey his will—these are the people of God. Though the nation be destroyed, and though the temple lie in ruins, such people can meet God *anywhere* (e.g., Jer. 29:10-14; cf. Ezek. 11:16). Both Jeremiah and Ezekiel (e.g., Jer. 24; Ezek. 11:14-21) seem to have looked especially to the most humiliated group of all, the captives in Babylon, when they thought of this Remnant. Here in bitterest trial God will create a pure people.

4. And with this true people God will one day make a New Covenant. We come finally to a concept such as only a Jeremiah could have had. For only those who have seen the total failure of the earthly order to produce the Kingdom of God, and who have lost the last vestiges of

123

hope in what human hands may do, may lay hold of a higher hope, may see clearly a city not made with hands. At a time when a people—whose capacity for wishful thinking was amazing—had had all hope snatched away, Jeremiah, who never had any hope, never ceased to hope.

This hope which seems so unexpected in Jeremiah [36] was securely based in his theology. In fact hope is the wrong word, for nothing in the current scene allowed the least hope. It was rather an indomitable faith in God. Jeremiah's God was the God of Israel; and the God of Israel is the one, almighty Creator and Ruler of all things. History is in his hands, and in history he will accomplish his purpose. For a Jeremiah to have surrendered hope would have been for him to say that Israel's calamity had frustrated and defeated God. And that he could not, and never did, say. Furthermore, although Israel had certainly broken covenant and paid for it with her national life, it was certain above all certainty that God never breaks covenant. All Jeremiah's world might crumble into rubble, but surer than the very stars of heaven—stands God (31:35-37)! This God, who with a father's infinite compassion yet yearned for his long-lost first-born, Ephraim (31:15-22), would certainly not forget his purpose in history; and his purpose is the creation of a righteous people over whom he can rule. In the light of this it is not strange that Jeremiah should have held fast to hope; it would have been unthinkable had he not done so.

So it was that Jeremiah could never believe that the national ruin was the end. True, he could see no cause to hope; but he never lost hope, because he never lost God. This faith overriding hopelessness is dramatically illustrated by Jeremiah's conduct in the last year of Jerusalem's life, while he himself was locked up in jail (32:1-15). With the land clearly doomed, with the Chaldean army battering at the walls, Jeremiah invested in—of all things—real estate! And this was not done because he wanted the land, or because of bullish optimism, but to symbolize his faith that the land had a future (vs. 15). Yet it was not that Jeremiah

---

[36] So much so that it has been doubted if Jeremiah had any hope for the future. We cannot debate the question here, but to take such a position involves regarding the bulk of chs. 30-33 (as well as other portions) as non-Jeremianic. It is probable that the poetry of these chapters has received some expansion, but the basis of it is to be regarded as Jeremianic. The fact that some of the noblest expressions of hope (e.g., the New Covenant 31:31-34) are cast in the style of the prose sermons cannot be used to impeach their essential genuineness (cf. my remarks in "The Date of the Prose Sermons of Jeremiah," *Journal of Biblical Literature*, LXX [1951], 15-35).

really dared believe such a thing. For his part the action seemed utterly foolish, and done against all his better judgment (32:24-25) only because he felt that God wanted him to. In short, hope was for Jeremiah impossible, but faith in God (vs. 27) made him act in hope nonetheless. Jeremiah, what you do not believe in, what you dare not even hope for, what all the current scene denies—that is possible with God!

But that hope is shaped as Jeremiah *would* shape it. It is not linked to the Israelite state, for Israel has broken the covenant. It is too late to speak of a Remnant of the nation which will be spared—although the idea is exactly the same. Here we hear of a new Israel, a spiritual Israel to which God will one day accord a New Covenant and a new start. It will be an Israel wholly obedient to God's law, not because she has reformed (Jeremiah knew how little an external reform could do), but because the law is within, written on the very heart. Here is a New Covenant which no external obedience can secure, but which is given to a people who have surrendered their hearts to God and received his forgiving grace:

Behold the days are coming, saith Yahweh, that I will make with the house of Israel and with the house of Judah a new covenant: not like the covenant which I made with their fathers in the day when I took them by the hand to bring them out of the land of Egypt—which covenant of mine they broke though I was a husband to them, saith Yahweh. But this is the covenant which I will make with the house of Israel after those days, saith Yahweh: I will put my law within them, and on their heart will I write it; and I will be their God, and they shall be my people. And no more shall they teach each his neighbor and each his brother saying, "Know Yahweh." For all of them shall know me, from the least to the greatest of them, saith Yahweh; for I will forgive their iniquity, and their sin will I remember no more.

(31:31-34)

Ezekiel in his own way expresses the same theme. In a vision (ch. 37) it seemed that he saw a vast plain covered with bleached bones, and he knew that they were the bones of the defunct nation. Nor was it possible to see how the dead nation might ever live again (vss. 3, 11). But God spoke to the prophet, and in his vision he summoned the very spirit of God from the four winds of heaven. And the spirit breathed on the bones, and they "stood on their feet an exceeding great army" (vss. 9-10). It is a nation dead in its sin, alive again through the grace of God. It is a nation purged of its sin in the cross of the national death, alive

125

again with the spirit of God in its heart. Here is the people of God and the Kingdom of God (37:23-28; 11:19-20)!

Here perhaps more than elsewhere the Old Covenant reaches out in longing for the New. Here we learn of all false hopes for the redemption of man. The state and its policies, its wealth and its prosperity, even its religion and its noblest efforts at reform—these cannot produce the Kingdom of God, cannot create the people over which he will rule. The earthly order is at its best a pale approximation of God's order, at its worst a travesty of it. In no case can it be that order or create it. On the contrary, it lives, now as then, under history's judgment. But here also we learn of the true hope. It lies in the grace of God, who accords to men a New Covenant—its law written on human hearts. The people of this covenant are the people of God's Kingdom, for they are the pure in heart who have been, as it were, born again. The Old Covenant thus points to a solution beyond itself—the creation of a new people.

Guard these words of Jeremiah well! You will hear them again. You will hear them in a little upper room; you will hear them when next you sit about the Lord's table: "This cup *is* the New Covenant in my blood" (I Cor. 11:25; Luke 22:20). And again: "Drink ye, all, of it" (Matt. 26:27).

CHAPTER FIVE

Captivity and New Exodus

THE HOUSE OF JUDAH FELL NEVER AGAIN TO RISE, AND WITH IT ALL HOPE THAT IT COULD EVER BE THE KINGDOM RULED OVER AND PROTECTED by God. The hope for the establishment of God's people under his rule had, therefore, either to be given up or reinterpreted in terms of something more spiritual and more enduring than the state. This last is, of course, precisely what generations of prophet preaching—culminating in that of Jeremiah and Ezekiel—had been doing. True, the Exile was a withering blow to popular expectations. But Israel's faith proved, as it has done many another time, that it had in it the stuff to survive. And the hope of the coming establishment of God's rule was an integral part of that faith, inseparably linked to the whole Old Testament notion of the God who accomplishes his purpose in history. It was not, therefore, abandoned but, ever more tightly held the darker the days, it flourished amazingly. Indeed it was during the Exile that it was given its profoundest expression. To that we must now turn.

I

1. If the faith of Israel was not extinguished, it was not because the calamity that befell the nation was trivial. On the contrary, the fall of Jerusalem and the collapse of the state signaled a major disruption in the life of Israel such as very few peoples could have survived.

Now we must disabuse ourselves of certain popularly held notions concerning the Babylonian exile. We are likely to imagine a total deportation of the population, tens of thousands of people led away in chains to be thrown into concentration camps and there to be subjected to the most savage persecution. But the facts scarcely bear out such a notion. The number deported to Babylon was never large. In Jer. 52:28-30 three deportations are mentioned, and the total listed for all three is but 4,600. Even if this be a count only of adult males, the grand total of the captives could hardly have been much over thrice that number.[1] And although the hardship and the humiliation which must accompany any such mass deportation ought not to be treated lightly, there is no evidence that the lot of these captives was unduly severe. They were taken to the homeland of Babylon, the very center of world civilization. They were settled in the towns there (e.g., Jer. 29:7), allowed to continue some semblance of community life (cf. Ezek. 8:1; 14:1; 20:1), and apparently permitted to mingle with the population and earn their living in whatever way they could. They were not subjected to persecution because of race or religion. King Jehoiachin, although he was subsequently thrown into prison, was at first honorably received as a pensioner of the Babylonian court.[2] In the course of the years many Jews began to enter trade, and not a few grew rich.[3] We may indeed believe that life in Babylon afforded to many opportunities which they would never have had in Palestine.

Nevertheless, the Exile was a calamity of total proportions for the

[1] This figure and those in Kings require some harmonizing. Jer. 52:28 sets the total for the first deportation (598 B.C.) at 3,023, while Kings (which gives no total for the deportation of 587 and does not mention the third one) places it at 10,000 (II Kings 24:14) or 8,000 (II Kings 24:16). There is probably no real discrepancy. The figures in Kings appear to be rough estimates. Besides, as Albright ("The Biblical Period," p. 47) suggests, terrific mortality on the route of march may account for some of the difference.

[2] II Kings 25:27-30 informs us only that Evil-merodach (the son of Nebuchadnezzar [562-560]) released Jehoiachin from prison, the implication being that he had languished there up to that time. But recently published tablets from Babylon, one of which dates from ca. 592 (thus before the final fall of Jerusalem), list Jehoiachin and five of his sons among others receiving rations from the royal court. He is called the "king of Judah." So it is clear that Jehoiachin was only jailed subsequently, probably for complicity in some rebellious activity. These tablets, first published by E. F. Weidner ("Joachin, König von Juda in Babylonischen Keilschrifttexten," Mélanges syriens offerts à M. René Dussaud [Paris: Librairie Orientaliste Paul Geuthner, 1939], pp. 923-35), are discussed by W. F. Albright ("King Joiachin in Exile," The Biblical Archaeologist, V-4 [1942], 49-55). For a translation see Pritchard, op. cit., p. 308.

[3] By the following century Jewish names become increasingly frequent in business documents, especially in those from Nippur.

128

little nation, and its effect on Jewish life is not to be minimized.[4] The land was a shambles. Practically every fortified town, including Jerusalem with its temple, had been destroyed by the Babylonians and left in ruins. Most of them were not rebuilt for many years to come. And while the actual number deported was not large, these represented the cream of the country's leadership. In addition we may be sure that thousands had been slain in battle or had died of the rigors of the siege, while other thousands had fled for their lives. Only the poorest of the peasantry, considered incapable of stirring up trouble, were left to harvest the crops (II Kings 25:12). Judah was a land drained of its inhabitants.[5] Much of southern Palestine began at this time to be settled with an Edomite population from southeast of the Dead Sea (whence its later name of Idumaea). The area occupied by the Jews seventy-five years later was a very small one in the immediate environs of Jerusalem.

In fact Palestine would not again be the physical home of the majority of Jews. We stand at the beginning of the great Dispersion. Of the Jews who had escaped death or deportation, an ever larger number turned their faces from their wrecked homeland and sought opportunity elsewhere. There was a tremendous flow of migration to Egypt. As early as Jeremiah's day quite a number had gone there (Jer. 40–44), and Jewish colonies are known to have existed there throughout the Persian period (cf. Isa. 19:18).[6] It was a process which went on unchecked, until by the Greek period Egypt had become a center of world Jewry. Similar streams of migration moved in other directions. Soon the number of Jews living abroad far exceeded the number remaining at home; the time would ultimately come when Jewish communities would be found all over the known world. And although Palestine remained the spiritual

[4] C. C. Torrey (Ezra Studies [Chicago: University of Chicago Press, 1910]; Pseudo-Ezekiel and the Original Prophecy [New Haven: Yale University Press, 1930]) and others have contended that the Exile is a vastly exaggerated occurrence, but their arguments have now been quite thoroughly refuted by recent discoveries. Cf. Albright, From the Stone Age to Christianity, pp. 246-50.

[5] Albright, "The Biblical Period," p. 49, on the basis of lists in Ezra and Nehemiah and other evidence, estimates the population of Judah after the first return at only ca. 20,000. The number present in the intervening years must have been few indeed, although an Israelite population continued to maintain itself in other parts of the country.

[6] Particularly at Elephantine at the first cataract of the Nile. Papyri written in Aramaic and coming from this community in the mid–fifth century have been discovered. They throw valuable light on its circumstances, customs, and religious practices. Cf. Albright, Archaeology and the Religion of Israel, pp. 168-74. For excerpts in translation cf. Pritchard, op. cit., pp. 222-23, 491-92.

homeland, and Jerusalem the holy city transfigured in feeling and memory, for most of them there was no going back. When the opportunity was given those in Babylon to return, most of them could not, or did not, see their way clear to do so.

2. The Babylonian conquest of Judah was thus a total calamity: the destruction of the nation and the dispersal of its population. But it was more than that. It was a severe spiritual crisis: a crisis in theology, if you will. Israel's religion could no longer continue as a sort of national church, supported by the state and existing to foster the well-being of state and society. It must adjust, it must reinterpret itself, or perish.

The fall of state and temple brought down with it all the popular conceit which had attached itself to these institutions, and against which the prophets had inveighed with so little success. It could not but have produced profound disillusionment. The popular theology, voiced by professional prophet and priest and gladly swallowed by a wishfully thinking people, had said it couldn't happen—God wouldn't allow it! This is his people, this is his temple, and here is David's eternal throne whereon sits his anointed "son," the king: God will never let this nation be destroyed! On the contrary, as the climax of history's drama he will glorify it—for it is his Kingdom!

But it had not so worked out. History had not led up to that climactic intervention of God and the establishment of his Kingdom; it had brought the end of that "kingdom" at the hands of a pagan army which worshiped pagan gods. Is not that the victory of paganism? Many Israelites could draw no other conclusion than that the Babylonian victory was proof that the gods of Babylon were mightier than Yahweh. Such would be gravely tempted to lapse from their ancestral faith altogether. Others, unwilling to go so far, whined that God was not fair, for he had allowed the children to be punished for sins committed by the fathers (Ezek. 18:2; Jer. 31:29; Lam. 5:7).[7] Still others—those who had taken the prophet preaching seriously—could only conclude that the doom announced by the prophets had indeed fallen, that the covenant bond had been broken, and destiny as the people of God ended: "Our bones are dried up, and our hope is lost; we are clean cut off" (Ezek. 37:11).

[7] It is not surprising that the question of the divine justice was to the fore in this period as it had not been previously; cf. Jer. 12:1-4; Hab. 1:1–2:4; Ezek. 18. While the date of the book of Job, which is the most earnest discussion of the subject which the ancient world has given us, is most uncertain, it is probable that it received its present form within a century of the time with which we are concerned.

This disillusionment could only have been aggravated as Jews were thrown into contact with a vaster world than most of them had ever dreamed of. Theirs was a small, poor, out-of-the-way country, and relatively few of them had ever traveled far beyond its borders. They were perforce a provincial people. Yet they prided themselves that their city was the very center of the universe, for Yahweh, God of Hosts, had his holy habitation on earth in its midst. But now they were uprooted and scattered through the world, the homeland and the heritage far away, the proud city and its temple in ruins. In that world they saw cities which made Jerusalem seem the country town it was; they saw wealth such as not even fabulous Solomon had had; irresistible military power; temples of a magnificence to shame the one on Mount Zion, where reposed the resplendent images of Marduk, or Nabu (cf. Isa. 46:1-2), or perchance Amun-Reʿ. It was a vast world in which horizons widened. Just what place was there in it for Yahweh, the erstwhile protector of a ravaged petty state whose ruined temple gaped to the sky on a mountain in Judah?

The way was wide open to a wholesale loss of faith. Not a turning to atheism, of course (that was a commodity unknown in the ancient Orient), but to the worship of more successful gods. The pagan, be he ancient or modern, will understand it as the function of religion to repay him in tangible terms for his worship. He will desire this cozy understanding with his god: that his prayers will return him protection, his dollars more dollars. Nor will he be likely to stick with a religion that does not do this. It was a great temptation, therefore, for a Jew—in whose paganized mind Yahweh had failed him—simply to sink into the background and cease to be a Jew. No doubt many did.[8]

Israel's faith could no longer continue as the parochial thing so many of its adherents had conceived it to be. The world had become vast and its tragedy deep. Faith would have to show itself wide enough and deep enough to embrace both that world and that tragedy—or perish. It could no longer turn within itself and survive by practicing its own little affairs. And, although by its very nature it could never be divorced from the Jewish people, the way back to what it had been before was forever shut and barred, and there was no returning.

[8] Direct evidence is lacking, but the violent polemic of Isa. 40–48 against the gods of Babylon would hardly have been necessary if many were not falling away to the worship of these gods. For evidence from a somewhat later period cf. A. T. Olmstead, *History of the Persian Empire* (Chicago: University of Chicago Press, 1948), p. 192.

3. Such was the challenge posed by the Babylonian exile. The gravity of that challenge can hardly be exaggerated. Yet it is clear that Israel's faith did rise to meet it. The Exile was anything but the spiritual extinction of Israel: there was vitality; there was a Remnant in her. That this was so might be regarded as little short of a miracle. But the miracle lay in the very nature of Israel's faith itself which, not least because its God was Lord of history, could not, as long as it understood that God, ever be defeated by history. And however much the majority may have misunderstood that theology, there were others who had not.

The prophets, particularly Jeremiah and Ezekiel, had prepared for the coming adaptation. While others doubted if God were in control, or blubbered that he was not fair, these prophets tirelessly asserted that he was both. They insisted that the calamity was God's doing and quite just: it was his judgment on the sins of the nation, sins in which the present generation had participated fully, and the sooner Israel realized this the better for her (e.g., Jer. 16:10-13; Ezek. 14:12-23; 18). To their voices was added that of the historian who gave us the books of Kings.[9] He not only explained the final calamity but every misfortune that had ever befallen Israel in exactly the same terms. This was surely a buffer against the blow. Here were men of undoubted integrity, whose words had been vindicated by events, who explained the tragedy precisely in terms of Israel's ancestral faith—and a tragedy explained in terms of a faith can never destroy that faith. Sincere Israelites, therefore, were not driven by the national debacle to numb despair or to railing against God, but to a searching of their own hearts.

The prophets, too, had prepared for the day when, the external forms of religion having been swept away, faith would have to go on without them. To most of their contemporaries it would have seemed unthinkable that God could be worshiped without sacrifice, without ritual, without temple. When these leave off worship leaves off; for neither can God be worshiped without them, nor does the law permit the erection of a substi-

[9] I and II Kings—like Joshua, Judges, and I and II Samuel—comprise a history written from the standpoint of the Deuteronomic law. It seeks to demonstrate that the principles which Deuteronomy asserts have actually been proven true by events. It is probable that all these books were given to us by one hand (cf. the fundamental treatment of M. Noth, *Ueberlieferungsgeschichtliche Studien I* [Halle: M. Niemeyer, 1943]). My opinion (against Noth) is that this historian worked in the last decades before the fall of Jerusalem, and that his work was subsequently supplemented in the Exile.

tute temple in a foreign land.[10] Had the popular notion been correct, Israel's worship would indeed and perforce have ended in the Exile. But the prophets had always declared the popular notion to be wrong. Sacrifice and temple ritual, they said, are not only not the heart of worship, they are not essential to worship at all (Jer. 7:21-23). The essential of worship is obedience and rectitude, without which external worship becomes a great sin. An obedient people meets God in the heart, and their prayers will find his ears wherever they are (Jer. 29:11-14; 31:31-34; Ezek. 11:16-20; cf. Deut. 4:29-31). For an obedient people, clean to the very heart, God has a future—for they are his people and he their God. It was thus by demolishing all false hope that the prophets were able to keep alive a true hope of the sort that could survive.

Thus it was, paradoxically, that the Exile, far from being the graveyard of Israel's faith, was a time of great spiritual vitality. We cannot trace the details; indeed most of them are obscure. Care was taken to preserve the historical records of the past, lest they be forever lost. The sayings of the prophets were remembered and passed on both orally and in small collections; although the details escape us, the process of collecting and editing which was to give us the prophet books as we know them was carried forward.[11] After all, had not the words of the prophets by their very correctness proved themselves to be words of God, and did they not also contain the only hope to which a man could hold? In particular there grew up a heightened interest in the law: to codify it, con it, and lay it to heart.[12] For now that the nation was no more and the temple and its cult had left off, what was there left to show a man a Jew except the law? Perhaps by keeping the law Israel might become what

[10] The Jews in Elephantine did indeed build a temple, but it is plain from the papyri that the community in Jerusalem must have regarded it as illegitimate. Its worship was of a most syncretistic sort (cf. note 6 above).

[11] The great pre-exilic prophets did not, as we are prone to think, actually "write" the books that bear their names, although we know that in some cases they wrote or dictated certain of their prophecies (e.g., Jer. 36). The prophets uttered their oracles orally. Where the prophet did not himself commit his sayings to writing, we may assume that they were remembered by his hearers and, after a longer or shorter interval, written down. These sayings circulated at first, we may believe, either separately or in small collections, and only after a long and complex process were they edited into the books which we now have. These books are, therefore, something in the nature of anthologies of the prophets' preaching rather than books written by their pens. Oral tradition no doubt played a part, but its importance must not be exaggerated: see the judicious remarks of G. Widengren, *Literary and Psychological Aspects of the Hebrew Prophets* (*Uppsala Universitets Arsskrift 1948:10* [Uppsala: Lundequistska Bokhandeln, 1948]).

[12] Cf. Chap. VI, pp. 170 ff.

God had always destined her to be: a people holy to himself (Lev. 19:2; 20:22-26 et passim; cf. Exod. 19:5-6). Here in the Exile there was already taking shape that form in which the faith of Israel was subsequently to express itself for centuries to come—indeed in which, with many modifications, it has survived until the present day. Israel was in transition from a nation with a national cult to the law community of Judaism.

Hope of eventual restoration was never given up. We have seen what the prophets did to keep that hope alive. While it is probable that many Jews longed for no more that the re-establishment of the nation, it is clear that the prophet hope went far beyond that. Jeremiah's emphatically did, as we have seen. Ezekiel, too, although he envisioned the resurrection of the nation (ch. 37), did not look for a revival of the old nation to continue in the old ways but for the birth of a new nation with the spirit of God in its heart. Perhaps the most grandiose expression of this hope is that found in Ezek. 40–48, a passage which might well be called Ezekiel's Civitas Dei.[18] Here we see the land again inhabited and divided among the tribes, with the reconstituted temple in which the Glory of Yahweh once more dwells (ch. 43; cf. chs. 10–11) in its midst. And from the temple there flows a stream of living water (ch. 47) to rejuvenate all the land. Toward that new Jerusalem and that temple, which so far existed only in faith, we may be sure that the eyes of many a captive Jew were strained. Hope could not die in Israel, because hope was integral to faith, and faith was indestructable.

4. Expectations were no doubt nourished by external factors as well. It is likely that the release of Jehoiachin from prison in 561 (II Kings 25:27-30) awakened in many the dream of an eventual restoration of the Jewish monarchy. The extreme instability of the Babylonian Empire undoubtedly fanned this hope to a flame. In fact, after the death of the great Nebuchadnezzar (562 B.C.) the empire was never again on even keel. Always threatened by the massive Median power to the north and east, it was beset by internal dissension as well. Within seven years after the death of Nebuchadnezzar the throne had changed hands three times,

---

[18] From the fact that the temple gate described in ch. 40 is Solomonic, a type of construction not attested in later periods, it becomes extremely hazardous to relegate the material of these chapters to a late date, as many scholars do. They must owe their origin to one who, like Ezekiel, actually remembered the pre-exilic temple. Cf. C. G. Howie, The Date and Composition of Ezekiel (Philadelphia: Society of Biblical Literature, 1950), pp. 43-46; idem, "The East Gate of Ezekiel's Temple Enclosure and the Solomonic Gateway of Megiddo," Bulletin of the American Schools of Oriental Research, 117 (1950), 13-19.

two of these by violence. Scarcely had Nebuchadnezzar's son, Amel-marduk (he is the Evil-merodach of the Bible who set Jehoiachin free), reigned two years when he was assassinated by his brother-in-law, Nergal-shar-uṣur (probably the Nergal-sharezer who appears as a Babylonian officer in Jer. 39:3, 13). The latter, however, died within four years, leaving a minor son on the throne who was murdered almost at once by one Nabu-na'id (Nabonidus).

Under Nabonidus (555-539) the end of the short-lived Babylonian world power came. It was, in fact, already tottering on its foundations. Nabonidus, apparently of a priestly family from Upper Mesopotamia, followed a policy, the details of which need not concern us, which made him bitterly and widely hated. In particular, he earned the enmity of the powerful priests of Marduk, high god of Babylon, who would gladly have gotten rid of him. For some years, for reasons that are obscure, he retired from Babylon to the oasis of Teima in the Arabian desert, leaving matters at home in the hands of his son, Bêl-shar-uṣur (whom we know from the book of Daniel as Belshazzar).

Now the most dangerous external menace to the state lay, as we have said, in the Medes. These, it will be recalled, had in the previous century teamed up with the Babylonians to destroy the Assyrian Empire. They had since gained control of a tremendous territory stretching from central Asia Minor far into what is now Iran. So greatly did Nabonidus fear the Medes that when one of their vassal kings, Cyrus the Persian, rebelled against them, Nabonidus encouraged him and made a treaty with him. Seldom has a head of state been more wrong. Cyrus was not only victorious, taking over the Median state, but in a series of astounding campaigns he enlarged it to yet more colossal dimensions. By his victory over the fabulous Croesus (546) he extended it clear to the Aegean Sea. Then he turned on Babylon. In one mighty blow he cut the Babylonian armies to pieces so thoroughly that in 539 his general was able to enter Babylon without a fight. Babylon was finished, and Cyrus the Persian ruled the world.

Early in his reign (538) Cyrus issued to the Jews an edict of restoration. The book of Ezra preserves it for us in two versions, one in Hebrew (1:1-4) and one in Aramaic (6:3-5). Its historicity cannot be doubted.[14]

[14] The authenticity of the Hebrew version is less widely granted than that of the Aramaic, but for an able defense of it cf. E. Bickerman, "The Edict of Cyrus in Ezra 1," *Journal of Biblical Literature*, LXV (1946), 244-75. In any case, that such an edict was issued is certain.

It was, in fact, not an isolated gesture but a part of Cyrus' general policy of toleration. It was commanded that the temple vessels be restored and that the people be encouraged to go home. Royal assistance was promised (6:4). The project was placed in charge of one Sheshbazzar (1:8), who was none other than the son of the last legitimate king of Judah, Jehoiachin.[15] When Sheshbazzar, for reasons unknown to us—probably through death—faded from the picture, he was succeeded by Zerubbabel (2:2; 3:2), his nephew and a grandson of Jehoiachin (I Chr. 3:19). That these events awakened the highest hopes in Jewish breasts goes without saying.

II

Addressed to this situation with all its despair and awakening hope is another of the great prophecies of the Old Testament. In many respects it might be called the greatest of them all. It is to be found in the latter chapters (40–66) of the book of Isaiah. That these chapters stand off rather sharply from the rest of the book is obvious to the careful reader. No doubt he is also aware that it is the virtually unanimous opinion of scholars that beginning with Isa. 40 we have to do not with the words of Isaiah, the son of Amoz, but with those of an unknown prophet who lived toward the end of the Babylonian exile and who is called for the sake of convenience the Second (Deutero-) Isaiah. To argue the question here would, of course, lead us far astray from our subject, although it must be said that the reasons which have led so many learned men to a like opinion are weighty indeed.[16] But the Word of God stands above all scholarly debate. It speaks through the mouth of the ancient prophet and

[15] Cf. Albright, "The Biblical Period," p. 49 and note 119. Sheshbazzar is almost certainly the Shenazzar, son of Jehoiachin, mentioned in I Chr. 3:18 (cf. idem, Journal of Biblical Literature, XL [1921], 108 ff. for full discussion). The name, like that of Zerubbabel, is a good Babylonian one.

[16] Historical allusions are without exception to the late sixth century. Jerusalem is in ruins (44:26; 49:19; 51:3; 52:9; 54:3; 63:18; 64:10-11) and has been for a long time (58:12; 61:4). The people are captives in Babylon (47; 48:14, 20; 51:14; 52:11-12). Cyrus the Persian is coming on the scene (44:28; 45:1). It is to be noted that in no case are these things predicted; they are assumed as present fact. Furthermore, chs. 40–66 in no place claim to be by Isaiah. Neither his name nor that of any eighth-century person is mentioned (quite contrary to chs. 1–39). In addition there are marked differences of style and concept. That the New Testament writers refer to chs. 40–66 as "the book of the prophet Isaiah" (e.g., Matt. 3:3; Luke 3:4; 4:17) is in no sense disturbing. These writers, who doubtless shared the beliefs of the day on such matters, intended no more than a reference to a scripture passage. It was not in their minds to argue questions of criticism. My profound conviction is that the doctrine of the inspiration of Scripture is in no sense diminished by the discussion. God may speak through whom he will.

summons us anew to hear and obey. And since these chapters are, by common agreement, addressed to the situation of Exile and Restoration, it is necessary to treat them in this context.[17]

It is quite impossible to do this great prophecy justice. One stands before it with humility; one comes away from it with the feeling that he has not said the tenth part of what ought to have been said. It is as if the prophet had laid hold on the mighty constants of Israel's faith and had, with surpassing power and beauty, drawn them out to their ultimate implications. There moves before our eyes, as it were with giant strides, the God of Israel's historic believing: one, almighty, and powerful to redeem. Lord of history, he moves events onward to the trumph of his rule. There is Israel, too, called long ago to serve the purpose of God in history, who here in deepest humiliation is summoned to destiny beyond farthest dreams. But she must now be told, in the highest and the deepest, what it means to be the servant of God.

But with that there enter in concepts, foreshadowed indeed in the Old Testament and not altogether foreign to the mind of the ancient world, which nevertheless take new shape and burst forth with all the force of a revelation. One may to a certain extent grasp them, yet the honest heart cannot avoid hearing that Philip's question (Acts 8:30): "Do you understand what you are reading?" And what answer can be given save that of the Ethiopian, "How can I . . . ?" It is as if all that seven hundred years of Hebrew history had been trying to say had at last been said, and there is nothing left to say until Another will speak: "I have finished the work which thou gavest me to do" (John 17:4 K.J.V.).

1. There is a vaulting hope in these chapters. From first (40:1-11) to last (65:17-25; 66:10-14) there runs through them an overtone of joy like the strains of triumphant music. The pages are suffused with light— light like the rising of the sun (60:1-3). It is as if the hell and the horror had been left behind, and one is moving up a high, sun-drenched summit to the very doors of the Kingdom of God. There is good news to tell

---

[17] Chs. 55–66 constitute a further problem. I am not convinced of a Third Isaiah; nor is it necessary, as so many do, to distribute this material among a number of authors of varying dates. While C. C. Torrey's defense of the unity of chs. 40–66 (*The Second Isaiah* [New York: Chas. Scribner's Sons, 1928]) is much too neat, and while his effort to date the prophecy late in the fifth century must be rejected, the fundamental unity of the whole may be defended (allowing for some expansion). Nothing in these chapters need date before ca. 540, and little or nothing long after ca. 516.

(40:9-11; 52:1-12): the night of humiliation has ended, a glorious future lies ahead.

That the coming of Cyrus and the impending collapse of Babylon fanned this hope cannot be doubted. But we shall be quite wrong if we try to understand it merely as abounding optimism over the happy turn of world events. On the contrary, it rested in an indomitable faith in the power and purpose of God. Here is Israel's God, drawn with giant strokes, beside whom all else is nothing. He sits in incomparable majesty high above the earth; the nations are powerless before him; the very stars obey him (40:21-26); nothing may be compared to him:

> Who has measured the sea waters[18] in the palm of his hand
>> laid off the heavens with his fingers,[19]
>>> held the earth's dust in a third-bushel measure[20]
> Weighed the mountains in scales
>> and the hills in a balance?
> Who has directed the spirit of Yahweh,
>> or as his counsellor may teach him?
> With whom did he take counsel, and who instructed him,
>> and taught him the pathway of judgment?
> Or imparted to him knowledge,
>> or taught him the way of understanding?
> Lo, the nations are like a drop out of a bucket,
>> are accounted as the dust on the scales;
>>> yes, he picks up islands like grains of sand.
> And Lebanon is not sufficient for fuel,
>> nor its beasts enough for a burnt offering.
> All the nations are as nothing before him,
>> they are accounted by him as absolutely nothing at all.
>
> Then to whom will you liken God,
>> or what likeness will you devise for him?
>
> (40:12-18)

[18] This reading (mê yām for mayim) follows the newly discovered "Dead Sea Scroll" of Isaiah. Cf. *The Dead Sea Scrolls of St. Mark's Monastery*, M. Burrows, ed. (New Haven: The American Schools of Oriental Research, 1950), Vol. I, Pl. XXXIII.

[19] Literally "with the span," i.e., the length of the distance between outspread thumb and little finger.

[20] This is frankly a paraphrase. Hebrew reads "with the shālīsh" (i.e., a one-third measure). The shālīsh is usually taken to be one-third of an ephah, and an ephah equals a fraction over a bushel.

What likeness indeed? It should be obvious that a God so great cannot be likened to anything. As for the pagan gods, they do not exist. They are so many chunks of wood and metal (46:5-7); they can effect nothing in history, because they are nothing (41:21-24). The centuries-long polemic against idols rises to its climax in a roar of derisive laughter. With savage irony the prophet taunts the heathen gods with their nonexistence, and satirizes the sodden stupidity of anyone who would carve a god out of a tree (44:12-20)—the same tree which had furnished the fuel to cook his supper! This is the purest monotheism. The monotheism which had been implicit in Israel's faith since Moses, and which had for years been becoming ever more explicit (e.g., Jer. 2:11; Deut. 4:35), is now a self-conscious doctrine: there is but one God, beside whom no other exists (e.g., 44:6; 45:18, 22; 46:9).

But if only one God exists, then he is in absolute control of history. Never had the Old Testament notion of the God who is Lord of history been given clearer expression. It is he who created all things (45:12, 18), and all things are in his hands. He formed a purpose of old and called Abraham and Jacob as servants of that purpose (41:8-10; 51:1-3). It is simply not conceivable that midway in the career of history he should quit that purpose in defeat: that would be unimaginable dishonor to his name (48:11). He embarked on a plan; he will finish it. He is the first and the last (44:6; 48:12), Lord both of creation and the end of things. He can, therefore, and he will. Nor let Israel imagine that the calamity which has befallen her is anything but a richly deserved penalty for sin (42:24-25; 48:17-19). It was not God's defeat, but God's doing; even there he was in full control (a thing Jeremiah and Ezekiel had said endlessly). And still he is in control. Even mighty Cyrus, unknown to himself, is the agent of God's purpose (44:28–45:4). God summoned him, God sent him victorious (41:2-4, 25; 46:11), and his career will redound to the glory of God (45:6). Since all this is so, let Israel cease her complaining (40:27-31) and have faith that God will bring history to the end for which he created the world, called Abraham, and led Israel from Egypt: the establishment of his people (51:1-16).

2. In the light of this unshakable faith that God, and God alone, is the Lord of history, the whole prophecy is suffused with an eager expectation: God has a future for his people; a "new thing" is about to come to pass, so stupendous that it will overshadow even the great things of

the past (42:9; 43:19; 46:9; 48:3, 6-8).[21] In this new thing Israel is to participate, not for any merit in herself—for she has been blind and deaf to God's calling (42:19) and utterly contumacious (48:1-8)—but for the sake of the very honor and purpose of God (48:9-11).

But what is this "new thing"? It is evident that the prospect of release from Babylon stands in the foreground (48:14, 20-21; 52:11-12), but it is equally evident that more is meant than that. The reader is struck by the recurring motif of the highway through the desert, a desert which flows with streams of living water (40:3-5; 41:18; 43:16-19; 48:21; 49:10-11). It takes no more than a little reflection to see that this is vastly more than a literal prediction of a marvelous journey back to the homeland. It is the imagery of the Exodus. On occasion (51:9-11) there is linked to a reference to the Exodus (vs. 10) an allusion to the ancient creation myth (vs. 9), in which the god (in the Babylonian version, Marduk) cleft asunder the Chaos Monster (in the Babylonian version, Tiamat; but here in the west Semitic form, Rahab) in order to create the world.[22] It is as if the prophet wished to say, in poetic language, that the struggle with primeval chaos begun at creation, and again taken up in the Exodus when God created for himself a people, is once more to be resumed. Israel is to experience a new Exodus! But the Exodus was looked upon by every Israelite as the national beginning. To speak of a new Exodus could therefore mean only a new beginning. There is for Israel, then, a new national beginning, a future more glorious than the past.[23] God will establish his people under his rule—that was the purpose both of the creative struggle and the entire historical process (51:16).

But the old Exodus was the scene of the covenant which made Israel a people. It was impossible, therefore, to speak of a new Exodus without mention of the covenant. Now Israel had certainly broken that Old Covenant (cf. Jer. 31:32), and there was every reason to believe that

[21] For recent discussion of this concept cf. C. R. North, "The 'Former Things' and the 'New Things' in Deutero-Isaiah," *Studies in Old Testament Prophecy,* H. H. Rowley, ed. (Edinburgh: T. & T. Clark, 1950), pp. 111-26; A. Bentzen, "On the Ideas of 'the Old' and 'the New' in Deutero-Isaiah," *Studia Theologica* (Lund: C. W. K. Gleerup, 1947), Vol. I, Fasc. I-II, pp. 183-87.

[22] Cf. J. Pedersen, *Israel: Its Life and Culture* (Copenhagen: Povl Branner, 1940), III-IV, 602; C. R. North, *The Old Testament Interpretation of History* (London: Epworth Press, 1946), pp. 48-49. For a translation of the Babylonian text in question cf. Pritchard, *op. cit.,* pp. 60-72.

[23] The new Exodus idea is not wholly novel. Hosea (2:14-20), Jeremiah (31:2-6, 15-22) and Ezekiel (20:33 ff.) had, in various ways, played upon it.

God had cast her off (49:14; Ezek. 37:11). But where Jeremiah spoke of a New Covenant to be made one day with a new Israel (Jer. 31:31-34), Second Isaiah speaks of a revitalized covenant. There has been no "divorce" between Israel and God: "Where is the bill of your mother's divorce, wherewith I sent her away? Or which of my creditors was it to whom I sold you?" (50:1.) In language charged with emotion he declares that the "divorce," so movingly described by Hosea, was but a momentary estrangement. God has in his everlasting mercy taken back his "wife," Israel, and with her has made an eternal covenant of peace:

Do not be afraid, for you shall not be shamed;
  do not be daunted, for you shall not be disgraced.
For the shame of your youth you shall forget,
  and the reproach of your widowhood you shall remember no more.
For he who weds you is your Maker,
  Yahweh of Hosts is his name;
And your Redeemer is the Holy One of Israel,
  God of all the earth shall he be called.
For a woman forsaken and distressed in spirit
  did Yahweh call you;
And, "Wife of youth—that she should be rejected!"
  saith your God.
For a brief moment I forsook you,
  but with great compassion I will gather you.
In an outburst of wrath I hid
  my face a moment from you,
But with grace[24] everlasting I have pitied you,
  saith your Redeemer, Yahweh.

This is just like the days of[25] Noah to me:
When I swore that never again should the flood waters overflow the earth,
So do I swear not to be angry with you nor to rebuke you.
For the mountains may move
  and the hills may totter,
But my grace shall not depart from you,
  nor shall my covenant of peace waver,
    saith Yahweh, who has compassion on you.

(54:4-10)

[24] The Hebrew word is ḥesed, for which "lovingkindness" (A.S.V.), "kindness" (K.J.V.) are inadequate translations. Cf. Chap. I, note 18.

[25] So with most ancient versions and, apparently, the new Dead Sea Scroll (cf. Burrows, op. cit., Pl. XLV). "For the waters of" and "as the days of" have the same consonants in Hebrew.

141

In this "new thing" are all the hopes of Israel to be gathered up. In it will those expectations which clustered about the line of David find their fulfillment (55:3-5). In it will the longing of Jeremiah and Ezekiel for a people cleansed of heart be realized; for then Yahweh will pour out his spirit on Israel, and they will be proud to stand forth as his people (44:1-5). In it, too, will the ancient promise to Abraham of a seed more numerous than the stars of heaven become reality. As God brought forth from Abraham—who was but one man—a mighty nation, so he will give to this pitifully tiny remnant an unbelievably numerous progeny (51:1-3; 49:20-21; 54:1-3). There is far more here than the mere dream of political restoration; it is the glorification of Israel before all the world in the coming establishment of God's rule over his people:

> Arise, shine; for your light has come,
> and the glory of Yahweh has dawned upon you!
> For, behold, darkness covers the earth,
> black darkness the peoples;
> But upon you Yahweh shines forth,
> upon you his glory appears.
> And nations shall come to your light,
> kings to the brightness of your rising.
>
> Lift up your eyes round about, and see!
> they all gather together, they come to you.
> Your sons come from afar,
> and your daughters are carried in the arms.[26]
> Then shall you see and be radiant,
> and your heart shall thrill and grow large.
> For the wealth of the sea shall be turned to you,
> the riches of the nations shall come to you.
>
> . . . .
> Who are these that fly as a cloud,
> like doves to their dovecotes?
> Truly to me the far lands are gathering,
> and the Tarshish boats as in former days,[27]

[26] Literally "nursed on the side": a reference, apparently, to the custom of carrying young children on the hip; cf. 66:12; 49:22.

[27] Possibly the reading (English, following the Hebrew) "Tarshish boats first of all," is to be preferred. The reading above has the support of a number of MSS and the Syriac version, and involves the addition of but one letter. Reference would then be to fleets of Tarshish ships such as Solomon once had (I Kings 10:22).

To bring your sons from afar,
    their silver and their gold with them,
For the name of Yahweh your God,
    and for the Holy One of Israel, for he has glorified you.
                  (60:1-5, 8-9)

Nor could the prophet believe that the coming victory of God and the establishment of his Kingdom was far away. On the contrary, it was *right there* at the door. History is moving onward to its consummation; the great eschatological drama is about to commence. It is as if the prophet were witnessing in the present suffering the birth pangs of a new creation (66:7-9). In almost shocking language he depicts Almighty God himself in the agony of travail (42:14-16), impatient to bring forth the new thing that he has prepared. Through the prophecy from end to end run two parallel motifs. There is on the one hand the imagery of the judgment, the Day of Yahweh. It is seen in the awful picture of ch. 34: ruin, blood, fire, smoke, stench, and desolation.[28] And we are left at the end with the worm that dieth not and the fire that is not quenched (66:24; cf. 63:1-6; 49:26; 50:2-3; 51:6). Opposite this is the imagery of the new creation, of nature rejuvenated (35:1-2; 41:19; 55:13; 60:13). There will be long life and peace (65:20-23), the warfare in nature will be ended (65:25), fellowship with God restored (65:24). The primitive Eden peace (51:3) will once more come to earth, and the rule of God, long disrupted by sin, will be re-established. In this coming triumph of God toward which all history moves, the people of God will find their redemption. Indeed the prophet sings so eloquently of a new heaven and a new earth (65:17-19) that the author of the great New Testament apocalypse, when he wished to speak of the ultimate triumph of God over all the powers of evil, could do no better than borrow the same language (Rev. 21:1-4).

3. This is a glorious vision and a glorious hope. But is it more than the transfiguration of Israel's dream of national glory? It might seem not, but for one thing. The prophet drew the logical conclusion of monotheistic

---

[28] I am aware that many of the passages cited in this connection are widely denied to Second Isaiah, but question if the evidence warrants such a course. I am not certain that chs. 34–35 are the integral parts of the prophecy that Torrey (*op. cit.*, pp. 122-26, 279-301) would make them, but I agree with Torrey's interpretation of them. They fit well into the thought of the prophet, and there are strong stylistic links as well (cf. R.B.Y. Scott, *American Journal of Semitic Languages*, 52 [1935-36], 178-91; A. T. Olmstead, *idem*, 53 [1936-37], 251-53; Marvin Pope, *Journal of Biblical Literature*, LXXI [1952], 235-43).

faith and interpreted the whole hope of the Kingdom of God in the light of it: if there is but one God, if this God rules all men and all history, if the judgment of God is upon all people—then there is but one God for all people. The domain of God is to be world wide. Let the heathen nations examine the fallacy of idolatry and turn to the one God who can save:

> Assemble yourselves and come,
>> draw near together, you that are escaped of the nations!
> They know nothing who carry the wood of their graven image,
> And pray to a god that can bring no deliverance.
> Announce (the trial)! Produce (your idols)!
>> Yes, let them consult together.
> Who has announced this from the beginning?
>> from of old declared it?
> Was it not I, Yahweh?
>> and there is no other God beside me,
> A God who is righteous and who rescues,
>> there is none beside me!
>
> Turn unto me and be saved,
>> all you ends of the earth!
> For I am God, and there is no other.
> By myself I do swear,
> Truth has gone forth from my mouth
>> a word and it shall not return,
> That "to me every knee shall bow,
>> and every tongue shall swear."
>
> (45:20-23)

With that the last implications of monotheism are drawn. Israel's faith has burst its banks like a river in flood and has become fitted to be the vehicle of world religion. It is not, of course, to be imagined that Second Isaiah either invented this world-wide reach or had a monopoly on it. On the contrary, this is a principle latent in monotheism itself. It had been hinted at in the ancient epic of the Patriarchs (Gen. 12:1-3; 18: 18), plainly expressed by Amos (Amos 9:7) and explicitly announced by the author of Kings (I Kings 8:41-43). Yet it was far from the popular notion. The people were all too prone to identify God's Kingdom with themselves, and to imagine that the foreign nations—as both their foes and God's—existed for the purposes of judgment only. This conceit was well illustrated in the ancient popular hope for the Day of Yahweh when, it was hoped, God would intervene in history to establish Israel and punish her foes. Amos, it will be recalled, combated that delusion (Amos 5:18-20), declaring that the Day of Yahweh was also a day of judgment on sinful Israel. Here, however, a still further step is taken. While the symbolism and the idea of the ancient notion are retained, the concept is both robbed of its national character and further broadened. God's Kingdom, far from being identified with the visible nation Israel, includes only those in Israel who obey him as his servants (65:13-15), while at the same time it reaches out to include those from all nations who acknowledge him and turn to him.

God intends to rule over the whole earth, and foreigners are invited to accept that rule (45:22-23; 49:6). And although Jews do not lose their place of pre-eminence, the worship of foreigners will be equally acceptable:

> And I will bring them to my holy mountain,
>> make them to rejoice in my house of prayer;
> Their burnt offerings and their sacrifices
>> shall ascend[29] with acceptance upon my altar.

> For my house a house of prayer
>> shall be called, for all peoples.
> Saith the Lord Yahweh,
>> he who gathers the dispersed of Israel,
> Yet others will I gather to him
>> to his that are (already) gathered.
>
> (56:7-8)

Not only will God receive the oblations of foreigners and their prayers, some of them will even be taken to serve as priests and Levites (66:18-21).[30] Here is, indeed, a widehearted theology. Nothing like it will be

[29] The verb, which is lacking in the Masoretic Hebrew, is supplied from the Dead Sea Scroll (cf. Burrows, op. cit., Pl. XLVI). Torrey (op. cit., p. 429) had already made the conjecture.

[30] The language leaves doubt whether Jews or foreigners are intended, but this interpretation is preferred by Torrey (op. cit., p. 471), J. Skinner (Isaiah; The Cambridge Bible [Cambridge: The University Press, 1922], II, 254), and others. If reference is only to Jews there would seem to be no point in saying it. Many Jews in other lands were already priests and Levites by birth. The idea, though startling, is quite in line with the prophet's theology.

145

heard until Another will declare (Matt. 8:11), "I tell you, many will come from east and west and sit at table with Abraham, Isaac, and Jacob in the kingdom of heaven." The true Israel of God is not racially determined, but includes those of any race who obey him. The prophet has stated what the New Testament will reaffirm.

III

The Kingdom of God, then, moves on to its victory. That victory is sure, because God controls history; and it is his purpose at the end of history's process to establish his reign over all the world. Nor is there long to wait. Events march on to their conclusion; the great turning point is not far; the glorious "new thing" will shortly come to pass. It is in the light of this lively expectation of the imminent victory that we may understand the abounding joy with which the prophecy is suffused.

This joyful and victorious path Israel is called to tread. But her victory is to be a queer one, so queer that it would seem not to offer the least excuse for joy. Clearly it is not to be a victory that is cheaply bought, nor one that is to be conferred effortlessly on a favored, spectator people. Second Isaiah knew well, as every prophet knew, that the call to be an elect people is a call to destiny and demands a duty in return. So it was that, in the light of this triumphant theology which filled all history with meaning, he summoned Israel anew to her destiny as the servant of God.

1. But what is this destiny, and what sort of victory will it bring? As the world would understand such things, no victory at all! On the contrary, it is a destiny of humiliation, suffering, defeat—and yet nevertheless of victory. There steps before us the strangest figure, a figure almost without ancestry or progeny in Israel, a figure so laden with offense that neither Israel nor we know what to do with him: the Suffering Servant of Yahweh. It is perhaps fair to say that thus far, for all the nobility of his concepts, the prophet has advanced nothing essentially new. The tallest possible edifice of Hebrew theology is his, but others had laid the foundations. But the Suffering Servant is something totally unique. And it is in terms of that Servant that the prophet sets forth both the destiny and the victory of the people of God, and the means by which God will establish his Kingdom.

The figure of the Servant appears in many places throughout the prophecy, but we see him with especial clarity in the so-called "Servant poems." [31] The Servant announces that he has been elected of old for a purpose and kept in reserve till the fullness of time (49:1-2). Clearly it is Israel speaking (49:3), the instrument of God's glory in the world. And just at that moment when it seems to him that all his labor has been in vain (49:4), there is revealed to him the full sweep of his mission: not only to call Israel itself back to its destiny under God, but also to proclaim the true faith in the entire world:

> And now saith Yahweh,
>   he who formed me from the womb to be his servant,
> To turn Jacob back to him,
>   and that Israel might be gathered to him,
> (For I am honorable in the eyes of Yahweh,
>   and my God hath become my strength)
> Yes, he saith:
> "It is too light a thing for you to be my servant
>   to raise up the tribes of Jacob
>   and to restore the residue of Israel;
> I will make you a light to the nations,
>   that my salvation may be to the end of the earth."
> (49:5-6)

Once more in 42:1-7 we see the Servant going about his world mission, bringing light and liberty to the Gentiles (vss. 6-7). Endowed with God's own spirit (vs. 1) and supported by God, it is certain that he will be successful. But his progress is not one of conquest and glory, but of quiet labor and infinite patience (vss. 2-3). Yet in spite of discouragement he will not give up till the victory is won (vs. 4). He will proclaim the good tidings of God's redemption (61:1-3), interceding meanwhile with God day and night for the victory of his purpose (62:1, 6-7). It is certain that his mission will bring him suffering, but, schooled as a willing pupil in God's school, he will accept it (50:4-5). We then see him, as a Figure out of Passion Week, beaten, tormented, spit upon (50:6)—yet enduring patiently, confident that God will vindicate him (50:7-9).

But in 52:13–53:12 the very ultimate is said of the Servant. It is true

---

[31] First isolated by B. Duhm (*Das Buch Jesaja: Handkommentar zum Alten Testament* [4th ed.; Göttingen: Vandenhoeck and Rupprecht, 1922]), the limits of the poems (42:1-4 [5-7]; 49:1-6; 50:4-9; 52:13–53:12) and their relation to the rest of the prophecy have been much debated. It seems certain to me that they are an integral part of the prophet's thought. The Servant is equally clearly seen elsewhere: e.g., 61:1-3.

that what is said here grows very logically out of what is said elsewhere. Yet it is quite unique. If we had not read it here, we should have had no right to infer that the prophet ever entertained such a notion. Here we read of the suffering and the victory; here we are given finally to understand what the Servant is to be. It is utterly unheard of—so much so that onlookers (53:1; cf. 52:15) cry out: "Who could have believed what we have heard?" Here is an unlovely figure, scorned of men and seemingly cursed of God (53:2-4). It would seem incredible that in this unlikely quarter, in this "root out of dry ground" (vs. 2), there should be manifested the very redemptive power of God (vs. 1). He endures brutal persecution (vss. 4-6), so brutal that belatedly it dawns upon men that no sin he could possibly have committed could account for it. They understand that he is suffering vicariously for others; he is bearing their sins. Finally we see him led off like a lamb to the butcher, done foully to death, yet making no complaint (vss. 7-9). It is clear that he has suffered innocently, indeed that he has made of his very life a sin offering for the misdeeds of others (vs. 10). It is utter humiliation and defeat. But just when the Servant has laid himself down to the death, God announces the victory. The Servant will be highly exalted (vs. 12); he will be satisfied to know that his sacrifice has borne fruit (vs. 11); he will be permitted to see his "offspring" (vs. 10)—the numerous progeny he has begotten into the Kingdom. The victory of the Servant lies beyond suffering. Indeed the discharge of his mission is impossible without suffering, for suffering is the means by which that mission is to be accomplished.

2. Now this is a concept quite without parallel either in the Old Testament or in the thought patterns of the ancient Orient, so much so that it cannot be explained externally as a logical development of them. This is not to say, of course, that it was without antecedents. Indeed there were not a few concepts common to Israel and her neighbors which may have prepared the way for it.[32] One thinks especially of the sacrificial

---

[32] Discussion of the subject has been voluminous. Recent treatments of note include: J. P. Hyatt, "The Sources of the Suffering Servant Idea" (*Journal of Near Eastern Studies,* III-2 [1944], 79-86); A. Bentzen, *Messias-Moses redivivus-Menschensohn* (Zürich: Zwingli-Verlag, 1948), pp. 42-71; I. Engnell, "The Ebed Yahweh Songs and the Suffering Messiah in Deutero-Isaiah" (*Bulletin of the John Rylands Library,* 31-1 [1948]); A. R. Johnson, "The Role of the King in the Jerusalem Cultus" (*The Labyrinth,* S. H. Hooke, ed. [London: S. P. C. K., 1935], pp. 73-111). For an excellent summary with full bibliography, see H. H. Rowley, *The Servant of the Lord and Other Essays* (London: Lutterworth Press, 1952), pp. 3-57.

system, which, complex and even primitive as were many of the ideas behind it, and liable as it was to the crassest of externalism, was still a constant reminder to the people of the enormity of sin. Sin demands atonement; sin merits death. And were not God gracious enough to accept the blood of an innocent animal, the life of the sinner would be forfeit.[33] One thinks, too, of that strong feeling for the corporate nature of society, so prevalent in the ancient world. As the sin of the individual was held to bring sin and a curse upon the group (e.g., Josh. 7), so might the righteousness of individuals be expected to procure justification for the group (e.g., Gen. 18:22-33).[34] Perhaps, too, we should think in this connection of the role played by the Oriental king as the cultic representative of his people, even to the extent of ritually assuming their sins. And no doubt there were many other things as well, which can be easier suspected than proved. Above all we may be certain that there had been much deep reflection on the part of Israelites upon the meaning of the national suffering and the national destiny, as well as upon the sufferings of righteous individuals. For this was a question that demanded to be answered.

Yet nowhere does one have a more inescapable feeling that the whole is more than equal to the sum of its parts. Not all these ideas together, nor all the adaptability of the Hebrew faith, nor yet the sensitive insight of the prophet himself, logically lead here. We cannot but conclude that the prophet was given, by the inspiration of God, to gaze into the very mystery of the Godhead. It befits one to have his shoes from off his feet, with the recognition that he stands at one of those places where logical analysis does not suffice, where one is brought into the presence of the Mystery. Here we learn that it is God's purpose to rule a world-wide Kingdom, which men of all nations are invited to join. But the victory of that Kingdom, sure as God is sure, will be procured not by force or spectacular power, but by the sacrificial labor of God's Servant. Here we learn of man's resistance to the Kingdom, a resistance so bitter

[33] This is, of course, not to say that sacrifice in the ancient world can be reduced to this, or to any single, motivation. But, in its many aspects, sacrifice served to restore or maintain that "peace" with God without which neither individual nor group could live. It was, therefore, a constant reminder of the gravity of separation from God, of sin. For an excellent discussion cf. Pedersen, op. cit., III-IV, 299-375.

[34] Numerous other examples could be given: e.g., Israel suffers a famine because of the sin of Saul (II Sam. 21:1-9); Israel suffers a plague because David took a census (II Sam. 24); Moses offers his life as a propitiation for the sin of the people (Exod. 32:32). The same ideas underlie Jer. 15:1-4; Ezek. 14:12-20.

149

that it will cost the blood of the Servant. But here we see a God who provides as the instrument of man's redemption no ritual atonement or external law, but the suffering of that same Servant. God proposes to win his Kingdom through the vicarious sacrifice of his Servant. Here the Old Testament faith leaps quite beyond itself and walks arm in arm with the New.

3. But who is the Servant? Or, rather, what does he represent? That is far the most important question. And no problem of Old Testament exegesis is more difficult.[35] The church has, of course, always seen in the Servant, particularly in ch. 53, a prophecy of Christ. That this is in a real sense true cannot be doubted; for Christ did, as we shall see, fulfill the pattern of the Servant. Yet it is hardly so simple as a mere prediction of the coming Redeemer. The figure of the Servant is a very fluid one; it seems to refer now to one thing, now to another; and any attempt to interpret it too rigidly will do violence to the evidence and almost certainly distort what the prophet wished to say.

The figure of the Servant oscillates between the individual and the group. In many places throughout the book the Servant is merely Israel (e.g., 41:8; 43:10; 44:21; 45:4), so much so that the prophet can call the Servant blind and deaf (42:19)—because that is exactly what Israel has been. In other places, although the Servant is still identified with Israel (e.g., 49:3), it is clear that he is something other than the visible people, because his first duty (49:5) is to lead Israel itself back to its destiny under God. Here it is plain that the Servant is not Israel itself but the righteous "Remnant" in Israel (e.g., 44:1; 51:1, 7), the true Israel which is obedient to God's calling and is a witness to his power in the world (49:1-6, 8-13; 42:1-7). But at all times the Servant is described in individual terms. And it is clear that sometimes this figure overshoots all that Israel, all that the true Israel, all that any individual in Israel ever was, and becomes a description of an ideal figure. He is the coming Redeemer of the true Israel who in his suffering makes the fulfillment of Israel's task possible; he is the central actor in the "new thing" that is about to take place; he is, we might say, the "new Moses"

[35] Merely to list relevant literature would take pages. The standard work is now C. R. North, *The Suffering Servant in Deutero-Isaiah* (Oxford: Oxford University Press, 1948), which is an extremely thorough and compendious review of virtually everything that has been said on the subject up to the date of its publication. For the reader who wishes a briefer but comprehensive discussion, the work of H. H. Rowley cited in note 32 is to be recommended.

in the new Exodus now shortly to begin. The Servant? He is Israel; he is the true and loyal Israel; he is the great Servant who will be leader of the servant people—all in one! [36]

But here is the most important point: however the Servant is pictured, even when conceived as the coming Redeemer, the Servant mission is always laid before Israel as her calling and destiny. It is not enough to describe the Servant; the call goes out: "Who among you fears the Lord and obeys the voice of his servant . . .?" (50:10.) Israel is to be the people of the Servant; only so will she be the people of God. As the Servant, prophetlike, proclaims the righteousness of God to the world, so must Israel; as the Servant, priestlike, mediates the salvation of God to men through his suffering, so must Israel. As the Servant gains a victory and a Kingdom through his sacrifice, so must Israel know no other royal path. Israel is to follow the Servant, take up the cross of the Servant, share in the Servant's redemptive mission. The Servant can no more be separated from Israel than Christ can from his Church, to which he said: "If any man would come after me, let him deny himself and take up his cross" (Mark 8:34). Israel is therewith forbidden ever to go back to the old lines. She is to take the road of missionary suffering in the footsteps of the Servant—for this alone is the pathway of the Kingdom.

4. Here at last is a word deep enough to reach down to the depths of the national humiliation and to speak to it. Here is a word, vast as the world was vast, capable of giving a people lost and astray destiny and direction. It is certainly a far deeper interpretation of suffering than any that had ever been heard before. Men have always wanted an explanation of tragedy, and those beaten Jews of that day must have needed it desperately. Prevailing Jewish belief would have tended to explain suffering as the punishment for sin (cf. 53:4b), as Job's comforters did. The prophets had explained the national calamity in precisely those terms, and Second Isaiah had seconded the explanation (cf. 42: 24-25). But it was obvious even then that this could not be a completely

---

[36] That the Servant is a fluid concept was persuasively asserted long ago by Franz Delitzsch (*Biblical Commentary on the Prophecies of Isaiah*, English translation by James Martin [Edinburgh: T. & T. Clark, 1881], II, 174, etc.) and has been held since by an impressive array of scholars with many variations in detail: recently Torrey (*op. cit.*, pp. 135-46); North (*op. cit.*, pp. 207-19); Rowley (*op. cit.*); Bentzen (*op. cit.*, pp. 42-67); etc. Although other explanations have been given, the evidence does not seem to admit of any other intepretation.

satisfactory answer. Deserts and awards did not always balance by any means, as Habakkuk saw on a national scale and Job on a personal one. It was easy for the Jew to feel that his people, sinful though they may have been, had been punished out of all proportion to their deserts. Israel had "received from the Lord's hand double for all her sins" (40:2). How is the overplus to be explained?

Now Israel's faith had, in fact, already reached far beyond an equation of suffering and sin, although small and dogmatic minds which liked neat explanations for everything clung to the equation stubbornly enough. It was plain that there was a suffering which came not from having sinned, but precisely from having done the will of God. The prophets had been living illustrations that to obey and to declare the Word of God costs exactly suffering. Jeremiah was a prime and recent example of the cost of choosing the Kingdom of God above the Kingdom of Judah. He became like the Servant, to use his own words, "a tame lamb led to the slaughter" (Jer. 11:19; cf. Isa. 53:7). Understanding men in Israel certainly knew this. But here is something far higher. For suffering is not merely the consequence of the Servant's task—it is the *organ* of it. His redemptive work and his world-wide victory will not only cost suffering as every battle costs casualties; it cannot be accomplished at all except by means of suffering. The victory of the Kingdom of God is achieved through the vicarious sacrifice of the Servant.

A more powerful summons to the people Israel could hardly be imagined. It was no less than an entire reinterpretation of their destiny as the people of God. It was a message of comfort, indeed, but not comfort as we are prone to understand that term. For here is no soothing syrup, no pink pills to be taken against fear, no technique for dealing with that frustrated feeling, no argumentation or answers to querulous questions. Here is a summons to stand again as the people of God and to take up a mighty task. It is the sort of summons that makes men into a people, for it calls them to the service of something greater than themselves.

The prophet addresses Israel as the people of the Servant. You have always, said he, thought yourselves a people chosen of God for a purpose, and so you were. But you forgot that destiny and were grievously punished, so grievously that you could not understand it and doubted all that you had believed in. Now, lift up your hearts! All is not ended! Before you is a new start and a greater destiny. God is calling forth for himself a true people, the people of the Servant. He is calling you to be that people and to serve his purpose. You are to be the vessels of his redemption, to bring Israel back to itself and to proclaim his salvation in the entire world. To be sure, you will find in this destiny no exemption from suffering, but precisely a summons to it. Yet suffering will be transfigured: no longer will it be to you brute agony without meaning, but the very instrument of redemption. In it you will enter into the very character of God's Servant and share in his redemptive purpose. Through your agony your original destiny in Abraham to be a blessing to all mankind is before you. And the victory is sure, for God is sure.

Clearly no profounder answer to suffering could be given than that. Suffering is not explained; it is transcended in destiny, as the people of the Kingdom of God.

IV

But we must close with an anticlimax. There will be no apologies for this; for the anticlimax is not of our making, but is written in history. The Servant had few progeny. The light of the Servant was, we may suppose, too blindingly bright for human eyes, and men could not face it. To be sure, the great missionary message of the prophet was not lost. It finds its echoes in later writings (notably in the book of Jonah), and Judaism certainly did make proselytes. But Judaism never properly became a missionary religion. On the contrary, it tended to draw ever more tightly into itself. Nor did the Servant ever catch the popular fancy. True, the figure of the Servant was related to the sufferings of Israel; so much so that in later literature, notably in some of the psalms, the "poor and needy" have become virtually a synonym for the true people of God (we shall hear more of "the meek" who shall "inherit the earth"; Matt. 5:5). But Judaism could not see the Servant as Messiah. While there are a few hints of a lowly and suffering Messiah in later literature (e.g., Zech. 9:9; 12:10), they are very few. The Jews did not want a suffering Messiah. They, like ourselves, desired other things.

So the Servant went underground, as it were, and there lay dormant like seed under frozen soil. "In the fulness of time" there would come One who would say, "Today this scripture has been fulfilled in your hearing" (Luke 4:21; cf. Isa. 61:1-2); who in his sacrificial labor, suffering, and death, quite literally "took upon him the form of a Servant"

153

(Phil. 2:7 K.J.V.). And when this same Jesus said to his disciples, "Go ye into all the world," he did no more and no less than lay upon them the Servant destiny.

And that, indeed, gives us to think. For as members of the Church of Christ our calling is that Servant calling. How seriously do we take it? Do we understand it at all? The world-wide mission of the Church we accept. We believe in one God; we declare that his Kingdom is over all the earth; we send missionaries to preach the gospel in far lands. Yet how little we have drawn the consequences of that great theology! Believing that one God is the God equally of all who call upon him, how often we seek to restrict the Kingdom along sectarian, or national, or racial lines—denying those beyond those lines comfortable fellowship with us in the Church of Christ! How often, by the small righteousness we offer, we withhold vast areas of life from the domain of God's Kingdom, and even declare that the Word of God has no business to speak there! Over the centuries the Servant is speaking to us, demanding that we get this straight over the gunsights: the Kingdom of God knows no man-made limitations. The church which seeks, as did old Israel, to restrict the Kingdom to itself—whatever its official theology—simply does not hold a pure monotheism, but is worshiping a small, strange god made in its own image.

As for the cross of the Servant, it is not strange to us. We own to a crucified Saviour. In that we stand with the mainstream of Christian faith from the beginning onward, and we do well to do so. We enthrone that crucified Saviour in stained glass, wood, and stone—and in doctrine. To that cross we look for salvation. But we want that cross not at all. Indeed we would have it the chief business of religion to keep crosses far away. We want a Christ who suffers that we may not have to, a Christ who lays himself down that our comfort may be undisturbed. The call to lose life that it may be found again, to take up the cross and follow, remains mysterious and offensive to us. To be sure, we labor to bring men to Christ, and we pray, "Thy kingdom come." But our labor we see as a labor of conquest and growth, successful programs and dollars. Can it be that we are seeking to build the Kingdom of the Servant—without following the Servant? If we do so, we will doubtless build a great church—but will it have anything to do with the Kingdom of God?

Let us, then, be reminded that the task of the Church is not and cannot be other than the Servant task. We pray as we have been taught to pray, "Thy kingdom come." And the answer we get is the answer of the Servant: "If any man would come after me, let him deny himself and take up his cross." We renew our prayer, "Thy kingdom come," because we have no other prayer to pray. But we renew it with the deepest confession of sin: have mercy upon us, for we are unprofitable servants!

CHAPTER SIX

Holy Commonwealth and
Apocalyptic Kingdom

WE HAVE SEEN HOW THE BABYLONIAN EXILE ENDED IN A BURST OF EAGER EXPECTATION THAT THE COMING OF CYRUS AND THE HOPED-FOR RELEASE from captivity would signal the dawn of a "new thing," beyond which would lie the victory and the Kingdom of God. We have also seen how the great prophet of that period, whom we know as Second Isaiah, transfigured that hope, laying before Israel the promise of a new beginning and challenging her with a great new mission. Israel is to be the Servant of God, by missionary labor and willing sacrifice to be the agent of establishing his rule to the ends of the earth; she is to bring people of all the nations of the earth into the Kingdom of God. It now becomes our task to inquire what became of that abounding hope as it met the drab realities of the Restoration.

I

It is clear that the Restoration did anything but fulfill the glowing promise which Second Isaiah had extended. Nor was Israel awakened to embrace the Servant destiny.

1. We may imagine, to be sure, that Cyrus' decree may have seemed to be the beginning of that fulfillment. Cyrus was one of the truly great men of ancient times, and one who stands in refreshing contrast indeed to the dreary succession of brutal conquerors who had preceded

him across the pages of history. His policy was one of surprising moderation. Quite the opposite of what an Assyrian would have done, he made no effort to destroy national life in an orgy of pillage, deportation, and ruthless repression. On the contrary, he habitually respected the customs and honored the gods of peoples subject to him. As far as he could do so, he trusted their native rulers. While the Persian government kept tight control of the whole structure and held it together by a complex administrative machinery, a very efficient army, and a well-developed system of communications, it was apparently the official policy that conquered peoples be allowed as far as possible to live their own lives within the framework of the empire.

We know that Cyrus exhibited this enlightened policy toward the Babylonians themselves.[1] Neither Babylon nor any of the other cities of the land was harmed. The Persian soldiers were issued the strictest orders against looting or otherwise terrorizing the population. Indeed Cyrus, by the amelioration of certain abuses, actively concerned himself for the physical well-being of the people. The worship of Marduk, high god of Babylon, continued without interruption, and Cyrus himself even made it a point publicly to honor him. Deported people from various places were resettled in their homes in peace, together with their gods. The gods of outlying cities, which Nabonidus had brought to Babylon, were restored to their sanctuaries with honor. Indeed, so temperate was Cyrus' behavior that many of the Babylonian people preferred him to the bitterly unpopular Nabonidus, and welcomed him as a liberator.

It is therefore with no surprise that we read that he exhibited the same policy toward the Jews. As we have already seen, he ordered the return of the sacred objects which Nebuchadnezzar had taken, encouraged as many as would do so to return to Jerusalem, and directed that the temple be rebuilt (Ezra 1:1-4, 7-11; 6:3-5). He even directed that the royal treasury assist in defraying the expenses (Ezra 6:4). What is more—and this, too, in line with his general policy—he placed the whole venture in charge of Sheshbazzar, son of Jehoiachin and scion of the ruling house of Judah, who was in turn succeeded by his nephew, Zerubbabel, also of the same royal house. While Cyrus' action toward

---

[1] Cyrus' conduct, and the enthusiasm with which he was received, is described both in his own cylinder and in the so-called "Verse Account of Nabonidus" (especially pt. vi). Cf. Pritchard, op. cit., pp. 314-16.

the Jews was no more than a part of his total policy for dealing with his subjects, we may well imagine that many Jews looked upon him as the God-sent deliverer (cf. Isa. 44:24-45:7). In any case the Restoration of the Jewish community in Jerusalem became a fact.

2. But the actual events of that Restoration were bitterly disappointing. In the first place, the response of the Jews in Babylon to Cyrus' invitation was anything but unanimous.[2] That is only what one would expect. Palestine was a faraway land which only the very oldest could remember. The journey thither was long and dangerous, and meant the cutting of all ties and an utter gamble on the future. By this time the Jews had sunk their roots in Babylon; there were their families and homes, there their livelihood. The summons to return was an invitation to hardship and danger which could hardly have been to many an inviting prospect. And for those who did go the first years were incredibly difficult. They had to make an entirely new start in a strange land, and a poor land at that. They were dogged by a succession of bad seasons and partial crop failures (Hag. 1:9-11; 2:15-19). They were surrounded by neighbors who bore them ill will, and it may be doubted if those few Jews who had continued to live in and around Jerusalem in every case welcomed the influx of immigrants. Besides this they lacked adequate military protection, with the result that public safety could not be secured.

In any case, it was over twenty years before the temple was built. It is true that work was begun and the foundations laid in the year after the first return in 538 B.C. (Ezra 3:8-10). But some eighteen years later, as we learn from the book of Haggai, little or nothing had been done. Reasons for this failure lie ready to hand and make it seem well-nigh excusable. The people were desperately poor, and the very struggle for existence no doubt ate up their meager resources. Nor may we doubt that the promised help from the government (Ezra 6:4) never materialized. On the contrary, their neighbors—particularly the governors and nobles of Samaria—who regarded Jerusalem as a part of their dis-

---

[2] The list in Ezra 2 and Neh. 7, which is thought to date from about a century after the edict of Cyrus, places the population of the Jewish community at just under fifty thousand. Albright (cf. Chap. V, note 5) estimates the population after the first return at hardly over twenty thousand. If this figure, which includes both returning exiles and Jews already settled in the land, is anything like correct, it is sufficient evidence that the response to the edict of Cyrus was not unanimous. Josephus (Antiquities, XI, I, 3) was certainly right when he said that many were "not willing to leave their possessions."

trict and who bitterly resented being frozen out of the plans there (e.g., Ezra 4:1-5), placed obstacle after obstacle in their path and repeatedly sought to get them into trouble with the Persian court. Only the most earnest exhortations of Haggai and Zechariah sufficed in the year 520 B.C. (Ezra 6:14; Hag. 1:1, 14-15; Zech. 1:1) to get the work going again. Not until four years later was the temple finished (Ezra. 6:15). And even so it was such a poor structure that many could not conceal their disappointment in it (Hag. 2:3). We read (Ezra 3:12) that when its foundations were first laid, the old men who remembered Solomon's temple could not control their emotions, but broke down and wept.

3. There can be no doubt that disappointment made itself keenly felt. It could hardly have been otherwise. Here is no Kingdom of God, no "mountain of the house of the Lord . . . established as the highest of the mountains" (Isa. 2:2) and defended by God from all its foes; here is the Persian *medinah* of Jerusalem, a tiny part of the most gargantuan empire yet. Indeed it did not, as we have said, have even minimal safety, but was subject to raids by enemy bands (e.g., Ezra 4:23) again and again. When some seventy-five years later Nehemiah secured a grant from Artaxerxes I to rebuild the walls of Jerusalem (Neh. 1:1–2:8), the situation was still so insecure (Neh. 4:15-20) that he was forced to keep one shift standing to arms while another did the work.

In any case, morale in the community was dangerously low. How little these were the purged and purified people of God, obedient to the service of his Kingdom in all things, we may see from a reading of Haggai, Malachi, and Nehemiah.[3] We see them concerned each with his own affairs, intent upon the struggle to get ahead, and willing meantime to let God's house lie in ruins (Hag. 1:2-4). We see them so busy about their employment, so reluctant to let a bargain slip, that they ignore the Sabbath completely (Neh. 13:15-18). We see them palming off sick and injured animals for the sacrifice (Mal. 1:6-14). We hear them whining that after all God is not just (Mal. 2:17), because there is no evidence to be seen that he rewards with material prosperity those that obey him any more than those that do not. There is therefore no

[3] The book of Haggai is dated precisely (1:1; 2:1, 10, 20) in the year 520. Malachi bears no date, but is best located, on the basis of internal evidence, approximately the middle of the fifth century B.C., perhaps a little before the arrival of Nehemiah. The book of Nehemiah is a part of the great history of the Chronicler (I and II Chronicles, Ezra, Nehemiah), but it contains as one of its sources the firsthand memoirs of Nehemiah (chs. 1–7; 12 [part]; 13), the authenticity of which has never beeen seriously questioned.

159

profit in serving him (Mal. 3:14). So always do men speak who would make God the servant of their small concerns, an instrument at their disposal, a sort of divine insurance against loss or damage. Such men will always be disappointed in God. For they do not know that God is not at all at their service but, quite the other way around, is summoning them to the service of his Kingdom.

But this bad morale pointed up a yet graver danger. There was a real possibility that if something were not done, the little community would be assimilated altogether into the Gentile world. It was, after all, a pitiful island in a sea of pagan people. Their total number a century after the first return can scarcely have been more than fifty thousand.[4] In the course of trade intercourse with neighboring peoples was naturally unavoidable (cf. Neh. 13:16), and intermarriage with foreigners became more and more frequent. Both Ezra and Nehemiah were greatly exercised over this fact (Neh. 13:23-31; Ezra 9–10), for it seemed to them that it foreshadowed the end of Israel as a people. Nehemiah in particular was alarmed (Neh. 13:23-25) when he discovered that children, the offspring of mixed marriages, could in many cases not even speak the ancestral Hebrew. As a matter of fact it was not many years until Hebrew did die out altogether as a spoken tongue, to be superseded by Aramaic, the lingua franca of the Persian Empire. Would Israel die out with its language? The danger was real, and it must not be forgotten. It is precisely this fear of assimilation that explains much of that narrow exclusiveness which makes the post-exilic community seem to us so unlovely.

4. What with the disappointment of hope, the crisis in morale, and the persistent fear of assimilation, it is scarcely surprising that the great ideal of the world mission of the Servant became obscured. To be sure, it was never quite lost. Judaism was and remained stoutly monotheistic; nor did it doubt that its God ruled all the earth. In the temple liturgy again and again, as if to enact and affirm the eschatological triumph, it announced that Yahweh is King (e.g., Pss. 47; 93; 96–99).[5] The strong feeling persisted, and was voiced by prophets of the Restoration, that he means to include foreigners also in his Kingdom (Zech. 2: 11; 8:23; Mal. 1:11). No sterner attack on smug exclusiveness, no more

---

[4] See note 2 above.

[5] The date and cultic situation of this type of psalm is a moot question; see the commentaries, e.g., W. O. E. Oesterley, *The Psalms* (London: S. P. C. K., 1939), I, 44-55. The most recent discussion is H. J. Kraus, *Die Königsherrschaft Gottes im Alten Testament* (Tübingen: J. C. B. Mohr, 1951).

ringing challenge to Israel to take up her world mission, could be imagined than the little book of Jonah.[6] Let Israel cease trying to run away from her destiny; let her take up her task of proclaiming the true God to the nations, however distasteful that may be, for God cares for foreigners also (Jonah 4:11). It must not be forgotten, either, that the law—which we are prone to think of as the very instrument of particularism—always made provision for the reception of proselytes, and demanded that these be treated equally with Jews (Lev. 24:22). Least of all must we forget that Judaism actually did make proselytes. Centuries later when Paul traveled up and down the Roman Empire, he found them in every town. In many cases they became the basis of his missionary success. Surely some Jews had heard the Servant calling and had obeyed!

Yet Judaism never really became a missionary religion. While there must have been many a devoted Jew who labored to win converts for his God, there is no evidence that Judaism as a religion made any concerted attempt to do so.[7] It would probably be accurate to say that while proselytes were accepted and welcomed, they were rarely sought. And in spite of the fact that such converts were received into the community of Israel, it is likely that there was a strong feeling against placing them on quite the same level as the Jew by blood. The truth is that there never seems to have been agreement within Judaism on the subject of proselytes. And while some wished to win them and labored to that end, Judaism as a whole tended to be driven into an ever more stringent particularism.

A contradiction, one might say, that a people with a God so universal and a sense of destiny so glorious should have withdrawn thus within themselves? Indeed it was a contradiction, and one that Judaism never succeeded in resolving. It is a contradiction, we may add, that lives yet. For it is possible for a church to subscribe to the widest of theologies and yet to sink back into a nauseous sort of self-congratulation, in the confidence that it is the one true and orthodox church whose

[6] Jonah was a historical figure, a prophet who lived in the eighth century B.C. (II Kings 14:25). The book of Jonah, however, was not written by him (nor does it claim to be), but is a story of which he is the central figure. On the basis of internal evidence it is to be dated well after the Exile, although the exact date cannot be determined.

[7] For an excellent, brief discussion of the attitude of Judaism toward the making of proselytes, with references to further bibliography, cf. H. H. Rowley, The Biblical Doctrine of Election (London: Lutterworth Press, 1950), pp. 87-94.

161

main business it is to guard itself from contamination. That this exclusivistic tendency had, in the case of Judaism, arisen precisely from such a fear of contamination, we have said. That this was a well-founded fear from the days of the Exile onward and ought, therefore, not to be sneered at, we have also said. Yet it inevitably led to an increasing contempt for foreigners and to a heightening of national pride which could hardly have been conducive of a zeal to undertake a world mission.[8] The reader of the New Testament knows of that prejudice against Gentiles which existed among the Jews. It was a prejudice which the infant church had difficulty in overcoming.

In such a climate there could be no general acceptance of the Servant mission. True, Israel was aware of that calling; indeed monotheistic faith logically demanded it. Yet, opposite to it was always the fear that to take up such a mission would cost Israel *itself*. The thought of the full participation of Gentiles in the Kingdom of God, and of a suffering mission to win them, could not therefore win widespread favor. The hope of the Kingdom of God had to find other channels of expression. This it did, particularly in attention to the keeping of the law and in that heightened expectation of the coming end which ultimately issued in the Apocalyptic. We cannot enter upon anything like an adequate discussion of these things, nor does the average person find them very sympathetic subjects. But it is very important that we get at least some idea of what they were.

II

After the Exile prophecy as we have known it hitherto gradually left off, and there began to emerge in its place that phenomenon known as the Apocalypse.[9] In it Israel's faith in the coming Kingdom of God found expression.

---

[8] Attitudes of individual Jews toward Gentiles, of course, varied. While some were bitterly hostile and contemptuous, others were not. See the article "Gentiles" in *The Jewish Encyclopedia* (1916), V, 615 ff., for a balanced discussion and references.

[9] It is quite out of the question to name here even the important works dealing with the apocalyptic literature, to say nothing of those dealing with the theology and literature of Judaism between the Testaments. It would, in any case, be out of place to befuddle the reader of this book with so formidable a list. The little book of H. H. Rowley, *The Relevance of Apocalyptic* (London: Lutterworth Press, 1944), which contains an excellent bibliography, is highly to be recommended as an introduction. The serious student will, of course, pay attention to the classical works of such scholars therein listed as E. Schürer, W. Bousset, G. F. Moore, R. H. Charles, E. Meyer, P. Volz, J. Bonsirven, M. J. Lagrange, and others.

1. Apocalypse means "revelation." Specifically it is a revelation couched in cryptic language of the great end events. It tells how God will intervene to wind up the affairs of this earth, to judge his foes and to set up his Kingdom. The Apocalypse, in the proper sense of that word, is rather a late development in the Old Testament period, and enjoyed its greatest popularity between the second century B.C. and the first century A.D. Only two books in full apocalyptic style are in the Bible, one in each Testament: the books of Daniel and of Revelation. But all who have any acquaintance with the noncanonical literature of the inter-Testament and New Testament periods are aware that many others were written which did not gain admittance to the Scriptures. That this type of literature should have been so popular at that time is no doubt an index of the lively faith, yet the repeated frustration and deep-seated pessimism regarding the current scene, which characterized the period.

But although the Apocalyptic knew its first great flowering in the second century B.C., it would be wrong to regard it as entirely a new thing. Still less ought we to look upon it as a vagary, in its spirit essentially hostile to the prophecy which it superseded. On the contrary, the Apocalyptic is in a real sense the outgrowth of prophecy. Old Testament prophecy, like the Old Testament faith itself, had always an eschatological orientation. That is to say, because it believed in a God who worked a purpose in history, it believed that events marched onward toward their appointed end—the triumph of the divine design. However little that faith might correspond to eschatology as we would define it, it was nevertheless eschatological: it looked for "last things," the effective terminus toward which history moves. It is with this termination of things, of course, that the Apocalypse is chiefly concerned.

But the prophets, for all their eschatological hope, focused upon the present—to attack present sins, to plead for present repentance, to announce in presently coming events the judgment of God. In the later prophets, however, one may detect a certain shift of focus from present to future, from historic event to cosmic event, with a heightened concentration upon the eschatological drama. It was when this lively hope clothed itself in new patterns, many of them borrowed from outside sources, that the Apocalypse was born. The Apocalypse is thus both the intensifying and the reshaping of Israel's historic faith in the triumph of God's rule. It is characterized by cryptic language, strange visions

163

peopled with awesome beasts, mystic numbers which only the initiated might understand. It provides, as it were with bizarre program notes, the libretto for the great end drama. And it declares that present events both foreshadow and reflect the mighty cosmic struggle between God and evil now reaching its pitch. But soon God's Kingdom comes!

Although the book of Daniel is the only full dress apocalypse in the Old Testament, there are many other writings there that exhibit similar tendencies and deserve to be called apocalyptic in character. Indeed that concern for the coming end which is at the heart of the Apocalyptic is characteristic of the whole postexilic period, and is evidenced in much of its literature. We have an early example in Ezek. 38–39,[10] a prophecy which some (quite wrongly!) believe will be fulfilled by present-day Soviet Russia. Here we see Gog from the land of Magog leading the heathen myriads from the mysterious north against the established people of God. But God intervenes to destroy Gog with a frightful slaughter. The Kingdom of God is then vindicated and established before all the world. It is the final victory of God over all the pagan, evil powers of this earth. The longing for God suddenly to step into the world to chastise his foes and to set up his Kingdom forms, as we have said, the very core of the Apocalyptic hope. But more than that it breathes through the entire eschatology of Judaism from the Exile onward, however diverse the forms that that eschatology might take.

Clearly this is in itself no new thing, but owes its origin to the ancient hope of the Day of Yahweh. This, as we have pointed out, was a very primitive thing in Israel's theology, entrenched as a dogma in the popular mind from the earliest times onward.[11] It fathered that fatuous confidence in the assured future of Israel which, like armor plate about the national conscience, blunted the prophet preaching of doom. What nonsense this talk of doom! God is our God and we his people, and in his great day he will intervene and set matters right for us! Amos, we recall (Amos 5:18-20), utterly rejected that conceit—and so did all the prophets—declaring that God's people, too, are under judgment. The conceit, however, did not down, but persisted unabashed until it fell

[10] On the interpretation of these chapters, cf. the commentaries; most recently G. A. Cooke, The Book of Ezekiel (International Critical Commentary [New York: Chas. Scribner's Sons, 1937]) II, 406-24. For a brief discussion, Rowley, Relevance of Apocalyptic, pp. 31-32.

[11] Cf. Chap. II, p. 60.

under the rubble of ruined Jerusalem. That ought, one would think, to have killed it. But it was an amazingly tough conceit, tough perhaps because it was an outgrowth—albeit an abortive one—of the mainstem of Israel's faith in the Lord of history. It survived the crash. And we recall how Second Isaiah took it up and gave it a new sense of immediacy, yet at the same time broadened it and moralized it beyond national lines.

After the Exile, it is to be feared, much of the old popular theology crept back, until eschatology became in this respect all too like what it had been at first. The eager expectation of that great day was retained and intensified by despair, but with little of the prophet's moral and widehearted spirit. The feeling was strong that Israel had purged itself, more than paid off its sin, in dire calamity. At the same time it was hard not to feel that the heathen powers were after all the true enemies of the people of God and the Kingdom of God. This does not say, of course, that the mission to extend that Kingdom to include Gentiles was ever quite lost. But in general there entered in a restless longing for the judgment of God upon his foes (i.e., the Gentile nations) and for the establishment of his Kingdom over his people (i.e., the Jews).

2. The hope of the imminently coming Kingdom flamed early in the Restoration community, only to meet cruel disappointment. If it seems unbelievable that it could have flamed at all, one has only to consider the mind-set of the day. Eschatological hope always tends to foreshorten its perspective, to feel that "the time is near." And the collapse of Babylon, Cyrus' generous policy and the hope of the "new thing" which was attached to it, had fostered the expectation that it would be soon. Add to that the tenacity of the dominant note in Old Testament prophetic eschatology: the Remnant. In one way or another all the prophets had pointed toward the pure Remnant: God's true people purged in fiery trial, over whom God would set up his Kingdom. Since Isaiah, and always dear to the Jewish mind, there had been linked to this hope the figure of the coming Messiah Prince of the line of David who would rule that Kingdom, as it were, as God's viceroy.

But now, here in the little Restoration community, it must have seemed that the conditions of the Remnant had been met. A purge of monstrous proportions had occurred, leaving but a cut-down stump of David's house and a pitifully few chastened people. The purge is past;

165

we are the Remnant! [12] And for our leader we have none other than Zerubbabel, grandson of Jehoiachin, prince of the line of David! And so Zerubbabel is addressed in messianic language. He is the "shoot from the stump of Jesse and the branch from his roots" announced by Isaiah (11:1): "Behold,the man whose name is the Branch,[13] and he shall sprout forth from his place, and he shall build the temple of Yahweh. Yes, it is he that shall build the temple of Yahweh, and it is he that shall bear the glory (i.e. assume the royal majesty), and shall sit and rule upon his throne" (Zech. 6:12b-13; cf. 3:8).[14]

In other words, it was believed that the Kingdom of God was about to be set up among the Remnant! Viewed soberly, to be sure, this might seem a fantastic hope indeed; for the power of Persia was unbroken, and certainly the little community in Jerusalem had not the power to break it. But that is scarcely the point. God has sent his "apocalyptic horsemen" riding through the earth, and he knows what they report: that the pagan world power has undisturbed peace (Zech. 1:7-11). He is displeased, and means to upset that peace and accomplish his purpose (Zech. 1:12-17). God is about to shake the nations (Hag. 2:6-7); it is the new Exodus time (Hag. 2:4-5), the great end drama is about to begin:

Speak to Zerubbabel governor of Judah saying, I am going to shake the heavens and the earth. And I will overturn the throne of kingdoms, and I will destroy the might of the kingdoms of the Gentiles. And I will overturn the chariot and its riders, and horses and their riders shall come down, each by the sword of his brother. In that day, saith Yahweh of Hosts, I will take you, O Zerubbabel ben Shealtiel my servant, saith Yahweh, and I will make

---

[12] K. Galling ("The 'Gola List' According to Ezra 2=Nehemiah 7," *Journal of Biblical Literature*, LXX [1951], 149-58) has argued from the form of the lists in Ezra 2 and Neh. 7 that the Restoration community incorporated in its organization a reminiscence of the ancient tribal amphictyony. This would be clear evidence that they regarded themselves as the "true Israel," i.e., the Remnant.

[13] The word used for "branch" (i.e., sprout, shoot) in Zech. 3:8; 6:12 is ṣemaḥ. This is not, to be sure, the same word as those used in Isa. 11:1 (ḥōṭer, nēṣer), but it can hardly be doubted that the idea is the same. The word ṣemaḥ is used by Zechariah as a technical term for the Messiah. The same word is used in Jer. 23:5. It also occurs in Isa. 4:2 but not, apparently, in the technical sense.

[14] It is true that Zerubbabel is not explicitly named as the "Branch," but there can be little doubt that it is he that is intended. Zerubbabel was the one who built the temple (Zech. 4:9; Hag. 1:12–2:9), and he was a prince of the royal house. It is probable that, as the commentators agree, the name of Zerubbabel originally stood in the text of Zech. 6:9-15 but was removed. The closing words of vs. 13 ("between them both") show that another leader stood beside Joshua the high priest, but none is named.

you as a signet ring, for I have chosen you, saith Yahweh of Hosts. (Hag. 2:21-23.)[15]

This hope was, of course, cruelly defeated. Zerubbabel was not to be the Messiah King. Whether he was himself carried away by the popular hope which clustered about him, we do not know. We have no evidence that he was, still less that he took part in active sedition against Persia. What became of Zerubbabel is a mystery. We hear no more of him after this time; it is as if he had dropped out of history through a trap door. His name even seems to have been expunged from the text of Zech. 6:9-15.[16] This has led some to speculate that Zerubbabel either plotted rebellion or that the claims made for him so disturbed the Persian authorities that they removed him. In any case, the messianic age did not dawn, the Kingdom of God did not come. And the power of Persia remained unshaken for two hundred years.

3. One would think that in the face of such frustration hope would have died. But it did not. Indeed the confidence in the ultimate divine victory was so integral to Israel's faith that it could not be given up without surrendering faith itself. Faith had, by its very nature, continually to cry for its fulfillment. Frustration and disappointment only intensified the yearning. So it was that as the present scene, as earth itself, continued to deny all hope, hope was pushed beyond earth and became a desperate longing for the catastrophic intervention of God.

This expected end event became in later writings virtually the exclusive center of interest—indeed, well-nigh an obsession. The climax is reached in the Apocalyptic, where the whole attention is shifted to the end drama and to the attempt to discern in the current scene signs of its beginning. In the noncanonical apocalypses this was to issue in no less than a fantastic, exotic, tropical jungle of the wildest speculation. No simple description of this end drama is possible, for Judaism never developed a systematic and consistent eschatological dogma, but presents us with the most widely varying pictures of it imaginable. Yet the feeling seems to have grown in intensity that the intervention of God would be preceded

---

[15] The hope expressed both by Haggai and Zechariah, that the powers of the earth would soon be overturned, must be read in the light of the chain reaction of rebellion which greeted Darius I upon his accession in 522. As the two prophets began their preaching in the year 520, it looked as if rebellion in Babylon might be successful. Cf. Albright, "The Biblical Period," p. 50.

[16] Cf. note 14 above.

by the most indescribable woes: the onslaught of all the forces of heathen-dom (e.g., Ezek. 38–39; Zech. 14:1-3; Joel 3:9-11), portents in the heavens and agony on earth (e.g., Joel 2:30-31; 3:15). But God would intervene victoriously to set up his Kingdom over those who are faithful (Joel 2:32; 3:14-16; Zech. 14).[17] Present darkness could not, therefore, quench hope —for one might possibly discern in it precisely the signs of the coming Kingdom. Perhaps this is the darkness that precedes the dawn!

This became, it need hardly be said, the pathology of Judaism. Forever scanning the times for signs of the coming end, drawing diagrams, as it were, of how that end should come, it moved in a dream world where the coming of the Kingdom was momentarily expected in clouds and glory. Or if it looked for the Davidic Messiah (although the genuine Apocalyptic gives little thought to the Messiah Prince, the hope con-tinued lively in Judaism), it would attach its hope to one false pretender after another. Its frenetic question would be: "Lord, will you at this time restore the kingdom to Israel?" (Acts 1:6.) In no case could it have room for a Servant whose Kingdom was "not of this world," and who came neither with a "Lo, here . . .!" nor a "Lo there!" (Luke 17:21.) Whatever else may be said of it, it would seem that when men seize upon the things of the end, fix their interest upon those things well-nigh to the exclusion of all else, there issues a disease of faith.

4. But our evaluation of this must not be one-sided.[18] To point out the pathology of it is all too easy. It is easy to laugh at airy speculations which, then and now, see signs of the end in every day's news, and find the personification of the arch-Foe first in this, then in that actor in present events. It is easier still to feel irritation at what can only be called the impudence of those who would draw diagrams, and even set dates, for the "times and the seasons" which Christ himself said that neither he nor the angels in heaven knew—but only God (Matt. 24:36; Mark 13:32; Acts 1:7). It could be pointed out, too, that there lurks here a rather fundamental pessimism regarding this earth which might, and on oc-

---

[17] These themes are developed to the fullest in later literature, notably the Pseude-pigrapha (e.g., I Enoch 37–71). The "woes of the Messiah" became a fixed belief (". . . learn this and take it to heart, how many woes will come at the turning point of the years"—Sibylline Oracles 3:562-63).

[18] For a much fuller appraisal of the values of the Apocalyptic than is possible here, cf. Rowley, *The Relevance of Apocalyptic*; also the little book of R. H. Charles, *Religious Developments between the Old and New Testaments* (Oxford University Press, 1914; 11th reprinting 1948).

casion has, cut the nerve of all effort toward its redemption. One could even say that there is something here which is not even very moral; it exhibits very little compassion, but rather seems actually to long for the destruction of millions of wicked if only a few righteous are saved.

Yet strange though this "apocalyptic mind" is to us, we must not forget that there lived in it a great faith which even those who sneer at it would do well to copy. For all its fundamental pessimism about the world, it was in the profoundest sense optimistic. At a time when the current scene yielded only despair, when the power of evil was unbroken beyond human power to break it, there lived here the faith that the victory of God was nonetheless sure: God holds the issues of history; he is a God *whose Kingdom comes.* Let those of us to whom the prayer "Thy kingdom come" has become a form to be rattled off without meaning, who find the Apocalyptic amusing, yet who tremble every time a Communist makes a speech—note it well. The Apocalyptic further insists that the world struggle is neither political nor economic, but essentially of the spirit and cosmic in scope. Behind all earthly striving it sees a continuing combat between good and evil, light and darkness, the Creator God and the destructive power of chaos, which summons men to take sides. There can be no neutrality. Whoever decides for the right, however humble he may be, has struck a blow for the Kingdom of God in a combat of decisive significance. In any case, there was in the Apocalyptic a faith that strengthened thousands of little men to an obedience unto the death, confident that their reward was with God (Dan. 12:1-4). Let all who scoff ask themselves if their more polite religion does as much.

There is further in the Apocalyptic a very sound instinct which we ignore at our peril, namely: the Kingdom of God is not man's creation, but God's. Perhaps the scorn of these eschatologists for what man can do was too total, and even naive—for God *does* use men.[19] But they bring us a needed reminder which we need desperately to hear: that we cannot simply take the Kingdom by the arm and "usher it in"; only God can do that. The Apocalyptic is, therefore, a rebuke to the *hybris* of man, forever seeking to produce a perfect world order by political maneuvering, social planning, and military preparation—without refer-

---

[19] An example of this attitude is to be seen in Dan. 11:34 where, as the commentators agree, the words "little help" are applied to the Maccabean uprising. However much a true apocalypticist might have been constrained to sympathize with, or even to assist, Judas and his brothers, he could never look to men for his salvation. What men can do is, at best, a "little help."

ence to God. It is a rebuke to the blasphemous *hybris* of the church of God, which will just "win the world for Christ" and bring in the Kingdom by preaching, conferences, and well-administered programs. The people of God are summoned to the side of God's Kingdom in the cosmic struggle; but they cannot produce that Kingdom in terms of their own activity. True, the apocalyptic expectation that few would be saved may well seem harsh. Nevertheless, tolerance and goodheartedness must not tempt us to blink the inexorable conclusion: the Kingdom of God comes only for those who will be his people and obey him. It can have no other citizens. Truly "the gate is narrow" (Matt. 7:14).

The Apocalypse was thus a legitimate outgrowth, albeit to us a strange one, of Israel's faith in the God who is Lord of history. In times of darkest despair, when the kingdoms of this earth exercised their tyrannical and unbroken rule, it affirmed and kept alive Israel's historic confidence in the triumphant Kingdom of God. It asked for a solution of man's dilemma in terms of the divine intervention. Like all the hope of Israel, it pointed to a solution beyond itself.

III

But Israel's faith issued in another and equally significant development: the Holy Commonwealth based upon the keeping of the law. To this we must now turn, for it too was an expression of Israel's feeling for the rule of God over his people.

In and after the Exile a succession of godly, yet very practical men took hold of Israel's faith and made it into Judaism. Their ideal was a community whose major business would be to become the holy people of God by the scrupulous observance of the law. If the Apocalyptic hoped for a Kingdom that only God could produce, it might be said that the Holy Commonwealth envisioned a Kingdom which man's righteousness could, if not produce, at least precipitate.

1. That postexilic Judaism should have become a law community is no accident, still less an abortion, but a very logical development. To obey the law of God had been a matter of central importance in Israel since Moses. We have seen that the two prime obligations which the covenant laid on the people were to worship God and God alone, and faithfully to obey the covenant law within the covenant community. We have also seen that the ethical attack of the prophets was aimed precisely at the failure of the people to realize that the covenant bond demanded

such obedience. The prophets insisted that the covenant brotherhood be established in righteous behavior, and they pronounced the doom because it was not.

The Exile inevitably brought a heightening of interest in this feature of religion. It is quite understandable that it should have. If the prophets, particularly Jeremiah and Ezekiel, as well as the Deuteronomic law and histories, had explained the national calamity as the result of the failure to take the demands of the covenant seriously—a failure, in short, to obey the law of God—it would be natural if, once the blow had fallen and the prophet Word had been vindicated, sincere and thoughtful men should take the lesson to heart. Ought we not at least learn the lesson and profit from it? Ought we not, then, from now on to keep the law? In addition to this there was the fact that, nation and temple having been destroyed, the law alone remained to mark a man a Jew. No longer is he a member of Israel who is a citizen of the Israelite nation—for it no longer exists; or who worships Yahweh on Mount Zion—for the temple lies in ruins. He is an Israelite who has signified his membership in the covenant by submitting to the rite of circumcision, and who keeps the law—especially that of the Sabbath (e.g., Isa. 56:2, 4, 6). In any case, during the Exile days scribes were busily at work collecting, codifying, studying the law, thereby laying out the lines along which Israel might actually show itself to be the Holy People of God.

So it was that in the Restoration community, side by side with that hunger and thirst for the catastrophic intervention of God to establish his Kingdom, there was a growing stress on keeping the law. Now we must realize that these two lines of development—one of which issued in the Apocalypse, the other in the law community—were in no essential hostile to each other. They did not represent opposing camps or factions within Judaism.[20] Indeed it would have been possible for an individual to have shared fully in both viewpoints. Both were expressions of the same hope. If the Apocalyptic longed for the establishment of the Kingdom by the direct activity of God, the law gave voice to the strong feeling that God would neither bless nor set up his Kingdom over a people which

[20] This is not to deny that many sects did arise in Judaism, some at least with strong eschatological leanings (e.g., the group from which came the Dead Sea Scrolls). Nor is it to deny that the Pharisees became increasingly chary of the vagaries of messianic expectation. But it would be artificial to divide Judaism into legalists and apocalypticists. The Pharisees, like all Jews, had their eschatological expectations, while the eschatological sects (like the one mentioned above) were greatly concerned about the law.

did not keep his law. We sense that this feeling is strong in the post-exilic prophets—particularly Haggai and Malachi—with their concern for temple, sacrifice, and tithing. Haggai seems to make the rebuilding of the temple virtually the precondition of the divine intervention (cf. Zech. 8:9-11). The final chapters of Ezekiel (40–48), which depict the *Civitas Dei* as a religious community centered about the purified temple and its cult, had already foreshadowed this ideal of a people holy unto God.

2. Overshadowing all others who had a part in shaping the Holy Commonwealth was Ezra the scribe. We cannot begin here the attempt to reconstruct the details of his career. One of the most vexed chronological problems of the Old Testament is involved. There is little agreement among scholars regarding the relationship of his work to that of his contemporary, Nehemiah, nor is it even agreed whether the King Artaxerxes in whose reign he labored (Ezra 7:1-5) was the first or second to bear that name.[21] Suffice it to say that Ezra was "a scribe skilled in the law" (Ezra 7:6) who, approximately a century after the establishment of the Restoration community, set out from Babylon for Jerusalem with the permission of the king. He had the "book of the law of Moses" under his arm, and reform in his heart (Ezra 7:10; Neh. 8:1).

His work, positively, was to saddle the Pentateuch Law [22] upon the community as the very charter of its existence. The dramatic story of

[21] The traditional view, that Ezra came to Jerusalem in the seventh year of Artaxerxes I (458 B.C.; Ezra 7:7-8), and Nehemiah in his twentieth year (445 B.C.; Neh. 2:1), can boast an impressive list of defenders. For a recent clear statement of it cf. J. Stafford Wright, *The Date of Ezra's Coming to Jerusalem* (London: Tyndale Press, 1947). It raises, however, not a few problems. An opposing view, first advanced by van Hoonacker, to the effect that Ezra arrived in the seventh year of Artaxerxes II (397 B.C.—van Hoonacker thought this was a second visit), while Nehemiah had come in the twentieth year of Artaxerxes I, has gained an equally wide following. For a recent able presentation, cf. H. H. Rowley, "The Chronological Order of Ezra and Nehemiah" (*Ignace Goldziher Memorial Volume* [Budapest: 1948], pp. 117-49; reprinted in *The Servant of the Lord and Other Essays* [London: Lutterworth Press, 1952], pp. 129-59). It must be said that while this view solves many of the problems, it raises others in its own right. A third view, similar to that advanced earlier by A. Bertholet and others, has found a recent champion in W. F. Albright ("The Biblical Period" p. 53 and note 133). In this view Ezra came to Jerusalem late in the reign of Artaxerxes I (ca. 428 B.C. if "seventh year" [Ezra 7:7] is an error for "thirty-seventh year"). I must confess that I have not been able to keep my own mind made up on the point.

[22] It is a question whether the law book introduced by Ezra was the entire Pentateuch (e.g., Albright, "The Biblical Period" p. 54) or only that portion known as the Priestly Code (e.g., H. H. Rowley, *The Growth of the Old Testament* [London: Hutchinson's University Library, 1950], pp. 34-35). The evidence does not allow a downright answer. In any case, the Pentateuch early became normative in the Jewish community.

Ezra's reform is given us in Neh. 8–10. From a wooden pulpit erected in the city gate for that purpose (8:4), Ezra read the book of the law to the people. The reading began at dawn and continued till midday (8:3). As Ezra read—apparently section by section—the Levites (8:7-8) explained it to the people so that they would understand. The reading was continued on the following day (8:13) before a select audience of leading citizens, after which there took place the celebration of the Feast of Tabernacles (8:16-18), with further reading from the law on each day. There then ensued a great public confession of sin (ch. 9) and a solemn covenant to keep the law (ch. 10). That Ezra's work was attended by a "revival" emotion is evident from another incident (Ezra 10) where the people, taxed with the matter of marriages with foreigners, stood in the court before the temple in a downpour of rain to hear Ezra (vss. 9, 13), until he took pity on them and sent them away. Let any who find Ezra and the Judaism he helped to create narrow, and who surely will be at church on Sunday if the weather is fine, note well!

The reform was also, as it virtually had to be, a separatist movement; it was marked by the repudiation of foreigners. Now it cannot be repeated too often that this xenophobia was really and primarily a fear of assimilation. This was a justified fear, and we would do well to reflect that had assimilation gone on unchecked, the likelihood is that the Jewish community would simply have vanished, and with it its precious heritage. Nehemiah, we have said (Neh. 13:23-24), was shocked to discover that the Hebrew language was being lost. In a passage of engaging candor (Neh. 13:25-28), he informs us that he flew into a fine temper and cursed, assaulted, and pulled the beards of certain offending parties who happened to be handy. When he cooled off he forbade further mixed marriages. Ezra was even more drastic—if apparently calmer. He not only forbade further such marriages but (Ezra 10:2-5) ordered the dissolution of those that already existed. The feeling in the community was one of "Jerusalem for the Jews." Zerubbabel had already repulsed the aid proffered by the neighboring Samaritans (Ezra 4:2-3), and Nehemiah's energetic policy only increased the enmity.[23] It is correct to see the be-

[23] It must not be forgotten that the adversaries of Nehemiah—Sanballat and Tobiah—were themselves worshipers of Yahweh, although we may assume that their Yahwism was of a highly syncretistic sort. That Tobiah was a Yahwist is clear from his name and from that of his son, Johanan, and others of his family (Neh. 6:17-19), as well as from the fact that his descendants are known to have been Jews centuries later. Cf. Albright, "The Biblical Period," p. 52 and note 129. The Samaritans, of course, remain a people of the law until today.

173

ginnings of that unbridgeable schism between Jew and Samaritan just here.

Ezra was a towering figure. While the legends that came to cluster about him vastly exaggerate his work,[24] it is not incorrect to regard him as the father of Judaism. He did not, of course, invent the law, but the full impact of the law on the life of the Jewish people dates from the movement in which he played a leading part. Judaism from now on is to be a law community. He is a member of the true Israel who keeps the law. The great prophet demand that the covenant law of God be obeyed had issued in a Holy Commonwealth where the first order of business is to do just that in every detail.

3. It is very difficult for us to view this aspect of Judaism objectively. It is an attitude of mind wholly foreign to us; it does not excite our sympathy. Nor is there any denying that it was not altogether a healthy development. For one thing it clearly marked the end of that fairest flower of the Hebrew spirit—the prophetic movement. The law, indeed, took over the function of prophecy: that of stating the Word of God. Where the Word of God is plainly written for all to read, there is little need or place for a prophet voice to speak it. The law, too—although this was as far as possibly could be from the intention of the law itself, and from the intention of its noblest teachers—opened the way to an externalizing of religion with which the prophet spirit could have had little part. For if the entire will of God is stated in the form of plain commandments, religion will tend to consist mainly in the keeping of those commandments—and who shall tell the trivial from the important, the mechanical compliance from the dedicated spirit? There were still voices in the Restoration community to speak with the clear accents of the old prophecy (e.g., Isa. 58:1-12; 66:1-4; Zech. 7:1-14; 8:14-23); and there were always rabbis who sensed the danger of externalism and fought it; but the law community was not one in which prophecy could thrive. The time soon came when there arose no more prophets in Israel.

With the passing years the exaltation of the law went on apace. It was

[24] For example, the legend, apparently stemming from the apochryphal book of II Esdras (IV Esdras in the Latin Vulgate) and repeated by a number of the church fathers, to the effect that the law having been burned in the destruction of Jerusalem, Ezra was enabled by divine inspiration to recreate it. On the other hand, the Jewish tradition that Ezra was the Chronicler, long scouted by the majority of scholars, has found a defender in W. F. Albright ("The Date and Personality of the Chronicler," *Journal of Biblical Literature*, XL [1921], 104-24; at that time Albright placed Ezra ca. 397); cf. *idem*, "The Biblical Period," p. 54 and note 138.

held to have been ordained of God from all eternity (e.g., Jubilees 39:6; 49:8; *et passim*); it has fully stated his will in all particulars; every letter of it is eternal and not to be changed.[25] To go beyond the law could only be viewed as a heresy worthy of death. Judaism thus moved toward a strange and paradoxical position: it honored its dead prophets—indeed, it was Judaism that preserved the prophet writings and passed them down to posterity—but it would give scant hearing to living ones (Matt. 23:29-36), for the age of prophecy had passed.

The law, too, became the pathology of Judaism. Religion is summed up in the law; to be religious is to study the law, discuss it, teach it, keep it. And since every law needs definition so that a man will know how to act in a given situation, and since there is always the danger that, if this is not provided, the law will be broken accidentally, there was need for yet further rulings to give the needed clarification. These the rabbis supplied, building a "fence" around the law. In the course of the process rules so multiplied that life was hedged in literally by hundreds of them, and law was burdened with a mass of casuistry in which it was very difficult to maintain perspective. The spirit tended to sink beneath the letter. A law grown so massive could not, of course, be mastered by everyone—the ordinary man had neither the time nor the skill—but was given over to a class of scribes and teachers. These, because they possessed a knowledge, and hence a rectitude, which most men could not, were tempted to an overweening pride. The law was supreme. The peculiar notion was to emerge that even God allotted time for its study,[26] and it was felt that if Israel could only keep it perfectly for a single Sabbath, Messiah would come.[27] In this sickroom climate there could be no room for One who would declare: "Moses saith in the law . . . but I say unto you. . . ."

[25] This was certainly the position of Judaism by New Testament times. Cf. the comments on Matt. 5:18 in Strack-Billerbeck, *Kommentar zum Neuen Testament aus Talmud und Midrasch* (Munich: C. H. Beck; Vol. I: *Das Evangelium nach Matthaeus*, 1922). See also the article "Torah" in *The Jewish Encyclopedia* (1916), XII, 196-97, for discussion and references.

[26] Cf. in the Talmud, Rab Judah in 'Abodah Zarah, 3b. For further discussion and references see the article in *The Jewish Encyclopedia* mentioned in note 25.

[27] We have, to be sure, express illustration of such a sentiment only in relatively late times: in the Talmud cf. Rabbi Johanan in *Shabbath*, 118b, who declares that the perfect keeping of two Sabbaths would cause immediate redemption to come. To gain an idea of the great importance laid by Judaism on the Sabbath, cf. the article "Sabbath" in the *Jewish Encyclopedia* (1916), X, 587 ff.

It takes no skill to criticize this pathology. Indeed the Christian has only to turn to his New Testament (e.g., Matt. 23) for a more scathing criticism than he could possibly give. It is the externalizing of religious faith; it is the works of the law by which no flesh is justified (Gal. 2:16; 3:11). Nor, unfortunately, is it a dead pathology even in the Christian church. For there are yet those to whom religious faith is largely a matter of rules, to whom the cardinal points of religion seem to be the abstention from certain habits and frivolous amusements considered to be sinful, the cultivation of certain pious practices, and regular attendance at church. And in these things they take great pride, for by these are the righteous known from the sinners.

4. Yet here again our evaluation must not be one-sided.[28] It is too easy and too cheap simply to make of scribe and Pharisee homiletical whipping boys, as the pulpit so often does. It must never be forgotten that the law housed and expressed a great ideal and attempted to make it actual. The law sought to create the true people of God over whom God could establish his rule. The end of the law was never rule keeping for the rule's own sake; it was God, and total obedience to God. Its stress on trivial and technical offenses, side by side with serious moral ones, did not aim to elevate the one to equality with the other, but to make it clear that any offense against God, however small, is serious (e.g., IV Macc. 5:20). Its pulling apart from the world was not an expression of mere snobbishness—though this was present—but of the realization that strict obedience could not mate with a toleration of all sorts of practices (e.g., Psalms of Solomon 17:27-28; Jubilees 22:16; Aristeas 128 ff.). It must not be forgotten that Judaism welcomed outsiders who were willing to shoulder the yoke of the law, and accorded them equality (Lev. 24:22; Ezek. 47:22). In the law there lived Israel's original ideal, to be "a kingdom of priests and a holy nation" (Exod. 19:6), fit subjects of the divine rule. In it, too, that search for a Remnant—a true Israel to which all the prophets had looked for the realization of Israel's hope—was further developed and individualized. A man is not one of the people of God just because he is a Jew by race; he is a true member of the people of God who has assumed the full burden of obedience to the law.

And it must be said that humanly speaking the law did no less than save Israel's faith alive. It was an armor about that faith to preserve it

---

[28] A complete appraisal is, of course, impossible here. The reader will find a brief but excellent evaluation in Rowley, *The Rediscovery of the Old Testament*, ch. vii.

from extinction.[29] Protected by it, the whole heritage of the prophets survived. Let us not forget that it was Judaism that preserved the writings of the prophets; without Judaism we should not have had them. It preserved the fruits of the prophet preaching as well. The law was stoutly monotheistic; it made no concession to paganism. It was highly ethical, even—at least in its noblest expression—to the level of the Golden Rule (Lev. 19:18). The law was the snow-covered, frozen ground which protected the seed till the fullness of time. It was an armor plate, rigid indeed; but we may well wonder if an armor less stout would have saved Israel from assimilation in the Gentile world, and her heritage from dissipation like so much water poured on the sand.

It is worth suggesting, also, that the law community has a lesson to teach us which we have not wanted to learn. Now we cannot as Christians ever go back to the law. Nor are we to measure righteousness in terms of things done or not done, as if righteousness could be achieved arithmetically by addition or subtraction. Yet these doctors of the law are, in one sense, an example to us which we ignore to our infinite hurt. Repelled by all legalism, we have come close to the point of apologizing for any duty religion seems to involve, nay, have offered a religion almost without the demand of duty at all. Can it be that in casting off all religious duty, we have ended up admitting no duty—save to ourselves? It is time that we heeded the lesson of the Holy Commonwealth: that religion, aside from all that it does for man, lays before him a duty and demands that he do it. Christianity *does* involve duty. And that duty is to obey God, not in general and as it is convenient, but in every detail and without exceptions. On this count, it is to be feared, scribe and Pharisee will enter the Kingdom of God ahead of us.

The Holy Commonwealth of Judaism was an expression of that dominant note in Old Testament theology: the rule of God over his people. Indeed Apocalypse and Law point to an inescapable paradox in the notion of the Kingdom of God. The former affirms that that Kingdom is beyond man's doing. The latter replies that it is nevertheless a Kingdom that demands everything of man; it expresses the deep conviction that God will rule only over an obedient and righteous people. It was the aim

---

[29] This was long ago given classical expression by J. Wellhausen in the closing paragraphs of his *Geschichte Israels I* (*Prolegomena zur Geschichte Israels* [Berlin: G. Reimer, 1878]). However much one may disagree with Wellhausen's total position, in this insight—as in many others—he was quite right.

of the Holy Commonwealth to make that true Israel, that Remnant, actual. The very righteousness which it struggled so manfully to produce was thus a finger pointing toward the coming Kingdom. But that Kingdom and that righteousness lay beyond the law community. The law had therefore to point to a solution beyond itself—a new righteousness.

IV

In any case, narrow and fanatical as the law community may seem to an unsympathetic observer, when put to its severest test, it showed that it had in it the stuff of survival. We might seriously ask ourselves if our infinitely pleasanter, politer, and nicer religion can do as much. For here and there the testing has already begun, and the question is at least relevant.

1. We must leap forward rapidly some three hundred years. From its beginning to its fall (539-332) the Jews remained subjects of Persia. We will not attempt to trace their fortunes during that period; much is obscure in any case.[30] The Persian Empire was a gigantic structure extending, at the height of its power, from the Aegean basin to the valley of the Indus, from Egypt far into the Trans-Caspian steppes of what is now Soviet Russia.[31] The Persians had early cast covetous eyes on the Grecian homeland, and had on more than one occasion sought to conquer that country. But at such places as Marathon, Thermopylae, and Salamis the plucky Greeks stood them off, and they could not. Late in the fourth century the shoe was placed suddenly on the other foot, and Persia had to face the meteoric rise of Alexander of Macedon. Everyone knows how Alexander hurdled the Hellespont in 334 B.C., and how in a series of brilliant victories—on the Granicus, at Issus, and at Arbela—his phalanxes tore the unwieldy armies of Darius III to pieces. In three or four years we see the young hero standing on the banks of the Indus weeping, so the legend has it, that there were no more worlds to conquer.

But the empire of Alexander the Great was the most ephemeral in all

[30] Until recently less was known of the Jews during the Persian period than at any other time in their history. Although the fifth century B.C. is now rapidly being illuminated by new discoveries, the fourth century remains almost a total blank. For details of world history during the period cf. A. T. Olmstead, *History of the Persian Empire* (Chicago: University of Chicago Press, 1948).

[31] It included at its greatest extent all of what is now Iran, Iraq, Syria, Lebanon, Israel, the Kingdom of Jordan, Egypt, Turkey, as well as parts of Greece and the Balkans, Soviet Russia, Afghanistan, and Pakistan.

178

of history. In 323, ten years after his great victory at Issus, Alexander was dead. His empire was ultimately divided among four of his generals. Of these only two concern us: Seleucus, who took over Mesopotamia and Syria; and Ptolemy, who made himself ruler of Egypt. The capital of the Seleucid kingdom came ultimately to be the newly founded city of Antioch, while that of Egypt was Alexandria—built by the Ptolemies and named, of course, after Alexander himself. As for Palestine—for history seems to have a way of changing everything, yet changing nothing—it remained as always a bone of contention between the power of the Euphrates and the power of the Nile.

The details of the struggle we may pass over.[32] After some vicissitudes Palestine passed into the hands of the Ptolemies late in the fourth century, and there remained for over a hundred years, although the Seleucids never gave up claim to it nor the effort to take it. The Jews for the most part seem to have remained more or less passive spectators. Although sentiment was no doubt divided between the two sides, and no doubt fluctuated considerably, the majority of Jews probably did not greatly care which side won. The Ptolemies seem for the most part to have allowed the Jews considerable freedom in managing their own affairs, indeed to have let them pretty much alone so long as they remained submissive subjects. The power of the Ptolemies, however, ended in Palestine with the accession of Antiochus III (the Great: 223-187) to the Seleucid throne. This king renewed claim to Palestine and—after a long seesaw war in which first one side, then the other, had the advantage—in 198 B.C. at Panium (Banias), on the Jordan headwaters, utterly crushed the armies of Ptolemy V and hurled them out of the land. The Jews thus passed under the rule of Antioch.

2. Now we should scarcely be interested in that struggle at all were there not cultural aspects involved far more important than the political: the dissemination of Hellenic culture all over the Orient, which was now going forward apace. The world was, as never before, one world.

---

[32] The standard history of the period has long been that of E. Schürer, *Geschichte des jüdischen Volkes im Zeitalter Jesu Christi*, 4 Vols. (3rd and 4th eds.; Leipzig: J. C. Hinrichs, 1901-11); English translation by Macpherson, Taylor and Christie, 5 Vols. (Edinburgh: T. & T. Clark, 1890; New York: Chas. Scribner's Sons, 1891). This may now be replaced by F. M. Abel, *Histoire de la Palestine: depuis la conquête d'Alexandre jusqu'a l'invasion arabe* (Paris: J. Gabalda, 1952, Vol. I). For a brief and up-to-date sketch in English R. H. Pfeiffer, *History of New Testament Times with an Introduction to the Apocrypha* (New York: Harper & Bros., 1949).

The ancient Oriental civilizations had been busy for centuries, in war after war, destroying themselves. Persia, a newcomer on the scene, had succeeded in creating out of the wreckage the largest political unit yet known. But this had in turn been grabbed into Alexander's empire, which embraced most of the known civilized world. Now Alexander was not merely a brilliant tactician and a very ambitious young man; he saw himself as a missionary of Greek culture. It was his aim to marry Greek and Oriental civilizations into a harmonious whole. And both because of his policy and because the political unity which he had created had destroyed older cultural boundaries and made free intercourse possible as never before, Hellenic culture—which had already made itself felt in the East— now began to penetrate at an amazing rate.[33] Furthermore, Alexander inaugurated the policy of settling his veterans and other Greeks in colonies scattered over his vast holdings, with the result that there were soon little islands of Hellenism everywhere.[34] And although the successor states lost the political unity which Alexander had created, all were ruled by Greeks, and all believed themselves to have the mission of extending the culture of Greece.

Judaism could not stand apart from the impact of that culture. This was, of course, doubly true of those Jews living in the lands bordering upon the Mediterranean—by now the numerical majority. These had long since lost their Hebrew and now spoke Greek as their native tongue. They had no access to their scriptures, which still existed only in Hebrew. It was to meet this need that, beginning in the mid–third century B.C. in Alexandria, a translation was made into the Greek (the so-called Septuagint).[35] Grave danger certainly existed that many of these Greek-speaking Jews would be lost to Judaism, and it is a powerful tribute to the tenacity of that faith that so many were not. In Palestine, too, there was the severest tension. On the one hand there were those that wanted no truck with Hellenism and heightened their zeal for the law to display their Jewishness. On the other hand there were those who, while

[33] On the impact of Greek culture on the Orient one should consult Albright, *From the Stone Age to Christianity*, ch. vi. Cf. also the works mentioned in the preceding note.

[34] The reader of the New Testament will recognize the Decapolis (Matt. 4:25; Mark 5:20; 7:31) as cities of this sort.

[35] The story of its translation as given in the noncanonical Letter of Aristeas is, of course, in good part fiction. For a convenient discussion of the Greek version, cf. H. M. Orlinsky, "The Septuagint—Its Use in Textual Criticism" (*The Biblical Archaeologist*, IX-2 [1946], 22-42; also Bleddyn J. Roberts, *The Old Testament Text and Versions* (Cardiff: University of Wales Press, 1951), pp. 101-87.

not at all wishing to abandon Judaism, went all out for Greek culture. Even the leaders of religion were swayed by the fashion. We hear of high priests with good Greek names (e.g., Jason, Menelaus). There was a general aping of all things Greek. On the streets of Jerusalem one might see people dressed like Greeks, and in its gymnasium Jewish youths participated in all sorts of Greek sports (I Macc. 1:15; II Macc. 4:10-15).

Matters came to a head when Antiochus IV (Epiphanes: 175-164) came to the throne in Antioch. This king was an able, devious, and complex character. A more fanatical Hellenizer there never was. Partly, no doubt, this arose out of the king's own zeal for the matter, but partly out of the need to consolidate his heterogeneous people against the grim threat of the growing power of Rome—which was by this time strong enough to intervene with a high hand in the internal affairs of the Near East. Many Jews, of course, would not have objected to Hellenization at all. But there was more. Like Alexander and others before him, Antiochus announced himself as *theos epiphanes*—the visible incarnation of Olympian Zeus—and he demanded worship. Here then was a man of the most dangerous type, a type which history has taught us not to take as a joke: he was god, and he was the missionary of *Kultur*. A pagan, perhaps, would not have minded even that, for Antiochus, in demanding worship for Zeus, by no means suppressed other cults but was tolerant of them—and what is one god more or less to a pagan? But for a monotheistic Jew, forbidden by over a thousand years of history to worship idols, to be asked to bow down to Zeus was simply unthinkable.

Antiochus' policy toward the Jews became severe.[36] At first covered with a velvet glove, as a result of stiffening resistance it turned into one of outright repression. Nor, it is sad to relate, were the Jews entirely free of blame for what happened to them. On the contrary, the party politics which characterized the period are an ugly page in Jewish history. Personal rivalries and skulduggery in the high-priestly office kept Jerusalem in a turmoil and undoubtedly helped to provoke Antiochus to his harsh action. The climax came when (168 B.C.) he marched his troops into Jerusalem, defiled the temple by offering swine's flesh on the altar, and virtually suspended the practice of Judaism (I Macc. 1:41-43). Copies of the law were ordered destroyed; the observance of the Sabbath was forbidden; the practice of circumcision, or even the possession of a copy

---

[36] See note 32 above for the details.

THE KINGDOM OF GOD

of the scriptures, was made a capital offense. And to crown it all an altar to Olympian Zeus was set up in the temple, and the people were commanded to worship before it. This is the "abomination of desolation" mentioned both in Daniel (9:27; 11:31; 12:11) and in I Maccabees (1:54).[37]

It was a full dress persecution, the first of many to which history has subjected the Jews. It was a question of making concessions to the point of consenting to profanation of temple and law, and outright idolatry —or die. Some, of course, being only human, gave in and denied their Jewishness (I Macc. 1:43). But many did not. They refused to sacrifice to Zeus, continued to circumcise their children, and died for it; they refused to violate the least dietary law (I Macc. 1:62-63). Some even kept the Sabbath so strictly that when war came, they preferred to be cut down by the enemy to defending themselves on that day (I Macc. 2:29-38). It became necessary to suspend that part of the law "for the duration" (I Macc. 2:39-41)! Notable among those who at first passively, but with heroic stubbornness, resisted the demands of Antiochus is a group known as the Hasidim (i.e., the pious, the loyal ones). It is probable that these are the ancestors of the Pharisees—a noble tradition!

3. The faith that gave the Jews courage to resist may be seen most clearly in the book of Daniel. This book raises a host of problems, both as regards its composition and its interpretation, which we cannot begin to discuss here. The stories of Daniel, it is true, are told of a figure who lived in the Babylonian exile, and it is likely that the stories in Aramaic (Dan. 2:4b–7:28 is in Aramaic, the remainder of the book in Hebrew) are quite a bit older than the rest of the book.[38] But it is generally agreed

[37] On the nature of Antiochus' cult cf. E. Bickermann, *Der Gott der Makkabäer* (Berlin: Schocken-Verlag, 1937). It was apparently an attempt to syncretize Judaism with Syro-Hellenic forms. Liberal Jewish leaders were implicated in it. The words used in Daniel (*hashshiqqûṣ meshômēm*, i.e., "the abomination making desolate") seem to be a pun on *ba'al hashshāmayim*, (Baal [i.e., Lord] of heaven). Cf. e.g., J. A. Montgomery, *Daniel* (International Critical Commentary [Edinburgh: T. & T. Clark, 1927]), p. 388.

[38] This, in one form or another, is the opinion of the majority of scholars, but important scholars—e.g., R. H. Charles (*A Critical and Exegetical Commentary on the Book of Daniel* [Oxford University Press, 1929]) and H. H. Rowley ("The Bi-lingual Problem of Daniel," *Zeitschrift für die alttestamentliche Wissenschaft* Neue Folge 9 [1932], 256-68); recently, "The Unity of the Book of Daniel" (*Hebrew Union College Annual*, XXIII [Cincinnati: 1950-51], pt. i, pp. 233-73; reprinted in *The Servant of the Lord*, pp. 237-68)—can be found who argue that the entire book is the product of an author of the Maccabean period.

among scholars that the book of Daniel in its present form belongs in the days of the persecution of Antiochus Epiphanes. Whatever the origin of the stories of Daniel, whatever the history of the book's composition, it would seem that an author of this period welded the whole together and shaped it into a message of encouragement for Jews in dire distress.

Daniel is the first, and one of the greatest, of the books in full apocalyptic style. But it is a sadly misunderstood book. It is not, as so many conceive it to be, a cryptic diagram of events yet to come so that, if one can only find the key, one may get from it a blueprint of the future. He who seeks to get this from Daniel has committed a major error of biblical interpretation: he has disregarded completely what the author of Daniel wished to say. The book of Daniel is, on the contrary, addressed to the author's own day, and is a mighty summons to courage and faith in the language of the Apocalypse. Hold fast, it says, to the law, to your Jewishness, and to your God! For God is there! The Kingdom of God towers over the puny kingdoms of men! God is even now preparing to intervene, to destroy the evil powers of this earth, and to set up his Kingdom among his people who are faithful!

Loyalty to the law breathes through the stories of Daniel—an illustration of how little the ideals of the Apocalyptic differed from those of the Holy Commonwealth. We see it in the story (ch. 1) of how the well-favored youths had the courage not to defile themselves with the king's dainties (vs. 8); and God rewarded them for their loyalty (vss. 15, 17-20). We see it in the story of blameless Daniel (ch. 6), who though commanded to pray only to the king (vss. 5-9), would not do it, but prayed to his God even if it meant a lion's den—and God saved him (vss. 20-22). We see it in the story of Shadrach, Meshach, and Abednego (ch. 3) who went to a fiery furnace rather than bow down to Nebuchadnezzar's idol. Their answer to the king (vss. 16-18) rings out as a challenge to all God-fearing men: "O Nebuchadnezzar, we have no need to answer you in this matter. If it be so, our God whom we serve is able to deliver us from the burning fiery furnace; and he will deliver us out of your hand, O king. But if not, be it known to you, O king, that we will not serve your gods or worship the golden image which you have set up." That is plain defiance! That is the categorical no with which man made in the image of God should give answer to the false god of the state, and even to Epiphanes!

Here, too, is utter confidence that the power of God looms over all

183

earthly power. There is that bizarre image of Nebuchadnezzar's vision (ch. 2) with head of gold, breast of silver, belly of brass, legs of iron, and feet of iron mixed with clay (vss. 31-33), typifying the succession of powers that hold sway over the earth (vss. 36-45). And there is that stone cut without hands out of the mountainside (vss. 34-35) which smote the image and broke it. The stone is the Kingdom of God: "And in the days of those kings the God of heaven will set up a kingdom which shall never be destroyed, nor shall its sovereignty be left to another people. It shall break in pieces all these kingdoms and bring them to an end, and it shall stand for ever" (vs. 44). Then, too, there is proud Nebuchadnezzar, ruler of all the earth, eating grass like an ox (ch. 4) until he learns (vs. 25) who is really King over the affairs of men. And there is Prince Belshazzar (ch. 5), who sees the handwriting on the wall announcing his doom because he did not recognize the lordship of one greater than he (vs. 23).

To its contemporaries the Apocalypse cries with a loud voice: Courage! In the present woes you may see signs that the great end drama is about to begin! The Kingdom of God is coming with power and glory over the kingdoms of men! In the form of mysterious beasts the powers of the world appear in ghostly parade. There is (ch. 8) a ram with two horns (Medo-Persia; vss. 3-4, 20) done to death by a he-goat with one enormous horn (Alexander; vss. 5-7, 21; cf. 11:2-4). Then the one horn is broken and becomes four (the four successor states; vss. 8, 22), and out of one of them comes (vss. 9-12) a little horn that made itself greater than God (i.e., Antiochus). Again (ch. 7), there are four strange and terrible beasts (the four rump states of Alexander's empire),[39] the last of which (vss. 7-8) had ten horns, out of which sprouted a remarkable little horn of overweening pride (Antiochus). That this is Antiochus there can be little doubt. It is he, the arch-Enemy, the very prototype of Antichrist. He will blaspheme the Most High, persecute the saints, defile the temple and suspend the sacrifices, attempt to abolish the law (e.g., 7:25; 8:9-13; 11:36). But do not fear! God is in control! This very little man has stood up against the Prince of Princes, and that is one too much for him! He will be broken out of hand (e.g., 8:23-25)! And cannot the eyes of faith see a greater throne than that of Antioch? It is the throne on which

---

[39] This interpretation of the beasts of ch. 7 is contrary to that of the commentators who see a succession of world powers as in ch. 2. But it has been persuasively advocated by H. Gressmann (Der Messias [Göttingen: Vandenhoeck & Rupprecht, 1929], pp. 344-45, 367).

sits the Ancient of Days in incomparable majesty (7:9-12). The Ancient of Days will slay this Beast. Then there will come "with the clouds of heaven . . . one like a son of man" (7:13),[40] and the Ancient of Days will give him a Kingdom over all men that shall never be destroyed. The triumph of the people of God in his Kingdom comes soon! Have courage! Do not fear to die for that Kingdom—for God will raise you to everlasting life! (12:1-4.)

4. But we must add an epilogue. It is a tale of raw courage seldom paralleled in history. Antiochus tried to enforce his policy, and men waited no longer for God; they acted. The king's officer came to the village of Modin and tried to persuade the priest there, one Mattathias, to set an example and sacrifice to the idol (I Macc. 2:15-19). Mattathias flatly refused. When a Jew stepped forward to do so, Mattathias leaped on him and knifed him where he stood, together with the king's officer. Then crying out (I Macc. 2:27): "Let every one who is zealous for the law, and would maintain the covenant, follow me!"—he took to the hills. Now Mattathias had a brood of rugged sons: Judas, Jonathan, Simon and the rest. Taking the name of Maccabee ("the hammer"?) they launched guerrilla war against the Seleucid armies—striking them, harrying them, hitting and running. Jews in increasing numbers flocked to their banner. Even those pious ones who expected God to act to save them and discounted what man could do (cf. Dan. 11:34), were constrained to join them. Defeated, they got up again. Outnumbered, without the ghost of a show, with utter courage and heroic patriotism, they fought on. And they won! Judah for the first time in over four hundred years could call itself free.

But the Kingdom of God—did they produce it? [41] Well, no! They pro-

---

[40] It would be a mistake in a book such as this to launch into a lengthy discussion of the origins and nature of this figure. There is debate whether the Son of Man is here an individual figure or, as most think, a collective figure symbolizing the victorious saints of God. But in the slightly later noncanonical book of I Enoch he appears as the pre-existent heavenly deliverer who will rule the victorious Kingdom of God (for a contrary opinion, T. W. Manson, "The Son of Man in Daniel, Enoch and the Gospels" [*Bulletin of the John Rylands Library*, 32-2, Mar., 1950]). Whether the Son of Man was, before the time of Christ, specifically identified with the Davidic Messiah as Albright (*From the Stone Age to Christianity*, pp. 290-92) argues, is also a debated question. But as the eschatological Saviour the Son of Man was, in the theology of Judaism, a messianic figure—at least in the broader sense of that term.

[41] That messianic hope did attach itself to the Maccabees (the Hasmoneans) may be argued from the appearance (in the Testaments of the Twelve Patriarchs) of the hope for a Messiah of the house of Levi. There is little mention of a Davidic Messiah in the literature of the period. The Hasmonean house was of the tribe of Levi.

duced the Kingdom of the Hasmoneans. And that was not the Kingdom of God; that was a singularly unlovely state, characterized by intrigue, murder, and self-seeking scheming. The end of it would be the tramp of the legions of Cnaeus Pompey, and "that fox" Herod. Still less did the heavens open and the Son of Man come in glory. That hope would have to be deferred for another fruition.

Indeed, it would seem that the Kingdom of God does not come so. How often do men think that beyond every war there will be a new world of peace, of justice, and of brotherhood—only to suffer the sharpest disillusionment! History and our deepest feelings conspire to teach us that we must be willing to fight and to die for freedom, for conscience, and for all that we hold dear. Only so can these things be maintained. But we are also warned that the Kingdom of God is quite another matter. It cannot be fought in; it cannot be signed in at a green conference table. The Kingdom of God comes in a wholly different way. And to that we must now turn.

CHAPTER SEVEN

The Kingdom at Hand: Jesus the Messiah

WE HAVE, UP TO THIS POINT, FOLLOWED THROUGH THE OLD TESTAMENT A SINGLE THEME, THAT OF THE PEOPLE OF GOD. WE HAVE TRACED IT FROM its roots in the Mosaic faith; we have seen how it was given shape by the blows of history and by prophet word; we have followed it until we saw it solidify into the beliefs and practices of Judaism. We have seen that there always accompanied it the concomitant hope of the consummation of God's purpose and the establishment of his Kingdom. Although this hope took many and various forms, it was always one hope. And although it was many times cruelly frustrated, it was never given up. It was never given up, because it was in the very texture of Israel's faith—indeed at the core of that faith—and to have surrendered it would have been to surrender faith itself. As long as Israel retained any sense of calling as the people of God, or any faith in the integrity and power of that God who is Lord of history, so long would there live the lively expectation of his coming Kingdom.

We pass now from the Old Testament to the New. We stand "in the fulness of time" before Jesus of Nazareth who is called the Christ. As we do so, it is clear that our discussion of the biblical concept of the Kingdom of God has reached its climactic phase. For it is the unanimous affirmation of the New Testament that this Jesus is no less than the long-awaited Messiah, and that in him all the hope of Israel has found its fulfillment and become present fact. It becomes our task, therefore, to inquire in what sense this is so.

I

This brings us face to face with a subject as wide as the New Testament itself, and we must first of all narrow our field somewhat. Although we have been greatly concerned to see the Bible message within the context of events, we can make no attempt to review the political history of New Testament times. Suffice it to say that a little over half a century before Jesus was born (63 B.C.) Pompey had annexed Palestine for Rome, thus bringing Jewish independence to an end. Thereafter the land was ruled partly through Herodian kings subject to Caesar, partly directly through Roman procurators. At the same time virtually all the other lands with which the New Testament is concerned had likewise been brought into subjection to Rome, so that its story is spun out entirely within the framework of the empire. But the details we must pass over. And although the shadow of Caesar falls often enough over its pages, it must be said that the New Testament is in general far less intimately concerned with political vicissitudes than were, say, the Old Testament prophets. To the New Testament mind eschatological event was far more real than political event.

Furthermore, it is manifest that we cannot undertake to reconstruct in detail the life and ministry of Jesus. This would involve a minute analysis of the gospel stories, and the discussion of a host of critical issues, which would carry us far beyond our bounds. Nevertheless, we must keep the figure of the historical Jesus steadily before our eyes as we proceed, for without him nothing of which we speak would have either meaning or existence. And we must be aware, even if this is not the place to discuss them in detail, of the profound questions which are involved, particularly the question of how faithfully the Jesus whom we see in the New Testament pages corresponds to the Jesus who actually lived. If this is a question which is properly foreign to the mind of the ordinary Bible reader, and even one which the conservative-minded Christian finds offensive, we must nevertheless be aware that it exists and be prepared to take a position with regard to it. Our whole understanding of our Lord will depend upon the answer given.[1]

Our concern is primarily with a fundamental question: Who is this Christ, and what did he come to do? Now if one were to put that question at random to Christian people today, he would probably get as many answers as people questioned. While all would in some way hail Christ as Saviour and Lord, each would express his faith in him in terms which had been shaped by his personal experience. The meaning of Christ cannot be reduced to any one formula; it is positively inexhaustible. When we turn to our New Testament, therefore, we are not surprised to find a similar variety of expression. Each of the New Testament writers addressed a particular situation, had traits and experiences peculiar to himself alone, and expressed his faith in Christ in his own peculiar way. The reader of the New Testament quickly senses this. As he passes, let us say, from the apparent simplicity of the Synoptic Gospels to the labored style and involved reasoning of Paul, and then perhaps on to the peculiar thought world of the Johannine literature, he does not need to be told that there are differences. The New Testament centers in Christ, but it expresses its faith in that Christ in many different ways.

But how, then, does the New Testament answer the question: Who is Christ, and what did he come to do? Does it afford no single answer, so that we must be content with a multiplicity of answers? By no means! While there are manifest differences within the New Testament which we would do ill to level off, we may say with confidence that there is a fundamental unity in it. And this unity lies precisely in its *gospel*.

This gospel, this proclamation (*kerygma*) of the earliest church, may be said to form the most primary element in the New Testament.[2] We

---

[1] The position here taken, as will be apparent from what follows, is that the Christ of the church's gospel corresponds in all essentials to the Jesus of history. If this seems a safely conservative position to take, it can only be said that it is not taken willfully but in line with what seem to be the best trends in current New Testament scholarship (for an excellent introduction, see A. M. Hunter, *Interpreting the New Testament: 1900-1950* [London: S. C. M. Press, 1951]). Form Criticism has, it is true, taught us that Jesus was from the beginning an object of faith; and the gospel tradition, shaped by the faith of the church, gives us Jesus as that church believed in him. But it is far easier to believe that the actual Jesus created the faith about him, however diverse the forms in which it was expressed, than that that faith created a Jesus in its own image. The gospel sources are too unanimous on all essential points, and the time-lag between the events and the writing of the earliest Gospels too brief, to make any such major distortion credible.

[2] The credit for this insight goes particularly to C. H. Dodd, *The Apostolic Preaching and Its Developments* (London: Hodder & Stoughton, 1936, 1944). There is a convenient summary in Hunter, *op. cit.*, pp. 34-36.

may see it particularly in certain passages in Paul (e.g., Rom. 1:1-3; 10:9; I Cor. 11:23-25; 15:3-7; Phil. 2:6-11) where the apostle echoes confessions of early Christian faith, and also in certain sermons in Acts (e.g., 10:36-43; 3:12-16). It was a very simple gospel and very clear. It announced that the New Age of God proclaimed by the prophets had begun; that the long-awaited Messiah had come, who is none other than this Jesus who did mighty works, died and rose again according to the Scriptures; that this Jesus has now been exalted to highest heaven to sit at the right hand of God, from whence he shall shortly come again "to judge the quick and the dead" (K.J.V.). Let men then make decision for this New Age by repentance and baptism to the remission of sins!

This primitive proclamation is in a real sense the binding element of New Testament theology.[3] Not only are traces of it to be found throughout the New Testament, but our earliest Gospel, Mark, might be said to be a conscious development of the same theme. It is a theme which is summed up in the words with which Mark introduces Jesus' ministry (1:14-15): "The time is fulfilled, and the kingdom of God is at hand; repent, and believe in the gospel." This, then, is the good news which the New Testament with unanimous voice proclaims: that Jesus is indeed the promised Messiah, fulfillment of all the hope of Israel, who has come to set up the Kingdom of God among men.[4] Variegated as the message of the New Testament became, especially as it adapted itself to Gentiles who knew nothing of the hope of Israel, to make that assertion remained at the very heart of the church's gospel.

1. That assertion is of especial interest to us, because in it the unity of all Scripture is plainly affirmed; in it New Testament is linked unbreak-

[3] So Dodd, op. cit. That there is essential unity in the New Testament message is increasingly recognized. Among recent books which illustrate this fact one might name: V. Taylor, The Atonement in New Testament Teaching (2nd ed.; London; Epworth Press, 1945); F. V. Filson, One Lord, One Faith (Philadelphia: Westminster Press, 1943); A. M. Hunter, The Unity of the New Testament (London: S. C. M. Press, 1944).

[4] For further discussion of the New Testament idea of the Kingdom of God, see the article "Basileus, etc." in Theologisches Wörterbuch zum Neuen Testament, G. Kittel, ed. (Stuttgart: W. Kohlhammer, 1933), I, 562-95. Other useful works include: R. N. Flew, Jesus and His Church (2nd ed.; London: Epworth Press, 1943); R. Otto, The Kingdom of God and the Son of Man (translated from the revised German edition by F. V. Filson and Bertram Lee-Woolf [London: Lutterworth Press, 1943]); E. F. Scott, The Kingdom of God in the New Testament (New York: The Macmillan Co., 1931).

ably to Old, and all biblical theology is made to hang together. For in affirming that Jesus is the Messiah, the New Testament affirmed that all that the Old Testament faith had longed for and pointed to has been given in him: he is the fulfillment of all that the law community had tried to do, and all that prophet hope had envisioned.[5]

Now the Old Testament stands, viewed as we have viewed it, in a very real sense as an incomplete book. It is, in all of its parts, suffused with the awareness of the rule of God over his people; it is upheld by the hope and the longing, expressed in a dozen divergent forms, for the coming establishment of the Kingdom of God. By the time of Christ this hope had, we might say, crystallized into certain major patterns. These patterns, it must be underscored, were by no means mutually exclusive or contradictory, but were expressions of the same longing and faith. There was the hope of political restoration, of independence from Rome through military action led by the Messiah. This hope we associate especially with that group known as the Zealots, the nationalist party within Judaism. There was also the ideal of the Holy Commonwealth, prevalent particularly among the Pharisees. These looked equally for the exaltation of God's people under the rule of his Messiah. But they expected this by God's action, not man's, and were consequently chary of following messianic pretenders in the struggle against Rome. They saw it as their duty to make actual the ideal of the Holy People of God through strict observance of the law, and if this were done, God would send and exalt his Messiah. Finally, there was the apocalyptic hope (such as that best expressed in Daniel and I Enoch) of the catastrophic intervention of God, and of the coming of the Son of Man in clouds and glory to receive an eternal Kingdom (cf. Dan. 7:13-14).

None of these expectations, of course, had found fulfillment, nor indeed, in their own terms, could they do so. The hope of political restoration was, and must remain, the wildest pipe-dream. Israel lay in the grip of the grimmest power of all, imperial Rome. *That* kingdom would not come—Caesar would not allow it! Yet the hope of it was a chronic pathology beyond cure. It produced false messiahs like a rash on the body politic. Zealot and *sicarius* would strike again and again for that Kingdom, but would only succeed in precipitating Roman reprisals of in-

---

[5] Note how Paul's sermon in Acts 13:16-41 links the gospel message to the promises, especially those to David. Cf. the excellent study of G. E. Wright, *God Who Acts: Biblical Theology as Recital* (London: S. C. M. Press, 1952), p. 70.

creasing severity until they brought about first the destruction of city and temple at the hands of Titus (A.D. 70), and finally the national suicide before Hadrian's legions (A.D. 132-35). There would be no Messiah Prince to defeat Rome.

What the apocalypticist hoped for, of course, simply did not come to pass. The heavens did not open to reveal the Son of Man coming in the clouds to receive the Kingdom of the Ancient of Days. Furthermore, they never would. Yet one senses behind the gospel pages the frenetic morbidity of it: a people looking eagerly for signs of the coming end, scanning the current scene for some omen or some portent that would show that the great end-drama was about to commence (e.g., Matt. 12:38-42; 16:1-4; 24:3; Mark 8:11-12; 13:4). Greedily they pounced upon every crumb of an indication, crying, " 'Lo here' you may see it! 'Lo there' is proof that it cannot be long" (Luke 17:21)! But always they were wrong—because what they wanted was wrong.

As for the ideal of the Holy Commonwealth, for all its high-mindedness and diligent practice it did not precipitate the Kingdom of God or even produce a very holy people. From the Christian point of view, at least, it simply could not do so. Yet it did not give up the effort, but rather intensified it. And, it must be admitted, it was these rabbis of the law who succeeded in creating normative Judaism out of the residue of the Jewish nation. Theirs was a structure of enduring and not-to-be-lightly-estimated worth, and to have built it was no small achievement, but the Kingdom of God which they sought was an entirely different matter altogether.

The Old Testament faith had fathered a mighty expectation of incredible vitality. But its hope had not found fruition. It must ever point ahead beyond itself to the rule of God triumphant. But that fruition did not come to pass, nor did Israel know how to bring it to pass. The Old Testament is, therefore, as it were, an incomplete book. It is a story whose Author has not yet written the ending; it is a signpost pointing down a road whose destination—and surely its destination is a city, the City of God (Heb. 11:10, 16)—lies out of sight around many a bend. It is a noble building indeed—but it lacks a roof!

2. That roof, by its own affirmation, the New Testament supplies: in announcing in Christ the fulfillment of the hope of Israel it stands as the completion of the Old Testament. But—and this must not be forgotten—to say that is at the same time to say that it cannot be understood to itself alone apart from the Old Testament. If the Old Testament

192

be a building without a roof, the New Testament alone may be very like a roof without a building—and that is a structure very hard to comprehend and very hard to hold up! It is a structure that may be put to all sorts of uses and may shelter all sorts of things, but it is a structure which may be very easily knocked down. By this we certainly do not mean to say that the New Testament is merely an appendage of the Old, or to deny that Christ is himself the cornerstone of a mighty building (I Cor. 3:11; I Pet. 2:4-7), but only to insist that it is impossible rightly to set the New Testament apart and to construct a purely New Testament religion without regard to the faith of Israel.[6] The New Testament rests on and is rooted in the Old. To ignore this fact is a serious error in method, and one that is bound to lead to a fundamental misunderstanding of the Bible message. He who commits it has disregarded the central affirmation of the New Testament gospel itself, namely that Christ has come to make actual what the Old Testament hoped for, not to destroy it and replace it with a new and better faith.

To put it this way, to be sure, may seem at first blush rather surprising. For there is much that sets the New Testament off from the Old, and the reader quickly senses it. There is a considerable time gap between them; there is the fact (how well the seminary student knows it!) that they are written in entirely different languages. There is also the fact that while the Old Testament is almost entirely concerned with the fortunes of the people Israel, the New Testament quickly breaks out beyond that limited horizon into a vastly broader setting. What is more, the New Testament has Christ—and that sets it off from the Old Testament so sharply that it might easily seem that we hardly need the Old Testament any more. We see Christ at odds with Judaism, bursting the framework of Judaism like new wine poured into an old wineskin (Mark 2:22). We see Christ rejected by Judaism, whereupon there emerges a new church.

Clearly there is a "new thing" in the New Testament. And we are tempted to look for it in some new ethic, some new theology or religion, which is to be found there. This was, in fact, exactly what much of so-called "liberal" Christianity did. Those who shared this viewpoint were accustomed to view Scripture as the record of man's ethical and spiritual progress (or, theistically stated, the progress of revelation), the

---

[6] See the splendid remarks of Wright, op. cit., pp. 111-12, with which I am in hearty agreement.

culmination of which was to be found in Christ and his teachings. The distinctive message of the New Testament was sought in some more lofty system of ethics, or some higher idea of God, than any previously attained. Christ became the great ethical teacher. As for the Old Testament, although it might be granted that it held a certain historical interest and contained certain moral values, it but reflected the lower steps of man's painful climb and a level of religion largely superseded. To the mind of many a Christian this meant simply that it could be dispensed with. But one does not have to discount the element of progress in the biblical faith in order to affirm that the cost of thus sundering the two Testaments was great. Aside from all else it heightened the danger that the "new" of the New Testament would be sought in the wrong place, and its fundamental meaning thereby missed.

For if anything is clear, it is that Christ did not come to contribute a new ethic. There has never been a higher ethic than his, yet it was essentially the ethic of Judaism.[7] It is true that nowhere among the rabbis do we find the concentration of lofty ethical injunctions which we find in the teachings of Jesus. Here moral demands are stated quite without that mass of ceremonial regulations upon which Judaism laid such stress. Indeed, Jesus held such ceremonial trivia in contempt. What is more important, he set forth his ethical requirements with a summons to radical obedience which we seldom or never find among Jewish teachers. Nevertheless, if compared point by point, the ethical teachings of Jesus find their parallels in Judaism and in the faith of ancient Israel. If Jesus commanded that we should love our neighbor as ourselves (Mark 12:31), so had the Levitical law (Lev. 19:18). If Jesus commanded that lovingkindness should extend even to one's enemy (Matt. 5:44; Luke 6:27; cf. Rom. 12:20), so had the ancient Jewish wisdom (Prov. 25:21).[8] The very attack which he launched upon the external righteousness of "scribes

[7] It must be emphasized that we do not mean by this statement that there is nothing to choose between the ethical teachings of Jesus and those of the rabbis. On this point cf. J. W. Bowman, *The Intention of Jesus* (Philadelphia: The Westminster Press, 1943), pp. 100 ff. Yet the ethic of Jesus was not essentially a new ethic, but a reorientation of an existing one. His teachings can be paralleled detail for detail among those of the rabbis, as the work of Strack-Billerbeck (*Kommentar zum Neuen Testament aus Talmud und Midrasch*, 4 vols. [Munich: C. H. Beck, 1922-28]), G. F. Moore (*Judaism in the First Centuries of the Christian Era*, 3 vols. [Cambridge: Harvard University Press, 1927-30]), and others have made clear.

[8] There is even a seventh-century B.C. Assyrian parallel. Cf. Albright, *From the Stone Age to Christianity*, p. 303 and note 77.

and Pharisees, hypocrites" (e.g., Matt. 23), was the ancient prophet attack—Amos and Micah alive again—in which existing righteousness was judged by the higher righteousness of the Kingdom of God. Christ indeed gave a radical reorientation to existing morality. But, it must be repeated, he simply did not come to teach Judaism a higher ethic and to understand the New Testament message in that light is fundamentally to misunderstand it.

Nor was Christ's mission to teach his people some new and loftier idea of God. At least neither Christ nor his church so understood the matter. We do not mean by a single syllable to deny that in Christ the character and purpose of God stand revealed as nowhere in the Old Testament or beyond it. As Christians we must say that we should not know God had we not seen him in the face of Jesus Christ. But Jesus did not announce to the Jews that a loftier notion of God was now available— but that their God *had acted!* While not minimizing the supremacy of the New Testament revelation, we cannot set the two Testaments apart theologically—as is sometimes done from the pulpit. We cannot say that the Old Testament reveals a God of justice and of wrath, while the New Testament shows us, in Christ, a Father God of love. To draw such contrasts is to misunderstand the God of the Old Testament. Besides, these two aspects of God are held in balance in the New Testament (even in the teachings of Jesus! For example, Matt. 8:12; 13:36-43; 22:13; 24:51) quite as much as in the Old.

To be sure, the New Testament repeatedly contrasts the Old Covenant with the New (e.g., Gal. 3-4; Heb. 7-9) and declares the New to be the "better" (Heb. 7:22; 8:6). But we cannot dismiss the relationship of the Testaments by saying that Christ came to replace a covenant of works with a covenant of grace, as though we had to do with two dispensations in which God dealt with his people in two essentially different ways. In spite of the powerful argumentative force of this contrast of the two covenants, one reading, for example, of Deuteronomy would be enough to convince one that the old covenant was itself regarded precisely as a grateful response to the unmerited grace of God.[9] What is more, the entire prophet attack had moved from an impatience with external, ceremonial "works" as fundamental as was ever that of Paul. That there was development in the biblical faith, none will deny; that Christ is the crown of revelation, no Christian may deny. But we cannot

[9] Cf. Chap. I, p. 28.

195

state the relationship of the two Testaments in terms of contrasting theologies, or regard the New merely as the last and highest upward step in the understanding of God. Christ came, indeed, to announce the decisive redeeming act of God, and to perform it. But he did not come to inform Judaism of a new and unknown God.

The New Testament, then, does not present us with a new religion which we may study for itself alone. We must express ourselves guardedly here, for the Christian Church was not, or did not long remain, a Jewish sect. On the contrary, it emerged as a separate entity which moved ever farther from Judaism, and, in the course of time, it developed its own peculiar doctrines and sacraments, traditions and ceremonies. Judaism and Christianity early became two distinct, if closely related, religions. Yet we must not forget that Jesus and his early disciples were all Jews. And it is clear that Jesus did not intend to found a new religion. His mission was precisely to "the lost sheep of the house of Israel" (Matt. 10:6; 15:24). He did not come to destroy Israel's faith and supersede it with another, but rather to bring it to its fulfillment (Matt. 5:17).[10] Nor did his disciples intend to found a new religion. On the contrary, they broke with Judaism only when forced to, and then with the greatest reluctance. Indeed it is the insistence of the New Testament writers that it is they who have the true Judaism and the true fulfillment of Israel's hope. In spite of the fact that, as the church had to adapt its message to the Gentile world, new terminology and new forms of expression were developed, the New Testament remains a book fundamentally Jewish in character,[11] organically related to the Old Testament faith. So much so, in fact, that the theology of the New Testament cannot be understood in isolation, but only in the light of all the hope of Israel.

3. The two Testaments are organically linked to each other. The relationship between them is neither one of upward development nor

[10] Cf. F. V. Filson, *The New Testament Against Its Environment* (Chicago: Henry Regnery Co., 1950), pp. 15-16.

[11] This statement is in line with the current trend of New Testament scholarship. On the Jewish background of the thought of Paul, cf. W. D. Davies, *Paul and Rabbinic Judaism* (London: S. P. C. K., 1948); C. A. A. Scott, *Christianity According to St. Paul* (Cambridge University Press, 1927). As to the Fourth Gospel, although the theory of an Aramaic original (C. F. Burney, C. C. Torrey) has not carried the field, its Jewish origin—and first century date—is widely conceded. "There is no thoroughly Greek or Hellenistic book in the New Testament": Filson, *op. cit.*, p. 31. It must not be forgotten, however, that Judaism itself had been powerfully influenced by Hellenism.

of contrast; it is one of beginning and completion, of hope and fulfill-ment.[12] *And the bond that binds them together is the dynamic concept of the rule of God.* There is indeed a "new thing" in the New Testament, but it lies precisely here. The Old Testament is illumined with the hope of the coming Kingdom, and that same Kingdom lies at the heart of the New Testament as well. But the New Testament has introduced what we might call a tremendously significant change of tense. To the Old Testament the fruition and victory of God's Kingdom was always a future, indeed an eschatological thing, and must always be spoken of in the future tense: "Behold, the days are coming"; "It shall come to pass in those days." But in the New Testament we encounter a change: the tense is a resounding present indicative—the Kingdom is *here!* And that is a very "new thing" indeed: *it is gospel*—the good news that God has acted! How real, how utterly central, was the present fact of the Kingdom to all the New Testament writers, I trust will become apparent as we proceed. Nowhere is it better put than in the words of Jesus with which Mark begins the story of his ministry, and which sum up, perhaps better than anything else, the very essence of his teaching: "The time is fulfilled, and the kingdom of God is at hand; repent, and believe in the gospel" (Mark 1:15).[13] What all the ages have desired to see now is here—in this Jesus (Luke 10:23-24). In him has the old order ended and a new order begun.[14]

Old Testament and New Testament thus stand together as the two acts of a single drama. Act I points to its conclusion in Act II, and without it the play is an incomplete, unsatisfying thing. But Act II must be read in the light of Act I, else its meaning will be missed. For the play is organically one. The Bible is one book. Had we to give that book a title, we might with justice call it "The Book of the Coming Kingdom of God." That is, indeed, its central theme everywhere. In the New Testa-

[12] See the excellent article of W. Zimmerli, "Verheissung und Erfüllung" (*Evangelische Theologie* 1952, Heft 1/2, pp. 34-59).

[13] Does the verb engidzō ("is at hand") mean that the Kingdom is near and will soon come, or that it has arrived? I should prefer the latter with C. H. Dodd and others (*The Parables of the Kingdom* [London: Nisbet & Co., 1935], pp. 44-45); cf. recently W. R. Hutton (*Expository Times*, LXIV [1952], 89-91). This need not, however, force one to a complete "realized eschatology."

[14] On the interpretation of this verse (cf. Matt. 11:12-13) see the commentaries, con-veniently T. W. Manson in Major, Manson and Wright, *The Mission and Message of Jesus* (New York: E. P. Dutton & Co., 1938), pp. 425-27. This book, incidentally, is to be recommended to the student who desires a thorough but nontechnical help to the study of the four Gospels.

ment, however, there is this difference: the Kingdom of God has become also the Kingdom of Christ, and that Kingdom is actually *at hand*. When Jesus, in the synagogue at Nazareth (Luke 4:16-21), read from the book of Isaiah one of the Servant passages (Isa. 61:1-2),[15] and then said (vs. 21), "Today this scripture has been fulfilled in your hearing," he announced not that the final act of the drama would one day begin, or that it was about to begin; he declared that it had, in truth, *already begun*: the Servant *is here* and has begun his work. The New Testament saw Jesus—as, we believe, he saw himself—as the Christ, the promised Messiah, who has come to set up his Kingdom. It hailed him as the fulfillment of law and prophecy. It affirmed with one voice that all the hope of Israel, in all its variegated patterns, had found its realization in Christ and his Kingdom.

II

But if the New Testament hailed Jesus as the Messiah, it is evident that the Jews did not regard him as such. Indeed, they rejected him outright and did him to death. Nor is it very difficult to see why they could not accept him. He was not at all the Messiah that was expected. Although he claimed for himself that office and made use of the various messianic titles, he understood that office and used those titles in such a way as to ensure his rejection. Evidently he was a Messiah of a novel sort.

1. Certainly he could not satisfy those who expected a Messiah who would lead the struggle for independence against Rome, or who would in any way set himself up as ruler of an earthly kingdom of the Jews.

The nature of the messianic consciousness of Jesus is a much debated subject into which we cannot go. Many scholars have, it is true, doubted that Jesus made any claim to be the Messiah at all.[16] I find it difficult

[15] I regard Isa. 61:1-3 as a Servant passage, with C. C. Torrey (*The Second Isaiah* [New York: Chas. Scribner's Sons, 1928], pp. 452-53) and others. Cf. Chap. V, p. 147 and note 31. In any case, Jesus clearly so understood it.

[16] Recently, for example, R. Bultmann, *Theologie des Neuen Testaments* (Tübingen: J. C. B. Mohr, 1948) I, 25-33. Bultmann's presentation of the message of Jesus is always brilliant and at times moving, but we disagree fundamentally at many points. Cf. also F. C. Grant, *The Gospel of the Kingdom* (New York: The Macmillan Co., 1940), who holds that Jesus made no definite claims for himself. I must align myself, for reasons that cannot here be debated, with the many recent scholars who have argued for the messianic consciousness of Jesus: e.g., Bowman, *op. cit.*; Wm. Manson, *Jesus the Messiah* (Philadelphia: The Westminster Press, 1946); Filson, *op. cit.*, ch. 1; Albright, *op. cit.*, pp. 304 ff.

to agree with them. On the contrary a sense of messiahship was the very central fact of his ministry. It is true that, although he was according to the Scripture of Davidic descent, he never played up that fact (although, on occasion, he allowed others to do so: e.g., Mark 10:47-48). It is also true that he seemed most reluctant to announce his messiahship openly— indeed, he discouraged his disciples from doing so (Mark 8:29-30; Luke 9:20-21; Matt. 16:15-20)—so much so that at his trial it was difficult to prove conclusively that he had ever made such a claim. Yet that he thought of himself as the Messiah seems certain. That the church so regarded him is, of course, beyond question. From its beginning onward it hailed him with one voice as Jesus the Christ (and "Christ" is but the Greek equivalent of the Hebrew "Messiah," i.e., "the Anointed One"). This conviction of the church cannot, we believe, be its own invention, but must rest on the self-consciousness and claims of Jesus himself. It is significant that it is the unanimous witness of the Gospels that when Pilate asked him point-blank, "Are you the King of the Jews?" his only answer was a blunt, "You have said it" (Mark 15:2; Matt. 27:11; Luke 23:3; John 18:33-37)—which, if cryptic, was certainly no denial. Before the Sanhedrin his answer to the same question was a flat, "I am" (Mark 14:62).

This meant that the ancient hope of a Prince of the line of David, who should reign in peace over the Remnant of Israel, Jesus saw fulfilled in himself. This hope, you will recall, had been given its classical expression by Isaiah (e.g., Isa. 9:2-7; 11:1-9) and had long since entrenched itself in the hearts of loyal Israelites. But for Jesus to admit in any way that he was the expected Son of David, the King of the Jews, involved a certain danger. The Messiah hope had become all too completely a longing for political independence. It had been often enough tragically befooled by pretenders who, claiming to be the Messiah, promised to produce just that. For Jesus to link himself with that hope would have been to gain easily a host of followers who would expect of him something that he could not, and did not mean to, deliver. And such followers he got. We are told that they tried to make him king (John 6:15). Even his disciples could ask, and that after the lesson of Passion and Resurrection, "Lord, will you at this time restore the kingdom to Israel?" (Acts 1:6.)

To those who entertained such hopes, Jesus simply could not be acceptable. He said never a word of re-establishing the Davidic kingdom

199

or of restoring the twelve tribes of Israel by military action, and it is clear that such a thing was the farthest thing in the world from his intention. Every attempt to acclaim him as a political leader he rejected. When John reports the words of our Lord to Pilate: "My kingship is not of this world" (John 18:36), he expresses the profound truth that Jesus' notion of the messianic Kingdom was not at all the popular one. No doubt it was precisely because Jesus knew how different was his understanding of the messianic office from the popular expectation, that he was so reticent about announcing himself as the Messiah, lest he be misunderstood. Certainly he was no popular Messiah. Indeed, his "Render to Caesar the things that are Caesar's" (Mark 12:17; Matt. 22:21; Luke 20:25), clever escape from entrapment that it was, must have seemed to many a Jewish patriot a craven evasion of the issue. In any case, it is clear that Jesus had no intention of setting up an earthly kingdom. On the contrary, he repeatedly warned that the material achievements of this earth are a snare, and recommended the spiritual treasures of heaven (e.g., Matt. 6:19-34; Mark 10:23-25; Luke 12:16-21).

And, to crown it all, claiming to be the King of the Jews, he understood it to be necessary that he suffer. This was, as we shall see in a moment, an entirely novel and strange combination. A Messiah King who should suffer and die was the last thing in the world that Jewish nationalism expected or wanted. Yet it is clear that Jesus understood his kingship as no warlike office, but as one of humility and peace. The story of the Triumphal Entry (Matt. 21:1-11) clearly identifies the messianic claim of Jesus with the figure of the lowly king riding upon an ass (Zech. 9:9), and it is difficult to believe that Jesus did not intend his action to be understood so.[17] In any case he sealed his messianic claim by allowing himself to be crucified, and on his cross were tacked the derisive words: "Jesus, the King of the Jews." A Jewish patriot could want no surer proof than this that here was no Messiah at all, but only another of those false messiahs of which there had already been more than a plenty.

2. When we turn to those Jews nurtured on the apocalyptic hope, we can only say that Jesus was nothing at all like what they expected. These hoped for the sudden intrusion of God's Kingdom in the clouds of heaven. Closely linked to this hope was the figure of the Son of Man.

---

[17] Cf. H. D. A. Major in Major, Manson and Wright, op. cit., pp. 138-40; also A. H. McNeile, The Gospel According to St. Matthew (London: The Macmillan Co., 1915), p. 297.

We encountered the Son of Man first, it will be recalled, in Daniel (7:9-14), where we see him coming in the heavens to receive the Kingdom of the Ancient of Days (God). Whether the Son of Man as he appears in Daniel is thought of as an individual, the representative or leader of the victorious Kingdom, or as a more or less corporate symbol or personification of that Kingdom, has occasioned a good deal of debate. But in the noncanonical book of I Enoch he seems clearly to be thought of as a pre-existent Being, residing from all eternity with God in the heavens, who should appear in the end time as the divinely sent deliverer. Leaving aside the moot question of how definite an identification had been made in Jewish theology before the time of Christ between this figure and that of the Davidic Messiah, we may say that the Son of Man was—at least in the broad sense of that term—a messianic figure.[18]

But here was one who claimed to be that Son of Man. In fact this was the title which he applied to himself more often than any other.[19] Although the words "son of man" in the Gospels sometimes have the force simply of "a human being" or "a man" (as so often in Ezekiel), they stand most often as our Lord's title for himself.[20] And he certainly understood it as a messianic title. When the high priest asked him if he were the Christ (i.e., Messiah), he replied: "I am; and you will see the Son of man sitting at the right hand of Power, and coming with the clouds of heaven" (Mark 14:61-62).[21] Jesus thus claimed to be the

[18] Cf. Chap. VI, p. 185, note 40. Among recent writers arguing that such an identification had been made are: Albright, op. cit., pp. 290 ff.; W. D. Davies, Paul and Rabbinic Judaism (London: S. P. C. K., 1948), pp. 279-80; Wm. Manson, op. cit., pp. 144-45; Bowman, op. cit., p. 125. H. H. Rowley has been among the most emphatic in arguing to the contrary: recently, The Biblical Doctrine of Election (London: Lutterworth Press, 1950), pp. 156-57; idem, "The Suffering Servant and the Davidic Messiah" (Oudtestamentische Studiën VIII [Leiden: E. J. Brill, 1950], p. 127 and note 107 there.

[19] Overwhelmingly so, as the table in Bowman, op. cit., p. 131 shows. What is equally striking, the gospel writers do not ever place the words on the lips of anyone else, even when addressing Jesus. To be sure, there are those who deny that Jesus used the term: e.g., B. H. Branscomb, The Gospel of Mark (The Moffatt New Testament Commentary [New York and London: Harper & Bros., n.d.]), pp. 146-59.

[20] For brief discussion of the different forces of the term "son of man" in the Gospels, cf. for example, Bowman, op. cit., pp. 121 ff., 142 ff.; Wm. Manson, op. cit., pp. 158-67; T. W. Manson, "The Son of Man in Daniel, Enoch and the Gospels" (Bulletin of the John Rylands Library, 32-2 [1950], 171-93). The latter finds the Son of Man to stand always for the corporate entity of the Kingdom, but in the Gospels embodied par excellence in Jesus.

[21] In this verse and a number of others (e.g., Matt. 16:28; cf. Mark 9:1) Jesus seems to speak of the Son of Man objectively as though he were another who was yet to come. Bultmann (op. cit., pp. 4, 26 ff., 34 ff.) and others have argued that Jesus did not regard

expected and eternally existing representative (if not the very embodiment) of the true Israel, the people of God. He claimed to be the heavenly Man.

But Jesus was clearly not the expected Son of Man. He did not summon the heavens to open and pour forth legions of angels to destroy the adversaries of the Kingdom. To be sure, he declared that he had the power to do just that (Matt. 26:53-54), but that if he did so, he would not fulfill the scripture. On the contrary, there runs through his teachings like an ever-recurring theme the assertion that the Son of Man would have to suffer (e.g., Mark 8:31; 9:12, 31; 10:33, 45).[22] The Son of Man is to be victorious, indeed, but only beyond the most abject and self-sacrificial humiliation. So the Son of Man goes to the cross. To one nurtured on the apocalyptic dream that emphatically did not fulfill scripture.[23] The very fact that he suffered and died was ample proof to such a one that Jesus was not the Son of Man at all.

3. That, of all things, Jesus could not be acceptable to scribe and Pharisee needs no saying. These, as we have said, for all their faults, were motivated by a noble ideal: to make actual the true people of God, "a kingdom of priests and a holy nation" (Exod. 19:6), by the meticulous keeping of the law. If this could be done, they felt, God would send his Messiah to establish his Kingdom.

Now the Messiah was, of course, thought of under a variety of patterns which it would be impossible to systematize. But it seems that there was a strong tendency, at least in some circles, to think of the

himself as the Son of Man but himself anticipated his coming. But if the contention of T. W. Manson (op. cit.) has validity—and I believe that it has—then the Son of Man (like the Suffering Servant) could fluctuate between individual and group. Thus the Son of Man must suffer (as the Servant) that the Son of Man (the victorious Kingdom and its Leader) might come in glory. Cf. Rowley, The Relevance of Apocalyptic, pp. 114-15.

[22] Some would argue that the wording of these verses reveals a knowledge of the Passion, and that they are therefore vaticinia ex eventu (e.g., Bultmann, op. cit., pp. 30-31; Branscomb, op. cit., p. 153, etc.). Without debating the point, we see no reason to doubt that Christ realized that he would suffer and said so, whatever words he used; cf. A. E. J. Rawlinson, St. Mark (Westminster Commentaries [7th ed.; London; Methuen & Co., 1949]), p. 113.

[23] Although some have argued to the contrary, there seems to have been little or nothing in Scripture or Jewish belief that would have prepared the Jews for the notion of a suffering Son of Man. For a convincing argument with full bibliography see the article of Rowley cited in note 18 (now reprinted in The Suffering Servant and Other Essays [London: Lutterworth Press, 1952], pp. 61-88). To be sure, as Wm. Manson (op. cit., pp. 235-36) points out, the Servant, the Son of Man, and the Davidic Messiah have predicates in common, and one may agree that all were aspects of the messianic idea (in the broad sense), but this is far from an identification of the three.

bringer of the new age, or at least the herald of it, as a prophet like Moses—a new Moses if not actually Moses redivivus. No doubt this arose in part from the overwhelming importance of Moses in the minds of the Jewish people. Great figure he was; and Jewish thought had magnified him as the greatest of the great, who had shared as had no other the secrets of God.[24] In what higher terms could one think of the coming deliverer? It is possible, too, that the prophet longing for a "new Exodus" (especially in Second Isaiah) and a "new covenant" (especially in Jeremiah) may have played a part. If redemption is to be a new Exodus, must there not be a new Moses to lead it? If it is to involve a New Covenant, does it not need a new Moses to give it? Partly, however, the hope seems to have been nurtured by the prophecy in Deut. 18:15-19, where a prophet "like" Moses is promised.[25] In any case, there was abroad in the time of Jesus a lively hope for "the prophet" (e.g., John 1:21, 25), whose coming would signal the redemption of his people.[26]

We are told that many were ready to hail Jesus as that prophet (e.g., John 6:14; 7:40). Certainly his followers from earliest times regarded him as such. Peter, in an early speech reported in Acts (3:22-26), expressly identified him with the expected prophet of Deut. 18:15. Matthew, in particular, seems concerned to make it plain that Jesus is a new Moses. Did he not present his teachings on a mountain, just as at Sinai (Matt. 5–7)? And did he not on that occasion reinterpret the laws of Moses into what amounted to a new law (e.g., Matt. 5:17, 21-22, 27-28, 33-37, 38-39, 43-44)? It has even been suggested that Matthew grouped the teachings of Jesus into five major blocks (Matt. 5–7; 9:36–11:1; 13:1-53; 18:1–19:1; 24–25) in an intentional parallel to the five books of the an-

[24] References from Jewish literature have been collected conveniently by P. Volz, *Die Eschatologie der jüdischen Gemeinde im neutestamentliche Zeitalter* (Tübingen: J. C. B. Mohr, 1934), pp. 193-95. The figures of Moses, of Elijah (cf. Mal. 4:5), of both together, or of some other, occur.

[25] Cf. the comments on John 1:21, 25; 6:14; 7:40: e.g., E. C. Hoskyns, *The Fourth Gospel*, F. N. Davey, ed. (London: Faber & Faber, 1947), pp. 169, 281, 324; R. H. Strachan, *The Fourth Gospel* (3rd ed.; London: S. C. M. Press, 1941), pp. 112-13, 180-81.

[26] The desired prophet is not always necessarily an eschatological figure (e.g., I Macc. 4:44-46; 14:41 [?]; cf. 9:27; Ps. 74:9). But we have a number of examples in Josephus of false prophets who, it would seem, promised to recreate the Exodus days. One Theudas (*Antiquities*, XX, V, 1) declared himself a prophet and promised to lead the people dryshod over Jordan. A certain Egyptian (*Ant.* XX, VIII, 6; cf. Acts 21:38) promised to cause the walls of Jerusalem to fall (as Jericho's?). Another (*Ant.* XX, VIII, 10) promised deliverance to all who would follow him into the wilderness (for a new Exodus?). Acts 21:38 has the Egyptian issue a similar call.

cient Torah.[27] The comparison of the work of Christ with that of Moses is very much to the fore in the thought of Paul. Indeed we might say that, to Paul, the Christian in dying and rising again with Christ has participated in the New Exodus and, in confronting the teachings of Jesus, has stood at the foot of a new Sinai.[28] But the same thought is found in other New Testament writers as well. Christ is in effect a new and better Moses (e.g., Heb. 3:1-6). He gives to his people a new and better manna, for he is the bread of life (John 6:48-51); he leads them on a new and more glorious Exodus, and mediates to them a new and better covenant (e.g., Heb. 12:18-24).

But if there were those in the Jewish community who looked for a new Moses, how could Jesus possibly satisfy their expectations? To be sure, he knew the law as few did, so that it was impossible to entangle him in it. He deserved, indeed, to be called "rabbi." But he made free with the law. He didn't keep the Sabbath very strictly (e.g., Mark 2:23-28; Matt. 12:1-14); he didn't trouble with ceremonial cleanness (e.g., Mark 7:1-15; Luke 11:37-41); he kept the very worst sort of company— taxgatherers, whores, and other sinners! And not since Jeremiah spoke in the temple had anyone given official religion such a tongue lashing (e.g., Matt. 23). In fact he declared the whole hope of the Holy Commonwealth to be deluded. Not only could it not by its law-keeping precipitate the Kingdom of God, it could not even produce a decent enough righteousness to enable a man to enter: "Unless your righteousness exceeds that of the scribes and Pharisees, you will never enter the kingdom of heaven" (Matt. 5:20).

In short, he talked like a new Moses, indeed, but a new Moses come "to abolish the law" (Matt. 5:17)! The audacity of the fellow with his oft-repeated "Moses said in the law, . . . but *I* say unto you"! Indeed he boiled the whole law down, so it would seem, into a matter of love toward God and toward the neighbor (Mark 12:28-31). Now the Pharisees did not object simply that he did this, for many of their own teachers had done the same. Nor did they protest—as many since have done—that his

[27] On these five discourses see, B. W. Bacon, *Studies in Matthew* (New York: Henry Holt & Co., 1930), pp. xv-xvii; cf. F. W. Green, *The Gospel According to Matthew* (*The Clarendon Bible* [Oxford: Clarendon Press, 1936]), p. 5. The suggestion of a "Christian Pentateuch" is as old as Papias (second century A.D.).

[28] Davies, *op. cit.*, p. 146. Cf. *ibid.*, pp. 111-76 for a very thorough discussion of this feature of Paul's thought. See now also *idem*, *Torah in the Messianic Age and/or the Age to Come* (Philadelphia: Society of Biblical Literature, 1952).

teaching about turning the other cheek, going the second mile, and giving your cloak to the man that takes your coat (Matt. 5:38-42), was an airy, impractical thing. They objected that in thus reorientating the law, he had made the lesser details of it nonessential, had virtually abolished them. And this they could only see as the destruction of the law.

To be sure, Christ declared that he did not intend to destroy the law, but to fulfill it (Matt. 5:17).[29] Far from abolishing its demands for righteousness, he placed an absolute construction on them. Righteousness is not a matter of rule-keeping, but of total dedication to the will of the Father. And the positive will of the Father is to be summed up in that very difficult word, "love" (Mark 12:28-31; cf. Rom. 13:8-10; Gal. 5:14; Jas. 2:8). Righteousness is therefore no longer an external conformity, but an inwardly motivated obedience which "fulfills" the law. No, Christ did not destroy what the law stood for. But in one respect the Pharisees were quite right: the teachings of Jesus were a radical break with the ceremonial law of Judaism; the "yoke" of Christ was substituted for the "yoke" of the law (Matt. 11:29-30).[30] As Paul was quite correctly to see, here is no law but the abrogation of law and the substitution for it of the rule of Christ in the believer's heart. Said he, "Have this mind among yourselves, which you have in Christ Jesus" (Phil. 2:5). In Paul's thinking Christ has taken the place of Moses, and that is the destruction of the ritual law. And to a Pharisee one who destroys the law is not "the prophet," a new Moses, but a false teacher and a false prophet worthy of death.

4. Far more serious, Jesus went beyond the bounds of blasphemy and claimed to be divine. Now Jesus did not, to be sure, anywhere say that he was God, or formulate his claim to deity as a systematic theologian might have done. But that he felt himself to stand in a peculiar relation of sonship to God, such as was vouchsafed to no other, is witnessed in all our gospel sources. Certainly he addressed God as his Father in a manner far more intimate than we would dare assume in using the term (e.g.,

[29] Some (e.g., Bultmann, op. cit., p. 15) find Matt. 5:17-19 non-genuine. In my opinion, however, whatever problems arise from vss. 18-19 (they may belong in another context), none is presented by vs. 17. Cf. McNeile, op. cit., p. 58; W. C. Allen, The Gospel According to St. Matthew (International Critical Commentary [New York: Chas. Scribner's Sons, 1907]) p. 45-46.

[30] Jesus' call to take his "yoke" is to be compared to that of ben Sirach and the "yoke" of Wisdom (Ecclus. 51:26); also "the yoke of the Kingdom of Heaven," "the yoke of the commandments," "the yoke of the law," etc. in the Mishnah (e.g., Berakoth 2, Pirke Aboth 3).

Mark 8:38; Matt. 10:32; 11:27; Luke 10:22; 22:29). He was God's Son in a sense that no other could claim to be, and God was his Father as no other could claim him. So characteristic of him was it to address God as his Father that the Aramaic word *Abba* (Father), which he used, persisted in the liturgy even of the Greek-speaking church (cf. Mark 14:36; Rom. 8:15; Gal. 4:6-7).[31] In a new and subtle way his characteristic form of address asserts his claim to speak with divine authority. For whereas the old prophets had habitually prefaced their oracles with a "Thus says the Lord," that form of address has, on the lips of Jesus, been transformed into "Truly, truly *I* say to you." Here it is as if God claims to speak directly, in his own person.[32]

The New Testament church, in any case, with a unanimous voice hailed Jesus as Christ the Lord and Son of God. Although these titles may have owed their origin to those of the Old Testament king, it is clear that the church early regarded Jesus as more than man. He is the Son of God in whom the power of God is uniquely revealed (so frequently in the Synoptic Gospels). He was shown to be the Son of God by the miracle of his resurrection (Rom. 1:3-4); nay, he is the pre-existent Son who "emptied himself" to take human form (Phil. 2:6-8). He is the very image of the substance of God, far above the angels, who sits on the right hand of the Divine Majesty (Heb. 1:1-4). He is the Cosmic Logos, existing from all eternity with God (John 1:1-3). Nay, he *is* God (John 1:1; 20:28; Tit. 2:13; II Pet. 1:1). Such was the faith of the church. And while this gave the deity of Jesus a far more precise doctrinal expression than Jesus himself ever gave it, and thus laid the basis for the subsequent theology of orthodox Christendom, we cannot believe that it was an invention of the church. On the contrary, the church in so believing but correctly developed the claim of Jesus himself to be the Messiah king.[33]

[31] Cf. E. D. Burton, *The Epistle to the Galatians* (*International Critical Commentary* [Edinburgh: T. & T. Clark, 1921]) p. 224.

[32] The expression seems to be without parallel among the rabbis; cf. Strack-Billerbeck, *op. cit.*, I, 242-44. On the indications of Jesus' divine claim see, e.g., J. Bonsirven, *Theologie du Nouveau Testament* (Paris: Aubier, 1951), pp. 39-41.

[33] That Jesus was hailed, even before Paul, as Lord and Son of God is widely conceded (e.g., Bultmann, *op. cit.*, pp. 120-32). But I cannot agree with those (Bultmann, Dibelius, etc.) who find the origin of these titles in Hellenistic circles. Both stem from the royal (messianic) terminology of the Old Testament and if Jesus claimed to be Messiah at all, they would naturally have been applied to him by Jewish disciples. Cf. Wm. Manson, *op. cit.*, pp. 146-54.

But to Judaism this was an intolerable claim. Judaism had rightly abhorred those god-men, divine kings, "living messiahs," with which the pagan world swarmed. Indeed a century and a half previously Jews had fought and died rather than bow down to one (Antiochus Epiphanes!). To be sure, the Messiah whom the Jews expected was not thought of as a mere human. Certainly the Son of Man as he appears in I Enoch, for example, was conceived as a heavenly Being, pre-existing with God since before the creation of the world, and thus divine or semidivine. In the Old Testament, too, there are passages (e.g., Pss. 2:7; 89:27) where the Israelite king is addressed as the (adopted) "son" of God, and these passages had messianic overtones. The Messiah as he is depicted by Isaiah (9:6) is clearly endowed with divine qualities and is more than an ordinary mortal. Yet it would seem that Judaism, like the faith of old Israel, in a real sense held the redeeming God and the Messiah redeemer in balance; it never systematically brought the two together into a God-Messiah. We have little or no evidence that Judaism was accustomed to speak of the Messiah as the Son of God.[34] In any case, the Jews recognized in Jesus only a man, not some pre-existent heavenly figure; and for a mere man to suggest that he was both Messiah and divine could only be viewed by them as blasphemy. For it they could have but one answer: "We have a law, and by that law he ought to die, because he has made himself the Son of God" (John 19:7).

And what more did they need to prove them right than that, claiming to be Messiah and Son of God, he actually suffered and died? That shows him for the blasphemer he is! For if he were Messiah and divine, as he claims to be, he would not allow this to happen; he would come down from the cross (Matt. 27:41-43)! To a Jew, in fact, nothing could be more absurd than that one claiming to be the Son of the Living God should suffer and die.

In conclusion, then, we see that Christ took up and arrogated to himself the concepts of messiahship. But all of them he transfused with the concept of suffering. And this ensured, if nothing else did, his rejection.

[34] Although Judaism interpreted such passages as Pss. 2:7; 89:27 messianically, it understood the word "son" figuratively (e.g., "dear to me as a son to a father"); cf. Wm. Manson, op. cit., p. 149 and the illustrations from the Targums there. Rabbinic literature likewise avoids the appellation "Son of God" in speaking of the Messiah (cf. Strack-Billerbeck, op. cit., III, 15-21), but perhaps partly as a reaction against the Christian use of the term. There are passages in the Apochrypha and Pseudepigrapha (e.g., II [IV] Esdras 7:28; 13:32, I Enoch 105:2) where the appellation occurs, but many think these to be Christian glosses. In any event, such instances are not numerous.

Truly the cross was "unto the Jews a stumblingblock" (I Cor. 1:23 K.J.V.).

III

Yet in spite of the fact that the Jews could not see it so, it is clear that Jesus took his stand squarely in what was properly a messianic tradition—specifically in that of the Suffering Servant. In fact, it would seem that he consciously adopted the pattern of the Servant and suffused all the other messianic patterns with it.

1. Herein lies one of the strikingly novel things that Jesus did. And here, too, is perhaps the deepest reason for his rejection. For Judaism had never understood the Servant as a messianic figure at all. To be sure, the figure of the Servant as it appears in Isa. 40–66 cannot, as we have seen, be interpreted merely as a messianic figure. On the contrary, it was a very composite concept which stood at times for the people Israel, at times for the elect in Israel, the true Israel. But, as we also saw, it was difficult to escape the conclusion that the prophet at other times intended the Servant as an individual: the redeemer of his people, the leader of the true Israel—thus as a messianic figure, at least in the broader sense of that term. But Judaism had not understood it so. Although the Jews had a keen sense of the fact that the righteous must often suffer, and that that suffering is efficacious, they had always interpreted the Servant as a type of the sufferings of the nation, or of righteous individuals within it. There is little convincing evidence that the Jews before the time of Christ had any expectation of a suffering Messiah.[35] Rejecting the Servant, therefore, as a messianic pattern, they rejected him who filled it.

It is, of course, scarcely necessary to point out that there are striking parallels between the figure of the Servant and the Christ whom we know from the Gospels. Indeed such parallels leap to the eye in such numbers that it would be impossible to mention them all. If the Servant was "a root out of dry ground" (Isa. 53:2), "Is not this the carpenter's son?" (Matt. 13:55), and "Can anything good come out of Nazareth?" (John 1:46.) If the Servant (Isa. 42:6-7; 49:6) was to bring light to those who sat in darkness, here was one who was called "the light of the world" (John 8:12), and who declared that his followers were to be the same

[35] There have been those, to be sure, who have argued to the contrary but, in my opinion, the statement holds good. For the clearest statement of the case of which I know, with full bibliography and a convincing argument against a pre-Christian notion of a suffering Messiah, see the article of H. H. Rowley mentioned in notes 18 and 23.

(Matt. 5:14). If the Servant went about his mission with a quiet lack of ostentation (Isa. 42:2), here was one who repeatedly tried to conceal his mighty works, who never made a show of himself, and who in a thousand ways, by example and precept, inculcated the lesson of humility. If the Servant (Isa. 42:3) was gentle toward the "bruised reed" and the "dimly burning wick" of faith, here was one who was able to see the spark of good in the unlikeliest people, who was forever seeking the lost sheep, and who was incredibly patient with such very human disciples who, it seemed, would never understand him. And, finally, here was one who was schooled in God's school and "was not rebellious" (Isa. 50:4-5), but said, "Father, . . . not my will, but thine, be done" (Luke 22:42); who "gave [his] back to the smiters, . . . hid not [his] face from shame and spitting" (Isa. 50:6); who suffered himself to be crucified "like a lamb that is led to the slaughter" (Isa. 53:7). But enough! The church clearly understood its Lord as the great Suffering Servant. It could only add to the story of his passion the epilogue of faith: "Therefore God has highly exalted him" (Phil. 2:9-11; cf. Isa. 53:12).

But surely the church's understanding of its Lord was no coincidence! To the contrary! It is, in my opinion, the surest fact of New Testament criticism that Jesus both understood the parallel between his ministry and that of the Servant and intended it to be so.[36] The church understood Jesus as the Servant because he so understood himself. Not only did he read from Isa. 61 in the synagogue at Nazareth (Luke 4:17-21) and then announce that that prophecy was even then fulfilled; when John the Baptist sent to inquire if he were indeed the Christ (Matt. 11:2-6), he answered in words that were virtually a paraphrase of Isa. 61:1. His teachings, particularly the Sermon on the Mount, exhibit parallels to the Servant passages (especially Isa. 61) that are remarkable.[37] That premonition of death that hung over his ministry, the certainty that he would have to suffer (Mark 10:45), that he had "a baptism

---

[36] This is a major contention of Bowman (op. cit.), with which I am in fundamental agreement. A similar position has been held by a long list of competent scholars, although not a few (e.g., Bultmann, op. cit., pp. 30-31; F. C. Grant, op. cit., pp. 63-64, 157, etc.) have held to the contrary. For further bibliography cf. Rowley, The Servant of the Lord, p. 55. It seems certain that the identification of Jesus with the Servant had been made in the earliest days of the church. It is far easier to credit such an insight to Jesus himself— who, on the very lowest count, was one of the great creative minds of history—than to his early disciples, who were, for the most part, humble and very ordinary men.

[37] Cf. Wm. Manson, op. cit., p. 115 ff. for details.

to be baptized with" (Luke 12:50),[38] is a part of it. He knew his ministry would end in death, because he knew that he was the Servant. But by the same token he must have been confident that his death would not end the matter, for, with him as with the Servant, beyond sacrifice lies glory. The words of the final prayer which John reports must reflect this confidence perfectly, "I have finished the work which thou gavest me to do. And now, O Father, glorify thou me" (John 17:4-5 K.J.V.)

2. In any case, it is clear that Christ summoned men to the Kingdom of the Servant. It is a Kingdom of the meek and lowly in which the leader is he who is willing to be "last of all and servant of all" (Mark 9:35) or, as John records it (John 13:14-17), who has so little pride that he will consent to wash his fellow's feet. And who is called to that Kingdom? Why, all weary and heavy laden souls who are willing to take on themselves the gentle yoke of the Servant (Matt. 11:28-30). It welcomes all humble, kindly men who "hunger and thirst" for it and who are willing to serve it to the utmost (Matt. 5:3-12; Luke 6:20-23). Wealth will get no one into it; indeed, wealth has kept many a man out (Mark 10:17-25). External rectitude is no ticket of admission; for that the scribes and Pharisees had in plenty, and it is certain that crooks and prostitutes will enter the Kingdom ahead of them (Matt. 21:31). The Kingdom belongs, in the final analysis, to those who have stripped themselves of all pride—whether of station or of wisdom or of rectitude—and have become as little children (Mark 10:14)—eager to receive. When Paul said "not many wise . . . , not many mighty, not many noble" are called to that Kingdom (I Cor. 1:26 K.J.V.), he was indeed right!

Nor is the call of that Kingdom a call to honor or to victory, as the world understands those terms, but to utter self-denial. Over and over again we hear of the tremendous cost of it. One leaves father and mother, home and family, at its summons (Mark 10:29; Matt. 19:29; Luke 18:29), and when one has done so, he may be assured that he will be, like his Lord, a wanderer without where to lay his head (Matt. 8:20; Luke 9:58). One will be hated (Mark 13:13; Matt. 10:22), nay, persecuted (Luke 6:22; Matt. 5:10-11). But there will be no retaliation—only a turning of the other cheek (Matt. 5:39; cf. Isa. 50:6). He who heeds the call of the Kingdom has no destiny save to take up his cross and follow the Servant (Matt. 10:38; Luke 14:27; Mark 8:34).

---

[38] The verse, again, is not an *ex post facto* creation of the church. See note 22 above.

But to those who are called, there is given nothing less than the Servant mission: to proclaim the gospel of the Kingdom to all the nations of the earth. To be sure, this mission must begin, as did that of the Servant (Isa. 49:6), with the "lost sheep of the house of Israel" (Matt. 10:6; 15:24). This explains, no doubt, why Jesus confined his ministry almost entirely to his own people, and why when he first sent out his disciples to preach, he set on them the same limitations. It is interesting, too, that it was Paul's habit, when in the course of his travels he would come to a new city, to begin his preaching in the synagogue, to the Jews (e.g., Acts 13:13-50). But the mission was not only to the Jews. Jesus had already declared that "many will come from east and west and sit at table with Abraham, Isaac, and Jacob in the kingdom of heaven, while the sons of the kingdom [i.e., the Jews] will be thrown into the outer darkness" (Matt. 8:11-12). He had foreseen the time when, the guests bidden to his feast (i.e., righteous Jews) having snubbed the invitation and there not being sufficient poor in the city (i.e., other Jews) to fill the table, his servants would scour the highways and hedges (i.e., the world) to find other guests (Matt. 22:1-10; Luke 14:15-24).[39] His servants are indeed like the Servant (Isa. 42:6; 49:6), a light to the world (Matt. 5:14). If the church remembered the last words of its earthly Lord as a command to preach the gospel in all the earth (Matt. 28:19-20; Mark 16:15; Luke 24:47; Acts 1:8), it only understood his intention perfectly: to give them the Servant task.[40]

3. Christ, therefore, clearly fulfilled the prophecy of the Servant of Yahweh. This profound truth is given classical expression by Paul in Phil. 2:5-11. This great passage might well be called a Christian commentary on Isa. 53 (cf. Isa. 45:23).[41] In making it Paul not only agreed

[39] As T. W. Manson (Major, Manson and Wright, op. cit., p. 422) points out, the parable might well be regarded as a midrash on Isa. 49:6.

[40] Of course, what with the varied forms of it which we have, it is impossible to say exactly what the words of the Great Commission were. There have been those who question its authenticity altogether. But, in my opinion, that Jesus gave his disciples such a commission is absolutely certain, otherwise it is unlikely that they would ever have become so energetically missionary. Besides, if Jesus regarded himself as the Servant, the missionary command follows necessarily—for it was part of the Servant's task. Cf. Rowley, The Biblical Doctrine of Election, pp. 143-44 for a splendid evaluation and bibliographical references.

[41] Phil. 2:6-11 is perhaps an adaptation of an early Christian hymn. Bultmann (op. cit., pp. 27-28) argues that the passage is given no messianic significance and that this is further proof that Jesus had no messianic consciousness. True, the picture here is not of

211

with the mind of the New Testament throughout but also with Jesus' own intention. When he said that Jesus took on himself the form of a Servant, he was not only correct,*he is to be taken quite literally.*For that was the pattern that Christ consciously adopted.

Christ did indeed fulfill the prophetic hope of Israel. He announced that in his own person all that the Old Testament had foreshadowed and predicted had been made actual. But this prediction and fulfillment is not to be seen as the mechanical and external thing so many people conceive it to be. It is not as if Christ were everywhere hidden in the Old Testament, so that we may find types of him almost at will in Old Testament characters and institutions. Nor is it that we may read into the prophet words literal predictions of events which Jesus in his life and death in detail after detail fulfilled, thereby to furnish proof positive that the Bible is divinely inspired and that he was what he claimed to be. This is to view the whole matter of Old Testament prophecy and New Testament fulfillment in a thoroughly artificial light. It is to make of the Old Testament a book written merely to predict Christ, and of the prophets little more than stenographers who wrote words the meaning of which they themselves could hardly have understood, but which nevertheless foretold incidents in the life of him who was to come. It is also to violate all principles of sound exegesis. For we are not permitted arbitrarily to superimpose meanings on Scripture, and we cannot read Christ at will into the Old Testament. Loyalty to the exact sense of Scripture forbids such a course. No amount of zeal to exalt Christ or to defend the inspiration of the Bible can excuse it.

Nevertheless, the Old Testament does in the truest sense foreshadow Christ and point to him. But that foreshadowing is far more than a matter of isolated and detailed predictions; it is something organic to Israel's faith itself. The Old Testament in all its parts is supported by a deep sense of the rule of God over his covenant people. And because Israel believed her God to be the Lord of history who works his purpose in history and summons Israel to be the servant of that purpose, she could conceive of no other end for history than the victorious establishment of God's people under that rule. The Old Testament faith by its

---

the conventional Messiah King. But if Jesus saw it as his mission to fulfill the messianic hope in the pattern of the Servant, then the passage hails Jesus as the Messiah, for it hails him as the Servant.

very nature pointed ahead and announced the coming Kingdom of God. It awaited its fulfillment.

Now we have observed—although this is by no means universally the case—a strong tendency in the Old Testament to crystallize the hope of the coming Kingdom about the figure of the God-sent Redeemer. The prophets conceived of that Redeemer, and predicted his coming under a variety of patterns—Davidic Messiah, Son of Man, Suffering Servant— but all were facets of the same hope. Surely the God whose Kingdom comes will not leave that Kingdom leaderless, but will accomplish his purpose through his designated representative! The messianic patterns are not isolated predictions, but expressions of faith in the Redeeming God as shaped by the thought forms and experiences of ancient Israel. Of all these patterns the profoundest, although the Jews did not see it so, is that of the Servant. And this is far more than a mere prediction; it is a comprehension of the character of Israel's God and the nature of his redemptive purpose. When it was granted to the prophet to see who his God was, it was given to him to understand that such a God would establish his Kingdom not with battle and glory and national victory, but with the devotion, the abnegation, the vicarious sacrifice of his Servant. And that hope, too, awaited its fulfillment—the appearance of the Redeemer in visible form. Although no Jew would have dreamed of putting it so, it awaited its *incarnation*.

The Old Testament hope of redemption, then, was an outgrowth of an understanding of the character of Israel's God. It found its fulfillment *because that understanding was correct, and because Christ was Christ.* Christ on the one hand (himself, we believe, in the express image of God) understood well the nature of God the Father and, because he did so, understood that the Servant was the truest and final messianic pattern. On the other hand, because he was moved by a deep messianic vocation, he knew that he must take on him the form of the Servant. Israel had been called to make that pattern actual, but could not any more than can we, nor could any individual in Israel do so. Christ, however, took it for his own, suffused the other messianic patterns with it, and lived it out to the death. He fulfilled the messianic hope of Israel by incarnating it in the form of a Servant.

This fulfillment was real, and it was on Christ's part quite intentional. Christ took on himself the pattern of the Servant, fulfilled the prophecy of the Servant, *because he understood it as his messianic calling to do so.*

213

The longed-for Messiah Prince must come as a Suffering Servant. The righteousness which the law sought to create must be fulfilled through the sacrificial obedience of the Servant. The ineffable glory of the Son of Man and of the victorious saints of God is to be reached through the doorway of the cross of the Servant. That true and purified Israel with whom there will be made a New Covenant—is exactly the people of the Servant. All the hope of Israel, and all the patterns which it assumed, are one, and are fulfilled in the servant.

Whether Jesus was the first to unite all these messianic concepts under the figure of the Servant is a debated question, although it seems very probable that he was. The important thing, however, is that he did so and, what is vastly more, declared that that Servant has come: "Today this scripture has been fulfilled in your hearing" (Luke 4:21). Here is the Suffering Servant of God, the Messiah of the Remnant. As such the church hailed him in Greek words which are virtually equivalent: Crucified Saviour, Lord of the Church.[42] These are all words pregnant with meaning, and we must inquire into them further. Particularly we must ask what sort of a Kingdom it is that this Messiah has come to set up, and who is the Remnant to whom it is given.

[42] Cf. Bowman, op. cit., pp. viii, 81.

CHAPTER EIGHT

Between Two Worlds: The Kingdom and the Church

THE NEW TESTAMENT ANNOUNCES WITH ONE VOICE AND WITH UNSHAK-
ABLE ASSURANCE THAT ALL THE HOPE OF ISRAEL HAS BECOME PRESENT
fact in Jesus Christ. It makes this assertion because it believed that in
him the promised Messiah had come. The position has been taken in
the preceding chapter that the New Testament so asserts because
Jesus himself so believed and so claimed; it has also been contended
that if Jesus was not accepted as Messiah by the Jews—and it is
obvious that he was not—it was because he came as a strange
Messiah and not the expected one. Refusing the popular messianic
patterns he seized upon a pattern which, although in the intention of
the ancient prophet it was indeed messianic in character, had not been
regarded by the Jews as such: that of the Suffering Servant of Yahweh.
He consciously and intentionally adopted that pattern as his own, and,
suffusing the other messianic patterns with it, he announced the fulfillment of the prophetic hope of Israel in the form of a Redeemer who
must suffer.

But if Jesus be indeed the Messiah, that confronts us with a further
question: what is the nature of his Kingdom? It is a question that follows inevitably. To acclaim anyone as Messiah is to announce in him
the coming of the Kingdom of God, for it is precisely the business of
the Messiah to establish the Kingdom. Messiah cannot be separated from

215

Kingdom. To be sure, both the Old Testament faith and that of Judaism frequently depicted the triumphant Kingdom with no mention of the Messiah, but the Messiah was never himself thought of apart from that Kingdom: when Messiah comes, the Kingdom comes. A Messiah who had come to set up no Kingdom would have been an anomaly indeed. If Jesus, therefore, is in any sense the Messiah, then he has come to make actual the victorious rule of God over his people which Israel's faith had long awaited. And this, the New Testament declares, Jesus has done. But in what sense did he do so? Or to put it differently, What is his Kingdom? Who inherits it? How does its victory come? To this question we must now turn. It is not an easy question, and the answer is not obvious.

I

It lies at the very heart of the gospel message to affirm that the Kingdom of God has in a real sense become present fact, here and now. We have already remarked upon the dramatic change of tense which the New Testament brings in speaking of the Kingdom. The future tense of the Old Testament ("behold the days are coming," and the like) has now become an emphatic present: "The kingdom of God is at hand" (Mark 1:15). The final act of the drama has even now begun, the messianic age has dawned; he who is greater than Solomon, greater than Jonah (Luke 11:31-32), nay greater than temple and law (Matt. 12:6-8), is here. The Servant is even now on the scene (Luke 4:17-21), and his works may be seen of all (Matt. 11:2-6). This is the day which all the past desired to see, but did not (Luke 10:23-24). No need any more to look wildly about for signs of the Kingdom's imminent coming: it is right here "among you" (Luke 17:21).[1] In the person and work of Jesus the Kingdom of God has intruded into the world.

1. The conviction that this was so is splendidly illustrated by the atti-

---

[1] The exact force of Luke 17:21 is so much debated that it might, perhaps, be the part of caution not to cite it in this connection. The reading "among you" (A.S.V. margin) seems preferable to "within you," although arguments almost equally strong may be advanced for either reading (cf. Major, Manson and Wright, The Mission and Message of Jesus [New York: E. P. Dutton & Co., 1938], pp. 36-37, where Professor Major prefers "within," and pp. 595 ff., where Professor Manson argues strongly for "among.") But does Jesus mean to say that the Kingdom is even now in the midst (so that there is no need to look for its coming), or did he mean that it will come suddenly (without preliminary signs)? A strong case can be made for either, and scholarly opinion is divided. While I cannot here give my supporting reasons, I have tentatively preferred the former alternative.

tude of the gospel writers—and, we may believe, of Jesus himself—toward the miracles which Jesus performed. Now the miracles are a sore subject in the minds of many people. They have frequently enough become a stumbling block to faith and a source of skepticism. Some of them, to be sure, in the light of all that is now known of psychosomatic relationships, are credible enough, and even the most agnostic have little difficulty in believing in them. But others resist all attempts at rationalization. They are incapable of explanation in terms of natural causation, as our finite minds understand it, and must be accepted or rejected for what they are. A great many books—most of them, it is to be feared, futile books—have been written on the subject of miracles which have sought either to prove that they happened just so, or that they could not possibly have happened at all. To take up that subject would carry us far afield indeed. It is a subject that ought to be approached honestly (for we have not been told that we must leave our minds behind us on entering the Kingdom of God) but with humility. For who, after all, shall say what is possible with God?

But the point that must be made here is that however one regards the miracles, he cannot escape the fact that they were an integral part of the New Testament faith in its Lord. He who regards them as an excrescence of the gospel story, an expression of the beliefs of a superstitious age which must be scraped away in order to get back to Jesus as he really was, may indeed recover a Jesus palatable to a rationalist intellect—but he may be assured that it will not be the Jesus of the New Testament faith. Nor may one regard them, as many who are inclined to accept them without question are prone to do, as more or less peripheral manifestations of our Lord's power which were performed in order to furnish proof that he was what he claimed to be. To be sure, the early church found such proof in them (e.g., Acts 2:22). But Christ himself consistently refused to use his powers for that purpose. In fact he said that anyone whose ears were deaf to the gospel Word would not believe such proof anyway, not even the raising of the dead before his very eyes (cf. Luke 16:29-31).

To the New Testament faith the miracles which Jesus performed were not incidental or peripheral, but integral to his person. And they were understood eschatologically.[2] That is, they were illustrations of the fact

---

[2] For further discussion of the point, see e.g., F. C. Grant, *An Introduction to New Testament Thought* (New York and Nashville: Abingdon-Cokesbury Press, 1950), pp.

that in Christ the new age was even then intruding upon the present one: the power of the Kingdom of God was present in them and was grappling with the evil power of this age. In the language of the Synoptic Gospels, at least, the miracles of Christ are never spoken of as "signs and wonders" (sēmeia kai terata), i.e., self-authenticating exhibitions of divine power designed to approve the claims of Jesus in the eyes of the people. Indeed, such "signs" (i.e., marvels) were precisely the sort of thing Christ refused to perform (e.g., Mark 8:11-12; Matt. 12:38-40). False messiahs are the ones who show off with "signs and wonders" (Mark 13:22; Matt. 24:24), and for Jesus to have done likewise would have been, from that point of view at least, the flat disproof of his claim to be the true Messiah. On the contrary, his miracles are "mighty works" ("powers," dunameis) of the Kingdom of God, which in them advertises its presence; they are a taste of "the powers of the age to come" (Heb. 6:5). In them the grip of the Adversary—who has enthralled men in bonds of disease, madness, death, and sin—begins to be loosened. When the Pharisees accused Jesus of casting out demons by the power of Satan, he replied that if that be so, Satan's house is divided and cannot stand; "But if it is by the finger of God that I cast out demons, then the kingdom of God has come upon you" (Luke 11:20; Matt. 12:28). In the mighty works of Jesus the power of that Kingdom has broken into the world; Satan has met his match (Luke 10:18; Mark 3:27); the cosmic end-struggle has begun.

The Kingdom of God, then, is a power already released in the world. True, its beginnings are tiny, and it might seem incredible that the humble ministry of this obscure Galilean could be the dawning of the new age of God. Yet it is! What has been begun here will surely go on to its conclusion; nothing can stop it. And the conclusion is victory. Over and over again this motif recurs in the teachings of Jesus. A lump of yeast may be small, but once put to work it will leaven a very large quantity of dough (Matt. 13:33). A mustard seed is a very tiny seed indeed, but if you plant it, it will become one of the largest of trees (Matt. 13:31-32). If you sow a field with seed, you have set in motion forces which one day will inevitably produce the harvest (Mark 4:26-29). And the Kingdom of God is just like that. It is small now, but in these small beginnings

148-59, 200; J. W. Bowman, The Intention of Jesus (Philadelphia: The Westminster Press, 1943), pp. 109-15; Wm. Manson, Jesus the Messiah (Philadelphia: The Westminster Press, 1946), ch. 3.

there lie hidden its victory.[3] And that victory will reach out into all the earth, for "all authority . . . has been given to me" (Matt. 28:18).

2. But if the Kingdom of God has in a real sense entered the world, then men are called to the service of that Kingdom. For the Kingdom is no empty domain, so many square miles of territory with geographical frontiers—it is people. Or to put it otherwise, the Messiah never appears as a lone figure ruling in solitary majesty, but always with corporate qualities. He rules over his people; he calls people to his rule. If Jesus, then, be the Messiah, where is the Remnant? If he be the Son of Man, where are the saints of his glorious reign? If he be a new Moses to give a new law, where is the new Israel to receive it? If he be the Servant, "Who among you fears the Lord and obeys the voice of his Servant" (Isa. 50:10)?

Christ, then, has come to call men to his Kingdom. His mission was not to instruct men in a better and more spiritual ethic, to impart to men a clearer understanding of the character of God, to attack those abuses which had made the Jewish law the stultification of the religious spirit and to suggest certain emendations to that law—in short, to point men the way to be better men. All this he did, indeed, and with a vengeance. But he did it in the dazzling light of the coming Kingdom. His was a call of tremendous urgency, a call to radical decision for that Kingdom. The Kingdom is *right there*, "at hand." It stands at the door and knocks (Luke 12:36, cf. Rev. 3:20). Who will open and let it in? Who will say Yes to its coming? Over and over again in the Gospels comes the radical urgency of its call. It is a pearl of great price; you sell everything you have to get it (Matt. 13:45-46). You leave father and mother, wife and family, as if you hated them, at its beck (Luke 14:26). It transcends all earthly concerns (Matt. 6:33). If it were a question of gouging out your eye and entering it blind or having two eyes to be excluded from it, you would without hesitation mutilate yourself in order to get in (Mark 9:47). No call to be trifled with, this—like the man who

---

[3] The stress of these parables does not seem to lie upon the length of time involved, as if to teach that the Kingdom comes by a process of growth, nor upon the contrast between small beginnings and large results (e.g., A. H. McNeile, *The Gospel According to St. Matthew* [London: The Macmillan Co., 1915], pp. 198-99), although this feature may well be present, but upon the fact that forces have been set in motion which inevitably move to fruition. See the commentaries: e.g., T. W. Manson in Major, Manson and Wright (*op. cit.* pp. 415, 596-97). C. H. Dodd, however (*The Parables of the Kingdom* [London: Nisbet & Co., 1935] pp. 175-94), in line with his "realized eschatology," argues that the parables announce a present, not a future, fruition.

puts his hand to the plow and then turns back (Luke 9:62)! No call to be answered with a modicum of moral improvement, a burst of zeal, a few New Year's resolutions to live a better life! It is a call to total and radical obedience, to an utterly impossible righteousness, to be perfect as God is perfect (Matt. 5:48): in short, a call to the righteousness of the Kingdom of God to which no man can attain, yet to which he may give the answer of faith. For to say Yes to the Kingdom and to submit to its rule is faith (Mark 1:15; cf. Rom. 3:22). And it is of faith's nature to cry, "Lord, I believe; help thou mine unbelief" (Mark 9:24 K.J.V.).

This call to radical decision for the Kingdom Christ issued to men. And those who heed it have entered the Kingdom, nay, are the Kingdom. More than any of the prophets that were before him, Christ addressed himself to the hearts of individual men. For the true Israel—the true people of the Kingdom—are not those who are Israelites by race, nor yet those who are of that elite group in Israel who know and keep an external law, but those individual men, however lowly and weak, who have in heart and deed signified their obedience to the calling of God. Not that obedience, in the sense of the performance of certain external duties, is made the condition of entrance into the Kingdom! No New Testament writer would have dreamed of saying such a thing. On the contrary, let any who have been inclined to separate those who are Christian from those who are not along the lines of duties performed or omitted, rules kept or broken, but read Paul again as with passionate zeal he declares the bankruptcy of all religious "works." The works of the law are dead: they cannot produce righteousness but can only, at best, awaken a consciousness of sin (Rom. 3:20). To sink back into the law is to put chains on one's self (Gal 5:1) and to fall from the grace of Christ (Gal. 5:4); for redemption is purely a matter of God's grace in Christ Jesus received by faith alone (Rom. 3:22-26; 5:1-2). Nor in saying these things did Paul mistake his Lord. For Christ himself freely welcomed into his Kingdom unsavory folk who had no visible righteousness at all, while declaring that the doctors of the law who had righteousness in plenty could never get in (Matt. 5:20; 21:31).

Obedience, then, is not the condition of entrance into the Kingdom of God. Yet, in another sense, condition of entrance it is, in that by it is signified the willingness and the desire to enter. What is more, it is the seal of him who has entered. Indeed, we may say that there run through the New Testament two parallel themes which might superficially seem to contradict each other. On the one hand we hear, particularly in Paul: only through the grace of God in Jesus Christ, received by faith without regard to the works of the law! And on the other hand: not without works, for he that does not do the works of Christ is a sham Christian and no member of Christ's Church! This last, of course, receives its most striking expression in the Epistle of James: a man is justified precisely by his works (2:24); faith without works is dead (2:14-18), for works are the index of faith. Indeed, as we read elsewhere (I John 4:20), the man who mouths of his devotion to God, and does not do such good works, is plainly a liar without a spark of truth in him. Nevertheless, we should do wrong to exaggerate this seeming contrast. However much James may have differed from Paul in his theology, on this point he and Paul are one: Paul demanded good demeanor of the Christian no less than did James.[4] And both of them are in line with fundamental emphases of the gospel.

In any event, it is repeatedly insisted in the Gospels that the members of Christ's Kingdom are those that obey him. Christ's own are those who have fed the hungry, clothed the naked, shown mercy to the prisoner and outcast—who have, in short, done the works of Christ (Matt. 25:31-46). Those who have not, whatever their profession and creed, simply are none of his. It does no good to hail him "Lord, Lord," to honor his name in doctrine, hymn, and prayer, if one does not obey him (Matt. 7:21-23). But whoever does obey him, whoever he may be, is his brother and next of kin (Mark 3:35).

3. It is in the light of the summons of the Kingdom of God that the New Testament ethics are to be understood. It is most important that we realize this, and it might be well if we paused a moment to underscore it. Jesus did not present his ethical teachings as a program which he expected the secular order either of his day or ours to carry out. To say this may, at first blush, sound shocking. For Christ certainly meant his teachings to be taken seriously, and he certainly believed that the unrighteous societies of this world were under the judgment of God. Yet the fact remains that he did not set out to reform society, but to do far more: he summoned men to the Kingdom of God and its righteousness. And his

---

[4] On the relationship of James to Paul, see the commentaries: e.g., J. H. Ropes, *The Epistle of St. James* (*International Critical Commentary* [Edinburgh: T. & T. Clark, 1916]), pp. 28-39. Whatever the limitations of James's theology (he does not mention the cross!), the differences are not to be exaggerated. Above all, we cannot with Luther brand James "a right strawy epistle."

221

ethical teachings are the righteousness of that Kingdom. As such, of course, they are incumbent upon all servants of the Kingdom. But by the same token they lie beyond men who do not acknowledge its lordship.

It is, therefore, a major error to think of the Christian gospel as a program of reform which society, as it presently is, may be expected to realize. This has been the error of much of "liberal" Christianity.[5] To be sure, we ought to thank the "liberal" for reminding us—what we sorely needed to be reminded of—that the demands of Christ are precisely ethical. It is true, too, that the preaching of Christian ethics has through the years had an impact upon secular society and has made it a better place in which to live. Indeed, one hates to think what society would be without the leavening influence of Christian morality. But to present the Christian gospel merely as a program of social righteousness is fundamentally to mistake the Christ of the Gospels and to tread a path of frustration and disillusionment. For a non-Christian world will not put into practice the ethics of Christ and cannot, for all our chiding, be made to do so. In a non-Christian world the teachings of Jesus are simply not "practical," as that world is quick to declare. To realize the ethics of the Kingdom it is first necessary that men submit to the rule of that Kingdom.

But the fact that the ethics of Jesus are the ethics of the Kingdom of God, and thus cannot be made into a program for the kingdoms of this earth, cannot be used as an excuse to absolve us of the burden of them. Such an excuse is often enough given. There will be the millennialist (and one frequently encounters such) who, when taxed with the fact that certain actions or certain social patterns are not in accord with the teachings of Jesus, will freely admit it but will declare that since the ethics of Jesus are the ethics of the Kingdom, it is not expected that they be practiced until that millennial Kingdom comes. If this seem a caricature, it can only be said that it is scarcely a worse one than the Christian who is all zeal for the propagation of the faith and who comforts himself that, if this be done, Christian social ethics will take care of themselves—but who advertises by his behavior that he does not feel them to be very practical. Nor can we, on the other hand, escape our dilemma by labeling

[5] The evaluation of Bowman (op. cit., pp. 192-96) of this aspect of "liberal" Christianity is highly to be commended. On the teachings of Jesus and their relation to the Kingdom, see e.g. T. W. Manson, The Teaching of Jesus (2nd ed.; Cambridge University Press, 1935), esp. pp. 285 ff.

the ethics of Jesus "interim ethics," as Schweitzer and others have done.[6] These have felt that the teachings of Jesus were surely too exacting for normal human life and must, therefore, have been intended merely as a pattern of behavior for Christians in the brief interim that was expected by the early church (and Jesus!) before the final end. But if that be so, what authority at all can they have over us today who live long after that expected interim has passed?

The ethics of Jesus are the ethics of the Kingdom; and Jesus expected his followers to take them seriously, not only in his generation but in all generations. For in New Testament theology the Kingdom of God is not only the goal of all history and the reward of all believers, not only the norm by which all human behavior is judged, it is a new order which even now bursts in upon the present one and summons men to be its people. Its summons demands response, and that response is obedience and righteousness here and now. Christ intended his followers to live each day in the light of the Kingdom which is intruding into the world, to live each day as if the end were tomorrow. It is a call to "eschatological living," if we may use the term. The ethics of the New Testament are like the ethical demands of the Old Covenant which thundered on the lips of the prophets, in this fact: they are the means by which men show that they are the true people of God's Kingdom. If obedience is not given, in New Covenant as in Old, then "you are not my people" (Hos. 1:9)!

Exactly here is the relationship of social gospel to gospel of individual salvation, and it is important that we get it. The two are not to be set apart as has so often been done, for they are two aspects of the same thing. Indeed, they are as intimate to each other as the opposite sides of the same coin. We can no longer, as "liberals" have done, preach the ethics of Jesus and leave aside his person and work as if it were a cumbrous and superfluous theological baggage. At least if we do so, we must know

---

[6] Albert Schweitzer, whose name is known to all, in his *Geschichte der Leben-Jesu Forschung* (2nd ed.; Tübingen: J. C. B. Mohr, 1913; English translation by W. Montgomery, *The Quest of the Historical Jesus* [London: A. & C. Black, 1910 (2nd ed. 1922); reprinted New York: The Macmillan Co., 1948]) set forth a devastating critique of the "liberal" Jesus which became a landmark in New Testament studies. But, in his zeal to stress the eschatological character of Jesus' ministry, he went far too far—even to the point of arguing that Jesus expected the Kingdom to come before his disciples had completed their first preaching mission (Matt. 10:23); and that, when disappointed in this, he went up to Jerusalem with the deliberate intention of precipitating the Kingdom by his own death. Since Jesus, in this view, expected the Kingdom momentarily, his teachings were given to govern his disciples' behavior only in the short interim that remained. In this extreme position Schweitzer would find few followers today.

that we do not preach the Jesus of the New Testament faith. Nor can we, as "conservatives" have tended to do, sneer at the "liberal" for not preaching a full gospel and then, because we urge men to salvation through faith, feel no need even to confront ourselves and our people with the demands of the righteousness of the Kingdom. This, too, is not to preach the Christ of the New Testament, but an incomplete Christ. We have not two gospels, social and personal, which vie for the limelight. We have one gospel, the gospel of the Kingdom of God, and it is both. We have simply nothing else to preach. Let us be sure that we are summoned to obey it in all our dealings within the Church of Christ, and also beyond that Church wherever we meet our brother. It is a thought of no comfort that Christ has told us that as we have treated our brother, so have we treated him (Matt. 25:31-46)!

II

Christ, then, announced that the Kingdom of God had come into the world, and he summoned men to that Kingdom. The New Testament affirms with one voice that those who have obeyed the call of Christ are his true Church and heirs of all the promises given to Israel (e.g., Rom. 4:13-15; Gal. 3:29; Tit. 3:7; Jas. 2:5).

1. Now we cannot turn aside to discuss at length the question of the sense in which Jesus intended to found a church. Some have denied that he had any such intention at all.[7] It is true that the word "church" is placed on Jesus' lips but rarely (Matt. 16:18; 18:17), and then in passages of extreme difficulty.[8] But that Jesus is indeed to be seen as the great

[7] For example, A. von Harnack, The Mission and Expansion of Christianity (New York: G. P. Putnam's Sons; 2nd ed.; London: Williams & Norgate, 1908), I, 407; recently, apparently, R. Bultmann, Theologie des Neuen Testaments (Tübingen: J. C. B. Mohr, 1948), I, 8, where will be found further bibliography on the question. M. Goguel (L'Eglise Primitive [Paris: Payot, 1947], p. 16) quotes A. Loisy (L'Evangile et L'Eglise, p. 152) to the effect that Jesus announced the Kingdom of God, but it was the Church that came. It would seem that we have to do very much with a matter of definition: what is meant by "church"? We may grant that Jesus did not intend to found a new religion, nor envision the organization of any of the churches that came to exist, but if as Messiah he came to call out the true Israel, the idea of the Church is inevitably present. See the excellent discussion of R. N. Flew, Jesus and His Church (2nd ed.; London: Epworth Press, 1943), pp. 17-88.

[8] These two verses contain the only occurrences of the word "church" on the lips of Jesus, and both are widely regarded as not genuine words of his. To discuss the critical issue here is out of the question. It seems reasonable that Jesus used some Aramaic word (kenîshta?) and the Evangelist selected the Greek word ekklēsia (church) as the translation most understandable to his readers. Cf. McNeile, op. cit., pp. 241-42; M. J. Lagrange, Évangile selon Saint Matthieu (3rd ed.; Paris: Librairie Lecoffre, 1927), pp. 324-25; Flew, op. cit., pp. 89-98.

Founder of the Church is, we believe, beyond question. To be sure, it was not his aim to found a new religion, and he certainly did not set up the organization of any particular church—not even that of your denomination! To test our ecclesiastical institutions by the teachings of Jesus and the apostles is right and proper, and only what we ought to do. But the attempt to prove that they, and they alone, had their origin and authentication there has often enough produced results both amazing and amusing—and not a little tragic. It is to be doubted if the Lord of the Church would approve of such procedures. In that sense of the word Jesus founded no church at all. But the Church is vastly more than that. Jesus founded no ecclesiastical organization, not even of the loosest sort, but as Messiah he came to call out the Remnant. In that true Israel which was obedient to his call lie the seeds of his Church, his *ekklēsia* (i.e., the ones called out). There is, therefore, no need to ask after the origins of the Church as though it were founded on a given date, say with Peter's confession (Matt. 16:16-17) or at Pentecost (Acts 2; cf. 1:8). The Church was founded on no date and can observe no formal anniversary. It began in those few about Jesus who had been obedient to the call of the Kingdom. Nay, it began in the Old Covenant itself and in the Old Testament longing for the true Israel of God's purpose.[9]

In the Church, so the New Testament declares, is all the longing for a true Israel fit to inherit the promised Kingdom—a longing best summed up in the concept of the Remnant—fulfilled. Now Israel was sustained by the confidence that she was the elect people of God. She believed that God had entered into covenant with her, and had purposed at the turning point of history to establish her under his rule in peace. But Israel had early given evidence by her behavior that she was no true and obedient people of God. She could not, therefore, inherit the promises, but lay under judgment—so the prophets announced repeatedly. Thus it was, we recall, that at least since the eighth century B.C. there had been the growing tendency to divorce the idea of the people of God from the physical people Israel. Yet at the same time the confidence was maintained that there would emerge from history's tragedy a righteous nucleus of Israel which would be truly the people of God and which would inherit the promised Kingdom. Isaiah gave this hope classical expression

[9] Cf. Grant, *op. cit.*, pp. 268-70 on this point.

as he envisioned a pure Remnant, refined in the fiery purge, over which the Messiah Prince would reign. But the longing for a Remnant is to be found in all the prophets even where the word is not used. Jeremiah's vision of a new Israel with whom God will make a New Covenant (Jer. 31:31-34), Ezekiel's vision of the resurrected nation (Ezek. 37), and Second Isaiah's description of the people who obey the Servant—all are variations of the same hope. Israel will indeed inherit the Kingdom of God, but it must be a new and spiritual Israel.

But here is One who, we have argued, consciously adopted the pattern of the Servant and fulfilled it, who summoned men into the humble and lowly company of the Servant and gave them the Servant mission of proclaiming the gospel of the Kingdom in the world; who even selected disciples to the number of twelve, as if symbolic of the twelve tribes of Israel (cf. Matt. 19:28).[10] It is as if Jesus wished to say in a living parable that in his person, his work, and his calling to men, he was laying the foundations of a new Israel and giving it its true destiny. That hope for the pure Israel of the Remnant which in blind human pride had so often attached itself to this or that fragment group in Israel—be it Jehoiachin and the deportees of 598 B.C., be it Zerubbabel and the Restoration community, or whatnot—and which the Holy Commonwealth had struggled so manfully and so futilely to make actual, is *here*. Here in Jesus and the community of his followers is the true Israel. And, it is worth noting, it is a community already in the intention of Jesus divorced from national lines (Matt. 8:11; 21:43; Luke 14:15-24), precisely along the lines laid down by Second Isaiah. In the work of Paul and others that intention became actual fact.[11]

In any case, the New Testament triumphantly hails the Church as Israel according to the spirit, the true heir of Israel's hope. We cannot begin to discuss adequately even the use that Paul alone makes of this

---

[10] J. Weiss (*Das Urchristentum* [Göttingen: Vandenhoeck & Rupprecht, 1917], pp. 33-34) and others have argued that the number 12 represents the effort of the church to schematize the number of Jesus' disciples to accord with the tribes of Israel (cf. Luke 22:30; Matt. 19:28). My belief is that Jesus himself selected 12 disciples for the same symbolic reason (cf. Bowman, *op. cit.*, pp. 209 ff.). K. Lake and H. J. Cadbury (*The Acts of the Apostles* [*The Beginnings of Christianity*, Pt. I, F. J. Foakes Jackson and K. Lake eds. (New York and London: The Macmillan Co., 1933, IV, 12) suggest that the 120 disciples of Acts 1:15 represent 12 multiplied by 10, 10 being according to the Mishnah the number required to form a congregation.

[11] On the missionary intention of Jesus, cf. p. 211 above.

notion.[12] Israel is not Israel simply because it boasts that it is Abraham's seed (Rom. 9:6-8), nor is a man a Jew just because he has been circumcised; he is a Jew who in his inmost heart has surrendered himself to God (Rom. 2:28-29). Israel is a tree, some of whose branches have been broken off through unbelief; and now new branches are grafted on (Rom. 11:17-19). The Church is the true "Israel of God" (Gal 6:16), "a remnant, chosen by grace" (Rom. 11:5). All who are Christ's are Abraham's seed and heirs of the promises (Gal. 3:29).[13]

But if Paul is emphatic, he but echoes the sentiments of the entire New Testament church. The Church is the true twelve tribes of Israel (Jas. 1:1). It is "a chosen race, a royal priesthood, a holy nation" (i.e., the true Israel) which has as its mission to exhibit before the world the glory of the God who called it to be his people (I Pet. 2:9-10; cf. Isa. 49:6). It is "a kingdom of priests" (Rev. 1:6; 5:10): i.e., it is the "kingdom of priests" and the "holy nation" (Exod. 19:6) which Israel was called to be. Nay, as Israel in the language of many a prophet (e.g., Hos. 1–3; Jer. 3:1-5; Isa. 54:4-7) was the wife of God, so the Church is the bride of Christ (Eph. 5:22-33; Rev. 21:2, 9-11). And, highest of all, as in the Old Testament the figure of the Servant blends with that of his followers, so that we are often put to it to say whether an individual or a group is intended, so Christ and his Church become one corporate body: "You are the body of Christ," says Paul (I Cor. 12:27). Or as John puts it, the Church is the branches of the vine which is Christ (John 15:5). Or, as Paul again repeatedly puts it (e.g., Rom. 12:5; I Cor. 1:30; Col. 1:28), the Christian is "in Christ": i.e., organically related to Christ and to his fellow believer in the community of the new people of God, the body of which Christ is the head.[14]

[12] For a thorough discussion cf. W. D. Davies, Paul and Rabbinic Judaism (London: S. P. C. K., 1948), ch. 4; for an excellent, brief summary of the evidence in general, cf. Rowley, The Biblical Doctrine of Election, pp. 144 ff.; Flew, op. cit., 100-104, 158, etc.; T. W. Manson, op. cit., pp. 171-91.

[13] It must be said that some (e.g., E. D. Burton, The Epistle to the Galatians [International Critical Commentary (Edinburgh: T. & T. Clark, 1921)], pp. 155-59, 358, etc.) argue that these terms (e.g., "Israel of God," Gal. 6:16) refer not to the church but to the faithful, but yet unenlightened, in Israel. We cannot debate the matter here. But I must agree strongly with the majority of scholars whose works I have consulted that Paul regarded the church as the Remnant. Aside from the works mentioned in note 12, cf. especially James Moffatt, Grace in the New Testament (London: Hodder & Stoughton, 1931), p. 117, for discussion of Burton's position.

[14] See, e.g.,: C. A. A. Scott, Christianity According to St. Paul (Cambridge University Press, 1927), pp. 151-58; J. Knox, Chapters in a Life of Paul (New York and Nashville: Abingdon-Cokesbury Press, 1950), pp. 111-59.

2. But if the Church is the true Israel, then it is the people of the covenant. The New Testament insists that that is what it is and also explicitly states that its Lord has made with it the long-expected New Covenant. Indeed, we might say that it is the major business of the New Testament so to insist, for the very name of that body of scripture which we call the New Testament ought more properly to be translated "the New Covenant": it is the record of that covenant, how it was made and what it signifies. Now the Old Covenant was, as we have said, the charter of the people of Israel. We may read the story of that solemn ceremony in Exod. 24:1-11. And a solemn ceremony it was, with the sacrifice, the sprinkling of the blood on altar and on people, the reading of the covenant law, and the sacramental meal in the presence of God. It was an act of utmost gravity which bound the twelve clans to the God of the covenant, and to one another, forevermore. In that act Israel became a people.

But that covenant bond had not been maintained. Indeed it was the major point of the prophet attack to insist that it had not: Israel had by its unbrotherly and idolatrous behavior clearly broken the covenant again and again, and had showed itself to be no true people of that covenant. It was simply not in Israel to keep the covenant. Yet the prophets could not believe that Israel's failure, however total it may have been, could frustrate God's purpose for his people and Kingdom. Surely out of the broken pieces of Israel he will raise up a pure Israel, a Remnant, and with them will make a New Covenant! That confidence expresses itself in the Old Testament in a dozen varying forms. It lies in the recurring hope for a new Exodus out of the wilderness of catastrophe; it lies in the figure of the Servant who is to be the representative of the covenant (Isa. 42:6-7; 49:8-10; 55:3), and to whose people is promised an eternal covenant of peace (e.g., Isa. 54:9-10). But it finds its clearest expression in those great words of Jeremiah (31:31-34): "Behold, the days are coming, says the Lord when I will make a new covenant with the house of Israel and the house of Judah. . . . I will put my law within them, and I will write it upon their hearts; and I will be their God, and they shall be my people. . . . For I will forgive their iniquity, and I will remember their sin no more."

It is in a little upper room that the New Testament permits us again to hear Jeremiah's words. But they, too, have suffered the characteristic New Testament change of tense. Gone is the predictive future; instead there is present indicative: "This cup *is* the New Covenant in my blood" (I Cor. 11:25; Luke 22:20). Now the exact original words of the sacrament present a textual problem which cannot concern us here.[15] It is true that in Mark (14:24) and Matthew (26:28) the word "new" does not occur in the best manuscripts. But that the church, even to the earliest times,[16] saw here the inauguration of the New Covenant is incontestable (e.g., Heb. 8:6-13; II Cor. 3:4-6). We find it impossible to believe that Jesus intended his action in any other way. Here in the upper room is the New Covenant forecast by Jeremiah and all the prophets announced and made actual. Here among the followers of the Lord is the new Israel to which has been given a new law of intention and heart (cf. Matt. 5:17-20).[17] Here is, what is more, the New Moses to give that new law and to make that New Covenant; here is the Servant who will mediate it in his suffering. Thus all the best hope of Israel is caught up and given fulfillment in those sacramental words.

Now the Last Supper was, we believe, a covenant meal. We cannot enter into the vexed questions which revolve about the exact time and the exact nature of that meal.[18] But whatever its exact nature, it seems

[15] We have the words of the institution of the Lord's Supper in the Pauline form (I Cor. 11:23-26), the Markan (Mark 14:22-25) and the Lukan (Luke 22:15-20). The account in Matt. 26:26-29 agrees with Mark with but slight variations. For details see the commentaries; there is a convenient discussion in Wm. Manson, *op. cit.*, pp. 185-201. There are those (e.g., B. H. Branscomb, *The Gospel of Mark* [*The Moffatt New Testament Commentary* (New York and London: Harper & Bros., n.d.)], pp. 258-64) who declare that the words "my blood of the covenant" (e.g., Mark 14:24) are not genuine. We can only agree with James Moffatt (*The First Epistle of Paul to the Corinthians* [idem, n.d.], p. 164), who quotes A. D. Nock to the effect that if these words are not genuine, few recorded words in history can claim to be.

[16] The word "new" is in the Pauline version, which may be the earliest of all. And the language of I Cor. 11:23 clearly indicates that Paul inherited the tradition from yet earlier sources which, he declares, reach back to Jesus himself. On the relationship of this account to the others, see, e.g., V. Taylor, *Jesus and His Sacrifice* (New York: The Macmillan Co., 1937), pp. 201-17.

[17] A connection between the inward morality of the Sermon on the Mount and the inward law of the New Covenant announced by Jeremiah has been pointed out recently, among others, by Wm. Manson, *op. cit.*, p. 124; Rowley, *op. cit.*, p. 142.

[18] The Synoptic Gospels place the Last Supper on the evening of the first day of unleavened bread (Mark 14:12; Matt. 26:17, 19; Luke 22:7, 13) when the Passover was sacrificed. John, however, places it a day earlier (John 13:1, 29; 18:28)—i.e., before the Passover had been eaten. The problem is a real one and little is gained by artificial harmonizing. At present I must withhold judgment on it. Scholars are well divided on the point, and the reader will find their arguments in the commentaries: conveniently, C. J. Wright in Major, Manson and Wright, *op. cit.*, pp. 866 ff. Whether the meal was the Passover itself, the Qiddush or preparatory meal, or some other sort of religious fellowship,

clear that it symbolized a fellowship—indeed the fellowship of the Kingdom—in which the twelve disciples were bound to one another and to their Lord. As the covenant at Sinai united the twelve tribes to one another about the service of the common God, so did this covenant meal. In it Christ identified his followers with himself: the people of the Lord God of Israel have become in the New Covenant the people of the Servant. Here, too, the number twelve is significant; how important it was is clear from the speed with which another was elected to take Judas' place (Acts 1:15-26), for the symbolism of new Israel must be preserved. And if a covenant must be sealed by a sacrifice, here the sacrifice is the Servant himself: "This cup is the New Covenant in my blood." It was only right and natural that the church should identify Jesus with the Passover sacrifice (e.g., I Cor. 5:7) and hail him as "the Lamb of God, who takes away the sin of the world" (John 1:29; cf. Heb. 12:24; I Pet. 1:19; 2:24; cf. also Isa. 53:7, 10). In his sacrifice has the whole sacrificial system of the Old Covenant been fulfilled and superseded.

But as Jeremiah spoke of a New Covenant written on the hearts of men, this covenant is exactly that. Its law, as we have said, is a law of the heart (Matt. 5:17-19). It is entered by those who have been crucified with Christ and in whom Christ lives (Gal. 2:20); who have been baptized into his death and have risen again to newness of life (Rom. 6: 1-11); who have become a new creation in Christ (II Cor. 5:17); who have put off the old man and put on the new man (Col. 3:9-10); who are as if they had been born again (John 3:3). Its members are those who are "in Christ" (II Cor. 5:17; Rom. 16:3), who rely on no external law but have the mind of Christ (Phil. 2:5): these are the people of the New Covenant.

III

The New Testament, then, speaks of the Kingdom of God as if it were in a real sense a present thing. Christ, it declares, is the promised Messiah who has come to establish his Kingdom among men; in him and in his Church is all the hope of Israel for a true Remnant and a New Covenant made actual. The New Testament faith is, therefore,

---

has also occasioned debate. But whichever be correct, the shadow of the Passover season hung over Passion Week, and the church early hailed the crucified Christ as the Passover sacrifice.

a triumphant faith. Yet it was inevitable that with that shift of tense with which the New Testament speaks of the Kingdom of God there should enter a severe tension. For on the one hand, that Kingdom is a present and victorious reality; on the other hand, it is a thing of the future and far from victorious.

1. This does not at all mean that the joyous confidence which supported the early church was in any sense diminished. On the contrary, there was every assurance of victory. If the Church is the true Israel, the people of the Kingdom of God, then it is heir to all the promises, and its victory is quite sure. Indeed, the New Testament went so far as to declare that the victory had *already been won*. Christ and his mighty works had signaled the breaking into the world of the power of the age to come, of the Kingdom of God. This power had grappled with the power of Satan, and Satan had met his match and fled in ignominious route: "I saw Satan fall like lightning from heaven" (Luke 10:18). That newly coming power nothing can defeat. To be sure, it might seem that the cross had been its defeat, for there Christ was delivered into the grip of the powers of this earth and was "crucified, dead, and buried." But do not be deceived! The Cross was not the defeat of the power of God, but precisely its victory. In Cross and Resurrection, affirms the New Testament, the decisive blow has been dealt the powers of Evil. Satan there suffered a defeat without tomorrow; his back is broken, he is beaten, done for! The struggle may drag on for many a weary year yet, but the outcome is not in doubt. The Servant's work has been done; victory has *already been won!*

The Cross thus stands in the eyes of the New Testament faith as the very pivot of history. It is the middle point of all things from which all events are to be dated. (And it is a sound instinct, though hardly evidence of deep Christian faith, that we divide all history into B.C. and A.D.).[19] For the Cross is the beginning of the new age and the end of the old. Here Christ laid down his life for sin and broke the power of sin (Heb. 2:14). Then, rising again on the third day, he showed that even that "last enemy" death had been done away (I Cor. 15:20-22). In fact Paul declared that in the events of Passion Week and Easter the whole history of mankind since Adam has been reversed (I Cor. 15;

---

[19] O. Cullmann, *Christus und die Zeit* (Zürich: Evangelische Verlag, 1946), pp. 15 ff.; cf. the English translation by F. V. Filson, *Christ and Time* (Philadelphia: The Westminster Press, 1950).

Rom. 5:12-21). As Adam in his sin bequeathed to the world the poison-ous heritage of rebellion against God and, through it, the sentence of death, so now has come a new Adam, a heavenly Adam (I Cor. 15:45-49) —a Son of Man[20]—who, obedient unto death, brings life.

Thus the New Testament faith in the victory! And in that victory, it declares, the Christian may participate here and now. In fact the new age has already dawned, and the church is living in that age. The miracle of Pentecost is proof that the end-time has begun, for the out-pouring of the spirit spoken of by Joel has taken place (Acts 2:16-21; cf. Joel 2:28-32; II Cor. 1:22; Eph. 1:13-14). The Christian has been delivered out of the present evil age (Gal. 1:4), has "tasted . . . the powers of the age to come" (Heb. 6:5), has transferred his citizenship to that age (Phil. 3:20). He has been freed from the demonic power of evil (Col. 1:13) into the Kingdom of the Son. His natural enmity to God has been removed, for he has been reconciled in Christ to his heavenly Father and King (II Cor. 5:19; Rom. 5:10-11). He has been adopted as a son in the family of God (Gal. 4:5-7), he has been accounted right-eous through his faith (Rom. 5:1-5). Indeed as he confronts his Christ face to face like one beholding the glory of God in a mirror, he himself takes on that image (II Cor. 3:18). Man, made in the image of God (Gen. 1:27), finds that image restored—becomes at length what he was created to be—in the Kingdom of Christ.[21]

In the service of the victorious and already present Kingdom of God the church is given a joyful and triumphant task. The New Testament church saw itself, as we have said, as the people of that Kingdom, the "eschatological community" which was living already in the age to come. It was, then, to busy itself in those last days between the Resurrection and the expected end in proclaiming the Kingdom in the entire world and in summoning men to its rule. There is a great out-turning of focus in the New Testament pages. Through the Old Testament the reader senses that the focus has been continually narrowed. It begins with the broad canvas of creation and tells of the dealings of God with the whole

[20] On the relationship of Paul's concept of the second or heavenly Man to that of the Son of Man, cf. T. W. Manson, *The Teaching of Jesus* (2nd ed.; Cambridge: The University Press, 1935) pp. 233-34; Wm. Manson, op. cit., pp. 216 ff., 250 ff. On the subject of the first and second Adam in the thought of Paul, cf. Davies, op. cit., ch. iii.

[21] On the biblical notion of the Image of God, and the use the New Testament makes of it, see the excellent article of F. Horst, "Face to Face: the Biblical Doctrine of the Image of God," *Interpretation*, IV-3 (1950), 259-70.

race of mankind (Gen. 1–11); then narrows to the people Israel whom God had called to be the special servants of his purpose; then still further to the search for a pure Remnant within Israel fit to be the vessels of the divine intention. At the center of the Bible's drama the focus has narrowed to one man: the Messiah, Christ. But from Christ the focus again turns outward—first to the new Israel which is his Church and then, through that Church, into the entire world.[22] The Church is called to take up the destiny of the true Israel, Servant Israel, and become the missionary people of the Kingdom of God.

And that mission is no forlorn hope doomed to defeat, but a victorious calling. Indeed the victory has already been won in the "payoff battle" of the cross. The cosmic struggle continues, to be sure, with seemingly undiminished fury, but it is now in the nature of a rear-guard action, a mopping up. The issue is not in doubt. The Kingdom of God moves on to its inevitable triumph: the unconditional surrender of the Foe, the restoration of all creation under the divine domain (Acts 3:21), and the submission of all powers in heaven and earth to the name of Christ (I Cor. 15:24-28; Phil. 2:10; cf. Isa. 45:23). In the victorious army of that Kingdom marches the Church. Not that the early church ever imagined that it could produce that victory, could by its labors bring in the Kingdom! That is a modern delusion of grandeur which the early church simply would not have understood. Rather, the Church was sent into the world as a missionary witness to a Kingdom *already set up*, a witness to what Christ had already done (Acts 1:8). It would on that mission, like the Servant, meet all manner of persecution, take all sorts of brutal casualties. But there is no question of defeat—for this is the Church, and the very gates of Hell do not prevail against it (Matt. 16:18). Nor does this little detachment march alone, for the Invisible Christ goes with them every step of the way: "Lo, I am with you always, even to the end of the age" (Matt. 28:20). To the call of that victorious faith the Church could have but one answer, and that a triumphant one: "If God is for us, who is against us?" (Rom. 8:31; cf. Isa. 50:7-9.)

2. Thus the confidence of the Church in the certain victory—indeed, the already accomplished victory—of the already present Kingdom of God. But therein lie the seeds of extreme tension. For it was equally clear, bitterly clear, that that Kingdom had *not* come and its victory

---

[22] Cullmann, *op. cit.*, pp. 99-103, stresses this point. This book is an extremely important treatment of the biblical view of history.

had not been won nor, from a human point of view, was there any way to produce that victory. That is indeed paradox! What is this Kingdom that has come but has not come, that is already victorious but is anything but victorious?

Victorious, as far as human eyes could see, it certainly was not. The power of the earthly state continued its unbroken rule. The New Testament church had to live all its life in the grip of imperial Rome. And Rome was not in the least subject to the Kingdom of God, nor had it any intention of being. Rome was by now a totalitarian state. And although the Roman government was not, at least at first, inclined to be intolerant of the Christians, there was in the Roman state religion a certain factor that must inevitably one day lead to conflict.[23] It began when Augustus, in an effort to bolster patriotism with religious sanctions, deified the dead Julius Caesar and declared that the "genius" even of living emperors ought to be worshiped. It is true that Augustus did not himself claim to be God, but the line between the "genius" of the emperor and the emperor himself was a very fine one. It only wanted some mad fellow such as a Nero or a Domitian to take the claim seriously, and the order would go out that the emperor was to be worshiped; and that would be the test of a man's patriotism. Then the awful, age-long dilemma of Christ or Caesar would be posed. Then the Christian would stand before the fire; for he could worship no King but God, and it was clear that Rome could not endure two kings. It would have to be decided in blood, as it seems that question always must, which of the two would be supreme.

The church simply had no way to defeat the power of Rome and procure the promised victory. She could obey the Great Commission: she could preach, could witness, could make disciples for the Kingdom. She could even attest her faith in that Kingdom unto the death. But she could not produce it. It must be underscored and underscored again that while there is not a sign of defeatism or of despairing passivity regarding its mission in the early church, there is in all the New Testament no brave talk of winning the world for Christ and of ushering in his Kingdom—not so much as a syllable!

---

[23] The reader will find a useful sketch of the religions of the Graeco-Roman world, including the official religion of Rome, in S. V. McCasland, "New Testament Times I: The Greco-Roman World," *The Interpreter's Bible* (New York and Nashville: Abingdon-Cokesbury Press, 1951), VII, 88-94.

Indeed, the attitude of the New Testament church toward state and society might easily seem amazing. There is no hint of an assault upon the tyranny of Rome, no scrap of a program for winning the state for Christ. It is certainly true that the gospel of the Church was a ferment in Roman society which would one day crack it wide open, but the gospel was never preached with that subtle intent in view. Nor is there any direct attack upon the abuses with which Roman society was filled, abuses utterly contrary to the teachings of Jesus. Paul, for example, assumes (Philemon) the institution of slavery without discussion, although the gospel which he preached could have had no truck with such defilement of the brother. Paul even urged an obedience to the state ("the powers that be are ordained of God," Rom. 13:1-4) which might seem, if followed out logically (and it has been!), to be an Erastianism that would sell the church abjectly to the state. It would seem that the early church had no hope of reforming the state or of bringing it into conformity to the Kingdom of God. Its advice to its followers is very clearly seen, for example, in I Peter, and might be summarized thus: remember that you are the holy people of God and so behave (2:9-12); stand firm, but so live as to avoid giving offense if possible (2:13-15); purge out all unworthy traits (2:1-3), so that by your manner of life you may be a living refutation of the charges of those who accuse you (2:12, 15; 3:16); commit your souls to God and await your reward in the day of Christ's appearing (1:7, 13).[24]

The picture of the New Testament church is, then, that of a frail and weak church, anything but victorious. At its beginning it is a group of unlettered Galilean peasants who flee like rabbits from the Jewish authorities. As the New Testament story ends, it has grown in numbers and has attracted to itself not a few persons of importance and, what is more, has gained an iron courage. But it is still a pitiful and helpless minority composed, for the most part, of people of no account (cf. I Cor. 1:26-28), the offscouring and the disinherited of the empire. This was its paradox: that it was the Church of Christ against which the gates of Hell could not prevail (Matt. 16:18), but it could not prevail against Caesar's Rome. This was its deeper paradox: that it was the true

---

[24] Perhaps the majority of scholars relegate I Peter to a later hand than that of the Apostle (recently, F. W. Beare, *The First Epistle of Peter* [Oxford: Basil Blackwell, 1947]), but its genuineness has recently been ably defended among others by E. G. Selwyn (*The First Epistle of St. Peter* [London: The Macmillan Co., 1946]). There is, in my opinion, no convincing objection to a date in the reign of Nero.

Israel, the people of the presently existing Kingdom of God, and yet an imperfect church with its full share of sinful men themselves but imperfectly delivered from the power of this age (I Corinthians!). Or to put it otherwise, although the New Testament teaches us that the people of Christ's Kingdom are his obedient followers, his Church, there is never the slightest hint that the visibly existing church can either be or produce that Kingdom.

There is no tendency in the New Testament to identify the visible church with the Kingdom of God. The church that makes such an identification will soon begin to invite God to endorse its own very human policies and practices, will equate the people of God with those nice people who share its particular beliefs and participate in its services, and will reckon the advance of the Kingdom in terms of its numerical growth. But it will not be the New Testament church! Such an identification is a great snare, as prophets since Amos have told us. It only fathers the fatuous conceit of rightness with God by external conformity, and the equally fatuous expectation of divine protection—for, forsooth, this is his church! Not so the New Testament! The Church is indeed the people of the Kingdom of Christ, but the visible church is not that Kingdom. On the contrary, let it take heed to itself, lest by its behavior it become so much lukewarm water to be spewed out of the mouth of God (Rev. 3:16)! Let it live in full awareness that it, too, is under the judgment of God (Rom. 2:5; 14:10; I Cor. 3:13; 4:5; II Cor. 5:10). It, too, the new and pure Israel, must be purged! The church is like a wheatfield in which a good many weeds have come up (Matt. 13:24-30). Weeds and wheat now grow side by side in it, but God (and only God: vss. 28-29!) will know how to separate them.

Because of these things the New Testament church could never be a proud, conquering church as the world understands those terms. It must remain the Church of the Suffering Servant, a martyr church. It had no way but Christ's way: to drink of his cup (Mark 10:38-39), to take up his cross (Mark 8:34). And in the later books of the New Testament we see it "girding up the loins of [its] mind" (I Pet. 1:13 A.S.V.) for its martyrdom. Victory? They might indeed hope that having come up out of the great tribulation, and having "washed their robes and made them white" as it were in the blood of the great sacrificial Lamb (Rev. 7:14), they might stand approved one day before the Eternal

236

Throne. But on earth they would have no victory save the Servant's victory—beyond the Cross.

3. In the light of what has been said it becomes clear that the Kingdom of God in the New Testament must be understood in a two-fold aspect: it has come and is even now in the world; it is also yet to come. In the tension between the two the Church must live, and must always live, as the "eschatological community."

This double manner of speaking which the New Testament employs is not altogether strange. We may observe it, to a certain degree, both in the Old Testament and in the teachings of the Jewish rabbis. The rule of God was always believed to be present fact in that it was not doubted that God was at all times in control, judging the affairs of men in the context of history and summoning men to his service. On the other hand, that rule was always viewed as a future thing to be consummated in the eschatological event at the issue of history.[25] But whereas in the Old Testament and in Judaism these two aspects of the Kingdom are held in balance, in Christ they are brought together: the future thing is made present, the Kingdom is at hand here and now, and one may enter it and know its victory. Furthermore, so the New Testament declares, Christ—through his ministry, his death and resurrection—has made the triumph of that Kingdom sure. The victorious Kingdom is thus no longer a passively awaited thing, but a dynamically active one.

But it is precisely that which introduces the note of extreme tension so characteristic of the New Testament. For although the ministry of Christ was understood eschatologically as the beginning of the new age, that eschatological hope could not be said to have been completely realized in the earthly career of Jesus.[26] The promised victory, although

---

[25] Cf. P. Volz, Die Eschatologie der jüdischen Gemeinde im neutestamentliche Zeitalter (Tübingen: J. C. B. Mohr, 1934), pp. 165-67. The very fact that Jesus' contemporaries spoke of the Kingdom under both aspects is a strong warning against relieving the gospel story either of the present aspect of the Kingdom (by way of a purely eschatological interpretation of Jesus) or of its future aspect (by way of a "realized eschatology"). See the timely remarks of F. V. Filson, The New Testament Against Its Environment (Chicago: Henry Regnery Co., 1950), pp. 66-67; also Cullmann, op. cit., p. 8, et passim.

[26] It is the position of the so-called "realized eschatology" of C. H. Dodd (The Parables of the Kingdom [New York: Chas. Scribner's Sons, 1935]) and others that in Christ's earthly career the Kingdom had come and God's purposes had been realized. For a brief statement of arguments to the contrary, see F. C. Grant, The Gospel of the Kingdom (New York: The Macmillan Co., 1940), pp. 145-46; also the remarks of Filson, op. cit.

it could not be doubted, was clearly not complete. So the New Testament assumes, as it must assume, a double view of the Kingdom: it has come ("the kingdom of God is at hand"); it is yet to come ("Thy kingdom come"). If it be asked, then, whether the New Testament looked upon the Kingdom as present fact or future hope, the only answer is *both*. Thus while it declared that the Kingdom was present and victorious, it also looked ahead with a heightened longing to the return of the Lord (e.g., Acts 1:11; I Thess. 4:15-17; Tit. 2:13) and to the final victory (e.g., I Cor. 15:25; Phil. 1:6; Acts 3:21).

That victory was not doubted, but eagerly and imminently expected. The early church felt that it was living in the last days and the time was short. It saw itself, as we have said, as the "eschatological community." Now this eager expectation of the infant church for the return of the Lord ought not to be exaggerated, as if the early Christians spent their time in futile gazing into the clouds and in morbid speculation.[27] On the contrary, they went about their work with dynamic energy and buoyant joy. Yet, it would seem, their joy was sustained by the thought that the victory would be soon. Paul clearly had such expectations. Every day brings it nearer (Rom. 13:11); it will come suddenly like a thief in the night (I Thess. 5:1-2); it is so close that it would be better not to marry (I Cor. 7:29). In fact it seems certain from Paul's language (I Cor. 15:51; I Thess. 4:17) that he expected to be alive to see the day. It is likely that certain words on the lips of Jesus himself (e.g., Mark 9:1; 13:30; 14:62) [28] contributed to this expectation of the imminent end. In any case the church was convinced that the time had not long to run (e.g., I Pet. 1:5; 4:7; Heb. 10:25; Rev. 1:3; 22:6-7, 20).

In this tense expectancy of the imminent end the New Testament church lived. To be sure, that end did not come as soon as many of the early Christians expected it. Indeed, it is yet delayed. And as the

---

[27] See the caution of R. H. Strachan, "The Gospel in the New Testament," *The Interpreter's Bible* (New York and Nashville: Abingdon-Cokesbury Press, 1951), VII, 6-7, against an exaggeration of this feature. It is true that "an early date for the second coming of Christ does not control the thinking of the apostles," if by this is meant that it was not the heart of their gospel. Yet while it is probably true that the hope of the *Parousia* increased in direct ratio to the intensity of persecution, and so ought not to be overbid, neither ought it to be discounted. For it seems that the early church generally expected the quick return of the Lord, and that with great eagerness (cf. I and II Thess.).

[28] On the critical problems relative to these and other passages of the same type, the reader must consult the commentaries. It would seem, at least, that the New Testament writers understood their Lord to have taught the speedy consummation of all things, and that within the lifetime of those then living.

years turned into decades and the decades into centuries, it was perhaps inevitable that some of the tension should have been lost, if it was not put aside entirely. But the New Testament church could never escape it. In its later books, when the time had already been longer than some had thought, we still hear the agonized cry of a church which lay at the mercy of the devildoms of Caesar: "How long, O Master . . .?" (Rev. 6:10 A.S.V.). And we hear, too, the answering whisper: "Patience!" (Jas. 5:7; cf. Heb. 10:36; II Pet. 3:4, 8). That hope carried the church through the fire. A weak church, it was helpless before Caesar and could do nothing. But as the "eschatological community" it could know that what it did was no small thing, but that with each stand for the faith, each Christlike deed, each act of obedient witnessing however small, it participated for the Kingdom of God in the great cosmic struggle. Down to the end its prayer went up: "*Marana tha*"— "Come, Lord" (I Cor. 16:22). In that prayer it announced its faith that its labor would not be in vain.

4. The New Testament church thus had to live in tension between its confidence that the victory of the Kingdom of God had already been made actual in Christ, and its eager expectation of the victory which as yet no human eye could see. It was a severe tension, and one which could not easily be put by. The church could not escape that tension except by surrendering all hope for the future. And that the church could not do, for that would have been to give up its God and its Christ and to cut loose from that eschatological element which was indigenous to its gospel—as, indeed, it had been indigenous to Israel's faith since the beginning. Had the church done that it would have betrayed itself and given proof that it was no true heir to the hope of Israel at all. Nor could the church resolve the tension by its own efforts, for it had no means of winning the victory over the power of Rome and of producing the Kingdom of Christ on earth. It was a tension that could only be resolved eschatologically, i.e., from the side of the divine activity. For that divine activity the church had to wait.

It is, therefore, most fitting that the New Testament canon should close with an Apocalypse, and that far the greatest Apocalypse of them all: Revelation. Revelation is a book of such magnificent proportions that it fairly takes the breath. It is also a book which has been made into a veritable playground for all sorts of wild and profitless speculations. Needless to say, we cannot here be drawn into an extended

239

THE KINGDOM OF GOD

discussion of it, particularly of the various millenial interpretations that have been given it.[29] To do so would be gratuitous even if it were possible. Suffice it to say that Revelation is not a puzzle book which, if only one can find the key, will furnish the curious with the exact program which future events must follow. That it tells of the drama of the end is true; that it does this in the cryptic language of the Apocalyptic, which needs considerable decoding, is also true. But to seek from it an exact program, and even the date, of the end of the world is to do it great violence. It is also to exhibit an idle curiosity which borders on the impudent; for Christ himself when on earth declared that not even he knew such things (Matt. 24:36), and that, furthermore, it was not man's business to know them (Acts 1:7). But if Revelation furnishes no libretto of future events, it is nevertheless a powerful summons to Christians of all ages to stand firm in the faith with utter confidence that the triumph of God's purpose is quite sure. It is also a reminder to the Christian that in the cosmic moral struggle there is no neutrality, that in his every action he is invited to take sides—for the Kingdom of God or against it.

Revelation presents a picture such as only the language of Apocalypse could draw. Sober speech would never have sufficed. On one side are arrayed that old dragon Satan (20:2), his angels, and his Antichrist;[30] all the powers of Evil visible and invisible, on the earth and beyond it. The evil powers of earth seem to be personified in the figure of the unspeakable Nero, number 666 (13:18),[31] the Beast. Yet it is not merely Nero, nor Domitian, nor yet Hitler or Stalin that is in question. It is

[29] One must consult the commentaries. The most exhaustive critical commentary is R. H. Charles, Revelation (International Critical Commentary [New York: Chas. Scribner's Sons; and Edinburgh: T. & T. Clark, 1920, 2 Vols.]); less technically, M. Kiddle, The Revelation of St. John (The Moffatt New Testament Commentary [London: Hodder & Stoughton, 1940]). There is a valuable brief discussion in Rowley, The Relevance of Apocalyptic, pp. 117-28.

[30] The word "Antichrist" is not used in Revelation to denote the earthly arch-enemy of Christ. In fact, it does not occur outside of I and II John, where it is used both of the arch-Enemy and of false teachers who obey him (e.g., I John 2:18). But "Antichrist" is only one of several names to express the same concept: e.g., the Beast (so in Rev.), the "man of lawlessness" (II Thess. 2:3).

[31] The number 666 appears to be achieved by taking the Hebrew letters used to write Nero Caesar (nrwn qsr) and giving them their numerical value (the Hebrews used letters of the alphabet for numerals also). The total would be 666. The figure of 666 is thus a sort of Nero redivivus (cf. Charles, op. cit., I, 366-67). The practice of designating persons by numbers in this manner was not unusual. A sentence scrawled on a wall at Pompeii reads: "I love a girl whose number is 545." Cf. M. Burrows, What Mean These Stones? (New Haven: American Schools of Oriental Research, 1941), p. 270.

240

any of them, all of them, none of them. It is all earthly powers, whoever and however many they may be, that subserve the will of the Adversary; that have made themselves antigod and antichrist. It is, if you will, eternal Nero—Nero redivivus—who walks the earth in many incarnations. It is the sum total of evil, and it launches a last demonic assault upon the heavenly Kingdom: the Lamb, the Son of Man, and him who sits upon the Throne. It vents its wrath also with fiendish fury upon the saints of God who live on earth. For them it is a time of decision: with the revelation of Christ there has come also, as it must, the revelation of Antichrist, and one must stand for one side or the other.

It is a fearful struggle, a struggle that beggars the vocabulary. There are portents in heaven, torment and tribulation on earth, as evil hurls itself at the Kingdom of the saints. But the writer gives us to understand one thing: *the issue is at no time in doubt.* The battle has already been won at Calvary by him who in his sacrifice had taken men out of every nation and made them into the true people of God (5:9-10; cf. Exod. 19:5-6). Meanwhile, let come what will; let the occupant of Caesar's throne—or of the Kremlin—do his utmost; this one thing is sure: "The Lord God omnipotent reigneth" (19:6 K.J.V.). The powers of evil simply cannot win, they have already been broken! The struggle may indeed be severe, but it is, on the one hand, the thrashing death agony of the Beast; on the other, it is the birth pangs of a New Creation (cf. Mark 13:8: "this is but the beginning of the sufferings").

With that New Creation the vision ends (chs. 21–22), and with it the New Testament canon. It is as if the seer had been projected beyond the present trial and all the woes and ills of this world, and had been permitted to behold that yet unconsummated end-event, the victory of the Kingdom of God. The power of Cosmic Evil is now at length ended. The Devil and his minions, the Beast and all that did his bidding, are consigned to the flames (20:7-10),[32] and the judgment books are opened before him that sits on the Great White Throne. Then it is that this old and weary creation is restored. New heavens are there and a new earth (21:1-4; cf. Isa. 65:17-19); the very City of God, the new Jerusa-

---

[32] We cannot pause here to discuss the question of the millennium. A chapter would be necessary for that alone. Rev. 20 is the only passage in the Bible which speaks of it and, whatever be its interpretation, it supplies a very slender base for the elaborate and exact theories that have been erected upon it.

lem, has come down from heaven to take its place among men. In it is ineffable joy; all sorrow, all pain, all evil have vanished away. It is a joy such as fairly outstrips mortal vocabulary: no gem or precious stone too bright to describe it, no sun whose light does not pale beside its glory! Joy is heaped upon joy in a mighty crescendo of language until language can bear no more and there arises, as it were, a grand "Hallelujah Chorus": "and they shall reign for ever and ever" (22:5)! It is the Kingdom of God triumphant and eternal at history's end. And toward that unseen City and Kingdom the church turned longing eyes, and its prayer went up (Rev. 22:20), "Amen. Come, Lord Jesus!" Thus the Bible closes with an echo of the theme which has been dominant in it from end to end: the coming Kingdom of God.

It is impossible to speak of this without the feeling that one is speaking of a strange thing, a thing utterly foreign to the modern mind. I do not mean, nor is it surprising, that the symbolism of the Apocalypse is strange to us. It is the very eschatological tension of the New Testament church that is strange. We do not understand it at all: this suffering church, living in the light of the coming Kingdom, waiting for the victory of God. We are not that kind of church, nor do we wish to be. We have gotten away from that tension so long ago and so completely, that we no longer remember what it is. The victory has been so long delayed that we no longer believe in its coming, and are content to nurture ourselves if, perchance, we may only survive. Or we have been filled with brash confidence that the victory was in our grasp if only we would launch programs energetic enough to win it—as if by programs we hoped to conquer the world, and to make it the sort of world in which we might comfortably carry on programs. But of the New Testament tension we know nothing.

Who will tell us that in thus escaping the tension of the Kingdom we have betrayed ourselves? Yet is this plodding survival which lives at peace in the secular order, without tension and with no inkling of that Other Order which is ever intruding, less than that? Or is the Kingdom so small a thing that we can just take it by the arm and usher it in on our own terms, if only we would set our minds to it? No, we cannot thus put the awful immediacy and the radical challenge of the Kingdom from our minds, nor turn it into a figure of speech, or perhaps a pale synonym for the sum total of human good, and remain the New Testament Church. For the New Testament Church is the people of the Kingdom of God. And that Kingdom is even yet "at hand," intruding into the earthly order. We can enter that Kingdom, can obey its bidding, can witness to its power, can pray for its victory, can (God help us!) steel ourselves to suffer for it. But we cannot escape its tension. For it is a Kingdom that we can neither create nor abandon—and remain the Church. It is ours, therefore, to find again, now in this time, the New Testament tension. Perhaps if we do so, we may be approved as good and faithful servants.

CHAPTER NINE

Even to the End of the Age

WE HAVE COME TO THE END OF WHAT WE SET OUT TO DO. THE BIBLICAL CONCEPT OF THE PEOPLE OF GOD, AND THE CONCOMITANT EXPECTATION of the Kingdom of God, have been traced from their roots in the Mosaic faith to the closing vision of the New Testament of "the holy city, new Jerusalem, coming down out of heaven from God" (Rev. 21:2). The effort has been made to show that this idea, so dynamic and so creative, is the unifying note of the biblical Word. How successful it has been the reader must judge. We cannot, however, dwell with the subject longer. Yet we cannot leave it without some attempt to make it clear that the biblical doctrine of the Kingdom of God, which is the unifying theme of the Bible, is still the motivating force of the living Church.

The New Testament church, as we have said, stood in a peculiar midposition between what had been done and what was awaited, between the present age which was dying and the new age struggling to be born. It was confident that the victory over all the dark powers of the old aeon had been won in Christ, so much so that the Kingdom of God could be spoken of as a present thing. Yet it was all too painfully aware that that Kingdom remained an unconsummated thing of the future which had yet to come in its power. In tension between the two the New Testament church lived and waited. It was a tension between the victory won and the victory anything but won, between the Kingdom which is at hand and the Kingdom unseen and unrealized, between the power of God and the power of Caesar, between the church militant and suffering and the Church triumphant. To that tension,

244

that dilemma, we must now return; for in it we, too, must stand—as the New Testament church.

I

Let us understand it quite clearly: the church, for all her variform changes, has changed not one little bit. We are still the New Testament church—*or we are no church!*

To be sure, this is a very difficult thing for us to be, and in one sense of the word, impossible. We cannot uproot ourselves from this age and walk back through the centuries to live in that age; nor can our churches, so complex and so entrenched, become again the simple community of that Jerusalem upper room or the Roman catacombs. That would be a self-archaizing, a futile attempt to wind back the hands of the clock, unhinged from reality. What is more, we are moderns and think like moderns and cannot think like ancients. It is perhaps more than can be asked of us that we should express our faith in exactly the terms that were so natural and so meaningful to the early church.

The early church, as we have said, understood itself as the successor of Israel, true Remnant and people of the New Covenant; it understood its mission as the Servant mission of proclaiming the Kingdom and extending the covenant to the world; it saw itself as the people of the Messiah living in the last days, an "eschatological community." All these ways of putting it are more than strange to our ears, so much so that we have difficulty in understanding ourselves in such terms at all. Especially and above all the eschatological tension of the early church is strange to us. It is hard for us to feel our way into it. Now that centuries have passed and the end is not yet, when every millennial prediction of the day and hour has been befooled, how can we possibly share that tense expectancy of the coming Lord? How can we live as though the end were tomorrow?

He who brushes these things aside, or minimizes them, has no comprehension of the problem. We cannot archaize the Church. Yet the New Testament church we are and must remain. We are the same church, and we have the same gospel—the gospel of the Kingdom of God. Our task is unchanged, and it has lost none of its urgency. Furthermore, as we discharge it, we live under the same tension—however much we try to forget it—for we, too, live in that end-time between a victory won in Christ and a victory anything but won, between a Kingdom which is

245

present and which we may enter and a Kingdom we can neither be nor create.

1. The preaching of the New Testament church was given an intense urgency by the conviction that the time was short and the last days had come. Such a note of urgency is never properly absent from the Church's message, and cannot be today, for it springs from a sense of impending judgment. And the feeling that the judgment is close upon them oppresses men today. At least there is abroad in the world, even among those that speak not the language of faith, an uneasy premonition of doom, and with it a hunger and thirst for salvation which does not fully know itself, yet which cries almost frantically for satisfaction.

In saying this we must avoid the peril of archaizing at every step. Few today find it possible to live in the tense expectation of the returning Lord exactly as did the early Church. Whatever the faith of the early church and however deeply we may share that faith and yearn for its fulfillment, we have no assurance such as they felt that we are in fact living in the last days. What is more, we find it uncommonly difficult to think in the eschatological patterns of the Bible. There is little preoccupation among us, it would seem, with judgment in the strictly eschatological sense: with the day when the trumpet shall sound loud and the earth dissolve to the accompaniment of apocalyptic portents and the books shall lie open before the Great White Throne. Nor is there much, so far as one can tell, of that lively fear of Hell which haunted our forefathers and sent them fleeing from the wrath to come in weeping repentance. But we have not outrun the eschatological urgency. There is with us a new sense of impending judgment and a desperate longing for salvation of eschatological intensity. It lends to our message a New Testament flavor.

It was not always so. There was a time when the old eschatological sense seemed to us so strange, not to say crude, that we came near to putting it by altogether. It involved ideas which we felt were unworthy of civilized man and a civilized man's God, so we put them, if not out of our theology, at least out of mind. They were the skeletons in our theological closet, as it were, which we hoped no one would inquire after. Sin, judgment, salvation—these were words which we used with apologies, if at all. Man we held to be essentially good. To be sure, he had his faults, and one might, if he insisted, call them sins; but they were really in the nature of an excusable ignorance which it was up to

246

education, civilization, and ethical instruction to remove. There could be no question of judgment, for man's future was one of unlimited progress; and progress and judgment have nothing to do with each other. No salvation did man need save what physical well-being, moral improvement, and mental peace could provide—and all these were possible. To put it so is perhaps a caricature but it is not far from the truth. We created a religion without eschatological sense to which the New Testament tension seemed a regrettable aberration best passed over in silence.

That misty delusion, of course, no longer exists. The very rooftree of history fell in on it, and it became a casualty. The lesson was spelled out to us that we had both overestimated man and underestimated his predicament. It became clear that man needed some salvation which the amenities of civilization could not give; for although there were placed in his hands all the tools for creating a new heaven and a new earth, he straightway constructed a new hell. It became clear that his trouble was deep. While we lauded his goodness, he bared his teeth; and we saw with our own eyes an uneradicated evil in him, infinitely worthy of the judgment, of which we had not believed him capable. Sin—that fusty, tut-tutting, finger-shaking word—gained content. We learned that we have not to do with sins: a list of the more obvious misdemeanors which a good man doesn't commit anyhow, or from which he may by force of will desist. We have to do with sin: man's total and corporate failure in the realm of righteousness, a failure which places a world of justice and peace forever beyond his grasp as if it were some lost Eden guarded by a cherub's flaming sword. And that is surely something beyond nagging or reforming; it is man's inescapable dilemma.

For that sin there is a judgment; we are sure of that now. History is a judgment, and in it civilization is judged. The old prophet sense of the judgment of God in history no longer seems in the least irrelevant or farfetched. For we know, if we are not blind, that a society that has flouted the law of God and placed gain above rectitude, that has worshiped a sorry procession of false gods dressed up in jack boots, that has defaced and violated the creature made in the divine image, that has been vaguely religious in a sentimental sort of way yet has cared for nothing so much as its material comfort—is under indictment. That society must now stand in history and show cause why it should continue to exist! This judgment hangs over us; we do not know how to save ourselves from

247

it, frantically though we try. And it is in this context of desperation that the Church today speaks.

2. Speaks, and proclaims her gospel. Nor is there any doubt what that gospel is: it is the gospel of the Kingdom of God. That is the gospel of salvation which the early church preached with end-time urgency long ago. Demonic powers of darkness and their earthly minions have held this world in deathly thrall. But good news! The Kingdom of God is at hand! The power of the new age has broken in, has grappled with the evil power and defeated it on a Cross, and now moves on to its final triumph! Let men now be summoned to live in that new age! Let them renounce their old allegiances and find life as citizens of the Kingdom of the Son of God! That, to be sure, is the New Testament language, not ours, and we might not put it just so. But we can have no other gospel. We, too, are to proclaim the rule of God, to summon men through faith to submit to it, to announce that in the Kingdom of God the longed-for salvation is possible.

Now the preaching of the Kingdom of God will not fall upon the ears of modern man as altogether a strange thing. Rather it strikes upon his deepest longing, albeit he knows it not. To be sure, he is not aware that he desires that Kingdom, for the very word is to him theologian's cant which he would not understand, even if, indeed, he ever heard it uttered. Yet for the stuff of that Kingdom he yearns; even thousands who have never in their lives darkened a church door grope blindly after it unwittingly. For the hope of it is engraved in the very necessity of man's nature, and he can no more escape it than he can escape himself.

There is, indeed, a remarkable coincidence between the vision of the Kingdom of God as the prophets saw it and that goal which men most deeply desire today. If the prophet spoke of swords beaten into plowshares and a total end to violence and war (Mic. 4:3; Isa. 2:4; 11:9), that same thing is still the object of our most desperate longing. If the prophet envisioned the desert that should "rejoice and blossom as the rose" (Isa. 35:1 A.S.V.), a time of unimagined plenty (e.g., Amos 9:13-15), we too could wish an end to grinding poverty and a freedom from want. If the prophet declared that in that day men "shall sit every man under his vine and under his fig tree, and none shall make them afraid" (Mic. 4:4), that but echoes our almost frantic desire to be free of the specter of fear which walks in the night of our spirits. When the prophet tells of the just reign of the Messiah Prince (Isa. 9:7; 11:2-5),

248

we, who are so heartily sick of incredibly little men who rule with no concept of rectitude, could only wish that we might see its coming. In truth the desire of mankind is a desire for the Kingdom of God which does not know itself. For with all our striving after material plenty, it is clear that we wish more than that: we desire a *moral world order*. A moral world order must be the end of history—or it might well be the end of history! Even this effete generation, in general so sheepish about matters of faith, finds this goal to be desperately relevant. We are, indeed, longing for the Kingdom of God, peering into the very windows of the Kingdom of God, but we do not know how to enter.

Do not know how because we are idolatrous. To borrow the New Testament language, the world is in the grip of demonic powers which block the path to salvation. It is the major error of modern man that he has desired a moral world order and has looked to false gods to give it to him. And the false gods can do no such thing. On the contrary, this is a day when the false gods have abundantly advertised their bankruptcy. The very word "idol" is, of course, an antique word, and one that may seem little relevant to a generation that never in its life manufactured an idol, nor even saw one outside a museum. The ancient prophet polemic against paganism seems to it, therefore, a matter for archaeologists. Not so! False gods—like Baal of old—have the power of resurrection, and many a false god, long dead, walks the earth with the grave mould upon him and finds for himself worshipers. For that to which a man looks for his ultimate well-being, his salvation no less, and from which he derives his standards of conduct—that is his god. And we have no lack of them.

But the idol gods, whatever their fair promises, simply cannot create a moral world order. There was, for example, the idol of material progress, and his cult was considerable. And it had definite messianic overtones: we thought we should be saved in terms of medical care, television sets, and indoor plumbing. But it should have been obvious that whatever blessings this "messiah" could confer upon us (and only a fool would deny that they are many), he could not create a moral world order. For material tools, be they butcher knives or atom bombs, *have* no morality. They can but assume the sometimes rudimentary or vestigial morality of their wielders, who desperately need a moral law to control them. The false god of the state and of party ideology is worse. Surely these sinister, parvenu god-men, whose gospel is propaganda and whose

249

salvation is a slave pen, can produce no moral world order—for the simple reason that it is their habit to spit on morality. Nor may we expect that some superorganization of nations, some world government by whatever name it may be called, will of itself deliver us. However well-intended such schemes may be, and however earnestly we may pray for their success, we sense that they are rather anemic saviors. If they are not urgently propped up, they straightway fall down. They cannot create a moral world; they can at best only strive to enforce the very relative morality of their constituents. And there be many other gods, but all with the same clay feet.

To a world long befooled by false messiahs and enslaved by false loyalties, the church proclaims its ancient gospel of salvation. It places its hope squarely with the biblical hope, because it knows there is nowhere else to place it; it announces the Kingdom of God as the goal of history and the only hope of man's redemption. It affirms that there can never be a moral world order until men renounce their allegiance to lesser powers and substitute gods and submit to a universal and just moral law. For until men can find some redemptive community which is capable of bridging the schism of society and uniting Western culture and Eastern—and all races and classes within them—under its righteous rule, a world of peace and justice must remain forever a dream. The Church affirms that there is but one redemptive community, and it is neither the United States nor any other nation, nor any government of nations, but the all-embracing commonwealth of the Kingdom of God. *That* is the hope of history. The Church points toward that Kingdom and summons men in faith to submit to its beneficent rule as its citizens. Then, and only then, is righteousness possible.

But not only that. The Church does not announce the Kingdom of God merely as a possibility, or as a thing to be wished for; she announces it as a fact made present in Jesus Christ, even now at work in the world building its structure in the hearts of men. And it is a victorious Kingdom! All history tends toward it; all the future belongs to it: it is a Kingdom that *comes!* It is as the emissary of that Kingdom that the Church makes bold to speak.

3. But the more seriously the Church takes her task, the more deeply she is thrown into a thoroughly New Testament tension. It is a tension which, it is to be feared, she has not completely understood and of which she has wanted no part; yet it is inherent in the very nature of her

250

gospel, and she can never rightly escape it. It lies between her estrangement from the present age and her imprisonment by it, between a victory declared and a victory which as a church she finds it impossible to produce. On the one hand, she affirms that in Christ the power of sin and death has been broken; she declares that his Kingdom is present fact dynamically at work in the world and moving irresistibly on to its ultimate triumph. Furthermore, she labors as she has been commanded to do for that victory, preaching her gospel with desperate urgency before the fires of history's judgment as the only hope of salvation, and urging men to accept it and submit to the yoke of Christ's Kingdom. On the other hand, for all her triumphant proclamation of that Kingdom she sees few signs of its imminent presence and coming victory; and she cannot, for all her stupendous efforts, bring that victory to pass.

To say that she cannot is not a welcome word: it smacks of futility and of a denial of the Church's missionary calling. For certainly Christ commanded his disciples to preach the gospel in all the world, and he expected them to take his commission seriously. Nor did he advertise that as a futile venture. Is it not, then, for the Church to labor energetically to win men for Christ that through her efforts the promise that to him "every knee shall bow" may find fulfillment and his Kingdom come? There was a time, perhaps, when that seemed to us quite possible. To be sure, we did not minimize the difficulty of the task—but was not the very difficulty a challenge to the girding up of loins? Let the Church launch a mighty effort, "win the world for Christ" and "usher in the Kingdom"! That is her rightful task, and one that she could do, too, if only she would half try! To suggest the contrary could only be regarded as the index of a serious lack of faith.

Now that was a bumptious confidence, and there is little good in saying that it was naïve. It was more: it was perilously close to ecclesiastical self-deification. Could the Church have been successful, could she have won every last man for her membership, it would have been a very large church indeed (and a better world than it presently is), but it would not have been the Kingdom of God. For the New Age cannot be produced by the visible churches in terms of aggressive action; the churches are themselves prisoners of the present age.

In any case we have to face it: we are not now winning any such victory. On the contrary, for all our great size and wealth we are as helpless before the powers of this world as was ever the infant church.

251

The problems confronting us are appalling and lie far beyond the parrot answers of a memorized theology. Desperation and despair oppress us. Arrayed against us is a demonic new idolatry, supported by a greater physical power than ever Rome could muster. A church so small, so weak, so torn asunder—what force or what program has she to oppose the brute power of so great a Caesar and to bring to pass anything remotely approaching a righteous world? Indeed, it would seem that she has been rocked back on her heels, checkmated, defeated. The task undone is enormous: a church owned by scarcely half the people even in this favored land, she is a pitiful minority among the world's millions. Here and there she crouches behind iron curtains a martyr church, having made the full circle to the catacombs in which she was born. For all her triumphant gospel no glimpse of her victory may be seen, nor does she know what to do to produce it. Thousands, even of her own children, have taken this as evidence of her futility and have come to expect of her little in the way of salvation.

And so we find ourselves in tension. It is a tension between two worlds: between the Kingdom of God victorious over all powers and the Church of God at the mercy of the powers of this earth. It is very like the New Testament tension, but, unlike the New Testament church, we are not resigned to living in it. We do not like it at all. We have the feeling that there ought not to be such a tension, that it is not a proper position for a church to be found in. We desperately desire to escape it, for to own that we cannot violates both our sense of mission as a church and our pride. But precisely that throws us on the horns of a dilemma. For fundamentally there are but two conceivable avenues of escape: we can give up all hope and responsibility for this world, retire from it, and let it go its own suicidal way to perdition; or we can by aggressive action conquer it for Christ. But neither way is possible. The former would indeed relieve us of tension, but it would be craven cowardice and a flat refusal of the command of Christ. And as for the latter, we confess that we do not know how. Yet we are driven to continue the effort. So we cast about among courses of action tried and found wanting for some course not yet tried, or not sufficiently tried, that might set us on the right path. The cry of the church still goes up. It is not the cry of the New Testament church, "Marana tha"—"Come, Lord" (I Cor. 16:22; Rev. 22:20), but a rather frantic what-to-do question. But it is a legitimate question, and it needs an answer.

252

II

What, then, ought we to do? If we put that question to the New Testament, we will get an answer that may seem at first blush disappointing, even negative. We should like to find there some suggested course of action, but there is none. No strategy for world conquest is mapped out (though the gospel is preached energetically); no program of political or social action is even suggested; no ecumenical organization (a modernizing word, to be sure) is pushed in order to further the solidarity of Christians in the face of danger. There is much, indeed, about what a Christian is to believe, much about how he is to live, how he is to witness to the gospel. But there is not a scrap of advice upon how the Church may escape the eschatological tension, nor any hint that it ought to be escaped. On the contrary, it is assumed that that tension is the Church's natural habitat: let her stand in it as the Church. We come, then, to the New Testament asking what to do, seeking a program of action. And the New Testament answer is: there shall no program be given you—except to *be the Church!*

But that may sound like a playing with words. And to play with words is a theologian's luxury which we can no longer afford. We cannot merely say that the Church is to be the Church; we must ask what the New Testament church thought she was, and what that means to us.

1. Now the New Testament view of the Church is rather plain, incredibly strange as this sounds to our ears. The Church is the "twelve tribes in the dispersion" (Jas. 1:1); she is the "Israel of God" (Gal. 6:16), a remnant elected by grace (Rom. 11:5), a kingdom of priests (Rev. 5:10), "a chosen race, a royal priesthood, a holy nation. . . . God's people" (I Pet. 2:9-10), and much more to the same effect. In short, she is God's holy community, the true Remnant, the people of the New Covenant, and the successor to the calling and destiny of Israel. Now Israel was a covenant people, a peculiar people. It was her faith that set her apart, nothing else. In size she was a fifth-rate state indistinguishable from the other fifth-rate states of the ancient world. Of wealth she had little. Her material culture did not differ essentially from that of her neighbors. But she had a God and a faith that set her totally apart from her context; she was the people of that God bound together in the covenant brotherhood to obey his righteous laws. As the true Israel the

253

Church is to carry on Israel's mission and, like Israel, to be the chosen and holy people of God.

That way of putting it, to be sure, conveys to our minds a connotation that is strange, if not offensive, and it is certain that few of us have been accustomed to think either of our church or ourselves in those terms. Indeed, as we understand the words, a chosen and holy people is the last thing we want to be. People who imagine themselves a peculiar and holy people are seldom lovely. These are they that pursue piety and arrive at unctuousness; these are they to whom righteousness is measured by the yardstick of abstention, and whose behavior is decidely peculiar; these are churches so sure that they are God's true and orthodox people that they become intolerable societies for self-congratulation. Of this we wish no part. The young people, we feel sure, would never stand for it. To be sure, it is a parody of the Church that we have feared, but our fear has blurred our calling and has driven us into a major effort to demonstrate that Christians are not peculiar at all. We have not wished to be the holy people of God, the Church; we have been content to be the normal people of the churches. And these can summon us, indeed, to a thousand tasks—but to no destiny.

Yet the Church is and must remain the new Israel, and in that fact a peculiar people. That is to say, she is a people who, like Israel, has received the grace of God and has responded to it in obedience. She has in the sacrament of the New Covenant bound herself to be the people of God and of his Christ, to live in fellowship with one another and with him as members of his covenant, and to embody before the world his righteous rule. In that sense the Church is a peculiar people, for she is the successor of Israel as the chosen servant of God's purpose in history. As such, and as such alone, she is heir to the promises of the coming Kingdom.

To resist this notion is to resist survival, for faith survives by finding for itself a people and incarnating itself in them. Not that the people of faith are perfect people! Israel was not, as we have had occasion to point out again and again. But Israel, for all her grievous failures, housed and kept alive a faith which could have survived *in no other way*, and in doing so was *herself kept alive* as in no other way would she have been. Just so, in fact, do all ideas and faiths, whether true or false, survive. Communism, for example, is surely more than so many Red Army guns and is certainly not an abstraction existing *in vacuo*: it is men who embody a

254

faith—and it will live as long as this particular Antichrist finds people for his incarnation. In like manner democracy is rather more than the Washington Monument or a historic document penned by Mr. Jefferson. It is men who "hold these truths to be self-evident," and it will survive as long as such men survive—not ten minutes longer. It is therefore certain that the Christian faith will live only in a peculiar people dedicated to it, and it is equally certain that that people will live as a people only so long as they are indeed the people of a faith. To speak of the Church as a new Israel, then, is apt: she is, like Israel, to preserve and propagate a faith by becoming its people and embodying it.

The Church, then, is not at all an organization, nor yet the sum-total of all its organizations: it is an *organism*; it is the people of a faith, the people of the Kingdom of God. We speak now not of the churches, but of the Church—and of a far higher sense of peoplehood than most of us have known. We are not the people of the Rev. Dr. ——'s church, held there by the power of the Rev. Dr. ——'s oratory—or in spite of it, by a very stubborn loyalty. We are not the people of the Presbyterian, the Methodist, or the Baptist churches, challenged by the worthy programs of these churches and finding fellowship in them. We are not men of good will, concerned for the foundations of society, aware that these are the gifts of religion to society, and so supporters of our churches. We are the people of *the Church*.

And the Church is greater than the churches. As the true Israel of God's purpose was not equal to the Israelite nation, so is the Church of the Lord Jesus Christ not equal to the Christian churches. It is in every one of them, yet beyond all of them—so much so that no church may claim to be the One True Church without self-deification and blasphemy. The Church is an invisible thing. It cuts across the membership rolls of the churches along a line no ecclesiastical statistician could follow, and reaches out to include the most improbable publicans and sinners. It breathes in and out of the forms and standards of the churches like a wind blowing "where it wills": one may indeed "hear the sound of it," but there is no telling "whence it comes or whither it goes" (John 3:8). The Church is a supra-earthly community transcending time and space. In it one sits down with Father Abraham and the Twelve, with the Christian brother in the pew and the Christian brother in China. It is the community of all who have heard the sound of the Kingdom of God

255

drawing near, and have said Yes to its coming. It is the new Israel, the new people of God, One Holy Church Universal.

It is not for this Church that we have feared. On the contrary, we have feared because we did not see her and, not seeing her, saw only those churches which we could see. It is for these that we have feared. We have been appalled at their shortcomings, dismayed at their weakness. They have no power to redeem society and to make it the Kingdom of God, because they are themselves attached to society, involved in society, and participants in its sin. They cannot win the victory of Christ, for it does not make sense to imagine that Christ's Kingdom of righteousness can be procured in terms of the activities and goals of only relatively righteous men. No visible church, nor yet all of them sitting in ecumenical session, can produce that Kingdom for so much as five minutes. On the contrary, the visible churches are condemned to lie ever at the mercy of Caesar. He can bring them to terms or destroy them. But that is not the Church. For over these frail weak churches there towers this other Church, the Church Invisible. She is a new race of Christian men. And for her the New Testament knows no shadow of fear at all, nor need we. She does not fear Caesar's Rome, for she will outlive both Caesar and Rome and all the successor states of Caesar's Rome. Visible churches may be tortured, brought into conformity, or destroyed; but the Church they cannot kill. Neither Nebuchadnezzar's army nor Nero's legions nor the Gestapo nor the MVD has that power. The Church is the new Israel— the people of a faith, the people of the Kingdom of God. And a people, so long as it remains a people, is indestructible. That is the New Testament church that we are called to be.

2. But not just to be! To act! If the Church is the new Israel, then she is given the destiny and the mission of Israel; and that is no passive thing, but a missionary calling. This goes back to the intention of Jesus himself. Long before Jesus, the prophet (Isa. 40–66) had declared that it was the proper destiny of Israel to be God's servant and to proclaim the true faith to the Gentile world, and, hard destiny though that was and fraught with the promise of suffering, he urged his people to accept it. But although it is certain that some heeded, Israel did not in general accept that destiny and become a missionary people; nor did she understand the Servant as a messianic figure at all. But Jesus not only saw himself as the promised Messiah, he understood his messiahship in terms of the Servant. So it was that when he called to himself the true

256

Israel, his Church, he gave to them Israel's true and proper destiny. The Servant's missionary calling was thus mediated to the Church. In any case, the Church so saw it: the history of the New Testament is a history of missions.

The Church, therefore, is not mistaken when she understands that her task is missionary. Indeed, her only mistake is that she has not understood it strongly enough. She is not to conduct missions as one of her many activities; she has in all her activities a mission; she is a missionary people—if she is not that, she is not the Church. Her gospel declares, as we have said, that the salvation of man lies only in the Kingdom of God, and that salvation she announces to the world. But she does not state it merely as an objective fact, she summons men to it. She is a Church that must wait for a Kingdom which she cannot bring to pass; but she is forbidden to wait passively. She is the Church Militant; she campaigns for the spirits of men; she captures men for the redemptive fellowship of the Kingdom of Christ.

The message of the Church is, therefore, essentially a summons to faith. And it strikes upon man's sorest need: for a saving peoplehood. We are, in fact, incomplete men until we find something beyond ourselves to impart to life meaning and purpose. We are forbidden by our very nature to live in and for self alone; we are driven to commit life to something, to repose faith in something. To be the people of nothing, to submit self to nothing—is damnation. For then, owning no master and no brother, we bow down to ourselves and to anything at all that promises ten dollars more. Or, lost and alone, we hearken to the false gods who say: Come with me and be my people, and I will save you. And that is double damnation. For we have indeed seen these false gods weld men into a people and then degrade them to the subhuman and the bestial, mutilating the very divine image in them which made them men. There is no hope for man until he can find some citizenship higher than that which national loyalty, class interest, and political ideology can impart. The salvation of man awaits precisely his decision whose man he is, what commands his ultimate allegiance, in what he reposes his faith.

Man must find a saving community. And it is the business of the Church to declare that there is such a community, and only one: the Kingdom of God and his Christ. Her gospel declares that there is no salvation for man until he submits to its rule, and it is hers to summon him to do so through an act of faith. It is truly said that salvation is of faith. But—and let us understand it—the faith which redeems is not the mere believing of certain propositions concerning God, concerning Christ, and concerning the future of mankind; nor yet the making up of the mind by sheer force of the will to question no more. That is a travesty of faith. It takes no faith to believe what is held without question to be true. Faith, on the contrary, is the commitment of life to that which is unseen and beyond proof. Saving faith is that a man cast himself upon God made visible in Christ and, however little he may have of untroubled assurance, that—because his very being desires it and the highest in his nature summons him to it—he submit to the yoke of Christ's Kingdom and to it surrender himself, his tools, and his will. In that act he finds righteousness, for in it he recognizes his Lord and turns his back on all false masters. It is to this act of saving faith in Christ and his Kingdom that the Church must summon men.

The missionary task of the Church is thus one of desperate importance. If the redemption of man awaits his faith in Christ and his Kingdom, then to summon men to that faith is no fussy meddling; it is the pivotal activity of history. Indeed, it is possible to say that it is the only hope of mankind. For mankind has no hope save in a redeemed race of men. That may seem a vague and airy thing to say, but it is the soberest realism. We ought to know by now that well-planned short cuts which promise a just world order through external programs are uniformly a delusion. This is, of course, not to say that certain political and social programs are not called for, or to discount the good that they can do. The Christian advocates no passive acquiescence to the evils of society. But it is to say that all schemes to produce a righteous world order in terms of external programs alone must fail for the simple reason that it is impossible to construct a changed world order in terms of men who have not been changed at all. To expect that such may be the case is the most wide-eyed naïveté imaginable. The redemption of man awaits precisely the birth of a new and redeemed race of men. And the Kingdom of God *is* that new race of men, God's living Church. In her is that ever-coming Kingdom.

To be sure, the growth of that Kingdom cannot be measured in terms of the statistical progress of the visible churches. The visible churches are not the Church. At best they are shot through with sin and pride and are but the palest approximation of the body of Christ. God knows—and so do most of his children—that their voice is often irrelevant and plainly dull, and inspires little confidence. It summons men sometimes—it is hard to say to what. Yet the mission of the Church must be performed through the visible churches, and it will not do to write it off. As the true and faithful in Israel served the purposes of God in the context of the existing nation, so does God's Kingdom work through the churches —even if, at times, almost in spite of them. We cannot, therefore, retreat from those churches to the vantage point of some imagined Church Invisible, and from there sneer at their activities. The propagation of the gospel of Kingdom remains the hope of history. And because this torn and fissured body of Christ—this visible church—is the only body which is even trying to perform this task, we will make no apologies for her, but will stand with her and support her with the utmost that we have. As she labors to win men for her gospel, we will labor with her that, as she is built up, a larger and more enduring structure may be built in her and through her: the Kingdom of God.

What, then, is the Church? The New Testament understood her simply as the true Israel, God's covenant and servant people, called to exhibit the righteousness of his Kingdom before the world, charged with proclaiming that Kingdom in the world and summoning men to its covenant fellowship. To that Church are all the promises given. And that is the Church that we are called to be.

III

But our practical questions have not been answered. We came to the New Testament in our helplessness and despair asking what ought we to do, what course of action ought we to follow. And we found no answer to that question, but only a very definite notion of the Church and her calling. Can we, then, draw any suggestions from that which might guide the present-day Church as she grapples with the manifold and tangible problems that confront her? We have a right to ask that question. The church needs guidance if she is to shape her programs aright, and where has she a better right to look for it than in the pages of her Scriptures? But the New Testament still stubbornly refuses to answer. Its reply is that same one, and it sounds to our ears all too simple, very nearly glib: What is the church to do? She is to be the Church! In that there is surely no course of action mapped out for us, and we are left as much in the dark as ever. But it is well that it is so. Were all our questions answered, we would be satisfied with that and would never confront the

259

deeper question to which the New Testament is driving us. And that question is: Are we indeed the Church, the people of the New Covenant that we are called to be, or are we unprofitable servants unfit to inherit the promised Kingdom?

Our immediate program, therefore, is to cease for the moment to talk of programs and to engage in self-examination and confession of sin. We are to stand before the New Testament church and receive correction. Everything has changed, and the Church has changed; yet she has changed not one bit. We are still the New Testament church—or we are no church. And if we are that Church, then we have no program but its program: to be and to produce in the world the true Israel of God's purpose, the covenant people of his Kingdom. But if we are not that Church, then nothing the New Testament has to say of its destiny and victory has anything to do with us—we are an ecclesiastical organization under the judgment of history like the temple cult on Mount Zion.

1. That gives us, to be sure, no program. Yet it furnishes an ample program, for it demands of us all our programs and more: it is a program in which all programs consist, and which gives all programs direction. Now it should be plain from what has already been said that it is not intended by so much as a syllable to cast slurs upon the worthy programs of the church. It has become fashionable in certain circles to do this and to sneer at the activistic churches which promote them, as though activity in the name of Christ were somehow futile or vulgar. The church's activities but represent its efforts to labor for Christ, and, shallow and noisy and inept though those efforts often are, to sneer at them would be the cheapest and unfairest thing imaginable. Programs of action are not only necessary, they accomplish untold good. There is no need for a church to pray for the victory of Christ and to expect it to be conferred as if it were an honorary degree. In fact, the church which will not engage in dynamic activity for the Kingdom has confused faith with futility: It has simply wrapped its talent in a napkin and will never hear its Lord say, "Well done, good and faithful servant."

God has commanded us to labor in his name, and it is certain that he will build no building in us and for us if we do not do so. And to do so calls for programs. But we do not need the New Testament to give them to us. After all, any program adequate for that day would hardly do today, and in any case one has unbounded confidence in the ability of American Christians to devise and carry out any program to which they set their minds. It is far more important, and precisely what we need, that we be reminded what our programs are for: they are the tangible means by which the church discharges the function for which it was ordained, and thereby shows itself to be the Church. Both Church and programs exist that the Christian faith may be preached to men, propagandized if you please, and that through this means the rule of Christ may be extended in the world. It is desperately necessary that this be kept in focus, lest our programs become ends in themselves and so much senseless expenditure of energy.

To this end a continual self-evaluation in the light of our calling is in order. If this is not made, the danger exists that we will fail to see the great gap which yawns between Church visible and invisible; and we will find it all too easy to identify our churches with the Kingdom of Christ, to understand the progress of that Kingdom in terms of their numerical growth, and to assume that any program that fortifies our organization automatically extends the Kingdom. Once we have done that, the major aim of all our activities will become—to build up ourselves! Then it is that we launch vigorous programs of visitation and evangelism that the rolls may show a net gain, the Sunday services be better attended, and the budget balanced. To be sure, this is never our confessed aim, but sometimes (the voice is the voice of Jacob!) it would be hard to tell it. Then it is that having set up our organizations to nurture a race of Christian people, we find ourselves racing madly to get people to nurture the organizations. Then it is that it is possible for us, while becoming a veritable beehive of activity, to raise up a generation of youth and adults ignorant of the first principles of the Christian faith. And that is seriously to fail to be the Church!

Our first program is to stand before the biblical notion of the people of God and receive correction. Let it be repeated: this is no denial of programs, but a program to give direction to programs. It will call from us all the programs we can devise, and more. For the task before us is no little task: to be and to nurture a people set apart to live under God's rule as the recipients of his grace and to exhibit before the world a likeness of the redemptive and universal fellowship of his Kingdom, while actively summoning men to that Kingdom in faith. But that is the task of the Church, and we have no other.

2. The Church, then, is called to be a people over whom God rules, who exhibit the righteousness of his Kingdom before the world. In

other words she is to witness by her distinctively Christian conduct to the fact that she is a people set apart to God. This is a statement that may seem obvious, but it is not superfluous. For this is a point at which we have been much less than the Church; it is an area of our profoundest failure—a failure which no amount of programs can conceal.

The member of the new Israel is to be as sharply distinguished from the world about him as ever was old Israel from her pagan environment. This is because the Christian has submitted himself to Christ, having received his grace, and has placed himself under the law of Christ's Kingdom. He has, like the member of old Israel, entered into covenant; and he must respond to the covenant God in obedience. Faith is attested in conduct: that is the whole drive of the New Testament exhortation to morality and good works. That is why James declared faith without works to be dead. That is why Paul exhorted the lately pagan Corinthians to put aside their pagan lusting and brawling and live in the recollection that they belonged no more to themselves, but to Christ. That is why Peter begged the Christians who lived in the shadow of persecution to purge themselves of pagan vices, that by their impeccable conduct they might confute the charges of their enemies. The New Testament was convinced that the Church must exhibit its faith in distinctively Christian conduct, or it would fail to be the Church.

Now it would seem, to be sure, that the Church has no need to be reminded of this. She has always demanded purity of character. She has always given voice against vice and drunkenness, foul language and dishonesty. She has done this so consistently and so successfully that it can truthfully be said that churchgoers are, in general, a good cut above society in matters of personal demeanor—which is as it ought to be. But it is probable that our very success in this area has concealed our failure. We have stressed matters of personal rectitude until these have become all. The result has been a very small righteousness achieved negatively by subtraction, and possible of achievement, which has blinded our eyes to our abysmal unrighteousness. We cut out our immoral habits, and we come to church—and we become good too easily. But the dynamic righteousness of the Kingdom of God, which would make society to its length and breadth obedient to the will of God, we refuse. We even dare to say that the Word of God has no business to meddle in such matters.

It is certain that by its limited righteousness this church will be judged. To pray, "Thy kingdom come," is to pray precisely that the rule of God triumph *everywhere*. It is a prayer that simply cannot be prayed while we declare that there are areas of life where the will of Christ *will not* rule, but our ancient prejudice. The Church is to exhibit the righteousness of Christ not merely in private morality but in all matters of human relations. The church which "sticks to the gospel" and utters no word of judgment or of exhortation to society's sin, is no prophetic church and, what is worse, is preaching an incomplete gospel. The Kingdom of God is supreme over the earthly order and by its righteousness pronounces judgment and summons to penitence. The Church is the people of that Kingdom and must be its earthly voice. She will witness to her faith in the God whose Kingdom comes by going out to meet that God in obedience.

In any case, God help the church that so blends into society that there is no longer any difference! Such a church will produce no quality of behavior other than that which society in general produces. It will take on the prejudices of society, and even demand that its gospel support those prejudices. It will make itself a tool of society whose main business it is to protect and to dignify with divine support the best interests of its constituents. And that is stark tragedy! The end of it is a poverty-stricken church which utters no Word, states no demands, summons to no destiny —but has a host of activities you would enjoy. And such a church is not the peculiar people of God's Kingdom: it has failed to be the Church and needlessly cumbers the ground.

3. But if the Church is a people marked and set apart as the people of the Kingdom of God, she is in that very fact called to exhibit before men the brotherhood of that Kingdom. She is one body in Christ! That is a statement, to be sure, that we make frequently, and with some unction, but we must stand in judgment before our own words. For it is to be feared that we have often showed ourselves as poor an excuse for the redemptive fellowship of the Kingdom of Christ as could be devised. Before we may speak of the program of the Church, we must become, here as elsewhere, more nearly an approximation of the Church of Christ's intention.

We are one body in Christ. As old Israel was bound together in a brotherhood under the law of the covenant God, so the Church is bound together in Christ in the fellowship of the New Covenant. And the bond of that fellowship is love, the Christian agapē. The Church, then, is a people who embody their Christian faith in Christian brotherhood. The

263

New Testament church, it hardly needs to be stressed, was one Church. It knew nothing of churches. The little churches scattered over the empire from Jerusalem to Rome and back were bound together by no formal ecclesiastical organization, but they knew themselves to be one body in Christ. Party strife existed, to be sure, and there were the seeds of schism—for these men were human even as you and I. But never once did Paul, or any apostle, recognize the rightness of such procedures, for it was a first principle with them that Christ was indivisible (I Cor. 1:10-17). To them a church which was not one Church would have been a contradiction in terms.

That, of course, cannot be interpreted as a demand that all barriers of denomination and creed be swept away—and that by tomorrow, or the next day at the latest. That is neither possible, nor, if my opinion may be injected, wise. Let meaningless differences be put aside as rapidly as may be, but it does not follow that a great superchurch will be one Church, still less a holy one. Nor are we to find in the New Testament a glib dismissal of all the tangled problems of race and class. These are existing facts, and while we are in duty bound to approach them as Christians, it does no good to pretend they are not there. Increasingly one mistrusts glib solutions; there are no glib solutions.

But this much is meant, and meant plainly: whatever divisions exist in society, and whatever may be the right solution of them, within the body of Christ such divisions *have no relevancy whatever*. In the Church of Christ there is neither Jew nor Greek, slave nor free (I Cor. 12:13): all are, without exception, one. And what is more, that is not so because we kindly agree to have it so; but because all of Christ's people are servants of the same Lord, fellow citizens of the same Kingdom, heirs of the same hope. If we are in Christ, we do not need to be made one; we are one. If we refuse to be one, and to that degree to which we refuse, we are not members of his Church. God, then, help the church that fragments the body of Christ! That is a crime for which there is punishment. I repeat, I do not mean that we should no longer worship God in the company of those like-minded with us. But God help the church that places other Christians—whether of other races, other classes, or other communions—beyond its fellowship, beyond its full fellowship! God help the church that would nominate itself the One True Church, as if the Lord God Omnipotent were a reflection of its prejudices! God has but one people—the new Israel, his Church.

264

There is, therefore, to be no rending of the body of Christ, no schism in his Kingdom. We may live in corners of it never so far apart, but we all have the same citizenship who are members of the living Church. The Church is to exhibit before the world a sort of community which transcends all barriers that human society has erected, so that men may see in it a reflection of God's redemptive community. Furthermore, she is to extend her good works and her brotherly compassion beyond herself into the world; for the Church can no more keep her *agapē* (love) to herself than she can keep her gospel to herself. It too must go out into society to witness to the coming Kingdom.

4. To go out and to witness! We have pointed out at length that the New Testament church was called to take up the destiny of the new Israel, and that this was the Servant destiny: the Church is to be the missionary people of God. Here, at last, we speak of tangible programs, and there is little need to argue about them. That the Church has been given a missionary calling is recognized by virtually every denomination, conceded—at least in theory—by the majority of Christians; and large sums of money are spent each year in the effort to carry it out. So much so that to speak of it is to bring no novel challenge at all. Yet here, too, as we stand for our correction before the New Testament church, it is plain that much more is required of us than we have done. We are to stop trifling with our historic task—and that as the price of our very existence.

Of course we must be a more missionary Church! We are engaged today in an ideological struggle; dynamic ideas do battle for the minds of men. We cannot stand aside from that battle—and to participate in it is missions. The Christian gospel may be never so redemptive, but it will redeem no one who has never heard its summons. And millions have not. Scarcely one of us but meets dozens of such each day as he goes about his daily employment. It is not enough that we support missions; were we to support ten times as much, it would not be enough. We must each of us rise to our calling; we must become a missionary people. The Church that will not contend for the spirits of men is no true Servant; it will not even survive, nor does it deserve to.

We concede that we must be witnesses of that faith whose people we are. But how lamely we go about it! To church on Sunday if nothing comes up—a program and a speaker on Tuesday, and afterward tea—a dollar for missions, but frankly they bore me—and missionaries are the queerest people! Well we know that the church must reach out into the

265

community and bring new people into its fellowship. That is what it is for, and we criticize it if it does not. For ourselves, we will pass on any names we hear of to the pastor. We are alarmed and dismayed at the manner in which Communism infiltrates and takes hold of the minds of men, and we feel that something simply has to be done to stop it. But we can never get over our well-bred feeling that to discuss one's religion with other people is just a little bit vulgar. We think it noble that missionaries should give their lives to preaching the gospel in far-away lands—but if one of our loved ones should toy with the idea, we implore him not to be quixotic. We are a missionary church that wishes the propaganda of the gospel to be carried on by someone else.

We shall plainly have to be a greater Church; that is our first program. Let us not mistake it: history is testing us to see what sort of people we are. Let no one say Christianity is being tested. Not so! It is we who are tested. Christianity will survive, never fear. It has survived worse and will survive worse again. It is we who are tested, and it remains to be seen if we are a people worthy to be the vehicles of so great a faith—to hold it upon our lips, to call ourselves its servants. History, in the form of Marxian Communism, is now teaching us that we must take our Servant calling seriously. As a Church and as individuals we must learn, and learn at once, that the vigorous propagation of the faith is the Church's life blood. We cannot approach the ancient mission of the Church with such a resounding "too little and too late" and survive history's judgment. We have simply no place to stand save as the servants of the Christian faith. As that faith stands to do battle in history, it is ours to stand with it as its people, to witness with voice and life to its coming victory and present power. In that we take part in the eschatological struggle, and each act we perform, however small it may be, becomes an act of decisive significance for the Kingdom of God.

We came, then, to the New Testament asking for a program of action by which we might further the victory of Christ, and we have received our answer: I give you no program, but a calling—to be the Church! And that is a call to be a far greater Church than we are. It is a call to nothing less than to be and to enter history as the Church of the Lord Jesus Christ, the people of his Kingdom. To be that and to do that is the summation of all programs; and if we cannot do it, there is no use to speak either of victory or of programs. For no victory is promised us save the victory of the Kingdom—and that belongs to its people, *the*

Church! The Church which is not that people will know nothing of it but must stand ever in history's judgment, from which none of its programs can save it.

IV

But let it not be thought that we speak of the church in despair. On the contrary, we make bold to lay claim to that biblical faith which through many centuries pointed forward through the darkness to its consummation; and we speak not of despair but of victory. For whatever the failure of the churches we have the confidence that just as in the nation Israel there was always a righteous Remnant, so in the churches there will always be a new Israel—a true Church. And to it goes the victory; to it is given the Kingdom.

Let us not, however, imagine that we are speaking of victory as that term is normally understood. The Church's path of victory is no triumphant path which moves from conquest to conquest till all men have been won for Christ. Nor are we promised in the treading of it any immunity from the blows of adversity, or even from physical defeat. On the contrary, it is a path that must be walked in that continual tension of which we have spoken, and which we find so strange: a tension between what we have been promised and commanded to do and what we are not and cannot do. The New Testament church lived in precisely that tension and could find no course to follow save to lay down herself and take up her cross. That was, indeed, her proper course. For if the Church is the new Israel to which has been given the Servant mission of proclaiming the true faith to the world, then she must also assume the Servant's cross. And it is in that Cross that this tension, which she can by no means escape, is resolved and the victory won. For the Servant's cross and the Servant's victory are inseparable!

1. The victory of the Church, then, is the victory of the Cross. This, too, lies in the intention of Jesus himself. We have argued that Jesus interpreted his messianic mission in terms of the Suffering Servant of Yahweh. The figure of the Servant we saw, it will be recalled, in the latter chapters of Isaiah, and a paradoxical figure he was. On the one hand, he was given a conquering task and promised the victory: he was to proclaim God's law to the ends of the earth, and he would not give up till the far lands waited on that law and bowed down to that God. On the other hand, he was anything but victorious: he was despised,

rejected, spit upon, beaten, done to death like a common criminal. Clearly his victory was the victory of the Cross. If it be asked how this was victory for the Servant at all, it can only be said that it was not *his* victory; it was the victory of the Kingdom of God in him and through him, and that became his victory. Out of his sacrifice innumerable progeny were begotten into the Kingdom, and he was satisfied with that (Isa. 53:10-11). It was this pattern that the prophet laid before Israel as the proper destiny of the people of God. It was this same pattern that Jesus not only took for himself but also gave to the new Israel—his Church—which it was his, as Messiah, to call out.

In "the form of a servant" Jesus fulfilled his destiny. His very understanding of himself led to his crucifixion, and no other outcome did he seek. His work he did, like the Servant, without ostentation; acclaim and honor he consistently refused. Claiming to be Messiah and Son of Man, he set his face toward Jerusalem convinced that it was necessary for him to suffer—for without the total surrender of the Servant there could be no victory of the Kingdom: "Except a corn of wheat fall into the ground and die, it abideth alone: but if it die, it bringeth forth much fruit" (John 12:24 K.J.V.). So we see him at the mercy of the powers of this earth—crucified, dead, and buried. But if the New Testament affirms that that Cross was not defeat but total victory, history in its own way but gives assent to the statement. For without that Cross the victory which Christ won over the human spirit would have been inconceivable. True, the powers of this earth have power to kill the body. But the power of God was neither dead nor defeated—it was let loose! And we see it alive, moving over the rotting bones of the powers of this earth, building a Kingdom not made with hands. We see it, from its supreme sacrifice, releasing into the hearts of men a redemptive stream, of which we have all tasted.

Nor did Christ give his Church any other destiny. He who commissioned his new Israel to the Servant mission of preaching the gospel in the world said also: "If any man would come after me, let him deny himself and take up his cross" (Mark 8:34). The Cross, therefore, has been and must be the Church's path of victory. And we know that the Church has been great when she has cast herself straight into the teeth of history at her Master's bidding. When she has grown fat and sought to avoid the Cross, she could neither be great nor produce greatness. The calling of the Church cannot, then, be an easy calling. The church whose calling is easy is no church and no agent of the gospel of redemption. For the redemption of man entails a cross. It is not a matter of conquest and gains, nor yet of gadgets and creature comforts; it is Almighty God laying down of himself to bring forth a new creation in his image. The Kingdom of God is, therefore, victorious by the Cross, and is entered by the Cross. And it is mediated to the world only by a Church that lays down of itself—and takes up that Cross. The redemption of man is a new creation in the spirit. As all creation has its labor pains, so must God's new creation have its Cross. Whoever, therefore, offers us the victory of Christ at a minimum of inconvenience to ourselves has suggested the worship of a false god!

2. But this calls for a major readjustment in our thinking. The Cross is still to us offense and folly; it is not at all the victory we had in mind. To be sure, we have no intention of abandoning the Cross. It is the pillar of all orthodox faith. We enshrine it in the stained-glass window and in doctrine; we bow before it in prayer. But we want no part of it. We are possessed of the notion that the Cross is for Christ, a once-and-for-all thing of the past tense with little relation to the destiny of the militant and victorious Church. Indeed, we feel it to be the business of church and religion to keep crosses far away. So our faith in the crucified Christ becomes to us a sort of charm to protect us from life's adversity. We wish the victory of God's Kingdom in terms of ecclesiastical aggrandizement, so that we may by energetic action win men to a cross now no longer a symbol of sacrifice but of established progress. We wish of God and religion what old Israel wished: protection for ourselves and our country. Let God with his great power defend us who are his people! Let the Cross march forth against hammer and sickle! Let the Church crusade for Christ, hurl its prophet word, organize its programs of advance, that Christ may be victorious—and that there be no crosses for his servants!

It is essential that we understand that no such victory will be given us, nor does the Christian faith promise it. I wish to be understood: I pray daily for the peace of this nation; I love her free institutions and would care to live under no other; if it becomes our tragic necessity, we must fight for those things that we hold dear. Further, both as a citizen and as a Christian, I abhor the Marxist idol beyond the power of my vocabulary to express it, and pray God that it may be brought to confusion. Nevertheless, the purposes of God are not equal to the peace and pros-

perity of any nation, nor to the physical well-being of any church or individual. Nor is our Christian faith here to protect us from history, but
to lead us into its dark valley and through it. In any case, history with
its bitter tragedy lies before us, and there is no escaping it; there is no
magic in religion to charm it away. The question is not *if* we shall face
history, but *how*: as moles cowering in our mental bomb shelters await-
ing the ultimate detonation, or as men made in the image of God who
have known the meaning of faith. A victory of Christ which protects our
comfort will simply not be given, and we should be as fatuous as was
old Israel were we to expect it.

But this is to say that there is a sense in which we cannot in any case
escape the Cross. It needs no great catastrophe: the path of life is, however pleasant it may be, dotted with crosses which men must bear. The
question is not if we shall bear them, for bear them we shall, but only
what sort of crosses they will be to us: will they be the Christian
cross or a thief's? Will we find in them dumb, brute agony or the stuff
of redemption? There is being spelled out for us now in tragic times a
lesson that we would not hear at our ease: that the purpose of God for
us is not to give us fat bodies in this earthly society, but to discipline our
spirits—if need be, at the cost of our bodies—to make us obedient servants of his Kingdom. It is ours to serve the purpose of God in this context of history as his people, and to yield to him total obedience. It may
be that the cross which history lays upon us, at once the punishment for
our sins, may become also in a measure a sharing of the cross of the
Servant.

3. We are called to be a greater Church, if we are to know the meaning of the Christian victory. But, let it be repeated, we must not be
betrayed into the notion that we may become this by a mere intensifica-
tion of our efforts, or perchance by a reorganization of our programs.
We must stand before that Cross which is, and must remain, our redemption. In that Cross we shall find our true destiny as the servant
people of God, and also our victory—for the Cross *is* the victory of the
Kingdom of God in us, and only through a Church that has known it
is the victorious proclamation of the Kingdom in the world possible.

But we must take care to rid ourselves of clichés. The Cross is no
doctrinal abstraction to which a man may give credence passively, as
though there were some magic in that. Nor does it demand on our part
an unhealthy desire to suffer—that were a parody of cross-bearing. Nor

does it entail a passivity before evil—that were, I think, to confuse the Cross with futility. Still less are we to imagine that the mere bearing of our suffering bravely is synonymous with the Christian cross. On the contrary, we are to lay hold upon something very essential, and essentially shareable, in the cross of Christ. For that Cross was not so much wood and so many nails—the thief's cross had these. Nor was it the mere fact of painful death—thousands have died equally brutally, and we are not redeemed thereby. Before the cross on Calvary was erected, there was another, inner, crucifixion whereby that Cross was accepted. It took place when the very righteousness of God surrendered itself without limits to serve the purpose of God in history. In Gethsemane, having prayed to escape the Cross, it said, "Nevertheless, not as I will, but as thou wilt" (Matt. 26:39). In that hour the Cross was manufactured; without it, it would never have been.

That will be our Cross too. For the Cross is essentially a fact to be known, which demands participation, in which—metaphorically speaking—the self is crucified and, in that crucifixion, is redeemed. The righteousness of Christ, to be sure, we can but follow afar off. But faith's *nevertheless* may repeat his words after him. It can say with Paul, "I have been crucified with Christ; it is no longer I who live, but Christ who lives in me" (Gal. 2:20). This, then, is our cross: that we lay down our unrighteousness, and that easy righteousness which is our deepest sin, that the righteousness of the Kingdom of God may rule in us; that we lay down all pride and prejudice that the brotherhood of the Kingdom may encompass us; that we lay down our fear, which is so basically selfish, that the redemptive power of the Kingdom may be seen in us; in short, that in the fiery purgation of history we should die to ourselves and rise again, the people of a faith greater than we. This is our cross: our total surrender, in faith, to the Kingdom of God. It is also our victory, for the Cross and the victory are one.

This is no small victory, nor is it a figure of speech. It is no less than the victory of faith that "overcomes the world" (I John 5:4); it is the victory of the Kingdom of God *in us!* In the strength of that victory we will be girded to take up the Servant mission. No longer will we cry: spare me; spare my church; spare my country! but: use me; use my church; use my country—to the utmost for thy purposes which are right and good! In that cross and in that victory our inescapable dilemma will be resolved. We shall labor, and shall await the fruits of our labor in faith.

271

And we shall no longer fear. What is more, we shall become—*the Church!*

4. We have spoken so far of a present victory. We have said that as Christ through his cross triumphed over all the powers of this earth, so we in sharing that cross may share his triumph and may know that the Kingdom of God is indeed "at hand," to be entered here and now. But of that final victory which faith announces, the Kingdom coming in power, we have said little. Indeed, in one sense, there is little that can be said; for it is a victory that cannot yet be seen; nor do we know when it will come, or how. And it is difficult for us to prevent a question from rising to our lips: Is there any proof, or any assurance, that Christ will ever be victorious? How do we know that we do not labor in a lost cause—although, to be sure, a noble one?

If such a question be asked, it can only be said that it is a very natural one, and one that cannot be turned aside with a shrug or, perchance, a dogmatic answer. For we do not, in fact, have proof. All honest men must feel a certain shyness at that point in religion where reason and attested data can go no farther, and one must either stop—or go on alone. It is possible at that point to wrestle all of a very dark night, like some Jacob at Jabbok's brook, yet achieve not the meagerest blessing. While it is certain that the Christian faith summons us to believe nothing that contradicts reason, it is equally certain that the very central things to which it summons us are beyond sight and beyond scientific proof. They have to be taken on faith. And nothing attests that coming victory of the Kingdom of God save the faith of the Bible writers and our own.

But let us understand what we are talking about. Faith is not, and never has been, something that takes its stand on assured and mathematically attested data. If it were, where would be its challenge? It is not, as popularly imagined, a believing which begins only when all questions have been answered; nor yet a wide-eyed credulity which has no questions because it has asked none. Faith is essentially the commitment of life to things which are often unseen and beyond mathematical proof, but to which man's very being summons him. Faith in God is of this sort. While it is true that it is easier to believe that a God exists than to doubt it, God cannot be demonstrated in a logical proposition but must remain beyond proof. But when a man says, I have heard the voice of One High and Lifted Up speaking in my conscience, and I will obey it; I will no longer obey myself or any lesser voice—that is faith in God. In like manner it would be very difficult to prove that we ourselves are in any essential different from the animals—albeit, to be sure, of superior intelligence. Yet there is that in our nature that forbids us to live as animal man, born to propagate and to die; all that makes us man summons us to stand face to face with One Higher and to live as man made in his image. To assent to that call is faith, and in that faith we become man. To refuse it is to deny the very highest in our nature and, sinking back to the level of the beast, to become less than man.

Just so is the summons of the Kingdom of God. Its victory cannot be proven, and in times of discouragement it is very easy for us frail mortals to wonder how it can ever come to pass. But faith—springing from that very divine Image in man which is his essential manhood, and freighted with all his most desperate necessity and most passionate longing—says Yes to that victory, and day and night never ceases to labor and to pray for its coming. Whatever may be said of the coming of the Kingdom of God, this much is certain: he who refuses its call has said No to his very self. But this, too, we may affirm: he who takes this step blind, going forth he knows not whither, but looking for a City "whose builder and maker is God" (Heb. 11:8-10), *shall surely be reckoned to the seed of Abraham, that elect race, that spiritual Israel in whom all the earth is blessed.*

Nor will he who walks the path of faith walk in darkness. True, he can never see the ineffable glory of the rule of God triumphant on earth; nor can all his efforts usher it in. But because he has in faith said Yes to the calling of Christ, he will understand the New Testament mystery that "the Kingdom of God is at hand": the future victory has become to him present fact. In the light of that assurance he will labor, performing those tasks which are set before him in the confidence that he does not labor in vain; for there sounds as it were in his ears the words of the Lord of victory: "Lo, I am with you always, even to the end of the age," and again: "I will not leave you comfortless: I will come to you" (K.J.V.). What though by his labor he can build only a visible church of wood and stone and mortal men? His eyes will be able to discern towering above it the walls of another and invisible structure which in and through his labors has been built, the very ramparts of the City of God. He will know that he could have spent his life in no higher employ. The future he will leave with God, who is Lord also of the issues of history.

The path of the future is indeed dark, and the end of it may not be seen. But because it has been granted us to hear the summons of the Kingdom of God which comes to us here and now, we will face it without fear and with the prayer of all Christendom on our lips:

Thy Kingdom come; thy will be done.

For thine is the Kingdom, and the power, and the glory, forever. Amen.

Index of References

Old Testament

Genesis

1–11	233
1:27	232
2:4 ff.	25
8:4	79
12:1-3	144
12:1 ff.	30, 40
12:3	30, 92, 106
18:18	30, 106, 144
18:22-23	149
22:18	30
26:1	38
34	23
49	26
49:10	30
49:25-26	30

Exodus

3:8	30
3:14	25
3:17	30
15:1-17	26
19:5	29, 134, 241
19:6	134, 176, 202, 227
20	24
24:1-11	228
32:32	149

Leviticus

19:2	134
19:18	177, 194
20:22-26	134
24:22	161, 176

Numbers

23–24	26
23:9-10	30
23:21-24	30

Num.—cont'd

24:5-9	30
24:17-19	30

Deuteronomy

4:29-31	133
4:35	139
5	24
6:1-15	104
8:11-20	104
10:16	108
11:26-28	104
12:1-3	104
12:13-14	104
13	104
16:5-6	104
17:14-17	49
18:6-8	103
18:15-19	203
28	104
30:15-20	104
33	26
33:13-17	30

Joshua

6–8	23
7	26, 149
7–9	22
10–11	22, 23
10:12-13	26
12:17, 24	23
17:2-3	23
24	23
24:14 ff.	23

Judges

1	23
1:19	22
3:10	31

Judg.—cont'd

5	26
5:4	26
5:20	26
5:21	26
8:23	32
9:7-21	32
14:6	31

I Samuel

1–4	31, 41
4	26, 33
7:1-2	41
8	33, 34
8–13	33
9	34
9:2	34
9:21	34
10:5-13	55
10:23	34
11:1-13	34
11:15	34
13–14	34
13:4	33
13:8-15	34
13:19-23	34
14:3	105
14:52	34, 35
15	34
18:7	35
19:18-24	55
22:2	36
22:6	34
22:20	105
23:19-23	34
24:6	36
26:1-2	34
26:10-11	36
27	35

I Sam.—cont'd

27:2	36
30:26-31	36
31	35
31:11-13	34

II Samuel

2–4	36
2:4	35
2:8-10	35
3:12-15	36
5:1-5	35, 36
5:2	34
5:6-10	37
5:11	38
5:17	35, 37
5:17-25	37
6	41, 42
6:20-23	36
7:5-7	47
7:13-16	86
7:14	42
7:16	41
8	37
8:1	37
8:2-12	46
8:4	38
8:9-10	37
8:18	36, 42
9	36
9–20	26, 40
10–12	37
12:1-15	48, 65
12:30-31	46
15–20	48
15:18	36
16:5-8	36
20:1	40
20:23	36

II Sam.—cont'd

20:25 41
21:1-10 ... 36, 149
21:12-14 36
23:5 .... 41, 86
23:14 35
24 .... 39, 46, 149
24:11-13 48

I Kings

1–2 .... 26, 40
1:7 42
1:25 42
2:26-27 ... 42, 105
3:1 38
4:7-19 ..... 39, 46
4:11 .... 39, 46
4:15 .... 39, 46
4:19 48
4:26 38
5:1-12 38
5:13-14 46
5:18 38
6:37-38 39
7:1-2 39
7:7 39
7:8 39
7:8-12 46
8 42
8:41-43 144
9:10-14 47
9:15-19 38
9:20-22 46
9:26-28 38
10:1-13 38
10:11-29 39
10:22 .... 38, 142
10:26 38
10:28-29 38
11:1-3 38
11:4-8 47
11:9-25 38
11:26-39 48
11:28 ..... 46, 48
11:40 ..... 48, 49
12:1-18 .... 46, 48
12:21-24 49
12:26-29 50
14:6-16 50
14:25-28 49
15:16-22 50
15:25-29 50
15:34 51
16:1-12 50

I Kings—cont'd

16:15-28 51
16:31 51
16:32 52
17:1 54
18–19 52
18:4 53
18:20-24 52
19 54
19:14 53
19:15-18 54
19:18 94
20:31-43 ... 55, 57
21 65
22 .... 53, 58
22:48 52

II Kings

1:8 54
2 54
3:10-19 55
3:15 55
8:7-15 58
8:18 52
8:26 52
9–10 54
9:1-10 55
10:15-17 55
10:22 142
10:32-33 56
12:17 56
13:6 57
13:7 56
13:14 55
13:25 58
14:8-14 58
14:19 58
14:22 59
14:25 ..... 58, 161
15–17 71
15:8-25 72
15:27 76
15:29 ..... 77, 90
15:30 77
15:33 76
15:37 76
16:3 ..... 79, 100
16:5 77
16:6 76
16:7-8 .... 77, 78
16:9 77
16:10-18 78
17:4 78
17:6 78
17:24 78

II Kings—cont'd

17:27-28 80
17:31 100
18–19 82
18:1-5 80
18:8 81
18:13-17 82
18:17–19:19 .. 82
18:22 80
19:6-7 82
19:7 83
19:9 82
19:20-34 82
19:32, 34 82
19:35, 37 83
20:12 80
20:12-19 81
20:20 81
21:3-7 100
21:9-15 100
21:19 104
21:19–22:1 ... 102
22–23 . 80, 103, 107
22:3 102
22:3-8 104
22:8-20 103
22:12 .... 107, 111
23 ...... 101, 103
23:1-14 103
23:7 100
23:8-9 .... 80, 103
23:15-20 ..104, 107
23:28-35 109
23:36 .... 104, 109
24:1-2 113
24:3-4 100
24:6 113
24:8-17 113
24:14 128
24:16 128
25:12 129
25:27-30 ..128, 134

I Chronicles

3:19 136

II Chronicles

20:14-18 55
26:6-8 59
26:10 59
30:1-12 80
32:3-5 81
32:30 81
33:11 99

II Chron.—cont'd

33:12-17 100
34:6 104

Ezra

1:1-4 .... 135, 157
1:7-11 157
1:8 136
2 .... 158, 166
2:2 136
3:2 136
3:8-10 158
3:12 159
4:1-5 159
4:2-3 173
4:2, 10 99
4:23 159
6:3-5 .... 135, 157
6:4 .. 136, 157, 158
6:14-15 159
7:1-6 172
7:7-8 172
7:10 172
9–10 160
10:2-5 173
10:9-13 173

Nehemiah

1:1–2:8 159
2:1 172
4:15-20 159
6:17-19 173
7 .... 158, 166
8–10 173
8:1 172
8:1-18 173
13:15-18 159
13:16 160
13:23-24 . 160, 173
13:23-31 160
13:25-28 173

Psalms

2 87
2:7 .... 42, 86, 207
9:27 203
29 26
45 87
47 150
67 26
68 26
72 87
74:9 203
89:3-4 87
89:19-37 87

Ps.—cont'd

89:27 .... 42, 207
93 150
96–99 150
110 87
132 87

Proverbs

25:21 194

Isaiah

1:2-4 85
1:2-9 85
1:5-9 90
1:11 85
1:14-17 85
1:21-26 89
2:2 159
2:2-4 ... 83, 92, 95
2:4 248
2:6-8 79
2:9-22 84
2:11-22 87
2:12 85
3:1-8 85
3:16–4:1 84
4:2 166
4:2-4 89
5:1-7 84
5:8 83
5:11-12 84
5:22 84
6 87
6:1-5 86
6:5 87
6:13 88
7:2 77
7:3 .... 77, 89
7:3-9 81
7:4 77
7:6-12 77
7:17 ...... 50, 90
7:18-19 87
7:20 77
8:1 89
8:4 77
9:1-7 ....83, 90, 91
          199
9:2 86
9:6 .... 18, 92, 207
9:6-7 ... 85, 92, 95
9:7 248
9:12 85
9:17 85
9:21 85
10:1-2 84

Isa.—cont'd

10:4 85
10:5-6 ..... 85, 86
10:5-19 87
10:20-22 89
10:28-32 82
11:1 .. 88, 93, 166
11:1-5 91
11:1-9 ..83, 95, 199
11:2 92
11:3-5 .... 92, 248
11:6-9 92
11:9 ...... 95, 248
14:32 86
19:18 129
20:2 81
22:1-14 90
22:9-11 81
22:14 91
28:1-8 84
28:9-13 84
28:14-22 81
28:16 86
30:1-5 81
30:15 81
31:1-3 85
31:4-9 86
32:9-14 84
33:17 121
34 143
35:1 248
35:1-2 143
36–37 82
36:6 78
37:6-7 82
37:7 83
37:21-35 82
37:30-32 ... 89, 90
37:33-35 ... 82, 86
37:36 83
37:38 83
39:1 80
39:1-8 81
40:1-11 137
40:2 152
40:3-5 140
40:9-18 138
40:21-26 138
40:27-31 139
41:2-4 139
41:8 150
41:8-10 139
41:18 140
41:19 143
41:21-24 139

Isa.—cont'd

41:25 139
42:1-7 ... 147, 150
42:2-3 209
42:6 211
42:6-7 ... 208, 228
42:9 140
42:14-16 143
42:19 .... 140, 150
42:24-25 ..139, 151
43:10 150
43:16-19 140
44:1 150
44:1-5 142
44:6 139
44:12-20 139
44:21 150
44:24–45:7 ... 158
44:26, 28 136
44:28–45:4 ... 139
45:1 136
45:4 150
45:6 139
45:12 139
45:18 139
45:20-23 144
45:22 139
45:22-23 145
45:23 ... 211, 233
46:1-2 131
46:5-7 139
46:9 .... 139, 140
46:11 139
47 136
48:1-8 140
48:9-11 140
48:11-12 139
48:14 .... 136, 140
48:17-19 139
48:20 136
48:20-21 140
49:1-6 ... 147, 150
49:5-6 147
49:6 ..145, 208, 211
            227
49:8-10 228
49:8-13 150
49:10-11 140
49:14 141
49:19 136
49:20-21 142
49:22 142
49:26 143
50:1 141
50:2-3 143

Isa.—cont'd

50:4-5 209
50:4-9 147
50:6 ..... 209, 210
50:7-9 233
50:10 .... 151, 218
51:1 150
51:1-3 ... 139, 142
51:1-16 139
51:3 .... 136, 143
51:6 143
51:7 150
51:9-11 140
51:14 136
51:16 140
52:1-12 138
52:9 136
52:11-12 ..136, 140
52:13–53:12 ...147
            150, 211
52:15 148
53:1 148
53:2 .... 94, 208
53:2-4 148
53:4 151
53:4-6 148
53:7 ..152, 209, 230
53:7-9 148
53:10 230
53:10-11 268
53:10-12 148
53:12 209
54:1-3 142
54:3 136
54:4-10 .. 141, 227
54:9-10 228
55–66 137
55:3 228
55:3-5 142
55:13 143
56:2-6 171
56:7-8 145
58:1-12 174
58:12 136
60:1-3 137
60:1-5 143
60:8-9 143
60:13 143
61 209
61:1-3 ....147, 153
            198, 209
61:4 136
61:21 193
62:1 147
62:6-7 147

Isa.—cont'd

63:1-6 143
63:18 136
64:10-11 136
65:13-15 145
65:17-19 ..143, 241
65:17-25 137
65:20-25 143
66:1-4 174
66:7-9 143
66:10-14 137
66:12 142
66:18-21 145
66:24 143

Jeremiah

1:2 105
1:6 105
1:11-16 105
1:18 119
2–3 106
2:1-2 56
2:2-3 27
2:4-8 106
2:10-11 106
2:11 139
2:13 .... 106, 118
2:14-17 106
2:15-17 110
2:21-25 106
2:29-37 106
2:35-37 110
3:1-5 .... 106, 227
3:6-10 106
3:12-13 .. 106, 107
3:21-22 106
4:1-2 106
4:3-4 108
4:5-9 110
4:8-10 111
4:14 108
4:23-26 113
5:1-9 117
5:12 110
5:14-17 110
5:23-29 107
5:30-31 107
6:13-14 107
6:14 110
6:16-21 107
6:22-26 110
6:27-30 .. 114, 117
7 86
7:4 ...... 110, 111
7:8-15 111

Jer.—cont'd

7:16 113
7:16-18 110
7:21-23 .. 108, 133
7:31 100
8:4-7 107
8:8 ...... 107, 110
8:10-11 107
8:11 110
8:13 113
8:18–9:1 121
9:2 118
11:9-11 110
11:14 113
11:18-23 111
11:19 .... 111, 152
12:1-4 130
12:6 111
12:7-8 117
13:23 117
14:11 113
14:13 110
15:1 113
15:1-4 149
15:4 100
15:10 111
15:15-18.. ... 111
15:17-18 118
15:20 119
16:10-13 132
17:15-16 118
18:18-20 111
18:18-23 120
19:1-2 112
19:10-13 112
19:14–20:6 ... 112
20:7 .... 111, 118
20:9 119
20:10 111
20:14-18 119
21:2-7 115
21:8-10 .. 115, 117
21:11–22:5 ... 116
22:13-14 109
22:15-16 . 106, 109
.... 116
22:18-19 ..109, 113
23:5-6 ... 114, 117
.... 166
24 .. 114, 117, 123
26 ... 86, 107, 111
26:6-8 111
26:16-19 ... 79, 80
.... 111

Jer.—cont'd

26:24 .... 107, 111
27:1-11 114
27:5-11 118
28:2-4 114
29:1-14 114
29:3 115
29:7 128
29:10-14 . 117, 123
.... 133
30–33 124
31:1-6..78, 107, 140
31:15-22 .. 78, 107
.... 124, 140
31:29 130
31:31-34 ..124, 125
133, 141, 226, 228
31:32 140
31:35-37 124
32:1-15 124
32:24-27 125
34:7-8 115
35 .... 55, 56
36 .. 107, 112, 133
36:5-6 112
36:12 .... 107, 112
36:14-16 112
36:19 .... 107, 113
36:20-21 112
36:23 112
36:25 107
36:26 113
36:30 113
37:5-10 115
37:13-14 117
38 115
38:2-4 118
38:5 115
38:19 115
39:3 135
39:9 115
39:11-12 118
39:13 135
40–44 129
40:4-6 116
41–43 116
51:27 79
51:59 115
52:4-6 115
52:28-30 128

Lamentations

5:7 130

Ezekiel

1:2 99
8 110
8:1 128
10–11 ... 117, 134
11:14 114
11:14-21 123
11:16-20 ..126, 133
14:1 128
14:12-23 ..132, 149
18 .. 123, 130, 132
18:2 130
20:1 128
20:5-7 27
20:33 ff. 140
33:24 ff. 114
37 .. 125, 134, 226
37:11 ... 125, 130
.... 141
38–39 ....164, 168
40–48 ... 134, 172
40:1 99
47:22 176

Daniel

1 183
2 184
2:4–7:28 182
2:31-45 184
3 183
3:16-18 183
4 184
5 184
6 183
6:5-9 183
6:20-22 183
7 184
7:7-8 184
7:9-13 ....185, 201
7:13-14 191
7:25 184
8 184
8:3-4 184
8:9-13 184
8:20, 22 184
8:23-25 184
9:27 182
11:2-4 184
11:31 182
11:34 .... 169, 185
11:36 184
12:1-4 ... 169, 185
12:11 182

278

Hosea

1-3 ...... 74, 227
1:2 74
1:3 74
1:4 ...... 56, 73
1:6-8 74
1:9 ... 66, 75, 223
2 27
2:2-13 74
2:3 76
2:4 74
2:8 75
2:9 76
2:12 75
2:12-15 76
2:14-20 140
2:14-23 75
2:19-20 76
3 75
4:1-2 73
4:4-14 59
4:6 73
4:8-9 73
4:11-14 .....73, 75
5:1 73
5:4 75
5:13 ...... 73, 75
6:4 75
6:6 74
6:9-10 73
7:1-11 73
7:13 75
8:4 73
8:13 75
9:3 75
9:10 ...... 56, 76
9:11-17 75
10:3 73
11:1 27

Hos.—cont'd

11:1-4 76
11:1-7 56
11:5 75
11:8-9 76
13:4-6 76
13:9-11 75

Joel

2:28-32 232
2:30-32 168
3:9-11 168
3:14-16 168

Amos

1-2 64
1:1 60
2:6-8 59
2:6-16 61
2:9-12 ...... 27, 64
3:2 64
3:8 60
3:12 63
4:1 61
4:4-5 59
5:2 63
5:4 63
5:7 61
5:10-12 61
5:14-15 .... 63, 65
5:18 ...... 60, 64
5:18-20 .... 66, 85
           145, 164
5:21-24 .... 59, 62
6:1 62
6:3-6 62
6:13 59
7:7-9 63
7:10-13 . 51, 59, 66
7:14 60

Amos—cont'd

7:14-15 66
7:15 60
8:4-10 61
9:1 86
9:7 ... 33, 64, 144
9:8 ...... 67, 85
9:11 105
9:13-15 248

Jonah

4:11 161

Micah

1:1 79
1:5 79
1:9 79
1:14-15 79
2:1-2 79
2:9 79
3:1-3 79
3:5 79
3:11 79
3:12 ... 79, 80, 86
4:1-4 ...... 83, 92
4:2 92
4:3-4 248
5:2 93
5:2-4 ...... 83, 91
6:2-5 27

Nahum

3:1 102
3:4 102
3:7 102
3:8 100
3:19 102

Habakkuk

1:1-2:4 130
1:6 99

Zephaniah

1:1 98
2:1-3 105
3:6-7 105

Haggai

1:1-4 159
1:9-11 158
1:12-2:9 166
1:14-15 159
2:1 159
2:3 159
2:4-7 166
2:10 159
2:15-19 158
2:20 159
2:21-23 167

Zechariah

1:1 159
1:7-17 166
2:11 160
3:8 166
4:9 166
6:9-15 ... 166, 167
6:12-13 166
7:1-14 174
8:9-11 172
8:14-23 174
8:23 160
9:9 .. 94, 153, 200
12:10 153
14 168
14:1-3 168

Malachi

1:6-14 159
1:11 160
2:17 159
3:14 160
4:5 203

New Testament

Matthew

3:3 136
3:4 54
5-7 203
5:3 94
5:3-12 210
5:5 153
5:10-11 210
5:14 .... 208, 211
5:17 ..196, 203, 204
          205

Matt.—cont'd

5:17-20 .. 229, 230
5:18 175
5:20 .... 204, 220
5:21-44 203
5:38-42 205
5:39 210
5:44 194
5:48 220
6:19-34 200
6:33 219

Matt.—cont'd

7:14 170
7:21-23 221
8:11 .... 146, 226
8:11-12 211
8:12 195
8:20 210
9:36—11:1 203
10:6 .... 196, 211
10:22 210
10:23 223

Matt.—cont'd

10:32 206
10:38 210
11:2-6 ... 209, 216
11:12-13 197
11:27 206
11:28-30 . 205, 210
12:1-14 204
12:6-8 216
12:28 218
12:38-42 .. 192,218

Matt.—cont'd

13:1-53 203
13:24-30 236
13:31-33 218
13:36-43 195
13:45-46 219
13:55 208
15:24 .... 196, 211
16:1-4 192
16:15-20 199
16:16-17 225
16:18 ... 224, 233
             235
16:28 201
18:1–19:1 203
18:17 224
19:28 226
19:29 210
21:1-11 200
21:31 .... 210, 220
21:43 226
22:1-10 211
22:13 195
22:21 200
23 .. 176, 195, 204
23:29-36 175
23:37 121
24–25 203
24:3 194
24:24 218
24:36 ... 168, 240
24:51 195
25:31-46 . 221, 224
26:17-19 229
26:26-29 229
26:27 126
26:28 229
26:39 271
26:53-54 202
27:11 199
27:41-43 207
28:18 218
28:19-20 211
28:20 233

Mark

1:14-15 ... 17, 190
             197, 216, 220
2:22 193
2:23-28 204
3:27 218
3:35 221
4:26-29 218
7:1-15 204
8:11-12 .. 192, 218

Mark—cont'd

8:29-30 199
8:31 202
8:34 ..151, 210, 236
             268
8:38 206
9:1 .... 201, 238
9:12 202
9:24 220
9:31 202
9:35 210
9:47 219
10:14 210
10:17-25 210
10:23-25 200
10:29 210
10:33 202
10:38-39 236
10:45 ... 202, 209
10:47-48 199
12:17 200
12:28-31 ..204, 205
12:31 194
13:4 192
13:8 241
13:13 210
13:22 218
13:30 238
13:32 168
14:12 229
14:23-25 229
14:36 206
14:61-62 201
14:62 ... 199, 238
15:2 199
16:15 211

Luke

3:4 136
4:16-21 .. 198, 209
             216
4:17 136
4:21 .... 153, 214
6:20-23 210
6:22 210
6:27 194
9:20-21 199
9:58 210
9:62 220
10:18 ... 218, 231
10:22 206
10:23-24...197, 216
11:20 218
11:31-32 216
11:37-41 204

Luke—cont'd

12:16-21 200
12:32 97
12:36 219
12:50 210
14:15-24 ..211, 226
14:26 219
14:27 210
16:29-31 217
17:21 ... 168, 192
             216
18:29 210
20:25 200
22:7 229
22:13 229
22:15-20 229
22:20 ... 126, 229
22:29 206
22:30 226
22:42 ... 120, 209
23:3 199
24:47 211

John

1:1-3 206
1:21 203
1:25 203
1:29 230
1:46 208
3:3 230
3:8 255
6:14 203
6:15 199
6:48-51 204
7:40 203
8:12 208
12:24 268
13:1 229
13:14-17 210
13:29 229
15:5 227
17:4 137
17:4-5 210
18:28 229
18:33-37 199
18:36 200
19:7 207
20:28 206

Acts

1:6 .. 93, 168, 199
1:7 .... 168, 240
1:8 .. 211, 225, 233
1:11 238
1:15 226

Acts—cont'd

1:15-26 230
2 225
2:1-13 55
2:16-21 232
2:22 217
3:12-16 190
3:21 .... 233, 238
3:22-26 203
8:30 137
10:36-43 190
13:13-50 211
13:16-41 191
21:38 203

Romans

1:1-3 190
1:3-4 206
2:5 236
2:25-29 108
2:28-29 227
3:20 220
3:22-26 220
4:13-15 224
5:1-2 220
5:1-5 232
5:10-11 232
5:12-21 232
6:1-11 230
8:15 206
8:31 233
9:6-8 227
10:9 190
11:5 .... 227, 253
11:17-19 227
12:5 227
12:20 194
13:1-4 235
13:8-10 205
13:11 238
14:10 236
16:3 230

I Corinthians

1:10-17 264
1:23 208
1:26 ..... 94, 210
1:26-28 235
1:30 227
3:11 193
3:13 236
4:5 236
5:7 230
7:29 238
11:23 229

I Cor.—cont'd

11:23-25 ..190, 229
11:25 .... 126, 229
12:13 264
12:27 227
14:1-33 55
15 231
15:3-7 190
15:20-22 231
15:22 92
15:24-28 233
15:25 238
15:45-49 .. 92, 232
15:51 238
16:22 .....239, 252

II Corinthians

1:22 232
3:4-6 229
3:18 232
5:10 236
5:17 230
5:19 232

Galatians

1:4 232
2:16 176
2:20 .... 230, 271
3–4 195
3:11 176
3:29 ...\. 224, 227
4:5-7 ...\.... 232
4:6-7 ...\..... 206
4:24-25 28

Gal.—cont'd

5:1 220
5:4 220
5:14 205
6:16 .... 227, 253

Ephesians

1:13-14 232
5:22-23 227

Philippians

1:6 238
2:5 ...... 205, 230
2:6-8 206
2:6-11 ... 190, 211
2:7 154
2:9-11 209
2:10 233
3:20 232

Colossians

1:13 232
1:28 227
3:9-10 230

I Thessalonians

4:15-17 238
5:1-2 238

II Thessalonians

2:3 240

Titus

2:13 .... 206, 238
3:7 224

Hebrews

1:1-4 206
2:14 230
3:1-6 204
6:5 ..... 218, 232
7–9 195
7:22 195
8 28
8:6 195
8:6-13 229
10:25 238
10:36 239
11:8-10 273
11:10 192
11:16 192
12:18-24 204
12:24 230

James

1:1 ..... 227, 253
2:5 224
2:8 205
2:14-18 221
2:24 221
5:7 239

I Peter

1:5 238
1:7 235
1:13 .... 235, 236
1:19 230
2:1-3 235
2:4-7 193
2:9-10 ... 227, 253
2:9-12 235

I Pet.—cont'd

2:12-15 235
2:24 230
3:16 235
4:7 238

II Peter

1:1 206
3:4-8 239

I John

2:18 240
4:20 221
5:4 271

Revelation

1:3 238
1:6 227
3:16 236
3:20 219
5:9-10 241
5:10 .... 227, 253
6:10 239
7:14 236
13:18 240
19:6 241
20:2 240
20:7-10 241
21–22 241
21:1-4 ... 143, 241
21:2 227
21:9-11 227
22:5 242
22:6-7 238
22:20 ... 238, 242,
                  252

Apochrypha

Ecclesiasticus

51:26 205

I Maccabees

1:15 181
1:41-43 181

I Macc.—cont'd

1:43 182
1:54 182
1:62-63 182
2:15-19 185

I Macc.—cont'd

2:27 185
2:29-38 182
2:39-41 182
4:44-46 203

I Macc.—cont'd

14:41 203

II Maccabees

4:10-15 181

Pseudepigrapha

Letter of Aristeas

128 ff. 176

Jubilees

22:16 176
39:6 175

Jub.—cont'd

49:8 175

Psalms of Solomon

17:27-28 176

IV Maccabees

5:20 176

Sibylline Oracles

3:562-63 168

I Enoch

37-41 168
105:2 207

II (IV) Esdras

7:28 207
13:32 207

Mishnah

Berakoth	Pirke Aboth
2 205	3 205

Talmud

'Abodah Zarah	Shabbath
3b 175	118b 175

Other Early Literature

Josephus Antiquities	Antiq.—cont'd	Antiq.—cont'd	Antiq.—cont'd
XI, i, 3 158	XX, v, 1 203	XX, viii, 6 203	XX, viii, 10 ... 203

Index of Subjects

Abiathar, 41-42, 105
Abner, 36
Abraham, 26-27, 40, 106, 139, 142, 153, 227, 273
Absalom, 47
Adad-nirari III, 58
Adam, new (second), 92, 231-32
Adonijah, 105
Adoram, 48
Ahab, 51-52, 54-58, 65
Ahaz, 76-80, 85-86, 90, 99-100, 104
Ahaziah (king of Judah), 54, 56
Ahijah of Shiloh, 48
Ahikam ben Shaphan, 111
Ai, 23
Alexander the Great, 178-81, 184
Amalek, 34
Amarna Letters, 22
Amaziah, 58
Amel-marduk, See Evil-merodach
Amenophis IV, 22
Ammon(ites), 22, 37, 59, 114
Amon, 102, 104
Amorite, 22
Amos: attack on society, 60-62; attack on the cult, 62; covenant, 63-65; Day of Yahweh, 66-67, 85-86, 145, 164; meaning of election, 64, 144; a Nabi? 60; rejection of the state, 63, 65-67; relevance of, 62-63, 67-70; times of, 51, 58-60
Amphictyony. See Tribal league
Amun-Re', 131
Anat, 52
Anathoth, 105, 111
Antichrist, 184, 240
Antiochus III (the Great), 179
Antiochus IV (Ephiphanes), 181-85, 207
Apocalyptic: characteristics of, 163-64, 167-68; Daniel, 182-85; evaluation

Apocalyptic—cont'd
of, 168-70; and Jesus, 191-92, 200-202; and law, 170-71, 177-78, 183; and prophecy, 163; Revelation, 239-42; rise of, 164-65; roots in Israel's faith, 163-65, 170
Aqabah, Gulf of, 37, 76
Aram(eans), 37, 50-51, 55-58, 59, 64, 76-77
Ark, 31, 33, 41, 50, 87, 105
Artaxerxes I, 159, 172
Artaxerxes II, 172
Asa, 49-50
Ashdod, 81
Asherah, 52, 57
Asshur (city), 102
Asshurbanapal, 83, 99-102
Asshur-nasir-pal II, 57
Asshur-uballit, 102
Assyria(ns), 55, 56-58, 72-73, 77-87, 90, 99-102, 104-5, 108-9, 112, 135
Astarte, 52
Athaliah, 52, 56
Augustus, 234
Azekah, 115

Baal, 51-57, 73-74, 88, 94
Baasha, 50
Babylon(ia), 42, 72, 78-81, 99, 101-2, 109-16, 118, 123-24, 127-32, 134-36, 138, 140, 157-58, 165, 167, 172
Balaam poems, 26
Baruch, 112
Belshazzar, 135, 184
Ben-hadad, 50, 55, 57
ben Tabeel, 77
Bethel, 23, 50, 60, 80, 86, 104

Caesar, Julius, 234

283

Canaan(ites): conquest by Israel, 21-23, 32-33, 37; influence on Israel, 32, 39, 42, 47, 51-53, 56-57; religion of, 52-53. See also Phoenicians

Carchemish, 112

Chaldeans. See Babylonians

Charisma: and the Messiah, 92; in the period of the judges, 31-32; persistence of the tradition, 50, 60; and the rise of the monarchy, 33-36, 39-40

Cherethites, 36

Cherubim, 50

Christ. See Jesus

Chronicler, the, 159, 174

Church: the body of Christ, 227; a covenant people, 228-30, 245, 254, 259, 262-63; early church and Judaism, 196; and earthly society, 43-44, 68-70, 234-35, 251-52, 256, 263; founded by Jesus, 224-25; and Israel, 224-27, 253-54, 256, 259; a missionary of the Kingdom, 232-33, 250-51, 256-59, 265-66; one body in Christ, 263-65; people of God's rule, 261-63; roots in the Old Testament, 94, 225; and the Servant of Yahweh, 154-55, 227, 230, 233, 236, 256-57, 259, 265, 267-69; in tension between two worlds, 230-44, 250-53, 267; unable to bring in the Kingdom, 233-34, 236-37, 239, 242-43, 251-52, 256-57; victorious through the cross, 231-33, 236-37, 267-72; visible and invisible, 236, 255-56, 258-59, 261

Cilicia, 38

Cimmerians, 101

Communism, 68, 254-55, 266, 269

Covenant: antiquity of concept, 27; broken by Israel, 64-67, 74-75, 110-11, 117, 124-25, 130, 140, 225, 228; central in faith of Israel, 26-30, 53, 104, 170-71, 174, 212, 228; Ezra's, 173; Josiah's, 103; obligations of, 28-29, 48, 64-65, 74, 84, 104, 108, 170-71; a response to grace, 27-28, 195; in theology of prophets, 27-30, 64-65, 74, 84, 87, 108, 124, 140-41, 170-71, 228; and the tribal league, 27, 31

Covenant, New: contrasted with Old, 28, 195; given by Christ, 228-30; in Jeremiah, 123-26, 228; kindred

Covenant, New—cont'd
ideas in prophets, 125-26, 140-41, 226, 228; members of, 214, 229-30, 245, 253-54; obligations of, 223, 262-64

Creation myth, Babylonian, 140

Creation, new, 143, 241-42

Croesus, 135

Cross: experienced by the Christian, 270-71; offense of, 154, 200, 202, 207-8, 269-70; victory of, 231-33, 241, 267-69

Cyrus, 135-36, 138-39, 156-58, 165

Damascus, 38, 50-51, 56-58, 76-77, 99

Daniel, book of, 182-85

Darius I, 167

Darius III, 178

David, 23, 35-43, 46, 48-50, 62, 65, 149; hope attached to line of, 18-19, 40-43, 80, 82, 86-87, 91-93, 104-5, 130, 142; idealization of, 40-41, 50, 86-87, 91. See also Messiah

Day of Yahweh: in popular belief, 60, 63-64, 145, 164; in prophet theology, 66-67, 85, 143, 145, 164-65

Debir, 23

Deborah, Song of, 26

Decalogue, 24, 65, 122

Decapolis, 180

Deuteronomic histories, 132, 171

Deuteronomic law, 103-5, 110, 171

Domitian, 234, 240

Ebed-melech, 116

Eden, return of, 92, 143

Edom(ites), 22, 37, 49, 114, 129

Eglon, 23

Egypt(ians), 20-22, 27-28, 33, 37-38, 41, 42, 48-49, 76, 78, 80-82, 85, 100-102, 106, 109-10, 112-16, 129, 139, 179

Egyptian, the, 203

Ekron, 81

Elah, 50

Election of Israel: antiquity of the belief, 27-30; by grace, 27-30; popular confidence in, 27, 58-60, 63-64, 94, 110-11; in prophet theology, 63-64, 139, 147, 152-53

Elephantine, 129, 133

Eli, house of, 41, 105

Elijah, 52, 54-55, 65, 94, 203

Elisha, 55

Esarhaddon, 83, 99-100
Eschatology: and Apocalyptic, 163-64; beginnings in early Israel, 29-30; and Day of Yahweh, 60; eschatological community, 232, 237-39, 245; foreshortened perspective of, 143, 165-66, 238-39; integral to Israel's faith, 29-30, 163; and Messiah, 92; and ministry of Jesus, 217-18, 223, 231-32; and New Testament church, 232, 237-42, 245; and present-day church, 242-43, 245-53; "realized," 197, 219, 237; "thoroughgoing," 223, 237
Ethics: of prophets, 60-65, 83-84; of Jesus, 193-95, 221-24
Evil-merodach, 128, 135
Exodus: in Hebrew theology, 27-28, 140; hope of new Exodus, 76, 140, 151, 166, 203; new Exodus in Christ, 203-4, 228
Ezekiel, 74, 98-99, 114, 127; beginnings of Apocalyptic in, 164; *Civitas Dei*, 134, 172; doom upon the nation, 117; explanation of the tragedy, 122, 132, 139, 171; hope for the future, 123, 125-26, 133-34, 140, 226; the individual, 122-23
Ezion-geber, 38, 52, 59
Ezra, 160, 172-74

Faith: meaning of, 119-20, 220, 257-58, 272-74; and obedience, 220-21, 262-63
Foreigners: attitude of Judaism toward, 153, 161-62, 165, 173, 176; mission to win them, 144-47, 160-62

Gad (the seer), 48
Galilee, 47, 50, 77, 104
Gittites, 36
Gedaliah, 116
Gerar, 38
Gezer, 38
Gideon, 32, 47
Gog, 164
Gomer, 74-75
Gospel (*kerygma*) of early church, 189-90
Greece, 31, 178-81; Hellenism and Jews, 180-82, 196; influence in New Testament, 196, 206

Habakkuk, 98, 152
Ḥabiru, 22-23

Hadrian, 192
Haggai, 158-59, 166-67, 172
Harran, 102, 109
Hasidim, 182
Hasmoneans, 186
Hazael, 56, 58
Hebron, 35-36
Hellenism. See Greece
Hepher, 23
Herod(ian), 186, 188
ḥesed, 28-29, 74, 141
Hezekiah, 77, 79-83, 85, 88, 90, 99, 103-4, 115
Hiram, 38, 47
Hophni, 33
Hophra, 115
Hosea: apostate nation, 51, 57, 73-74; covenant bond, 74; hope for the future, 75-76, 78, 140-41; marriage of, 74-75; rejection of the state, 56, 66, 75
Hoshea, 77-78

Image of God, 232
Isaiah: contemporary relevance of, 95-97; continuing influence of, 86, 92-94, 114, 165-66, 199, 225-26; and the cult, 84-85; the Messiah, 18-19, 83, 85-87, 89, 91-92; the Remnant, 87-91; and sins of society, 83-85; and state, 50, 77, 81-82, 85-89; summons to faith, 77, 81-82, 85
Isaiah, Second: exilic setting of, 136; monotheism, 137-39, 144-45; new creation, 143; new Exodus, 140, 151; "new things," 139-40, 142-43, 146, 150; polemic against idols, 139; renewal of the covenant, 140-41; Servant, 146-153; triumph of God's purpose, 139-40, 143, 146; world-wide reach, 143-47, 149. See also Servant of Yahweh
Isaiah, Third, 137
Ish-baal (Ish-bosheth), 35-37
Ittobaal (Ethbaal), 51

Jabesh-gilead, 34
Jacob, 139
James, message of, 221, 262
Jehoahaz (king of Israel), 56, 58
Jehoahaz (king of Judah), 109
Jehoash (king of Israel), 58, 59
Jehoiachin, 99, 113-14, 117, 128, 134-36, 157, 166

Jehoiakim, 98, 104, 109-10, 112-13, 116-17, 123
Jehoram (king of Judah), 52
Jehoram (king of Israel), 54
Jehoshaphat, 52
Jehu, 54-58, 66
Jeremiah, 56, 78, 98, 99, 105-27, 140; and the cult, 107-8, 111; and the doomed nation, 108-16; early preaching, 105-6; and Josiah's reform, 106-8, 110; New Covenant, 123-26, 226, 228-30; religion of the heart, 108, 122-23, 125-26; and the state, 116-18; suffering and inner struggle, 111-13, 115-16, 118-21, 152; and survival of Israel's faith, 121-23, 132, 171
Jericho, 22, 23, 26, 203
Jeroboam I, 48-51
Jeroboam II, 51, 58-59, 71-72, 73, 76
Jerome, 103
Jerusalem, new, 134, 241-42
Jesus: death and resurrection of, 231-32; ethics of, 193-95, 221-24; founder of the Church, 224-25; fulfillment of the hope of Israel, 190-98, 212-14; historical Jesus, problem of, 188-89; in kerygma of early church, 189-90; and Kingdom of God, 17-18, 190, 197-98, 210, 215-24, 230-31; Last Supper, 228-30; and the law, 202-5, 229; as Messiah, 190, 198-200, 214-15, 224-25; messianic consciousness of, 198-99, 201, 206, 208-10, 211, 213-14; miracles of, 216-18, 231; and Moses, 203-5, 219, 229-30; in Old Testament, 212-13; Passover sacrifice, 229-30; return in glory, 238-39, 242; revelation of God, 195; as Servant of Yahweh, 153-54, 198, 208-14, 226-30, 256-57, 267-68; as Son of God, 205-7; as Son of Man, 200-202, 214, 219
Jezebel, 51-56
Job, 130, 151-52
Joel, 99, 232
John the Baptist, 54, 209
Jonadab ben Rechab, 55
Jonah, 153, 161
Jonathan, 36
Joshua (high priest), 166
Josiah, 80, 90, 98, 102-4, 106-9, 116
Jotham (son of Gideon), 32, 47

Jotham (king of Judah), 76
Judges, period of, 31-32

kemārîm, 103
kerygma. See Gospel
Kingdom of God: centrality of concept in the Bible, 10-11, 18, 197-98, 242, 244; and the church, 224-26, 230-43, 248-52, 254-74; hope of Israel, 17-18, 86-94, 123-26, 137-53, 160-72, 176-78, 184-86, 191-92; hope of mankind, 95-97, 245-50, 257-58; Kingship of Yahweh, 160; origins of the concept, 18-19, 28-30; popular conceit, 40-43, 60, 63-64, 79, 86, 110-11, 130; present fact in Christ, 97, 190, 197-98, 216-20, 230-31, 250, 273-74; prophet negation, 65-67, 75, 79, 85, 90-91, 94, 110-11, 114, 116-17, 122; in teachings of Jesus, 17-18, 197-98, 210-11, 218-24; victorious through the Cross, 231-33, 236-37, 267-71; yet to come in power, 233-34, 237-42, 244, 250-52, 272-74
Kiriath-jearim, 41

Lachish, 23, 115
Law: and Apocalyptic, 170-72, 177-78, 183; and covenant, 28-29, 48, 63-65, 104, 107-8, 170-71; ideal of, 133-34, 171-72, 176-78, 191, 202; interest in, in Exile, 133-34, 171; Jesus and, 203-5; and Judaism, 170-78; of New Covenant, 229-30
Lord's Supper, 229-30

Maccabees, 169, 182, 185-86
Maher-shalal-hash-baz, 89
Malachi, 159-60, 172
Manasseh (the tribe), 23
Manasseh (king of Judah), 83, 99-104
Marduk, 131, 135, 140, 157
Marduk-apal-iddina (Merodach-baladan), 80-81
Mareshah, 79
Marniptah, 20, 33
Mattathias, 185
Medes, 101-2, 134-35, 184
Megiddo, 38, 104, 109
Menahem, 72
Mephibosheth, 36

Messiah: in Isaiah, 18, 83, 85-92; of Levi, 185; in popular hope, 93, 114, 165-68, 171, 175, 191-92, 207; and Primitive Man, 92; and Son of God, 40-42, 86-87, 206-7; and Son of Man, 185, 201-2; sources of concept, 18-19, 40-42, 86-87, 91-92; and Suffering Servant, 93-94, 153, 168, 208, 256-57. See also Jesus
Micah, 79-80, 83, 86
Micaiah, 54
Moab(ites), 22, 37, 114
Monarchy: institution in Israel, 39-43, 46-47, 50-51; rise of, in Israel, 33-39; tension against, 32-34, 40, 45-56, 66-67, 75, 116-18
Monotheism, 24-25, 138-39, 143-45
Moresheth-gath, 79
Moses, 19, 24-25, 27, 139, 149, 170, 203-4; Blessing of, 26; new Moses, 150, 203-5, 219, 229; religion of, 24-30

nābî'. See Prophets
Nabonidus (Nabu-na'id), 135, 157
Nabopolassar, 102, 112
Naboth, 65
Nabu, 131
Nadab, 50
Nahum, 98, 102
Nathan, 48, 65
Nazirite, 54-55, 65
Nebuchadnezzar, 112-16, 128, 134-35, 157, 183-84
Necho, 109, 112
Nehemiah, 159-60, 172-73
Nergal-sharezer, 135
Nero, 234, 240
Nineveh, 98, 102
nôqēd, 60

Omri, 51

Padi, 81
Paganism: fall of Jerusalem as victory of, 122, 130; and Israel's faith, 24-26, 52-53; menace to Israel, 41-43, 47, 50-53, 56-57, 64, 73-75, 78-79, 88, 100, 103, 106, 110-11, 131, 139, 160; modern idolatry, 249-50, 257
Parousia. See Jesus: return in glory
Paul: the church, 226-27, 264; Cross and Resurrection, 231-32; faith and

Paul—cont'd
works, 220-21, 262; Jewish background of, 196; kerygma in, 190, 191; and law of Moses, 108, 204-5; Lord's Supper in, 229; return of Christ, 238; Servant calling, 161, 210-11, 226-27; state and society, 235; two covenants, 28, 195
Pekah, 72-73, 76-77
Pekahiah, 72
Pelethites, 36
Pentecost, 225, 232
Persia (ns), 135-36, 157, 159-60, 166-67, 178, 180, 184
Peter, 203, 225, 235, 262
Pharisees, 171, 176-77, 182, 191, 195, 202, 204-5, 210, 218
Philistines, 21, 33-35, 37, 55-56, 59, 65, 81, 82
Phinehas, 33
Phoenicians, 38, 51, 56, 59. See also Canaanites
Pompey, 186, 188
Priestly Code, 172
Prophets: early prophets, 32-34, 47-50, 52, 54-57; end of prophecy, 162-63, 174-75; professional prophets, 57, 60, 79, 110, 114, 122, 130; prophecy and Apocalyptic, 163; prophet books, 133, 175, 177; "sons of the prophets," 55
Proselytes. See Foreigners: attitude of Judaism toward
Psammetichus I, 101-2, 109
Psammetichus II, 115
Ptolemy, 179
Pul. See Tiglath-pileser III

Qarqar, 57
Que. See Cilicia

Rahab, 140
Ramesses II, 20
Ramesses III, 20-21, 33
Ramessides, 21
Ras Shamra, 22, 52
Rechabites. See Jonadab ben Rechab
Rehoboam, 46, 48-49
Remnant: beginnings of the concept, 86-92; in popular conceit, 93, 114, 165-66; search for the true Israel, 94, 117, 123-26, 142, 150-51, 176-78, 226; true Israel and the church, 94, 214, 219, 225-30, 253

Rezin, 76-77
Rome, 101, 181, 188, 191-92, 234-35

Sabbath, 159, 171, 175, 181-82, 204
Samaria, 52, 55, 57, 59, 61, 72, 76, 78, 80, 104, 158
Samaritans, 78, 173-74
Samson, 33
Samuel, 32-34, 41, 47, 55
Sanballat, 173
Sargon II, 78-81, 90, 99
Saul, 34-37, 39, 149
Scripture: Christ in the Old Testament, 212-13; development in, 193-96; diversity in, 189; problem of unity of, 189-98; promise and fulfillment in, 94, 126, 153-54, 170, 177-78, 190-98, 212-15, 225-30
Scythians, 101, 110
Seleucid, 179, 185
Sennacherib, 81-83, 90, 99
Servant of Yahweh: antecedents of concept, 148-49; calling and destiny of Israel, 151-53, 256-57; fluidity of concept, 150-51, 208; mission to Israel and the world, 147; "Servant poems," 147-48; as understood by the Jews, 153, 160-62, 168, 208; uniqueness of concept, 146, 149-50; vicarious sacrifice of, 147-48. See also Church, Jesus
Shabako, 81
Shallum, 72
Shalmaneser III, 57-58
Shalmaneser, V, 77-78
Shamash-shum-ukin, 99, 101
Shear-jashub, 89
Sheba (ben Bichri), 48
Sheba, queen of, 38
Shechem, 23
Shemaiah, 49
Shenazzar. See Sheshbazzar
Sheshbazzar, 136, 157
Shiloh, 31, 33, 41, 105, 111
Shishak, 49
Sidon (ians), 51, 114
Siloam tunnel, 81

Sinai, 26, 28, 204, 230
Sin-shar-ishkun, 102
So (Sib'e), 78
Solomon, 37-49, 51, 59, 105, 142
Son of Man: in Apocalyptic, 185-86, 191-92, 200-201, 207; and Messiah, 185, 201, 202; and second Adam, 232; and Servant of Yahweh, 202. See also Jesus
Syria. See Aram

Tarshish, 142
Teima, oasis of, 135
Tekoa, 60
Temple: Ezekiel's, 134, 172; Solomon's 41-42, 47, 50, 134, 159; Zerubbabel's, 159, 166
Thebes, 100
Theudas, 203
Tiamat, 140
Tiglath-pileser III, 72, 77, 90, 99
Tirhakah, 82
Tirzah, 23
Titus, 192
Tobiah, 173
Tribal league, Israelite, 31-34, 39-41, 166
Twelve, the, 227, 230
Tyre, 38, 47, 51-52, 56, 114

Urartu, 79
Uriah, 48
Uzziah, 58, 77

Yahwist, the (J), 26

Zadok, 41
Zealots, 191
Zechariah (king of Israel), 72
Zechariah (the prophet), 159, 166-67
Zedekiah, 113-17
Zephaniah, 98, 105
Zerubbabel, 93, 136, 157, 166-67
Zeus, Olympian, 181-82
Zimri, 50
Zion, inviolability of, 41, 43, 79, 82, 86, 93, 110-11, 115, 122, 130